# DESERT AMERICA

# DESERT AMERICA

## BOOM AND BUST IN THE NEW OLD WEST

### RUBÉN MARTÍNEZ

Metropolitan Books   Henry Holt and Company   New York

Metropolitan Books
Henry Holt and Company, LLC
*Publishers since 1866*
175 Fifth Avenue
New York, New York 10010
www.henryholt.com

Metropolitan Books® and m® are registered trademarks of
Henry Holt and Company, LLC.

Library of Congress Cataloging-in-Publication Data

Martínez, Rubén.
  Desert America : boom and bust in the new Old West / Rubén Martínez.—1st ed.
    p. cm.
  Includes index.
  ISBN 978-0-8050-7977-7
  1. New Mexico—Economic conditions—21st century.   2. New Mexico—Social
conditions—21st century.   3. Immigrants—United States.   4. New Mexico—Race
relations.   I. Title.
  HC107.N6M37 2012
  330.9789—dc23                                                    2011040587

Henry Holt books are available for special promotions and
premiums. For details contact: Director, Special Markets.

First Edition 2012

*Designed by Kelly S. Too*

Printed in the United States of America
1   3   5   7   9   10   8   6   4   2

*For my father, who bequeathed me his love of the desert.*

*For Angela, who lived it with me.*

*And for Ruby and Lucía, who will see it with their own eyes.*

For we are strangers before thee, and sojourners, as were all our fathers.

—1 Chronicles 29:15

# CONTENTS

# SNOW IN THE DESERT

Long before the boom of the aughts, long before the bust, I made a pilgrimage to the desert. When I arrived, snow suffused the sand, icicles hung from yucca spikes. It was late 1997, the beginning of an El Niño winter.

I'd come running from Mexico City and stopped in the Mojave because it was close to Los Angeles, my hometown, and because that's where people from L.A.—in trouble with the law, their lovers, their creditors, themselves—go to hide out, lick their wounds, end the affair, bury the body.

I went because my friend Elia was there. She, along with a small crew of L.A. expatriates, optimistic bohos, was creating a life for herself in the village of Joshua Tree, at the edge of the famous national park. Their presence unwittingly helped set the scene for a full-blown art colony and a season of wild speculation in the mid-2000s.

Me, I was simply trying to save my life. I was supposed to be finishing a book. I had "completed the research," as writers like to say to editors when they miss the deadline.

I had just enough in the bank to put down the first and last month's rent on a house down the road from my friends, in Twentynine Palms, a small town sandwiched between the iconic vistas of Joshua Tree National Park and another massive, equally iconic tract of public land: the Marine Corps Air Ground Combat Center, the largest corps training facility in the United States, whose sand dunes had served as a simulacrum of the Middle Eastern desert for the first war in Iraq and would again for the second. The rent was $275 a month; I'd talked the rental agency down from $400. There weren't many takers at that time for shacks in the Mojave sand.

My pre-boom hovel was a small, ordinary stucco A-frame with thin walls and a composition shingle roof, pale yellow with white trim. Names were etched in the cement of the patio, and a year: 1952. There was a fenced yard in the back, and a big garage empty except for a truck engine block lying on its side. Next to the house were a couple of big tamarisk trees that whooshed in the wind. The "street" I lived on (it had been paved once, but now it was mostly broken asphalt and big pools of sand) ran north–south, and the house faced west, the direction the wind blew from, pecking the living room's picture windows with sand. A sign nearby read, "NEXT SERVICES 100 MILES."

I had never seen snow in the desert, had hardly even imagined it, but that is how the Mojave greeted me. A frigid wind blew, and thick flakes fell to efface the land I thought I knew.

On one of my first nights in that thin-walled house on the edge of the one-hundred-mile nothing, I heard what I thought was the hiss of a gas leak. A thorough inspection turned up nothing. It wasn't a rattlesnake or wind through the tamarisks. It took me a long while to realize that I had never before been in a place of such perfect silence. What I was listening to was the blood coursing through my own body.

Natives of Los Angeles consider the desert their backyard, and sometimes—especially when the Santa Ana winds blow hot and dry—tell themselves that the city itself is in the desert. But no, L.A. is "west of the West," as Theodore Roosevelt once famously surmised. What L.A. does is *imagine* the desert, and it projects those representations to the rest of the world.

I'd been to Joshua Tree before, to the actual place on a couple of occasions, but mostly it had been imagined for me. I'd seen its expressionist boulders in *Star Trek* episodes (the original series) and "heard" it on U2's eponymous album. In the L.A. music scene there were stories about "country-rock" legend Gram Parsons and his untimely demise in Joshua Tree from a cocktail of morphine and tequila. Joshua Tree was American desert cool incarnate.

During an earlier trip to the desert I started wearing a cowboy hat to declare myself a Cowboy—a man of the West, feet wrapped in snakeskin, guitar slung over my shoulder. I am actually a second-generation cowboy. My father, born in Los Angeles to Mexican immigrant parents, was the first to play the part, having been weaned on the Western via radio, film, and phonograph records: the Lone Ranger, Jimmy Stewart and John Wayne, Gene Autry and the Sons of the Pioneers and Marty Robbins. This became my pop culture cradle.

As I grew older, this influence largely turned into a source of embarrassment; the Western as genre was well past its prime, and although I liked the Eagles (everyone did in 1977, my freshman year of high school), I had only a vague notion of who Gram Parsons was, and the alt-country movement was still a generation away. Being Mexican back then was almost cool, insofar as being able to play "Malagueña" on guitar to romance white girls looking for something a little more exotic than the parade of boys with feathered blond hair. But my brownness mostly embarrassed me, too.

The embarrassment gradually turned to ethnic pride, as I felt summoned to fight the good fights: against, first, U.S. intervention in Central America and, later, the cowboy Know-Nothings who sponsored the reactionary California ballot initiatives of the mid-1990s. Propositions 187, 209, and 227 sought to deny public services to "illegals," end affirmative action in California's public institutions, and ban bilingual education. With a ponytail, goatee, and flamboyant ties, I railed against the propositions as a commentator on TV and radio, as a spoken-word and performance artist, and as a writer. Support for the measures came from an aging, demographically diminishing, and economically insecure group of voters, middle- and working-class whites reacting to growing income inequality and the latest waves of immigration. This slice of the electorate canonized the measures with overwhelming electoral majorities—chiefly because most of the new immigrants lacked citizenship or even papers and, thus, voting rights—and crushed my political idealism.

For all my activism, there was no room for a brown cowboy in this debate. I felt the familiar discomfort. It just wouldn't do to sing a Marty Robbins song, even if it was about the border, at a rally for immigrants' rights.

So I went south, to Mexico, to experience another kind of difference. I was a restless thirty-something, and Mexico was a restless place. I found my subject: migrants crossing the border into California, Texas, New

Mexico, and Arizona. So I crossed the border too, all along the line of barbed wire and occasionally trampled chain-link that has since been replaced by hundreds of miles of a great wall. Each leap fulfilled a deep and quixotic desire to reconcile my mixed parentage (as the son and grandson of immigrants from Mexico and El Salvador). I crossed from Tijuana into San Diego, from Agua Prieta into Douglas. From Columbus to Palomas, from Juárez into El Paso.

I'd come in a big circle. It happens all the time in the desert—the view is so vast that you can't be sure sometimes where you're headed. The land does not change from one side to the other. The flora, the fauna, the mesas and buttes and playas are the same. But the landscape is not.

"The problem," wrote the literary critic Raymond Williams in *The Country and the City*, "is one of perspective." Any particular place can be imagined and represented any number of ways, and the various versions often contradict one another. Landscape is about who is gazing upon the land; the position of the observer creates a frame and necessarily edits the view. It says more about who is doing the gazing than what is being gazed upon. It is impossible to gaze upon the land itself—Sierra Club true believers notwithstanding—because of the layers of imaginaries that overlay it. Raymond Williams referred to such an accrual of imagery and sentiment and ideology as a "structure of feeling." The notion of the desert as a spiritual and healing place, or Native land, or cowboy cool, or the Big Empty—all these are supported by structures of feeling, by human history, by contradiction and desire.

In my romantic elision of a very real divide, I had wanted to deny the imaginaries by creating a new one, willing the landscape to be of a continuum from one side of the line to the other. In the end, by following brown footsteps back and forth over the border, I "returned" to the West, which in a sense I'd never really left. I came running to it with a nosebleed from Mexico City's altitude, smog, and cocaine.

In my shack in Twentynine Palms, I began a long process of "recovery"—one that, in fact, lasted throughout my decade-long desert sojourn—and I consciously revisited the West I'd been raised on. I rescreened the films Pop had fed me when I was young, the best from directors John Ford and Anthony Mann. Hollywood had thrust me into the West via the big screen and the little one, representations I carried with me to the actual desert and border and farther south (a typical narrative route in a Western). Now I read the films as an adult, recognizing both their ancient prejudices (Mexican or Native as dark other) and the nuances that had escaped my childhood vision—especially Mann's "psychological" renderings of conflicted Western characters played by Jimmy Stewart, cowboys who questioned themselves and, by extension, the entire cowboy project.

Perhaps the brown cowboy could have the best of both worlds even as he negated the worst of each. In my journey to the desert I was also indulging cowboy cool for its own sake, which is what people who visit Joshua Tree (or Tombstone or Monument Valley) invariably wind up doing. The interpretive signs of Joshua Tree National Park underscore cowboys and Indians (the latter ancient, nameless wisps who disappeared; the former, with names like Rusty or Bill, unfailingly "colorful"). Walking in the desert with my Akita mix, Bear, rescued from a local animal shelter filled with pets abandoned by Marines transferred overseas, I felt very much like Harry Dean Stanton's character in the touching Euro-pop desert of Wim Wenders's *Paris, Texas*, a favorite of desert rats who aren't really from the desert. Ry Cooder's slide guitar, a unique hybrid that echoes both the blues and Mexican folk, played as hipster Southwest sound track. And although in the beginning I didn't consciously imagine myself in any representational context for the pain I was in, I came to understand that it wasn't just my friend's fortuitous presence in Joshua Tree that had brought me there.

After a few years in the Joshua Tree area, I moved deeper into the West, to the village of Velarde, in northern New Mexico, where I married into the Garcia clan of Albuquerque. More than an exotic location to find or lose myself in, New Mexico became my home, even if I was constantly reminded that I was an outsider by the "natives."

During the time I lived in Velarde, in a development I could not have foretold, parts of New Mexico and locations in Texas, Arizona, and California were swept up in one of the largest economic boom periods in American history, the main effects of which were a rapid transformation of the built environment and people moving—or being moved. The term "gentrification" was originally coined in 1960s London and in subsequent decades was refined in the United States to describe the reversal of "white flight," the movement back to the urban core by the professional class. This movement resulted in the displacement of the erstwhile working-class denizens of color. It was both a literal, physical marginalization and a more symbolic, representational one. The structure of feeling of particular places was transformed, rewritten by the new arrivals, and "branded" to help set the stage for the speculation—and the ultimate, spectacular collapse of the boom—that came to define the first decade of the millennium.

In the desert West this movement occurred everywhere, from the "techno-urbs" of Phoenix and Denver to much more remote and sparsely populated areas, some of which had been boomtowns a generation or a century ago under utterly different economic and cultural orders. As with the urban model, rural gentrification brought new arrivals—often as not, scruffy or not-so-scruffy artists and assorted bohemian types, the "art colony"—who shoved the "native" population aside with the raw combined powers of speculation and representation. I was a witness to the birth of the boutique desert.

I came to the West during a time of change as profound as any since the opening of the frontier. Migrants were arriving from the South, from the East, from west of the West, a motley cohort that would transform the demographic profile of the region. All this movement meant extraordinary wealth for some and darkening prospects for many others.

As surely as the bloody scrim of Manifest Destiny swept across it, the West tells Americans about themselves. It is a place writ large with desire over many generations—for water, for silver and copper and gold, for timber and oil; as the place where consumptives came to soothe their lungs, where environmentalists see sacred space, where multinational corporations beat back environmentalists to exploit the land. The story of the great American boom of the 2000s and its culmination in the Great Recession is told well as a Western.

By choice and by pocketbook, first in Twentynine Palms, California, and then in Velarde, New Mexico, I observed the margins of the boom. In a futile attempt to embrace the entire expanse—of land, of landscape, of history and representation—like many others before me who craved the immensity of the desert, I roamed farther out, to the Tohono O'odham reservation in southern Arizona and to what is certainly the remotest art colony in the West: Marfa, Texas.

With their wildly contrasting landscapes and human geographies, these four places nonetheless share multiple characteristics—all border-lands, all changed by the boom. In each, colonial history is not abstract but embodied: the descendants of the peoples whose lands had been stolen generations ago still live there, and they will tell you that you are not where you think you are. Also, these places all have bona fide Western tourist destinations in them, or nearby: Joshua Tree National Park, D. H. Lawrence's cabin (just north of Velarde), the oldest "continuously inhabited house in America" in Santa Fe and the Indian pueblo just up the road where you can see the Turtle Dance on New Year's Day, the Rio Grande where it takes its "big bend" in West Texas, the land set aside to preserve the iconic saguaro cactus along the border in Arizona, the landscapes Georgia O'Keeffe and Ansel Adams framed.

And they all, to varying degrees, have a "drug problem." The "problems" are acute and specific to place. The U.S.-Mexico borderlands are a region of smuggling and related abuse. Because of the sense of loss of land, of status, of history, many people may consequently be more vulnerable to what drugs offer. Get high, in other words, to take the edge off—of history. The boom only exacerbated the experience of dispossession. And I had come with my own drug problem, related to theirs but not entirely. I was inside and out, among and beyond: the brown cowboy, always on the border.

One way or another, all the actors on this stage displayed tremendous hunger—for a reckoning with history, for justice, or, as in Velarde, for heroin. Or, like in Marfa, to scrub their souls clean in the desert wind (and surround themselves with high art and haute cuisine). In Joshua Tree there was a peculiar and all-consuming lust for landscape, to own the best view of yucca-spiked vastness. In Arizona the neo-Know-Nothings were utterly obsessed with their dark other out in the desert, while the Mexicans were utterly consumed with their single-minded drive to get to "el otro lado"—and, of course, with narco noir, a few as producers of it but most as its hapless spectators or victims. In the tourist traps on or near the Indian reservations, there was the lust of non-Indian for mystical Indian.

Each of these intense desires created a tendency for people to erase their neighbors.

I lived in and among them all. The only way to tell my story, it seemed, was to tell theirs.

## MORNINGS IN NEW MEXICO

**1.**

I came to live in New Mexico like an old-school anthropologist, an adventurer in a remote land. I had visited a handful of times as a tourist. Long ago, there was a lover. I was barely out of my teens and was drifting. She was in her late twenties, drifting and practicing the healing arts. She was from Los Angeles, had moved to Albuquerque for more space, cleaner air, fewer of the ills associated with the city—and for the imaginaries of the West as a place of history and restorative powers that can heal the modern, alienated urban psyche.

Albuquerque is not a city, even as its metropolitan-area population approaches one million. That is, it cannot imagine itself a city because to do so would negate its reason for being, its biggest draw for tourists and refugees from Los Angeles and other large cities. Despite the sprawl, it thinks of itself as a town, a provincial way station set between a mountain and a mesa, bisected by the Rio Grande and its verdant cottonwood "bosque."

My lover and I were each other's other: I stood in for Latin American poets and revolutionaries. She stood in for heroic Jewish intellectuals and activists.

Our cause was the revolution in El Salvador and the refugees amassed at the U.S.-Mexico border. Ronald Reagan did not call them refugees; he called them Communists. Along the line in Arizona, New Mexico, and Texas, faith-based activists guided the persecuted pilgrims across the desert and into their churches and homes. The first wave of punk was in the air back then (the Clash had recently released *Sandinista!*), and my own existential desire found its home among the exiled militants and working-class heroes that transformed MacArthur Park in Los Angeles into a Little Central America. I imbibed and imitated Salvadoran bard Roque Dalton's revolutionary verse ("Poetry, like bread, is for everyone . . ."), declaiming at solidarity events and proselytizing Hollywood liberals. It was a melodramatic Cold War affair, and a sexy one. The passion of solidarity meetings and anti-intervention demonstrations spilled over into bedrooms, and suddenly it was cool to have a brown-skinned boyfriend with a Che beard.

My lover and I had met at a transformational seminar in L.A. in the summer of 1984, and reunited under the Albuquerque sky, a cerulean vastness I'd seen only in the films of John Ford. We picnicked under the rasp of cottonwood leaves. We drove north—my first visit to northern New Mexico—to a rustic adobe for our rendezvous.

We visited Chimayó, the Lourdes of the American West. She dressed me in vests of wool woven with Native designs. We crouched at the pit of holy dirt said to hold restorative powers and smudged our bodies. I had no idea that within a few yards of the sanctuary there were Hispanos, as Mexican-Americans refer to themselves here, shooting up heroin.

When we drove back down I-25 to Albuquerque, the thunderheads billowed up and two rainbows joined above us. Really.

So New Mexico, to me, was a place where difference became desire and our desire was consummated on a landscape that relieved us of difference, welcoming us back to Eden. Even then I knew it was a lie, but I indulged the magical mystery tour because I was in love.

Twenty years after my New Mexican affair, my wife-to-be, Angela Garcia, and I begin scouring the rental market in the Española Valley—the heart of the Upper Rio Grande region between Santa Fe and Taos.

The reason we've decided to move here is, simply, addiction. Angela, a medical anthropologist, is writing her dissertation on the social and historical dimensions of heroin addiction. She's chosen the villages of northern New Mexico as her site of research because the area comprises a particularly acute node of the problem. The Española Valley, in fact, has a rate of heroin addiction and death by overdose greater than that of any American city. Angela and I are very familiar with the theme.

Among Angela's relatives in New Mexico there is alcoholism and heroin and coke and pills, and then there are Angela's own habits, which I have only a vague notion of at this point. She, in turn, doesn't know much about my past. Part of the reason she's fallen in love with me is my passion for the desert. She isn't yet aware that my drug abuse had brought me to it, to get clean out here beyond the temptations of Mexico City and L.A., my own private Sodom and Gomorrah. But the problem with recovery in the desert is that there are a lot of drugs there, too. Meth produced in remote labs, human "mules" trudging along the burning sands carrying backpacks filled with contraband. Planes, trains, and automobiles carrying it across the border and across the West. Along every route the cargo is shipped, the dealers, just like pharmaceutical company reps, drop off samples to open up new markets and revive old ones.

I have been getting high since my first year of high school, have experimented with most every substance deemed controlled by the DEA. I am the son and grandson of alcoholics, a child of 1970s California, a bohemian, a writer in search of "experience." I dropped out of college to emulate Kerouac and was utterly confused as to where the road was taking me even as I snorted up its white lines. By the time I met Angela, I had been on the wagon a few times and fallen off just as many, alternating periods of abstinence and bingeing that lasted months or years.

Angela does not know that I am still occasionally using as we prepare to live together for the first time. The addict prides himself on his discreetness. Perhaps Angela has turned away from an obvious truth too terrible to admit, or turned toward me because at some level she knows that I, too, am the subject of her research.

We need a house with enough square footage for two home offices. We need a yard for my dog, Bear. And beyond the practical, we both want to live in an adobe. Not a simulacrum, mind you—not in a subdivision of recently built homes with street names like Rising Moon and Camino Cielo; we want one with roots deep in New Mexican history, a real one. We are seeking an authentic Western life, after all.

Our first appointment is in the village of Cordova, nestled just above the Española Valley in the foothills of the Sangre de Cristo Mountains. "Perfect for an artist's retreat," reads the ad in the real estate section of the *Rio Grande Sun* ("News from the Heart of the Pueblo Country"), the valley's weekly newspaper.

We drive north on I-25 from Angela's mother's place in Albuquerque, blowing through Santa Fe's peculiar mix of Whole Foods, Indians peddling to tourists, Spanish folk kitsch, and jet-set fashion. We pass Camel Rock Casino and then its namesake, the natural sandstone formation perfectly representing a head and hump. Soon after comes our first glimpse of the Española Valley. Just past a bend in the road, it suddenly opens up before us, an immense yellow bowl flanked on the east by land wrinkled with innumerable barrancas, alluvial furrows draining the Sangre de Cristos down to the river. To the west, the mass of the Jemez Range, sections of its flanks barren still from the great Cerro Grande Fire of 2000, which overran Los Alamos National Laboratory. To the north, the high country of the San Juan Mountains, which disappear into Colorado on the horizon. In this view, there is something of virtually every landscape that defines the American Southwest and northern Mexico: arid scrublands, hills of juniper and piñon, dense mixed-conifer forest, highlands of aspen, and even alpine meadows. Everything else about the drive from Albuquerque to the north will become numbingly familiar over the next few years, but the moment the valley appears will always astonish—even after I become well aware of the human devastation hidden by the sweep of the landscape.

We aren't the only ones house hunting in northern New Mexico. We don't realize it yet, but we are part of a massive new rush on the West, the latest wave in almost two hundred years of American migrations in the region, from the trappers of the early nineteenth century onward through several boom periods of varying intensity and longevity— among them gold and oil speculation, the early artist colonies in Taos and Santa Fe, the hardscrabble folk lured by the Homestead Act, and the exodus into the West spawned by the Great Depression. The rush that Angela and I join will quite possibly signify the greatest period of upheaval yet.

In the 1990s, the interior West (which includes all the states that share the Rocky Mountains—Montana, Idaho, Wyoming, Colorado, Nevada, Utah, Arizona, and New Mexico) had the highest growth rate in the country, marking an overall population increase of 25.4 percent, not just in urban centers like Denver and Phoenix but in the exurbs and rural areas as well. This was the culmination of a process that spanned the better part of the twentieth century, from the closing of the frontier to the eve of the millennium, which saw a gradual decline of the traditional population corridors in the East and Midwest. More recently, large numbers of migrants from the West Coast arrived in the interior, too.

The influx only increased during the boom years of the early 2000s. In 2003, the top five fastest-growing cities were split between Nevada and Arizona: Gilbert, Arizona (a Phoenix suburb that logged an astonishing 42 percent population increase in a single year); North Las Vegas, Nevada; Henderson, Nevada; Chandler, Arizona; and Peoria, Arizona. (In the same time frame, San Francisco lost over 4 percent of its population.) The *New York Times'* story on the Census Bureau's report attributed the following breathless quote to Rachelle Iadicicco, who'd moved to Gilbert from St. Louis two years before with her Lutheran minister husband to start a church: "They say there are two kinds of roads here, under construction and not enough lanes."

Multiple streams were simultaneously propelled into the West by the fundamental force of an economy fueled not by gold or oil or ranching but mostly by the housing boom, which, in turn, had its roots in the tech bubble of the late 1990s, when a good part of California's urban white working class was forced to flee the cities because of inflated property values. Families that a generation before would have lived in the inner city or perhaps in one of the old suburbs moved east into the desert, searching for affordable housing. ("Starting in the mid-100's," read billboards advertising tract homes on the outskirts of Albuquerque, while single-family middle-class homes in Los Angeles were edging up to $1 million.)

A new gentry arrived as well, seeking second homes or turning its back on the urban altogether in favor of telecommuting from a rustic chalet in Montana. At one time in America, the country house was imagined mostly on a beach or a cape, perhaps a cabin in the woods or on a lakeshore. But in the late 1990s and well into the new century, the house in the country moved west.

Then came the middle class, having discovered McMansions, subprime housing loans, and the lure of a tiny patch of grass with a play area for the kids (the group that came to personify the great mortgage collapse of the early 2000s).

The new money drew immigrants from Mexico and Central America, with construction and service-sector jobs. These workers built and renovated the houses of the boom, washed dishes in the new eateries, swept casino floors, folded linens in luxury hotels. Thus immigration became a political issue throughout the West, with renewed debate over illegal status and the browning of the desert, its skin and its tongue, which increasingly pronounced the vowels of Spanish.

Add to that a dramatic African-American out-migration, a displacement partly related to the arrival of Latin American immigrants to formerly all-black urban neighborhoods. African-Americans arrived in parts of the West with historically modest black populations—Las Vegas and Phoenix, as well as the Los Angeles desert satellites of Lancaster, Palmdale, and even Needles, an extreme outpost on the Colorado River that regularly bakes in 120-degree heat during the summer. In one study, historian Andrew Wiese called this movement "as large as the exodus of African Americans from the rural south in the mid-twentieth century."

All the movement accompanied a general turn away from the Old West economies based on mining, logging, and grazing and toward tourism, recreation, telecommuting businesses, and the service sector. (In the late twentieth century and through the first years of the aughts, this created a new subgenre of amenities for the leisure class, a growth industry catering to "amenity migrants.")

The transformation of both economy and population, especially the nonwhite minority, has its origins in long-standing global economic trends, and in recent years these changes reached a kind of critical mass. The West's increased ethnic and racial diversity coincided with a notable change in its ideological character, a cleaving in opposite directions. On the one hand there was the "New West," with several states (Colorado, New Mexico, Nevada) moving from the "red" to the "blue" column, a pivotal factor in the election of Barack Obama. On the other hand, some red states became redder—notably Arizona, which took a radical nativist turn with SB 1070 and the antics of "America's toughest sheriff," Joe Arpaio, rounding up the "illegals," a classic Old Western performance.

While the economy drove all this movement, the force shaping the cultural trimmings of the boom resided in the imagination—the *idea* of the West. After having been declared dead or moribund many times before, the Western (in the broadest sense of the term) made a vigorous comeback, with most of the old tropes intact and enhanced with a couple of postmodern variants. Patricia Nelson Limerick, the author of the foundational New Western history *The Legacy of Conquest*, noted several, including the West as a place of "authenticity" relative to the "alienation" of urban space, the West as place for manly men (reacting to their sense of postfeminist displacement), and the West as repository of whiteness and the destination of white flight from the diversity of the late-twentieth-century American city. There was also the enduring West of natural grandeur or, as environmentalists portrayed it, the last redoubt of nature—ironically, a campaign so successful that it lured urban dwellers to the interior for the greatest "amenity" of all: nature itself, open space, a sound track of coyotes howling and desert wrens whirring on your very property.

Although historians had spent over two decades assiduously deconstructing the mythic Cowboy West as racist, homophobic, misogynist, and imperialistic, these tropes flourished, too, aided by the literary establishment and Hollywood. Cormac McCarthy became the Faulkner of the borderlands, Joel and Ethan Coen were schooled in the Western by McCarthy, and the Oscar for Best Picture of 2007 went to *No Country for Old Men*. It did not matter whether you lived in Manhattan or Malibu; *Sunset* magazine was hot, and *National Geographic* turned from Africa and Brazil to pictorials of sand and sky accompanied by texts in which the writer battles dehydration in the American desert on the trail of rare animal species.

Different actors employed the same images at cross-purposes. Developers selling ranchettes in Colorado invoked "pristine" nature just as much as environmentalists battling the developers and, for that matter, Al Gore fighting against global warming. In the process, each erased the human presence from the landscape. And as the new cultural class— filmmakers and writers and photographers and painters—moved in, they took up the old representations, which fueled the real estate boom and lured ever more migrants.

These forces had the power not just to inflate real estate values but also to displace the people who were living here when the newcomers arrived. As with the overall national economy, the new money did not necessarily produce wealth for the local population. If anything, the new money brought business that sucked the air out of what remained of the old regional economies. The boom on one end of the economy often meant a bust on the other—the displacement of a ma-and-pa operation by a corporate brand, for example, or the subdivision marching across old ranch land. The social and personal fallout of this could often be seen—if one was willing to look—in the shadow of the artists' lofts, vineyards, gated communities, and boutique hotels.

It is in this context that Angela and I arrive in Cordova to see the first house on our list of prospective rentals. We get to the property under a late-winter gray sky and are met by a middle-aged "norteño," or north-erner, as the Hispanos of northern New Mexico often call themselves. He sounds like he's made the pitch to outsiders before. "The last tenant was an artist from New York," he says. The house is a one-story adobe with a large attic, from the late nineteenth century or earlier. The twenty-four-inch-thick walls are in great shape considering their age, but inside everything made of wood is crumbling—doorjambs, window frames, the massive viga crossbeams of ponderosa pine. Outside the temperature is mild with a hint of spring, but inside the air pinches our skin like an ice-water bath. Apparently, the woodstove hasn't been fired up since the New York artist left, months ago. It is a dark, cobwebby house (usually only refurbished or newer adobes are "light and airy," with picture windows facing mountain views). The interior space is what in today's market is referred to as an open floor plan—living and dining rooms and kitchen flowing into one another without walls or doorways. At the far end is a cramped bedroom and bath. The attic is nearly as big as the living space below. Here the family once hung meat for jerky or dried "ristras" of chiles. There is a large hacienda-style patio outside. Angela imagines us sitting at a table there, writing in the morning sun—D.H. and Frieda Lawrence in the mountains above Taos, in 1924—gazing up at the Truchas Peaks, the snowcapped pinnacles of the Sangre de Cristos.

This is perfect.

I'd live and write about the West in a veritable Western museum. An American writer, I would claim my birthright, my place in the lineage. No more marginal Mexican-American musings! I would have a real encounter with the Land.

I'd been preparing for this—groomed for this—since childhood and Boy Scout merit badges and my first Swiss Army knife. I'd been schooled in the colonial adventure storybook: Columbus "discovering" the Americas, Sir Edmund Hillary and his Sherpa sidekick Tenzing Norgay fearlessly scaling Everest. Still, the most seductive figures were Western. John Wayne, so thoroughly familiar I could imagine him sitting at our table for Thanksgiving dinner ("Pass them mashed potatoes, little brown buckaroo!") and, in the eternity of film, forever stumbling through the desert with a baby in his arms in *Three Godfathers*, forever seething against the Comanche chief Cicatrice (a.k.a. "Scar," played by the blue-eyed, German-born Harry Brandon in copperface) in *The Searchers*, both directed by John Ford, that great twentieth-century framer of the West.

My first vision of the desert was in my grandparents' house in Los Angeles, where a small glass-framed diorama, a memento from the 1950s, hung in the entryway. During the daytime the windowless space was dark compared to the airiness of the adjacent living room, but the frame seemed to glow from within. About eight inches wide by six high and three deep, it depicted a sandy path cutting through a landscape of thick-columned saguaro cacti and ocotillos with their thin fingers reaching skyward. The earth was a rich tan, with rocks and boulders (rendered by tiny clods of actual dirt held down with glue). What struck my eyes, as a child, was the sky, which was blue-green near the top of the frame and passed through sea green to peach to golden yellow at the horizon line. In the dark of the entryway, the rich green of the cacti looked even darker, nearly black in silhouette against the luminescent sky. It was, of course, a Western sunset, in the Sonoran Desert, which had thrilled my father during his journeys across the border with my grandparents, back and forth from Los Angeles to Mexico City. I don't really know which I saw first: the diorama, John Ford, or the actual desert through the windshield of our red Chevy station wagon as we rolled through California in the dead of summer en route to a family vacation, taking advantage of off-season motel rates.

There were no human figures in the diorama, although the artist could have followed the "three cultures" model of New Mexico's official mythology, in which Anglo, Native American, and Hispano unite in the enchanted landscape. But the image is intended as an idyll, and these come easier without people and their messy histories.

The diorama was beautiful, like any postcard you might buy at a desert truck stop, like Ansel Adams. By framing these scenes, we inscribe the land with our desire. The Western image thrives in its largeness, the sweep of the vista, a hundred miles on a clear day. The experience fulfills a Wordsworthian yearning for the sublime: the immensity of nature makes us feel smaller than we are, inspiring awe. We are drawn to the natural beauty of the West out of our alienation from the human, our desire for a landscape without human contradiction.

The desert!

They used to say that Los Angeles would still be desert but for founding father William Mulholland, who stole the water that made paradise friendly to suburban development. In any event, the only thing standing between me and the real desert was the border formed by the San Gabriel Mountains, which I saw every single day as I walked out of my house for school. The desert was in Pop's stories of all-night drives through Chihuahua in his youth. The desert was my Everest. I would live there one day. I would face death there one day. I would survive it, subdue it, represent it.

I'd already had to adjust this mythology somewhat during my stay in Twentynine Palms, after I'd fled Mexico City. But my encounter with New Mexico restokes my desire for the iconic, in spite of the fact that the Chihuahuan Desert actually ends in southern New Mexico. In the northern half of the state, where the Española Valley is nestled, there are thirteen-thousand-foot peaks and vast swaths of coniferous forest. In fact, the valley seems to split the difference between mountains and desert. At the lower elevations, there are sage plains and hills of juniper and piñon. Geologically speaking, it looks like desert; the soil is loamy and there are plenty of mesas and even some modest buttes. It also snows there and the winter is very long; it is desert enough for me.

D. H. Lawrence had his cabin in the mountains above Taos; now I'd have mine alongside the Rio Grande, the Great River itself. I'd come back to the land (of forebears several generations ago in altogether distinct geographies, but still) and live off it, chop wood, grow vegetables, bake bread. I'd enter my own diorama.

That day in Cordova, I know next to nothing about New Mexico's particular and peculiar history. Here I am, I believe, far from the border I've been writing about most of my adult life. It is time to leap beyond that line and its maddening binaries (poor-rich, brown-white, Spanish-English). I will speak as an American to Americans! A cowboy to cowboys!

When we drive out of the village—the designation for the smallest New Mexico rural communities—I notice details I hadn't on the way in. In addition to the typical signs of provincial decay (a 1940s work truck sinking into the weeds, that favorite of plein air painters marketing New Mexican pastoral), there is gang graffiti scrawled on crumbling adobe walls, and plenty of beer bottles and cans along the road that seem to have been tossed from moving vehicles. The highway that passes through Cordova, I later learn, is one of the deadliest in the state, owing to the rate of alcohol-related accidents. There are also several rustic boards nailed to posts announcing the "art studios" of Cordova's many "santeros," who carve Catholic icons out of the wood of the forest surrounding the village.

These details are disconcerting and familiar to me, the death and life of the rural poor. Cordova is a noted stop on the scenic High Road to Taos, one of northern New Mexico's biggest tourist draws. A church O'Keeffe painted is on that road, and the Santa Fe National Forest—as well as a string of communities that constitute one of the poorest regions in the United States.

The Española Valley and nearby mountain villages like Cordova are at the center of a rough triangle formed by the cities of Santa Fe, Los Alamos, and Taos, islands of opulence with the highest per capita incomes of the Southwest and among the highest in the nation. The correlation of ethnicity to poverty is almost perfect. The higher a location's Hispano population, the poorer it is. Los Alamos is the whitest city and, therefore, the richest. (There is, of course, also profound poverty among the Native American pueblos, although casino revenue is beginning to have an impact on the quality of life in some of them.)

This divide is as familiar to me as the Westerns and tales of colonial conquest. It is the contrast between my grandparents' two-bedroom house in San Salvador and the nearby villages of barefoot peasants who lived in huts and cooked over wood fires. Between the spaciousness of San Diego's middle-class suburbs and the ultra-high density of Tijuana's shanties. I recognize this border. I will, after all, live and write on it again.

The romance of the Cordova house evaporates quickly. I can't imagine writing on the patio because my meteorological research shows that almost half the year a frigid wind blows down from the Truchas Peaks. The interior of the house grows darker and even sinister in my imagination.

We set up another appointment, this time in the village of Velarde, about eleven miles north of Española. The owner tells us to meet her on Riverside Drive, Española's main drag. It is midday, and traffic is heavy. The longtime commercial capital of the rural north, Española is a strikingly urban space in a provincial setting. It has a Walmart, a Lowe's, a Radio Shack, a Walgreens and a slew of fast food joints, including favorite local franchises like Blake's Lotaburger (where virtually everyone orders a "Lotaburger with green chile and cheese") and two Sonic Burgers within a mile of each other.

For a few generations now, Española has been known as the lowrider capital of the world. The local trucks and sedans are tricked out with tinted windows, spoilers, stereo speakers pumping bass, shiny rims that spin even when the tires stop. They cruise up and down Riverside and pull in at the Sonic Burger on the north end of town, where lots of kids hang out, having fun and flirting, and there are occasional clashes between gangs. Española youths might be proud of their rides, but for the affluent of northern New Mexico, the scene prompts fear and derision. "Española jokes," primarily told in Santa Fe, say it all. For example: "Why do lowriders have those tiny steering wheels? So you can drive them even when you're handcuffed." On more than one occasion in recent years, speculators have tried to create buzz about Española becoming a "new Santa Fe." But besides a white-owned cybercafé that serves up espressos and cappuccinos, there is little sign of that coming to pass. In the end, Española fits the profile of that *other* increasingly typical small city of the West: poor and brown.

We meet our prospective landlady, Lisa Salcido, at the Mickey D's lot, which is jammed full of lowriders and rural work trucks. Not everyone is picking up Happy Meals; a few small-time drug transactions appear to be going down between relaxed, well-dressed dealers and gaunt, jittery users. Lisa is unfazed by the scene. A landscaper in Santa Fe, she is scrappy and street-smart and, culturally, seems to split the difference between her California roots and the New Mexican influences she's picked up since she arrived, more than twenty years ago. She'd been drawn by echoes of the hippie communes and the New Age that Californians have long imagined in Santa Fe. Lisa has lived in a few norteño villages along the Rio Grande—Pilar, Embudo, and finally Velarde, where she bought an old adobe. She's been slowly refurbishing it over the years even as she's rented it out. She hopes to live in it one day, maybe retire there. She tells us to follow her in my car, a year-old Chevy Silverado, eight cylinders and four-wheel drive, that I hope will ease my way into living among the locals. I am no Prius-driving invader from the coast, I tell myself, precisely because I feel very much the foreigner in New Mexico, more out of place than I've ever felt in Latin America—or even in truly foreign places, like Boston. It isn't enough to have brown skin and a Chevy. For many Hispanos, there's a clear line between locals and outsiders, a divide rooted in centuries of invasion, occupation, and resistance, exacerbated by notions of historical authenticity that inform local politics.

People immediately know I'm not local; they can sense it in the way I speak, the way I dress, the way I walk. That I come from Los Angeles and not New York brings only limited acceptance—the Cali connection often deepens the distrust, I am just another gentrifier from the coast. My best card is that I am with Angela, a native of the South Valley, the legendary Albuquerque barrio given the high Chicano literary treatment by the poet Jimmy Santiago Baca, a place that, like Española, marries two different kinds of authenticity: historical tenancy (dating to the early Spanish settlement of the area in the late sixteenth century) and the urban edge of Chicano pop. Although the macho Hispanos wonder why I'm following my wife around. I am the stranger, period.

We head north on Highway 68, sometimes called the "low road" to Taos and certainly without the tourist distinction of the high one. Just beyond the edge of town is Ohkay Owingeh, until recently known as San Juan Pueblo. The Ohkay Casino Resort (600 slots, 101 hotel rooms) dominates the east side of the highway; it is rendered in adobe style, vigas protruding through a sandstone-colored façade, and crowned by a view of the Truchas Peaks. Farther up lies a large swath of public land administered by the Bureau of Land Management (BLM). With relaxed regulations compared to those that protect national parks, it lures a working-class crowd of small-time ranchers grazing their cattle, kids riding ATVs, and gun enthusiasts—all of which are anathema to most environmentalists. We pass homes on rural parcels of a few to dozens of acres, some of the spreads stretching all the way to the Rio Grande. About half a mile west of the highway sit several trailer homes, some abandoned and graffiti-scarred. A number of adobes have been burned, leaving scorched mud walls and piles of charred timber. A line of cotton-woods, leafless during winter, marks the course of the river. But the dominant feature of the landscape is the Black Mesa, a dozen miles long and a thousand feet high, a sudden and sharp thrust from the river valley. Like all the black mesas of the Southwest, it has volcanic origins. A long, narrow, and deep lava flow cut through the land, and across millions of years the sediment on either side fell away, leaving the top mostly flat and the sides craggy with exposed basalt. I immediately think about hiking it. It will be years before I do.

We take a left off Highway 68 at an intersection marked by an imploding pile of graying wood that once formed a curio shop named Ruben's Poco de Todo—bit of everything.

After heading toward the river for a quarter of a mile, we turn right onto a paved county road and then onto a dirt "private drive," part of a network of roads that aren't maintained by the county.

Ahead of us, Lisa's truck kicks up grayish dust. A well-kept double-wide trailer appears on a small parcel to the left, and just beyond it a large gray wall. Lisa pulls her truck up to a gap in the wall and unlocks the ranch-style gate.

The house is an adobe. Not the oldest in the area—it was built about seventy-five years ago—but traditionally New Mexican in most ways, with a steeply peaked roof of corrugated tin and a stucco façade speckled blue and white. A narrow concrete path ends at a covered patio alongside the house. There are two doors. One leads to a bedroom; the other is the front door, which Lisa now opens. We find ourselves in an entryway and sunroom, brilliant light flooding in through two large sliding glass windows. The floor is made of flagstones. The kitchen is a large open space with cheap flooring made up of large plywood panels. A window above the sink looks down a dirt slope to the southern edge of the property; I can see a garage at the bottom, leaning and disintegrating. At the far end of the kitchen a very low door—I am five-eight and have to duck a bit—leads to a tiny hallway dominated by a large gas furnace with a tin exhaust pipe disappearing into the ceiling. Another door connects to the laundry room, which in turn leads back toward the interior of the house. Here is a room with a fireplace. Was it the original "sala," or living room? We climb a staircase to the attic. Watch your head, says Lisa. You can stand fully erect only in a four-foot-wide corridor under the apex of the roof. Both floor and ceiling are covered with large sheets of plywood painted white. It is an L-shaped space, like the house below. The window at the top of the L looks down on the front yard and driveway and across to the neighbors' trailer; the one at the bottom looks over another trailer, a single-wide with blue siding; to its left is an adobe with a rusting tin roof and a jungle of weeds in the yard, abandoned. I hear a whooshing sound outside. At first I think it's traffic from the highway, but Lisa says it's the river, which is only a couple of hundred yards away.

Living within earshot of the Rio Grande! I'd walk alongside it with Bear every morning! There is a third window, and it frames the adobe next to the abandoned one. That home looks to be in good shape, with a short plastic basketball hoop, a Big Wheel, and scattered toys and balls in the yard. A young family.

Back down the stairs; watch your head again. Through the sala, the kitchen, into the sunroom and left into a large room with a built-in bookshelf at one end and another furnace with an exhaust pipe at the other. A den? At the far end is a large picture window, overlooking the front yard, which has several leafy sumac trees for shade and a "horno," the traditional Pueblo Indian–style domed adobe oven.

Back outside, I notice a small adobe shed. Storage? The pump house, Lisa says. Yes, of course—there is a well, because there's no city water system to hook up to; there's no city.

At our cars we chat for a bit before heading back down to Albuquerque.

Even before having a chance to talk to Angela, I know we will live in the house. There is more than enough room for both of our offices in the attic. It is a real adobe in a village alongside the Rio Grande surrounded by millions of acres of public lands—the Carson and Santa Fe National Forests.

Somehow, the fact that Angela's research will focus on heroin addiction in rural communities has receded to a dim corner of my mind. As have my own addictions. Spring is on the way, the river is rushing, the house is full of light, and the Black Mesa beckons.

We move in a month later.

Angela begins her research by taking a job at a detox facility called Piñon Hills, a program of Hoy Recovery, the largest drug rehab center in northern New Mexico. It is about a mile down from our house, in the village. She is hired as the graveyard-shift caretaker; her responsibilities include dispensing medications and calling 911 in emergencies. The clinic's staff is vague about what kind of emergencies may arise.

Angela has some reservations about the job, as do I, but we both recognize how close this could bring her to her subjects.

On her first night at Piñon Hills, a violent windstorm hits in the wee hours. I wake up to a roar and a mad metallic clanging echoing through the house. I groggily imagine that the Rio Grande has flooded and that I'll have to swim to safety in the dark because the power has been cut. I jump out of bed and look through the picture window in the front room—this is where we've made our bedroom—and the young leaves of the cottonwood in the neighbor's yard hiss, twirling and shimmering under an amber streetlight, one of the few in the village. The clanging comes from outside. A piece of tin roofing above me has partially torn loose, and the wind, rushing down the mesa and across the river, plays it like a child with a spoon on a pot. If the power is out here, I think, it is surely out at the clinic as well. I pick up the cordless phone, but it's electric, of course. Should I drive down there, make sure she's okay? I hesitate. I don't want her to think that I think she isn't capable of handling the situation. I decide to wait.

Angela spends the night keeping vigil with an addict whose legs ache terribly. He begs her to massage them. This is not sexual; this is his body in withdrawal from heroin. She rubs his legs.

Dawn comes with a beautiful stillness and Angela returns home. She does not know that when she gets in bed with me how close she remains to the subject of her study, the subject of addiction that I am.

## 2.

When I search for "Velarde" on the New Mexico Department of Tourism website, I am told, "The page you requested is no longer available or has been moved," a symbolic cyberglitch. The town is mostly invisible in the physical sense as well. Highway 68 runs along a shelf that hides the town from motorists driving between Santa Fe and Taos. There are a handful of roadside businesses—a couple of modest fruit stands, a gas station with a luncheonette for local workers. There is a winery, but it is north of the main village, and if the owners (who are from Oregon) could claim that their storefront is actually in Taos, I'm sure they would. If Velarde is known for anything, it is for apple orchards, but that evokes a golden era long past. Only a handful of the orchards still produce; most are filled with trees left unpruned and unirrigated, apples falling to rot in the weeds. The once-bustling apple warehouse is now a lumberyard, and it, too, is owned by outsiders. (Still, the lingering quaintness of the old orchards is used by real estate agents to bill neighboring villages like La Canova and Lyden as Velarde proper.) The village appears only very rarely in historical accounts; it gets all of one sentence in Paul Horgan's epic *Great River: The Rio Grande in North American History*.

The vast majority of Velarde's people, of which there are about eight hundred, are native New Mexicans. A few gringos have bought in, all on the Black Mesa side of the river in La Canova or Lyden. Real estate ads notwithstanding, Velarde is not the gentrified West by any stretch. It is the village before speculation, but not Edenic, either; it is poor, and surrounded by wealth. Further, it is poor because it is surrounded by wealth, the product of a long history of colonial dispossession.

As is typical of norteño villages, most of Velarde belongs to a handful of families who claim that their tenure stretches back to the land grants of New Spain, which were given to individuals and communities during the sixteenth-century settlement period. This system of "mercedes," as the grants were called, served several purposes, including rewarding Spaniards who'd fought in the conquest and creating a buffer between Indian and Hispano communities. (Land grants were made to Indians as well as Hispanos.) The legal framework of the mercedes emerged in Spain, where they helped consolidate territory taken back from the Moors. A grant usually awarded and specified an "ejido," common land that provided water, timber, pasture, and hunting. Individuals included in such grants were free to sell their personal land after a few years of tenancy, but the ejido was to be held by the community in perpetuity. During the Spanish period, land grants were initially weapons of conquest and colonialism. After the 1848 signing of the Treaty of Guadalupe Hidalgo, in which Mexico ceded much of New Mexico (as well as present-day California, Nevada, Utah, and most of Colorado and Arizona), the grants were viewed by Americans as obstacles to expansion—and by Hispanos as their point of resistance to American occupation.

This history, which is central to Hispano identity in New Mexico, is typically a minor sidebar in most accounts of the Southwest. In Velarde, it is very much alive. The "acequias," the communal irrigation ditches—the system introduced by the Spaniards when they arrived in the area in 1598—are cleaned out in a big village ritual every spring. The ejido, however, is now part of the Santa Fe or Carson National Forests, and although some men clean and oil their chain saws and head up into the mountains to gather firewood, although they stock up on ammo during hunting season, the Hispanos now have to buy permits to log or hunt or fish on land that was once their commons.

The Spanish legacy also remains present in the region's Catholicism, generally stereotyped as extreme. The reputation is due, in large part, to Charles Fletcher Lummis, a nineteenth-century explorer, Southwest booster, and Indian rights activist who spied on the "penitentes," a Catholic brotherhood rumored to have staged actual crucifixions well into modern times. Although the penitentes did not want to be photographed, Lummis took a picture of a penitente rite from afar. The resulting image, which continues to circulate in Western pop culture today, is a classic example of the modern gaze upon the "primitive," with its inescapably colonial overtones. The material was perfect fodder for Lummis, who went on to write about his New Mexico sojourn in *The Land of Poco Tiempo*—the title refers to a variation of the "mañana" stereotype—to underscore the exotic nature of the local color.

In Velarde today there is no full-time priest, but one visits on a rotating basis and offers Mass at Our Lady of Guadalupe, a handsome and well-kept sanctuary. The cemetery is tidy, too. There are tin awnings for the wood-carved santos adorning the most prominent graves, and the living pick up the trash that blows in on the wind, especially the shopping bags from the Walmart in Española.

It is a new world, and I want to explore it: the house, the neighborhood, the land, the north, the West. I am a new arrival, a pilgrim, a pioneer, an outsider, a conquistador.

I feel excitement, awkwardness, nervousness—all the affect that comes with not belonging. One afternoon I am driving back to the house from Walmart in Angela's Subaru, which underscores our class status among the villagers. A handful of locals have late-model SUVs; the rest mostly drive older work trucks. I turn onto our dirt road just as a truck is coming up from the direction of the river. It charges toward me fast, forcing me to slow down and swerve a bit. I don't think much of this. But then in my rearview I see the truck make a sudden U-turn and barrel back down the road toward me. Within seconds he is right on my bumper, churning up a torrent of dust. There is no room to pull over for him to pass. I cannot see the driver; his windshield is tinted. I maintain enough composure to keep a steady speed, and within a few seconds I turn through our gate and park in front of the house. I'm thinking of running in and grabbing my .22 rifle; since moving I've kept it loaded in the bedroom. It is the one my dad and I used to go plinking with when I was a kid and whose bullet clip I lost years ago, making it a single-shot rifle. But the driver doesn't pull in through the gate. He just rolls past it, very slowly, gravel popping under his tires. The side window is down partway, to just beneath the driver's chin, which he juts up and out as he gives me the classic hard look. Then the truck disappears. I hear him make another U-turn and he drives past the gate again, not quite as slowly.

He is letting me know that I am not from Velarde and never will be, even if I live out the rest of my days here.

Who belongs here and who doesn't? On its face, the question is ridiculous, because most of us aren't going anywhere. Yet it is the question of the American West, and these days it is much on my mind.

I visit the Santa Fe Opera on three occasions, twice to see wonderful productions, and yet every time I pass it on the highway and look up at the bizarre ship rising from the forest—all masts and cables and gleaming slope of white roof like the sail of a caravel—I see Herzog's *Fitzcarraldo*, with the maniacal, pitiful eponymous character played by Klaus Kinski dreaming of planting an opera house in the middle of the nineteenth-century Peruvian jungle.

The Santa Fe Opera does not belong, although it is not going anywhere. That is not to say that norteños shouldn't have access to *The Barber of Seville,* but the opera is not for them, given the segregation of race and class in the region. Yet the Santa Fe Opera's authority is immanent. The culture and economy that produced it feel little need to justify or rationalize its presence.

There are three major claims to "native" status in New Mexico: Pueblo, Hispano, and Anglo. Regional boosters have invoked the "three cultures" notion while eliding a fractious history in which the great unifying factor is conquest.

Native Americans hardly need display their credentials. The Spanish prosecuted not one but two conquests against the Pueblo Indians (the first was so brutal that it prompted the revolt that made the second one necessary). But the conquerors were then conquered by the Americans, forging the Hispano identity. The military activity during the Mexican-American War in northern New Mexico was relatively minor, but real estate speculation was war by another means. At the time of the American occupation, Spanish and Mexican land grants to non-Indian communities accounted for over 5 million acres. Under the Treaty of Guadalupe Hidalgo, "property of every kind now belonging to Mexicans . . . shall be inviolably respected." But Article 10 of the treaty, which specifically mentions land grants and their protection, was stricken by the U.S. Senate during the ratification process. A clarifying agreement known as the Protocol of Querétaro, which again conferred legitimacy on the land grants, was signed by representatives of both countries but largely ignored by the United States. A catastrophically corrupt adjudication process ensued, in which first the Office of the Surveyor General of New Mexico and then the Congressional Court of Private Land Claims ruled on land grant claims. However, the surveyors, judges, and governors with the authority to accept or reject claims were at the same time buying and selling the lands in question. These men came to be known as the Santa Fe Ring, and their names can be found all over New Mexico on buildings and street signs. One of them, Thomas Catron, who became a U.S. senator, collected some three million acres of land for himself. Through the denial of Hispano land grant claims, partition suits (a radical Anglo reinterpretation of Spanish land grant law, essentially making the "commons" vulnerable to sale at the behest of a single grantee), and other strong-arm means, the vast majority of acreage was usurped by the Americans. In New Mexico today, only a little over 300,000 acres is held by the heirs of the original grantees.

Hispanos and Native Americans are divided by their different land claims—a division as old as the decision to give distinct grants to the two groups, which was rooted in the theoretical rigidity of Spanish ideas of race and caste. The historical split has only widened with the advent of the modern casino economy. Pueblo tribes with vastly improved portfolios are less in need of political collaboration, although Hispanos patronize and work in the casinos.

On the third side of the triangle are the Anglos, and every Anglo arrival (or Subaru-driving brown guy from Los Angeles) reminds Hispanos of their festering historical loss, just as the Hispano presence recalls conquest for the Native.

Five hundred years of history are extraordinarily present in New Mexico, which makes the state so palpably American—in the broad continental sense and in its embodiment of colonial history.

Shortly after my arrival, New Mexico's governor, Bill Richardson, signed a bill recognizing Spanish land grants (or at least those that were accepted by the Court of Private Land Claims) as "entities of the state," making them eligible for economic development funds. And in 2004 the federal General Accounting Office completed a study of land grant heirs' charges of usurpation. After public hearings, interviews with heirs, and exhaustive historical research, the two-hundred-plus page report concluded that the United States generally had abided by the laws enacted to address land grants in New Mexico within the context of the Treaty of Guadalupe Hidalgo, even as it recognized the claimants' sense of historical loss. In the end the GAO's list of recommendations ranged from doing nothing to creating a new governmental entity to once again review the claimants' grievances. The preeminent New Mexico land grant historian Malcolm Ebright called the report a "whitewash." If anything, it stoked Hispanos' resentment and ensured that their political-historical passion would be passed along to yet another generation.

Grant heirs delight in dissecting land tenure codified, in some cases, nearly a century before the American Revolution. Visit Santa Fe and the tourist guide will inevitably lead you to the "oldest house" in the United States, an adobe supposedly built in 1646. When Pueblo Indians today talk of the Pueblo Revolt against the Spanish in 1680, which ushered in twelve years of independence from Spanish rule in what is today New Mexico—an unprecedented respite in the colonial era—it comes in the tone of familiarity that one associates with lived history. So celebrated is the figure of Po'pay, leader of the revolt for the northern Pueblos, that his statue was placed, in 2005, in the National Statuary Hall in Washington, where each state is represented by two individuals. Jemez Pueblo artist Cliff Fragua's rendition of the revolt leader was rendered in pink Tennessee marble.

In this history, I'm a mote of dust.

### 3.

One spring evening, I walk beyond our outer wall to the road in the balmy dark and listen to the river roar in the high-country thaw. On the other side of the road lies a gully overgrown with wild grass and cholla cactus. There are dozens of discarded beer cans and bottles, an old cottonwood tree, a haphazard barbed-wire fence, a piece of corrugated tin that must have flown off someone's roof during a windstorm. I want to walk down to the river, up to the highway, anywhere, but I've learned that people don't walk much in Velarde. That's an outsider's pastoral indulgence. In any case, I couldn't bring Bear here because the ground is carpeted with prickers that stick in his paws. There's also the matter of property lines. No one owns the river itself, of course, but every inch of land parallel to its banks is private. I would have to trespass to get to the water. But I am still intrigued by the Black Mesa, which looms over the valley. There is very little development on it, only a few houses relatively close to the river. There must be good hiking up there, I tell myself.

Back on our property, I hear my neighbor. A cough, an abbreviated rasp and wheeze, as if he's trying to check the reflex and hold his breath. It comes from across the six-foot-high fence of unfinished pine planks that marks the property line on our east side.

I meet him a couple of days later, in daylight, and we shake hands across the wire fence that continues where the wood planks end. His name is Joe Rendón, and he is amicable and chubby, with thick glasses that tint in the light but don't quite hide his small, dark eyes. He seems to want to grow a thick mustache, but it's come up thin. He's fond of base-ball caps and sports jerseys; he is fanatical about the Dallas Cowboys.

"All this land you can see," he tells me, sweeping his arm from the direction of the highway to the east and all the way around to the river in the west, "belonged to my ancestors. You don't live in Velarde. You live in Los Rendones."

He has an uncle who lives just on the other side of the county road (called "el camino de en medio," the middle road, one of the two paved paths in the village). A cousin lives in a handsome two-story adobe a bit farther south. Another cousin is in the blue trailer directly west of Angela and me. His great-grandfather lived in the now-abandoned adobe next to the trailer. His great-great-grandfather lived where a utility pole stands today; the old adobe was torn down long ago.

Joe's paternal grandparents had eleven children. The family worked the land. At their height, Los Rendones had about 200 acres in the area, with sixty under cultivation with apples, chiles, and corn. Each year the family would gather for the harvest, sorting and storing the apples in a crumbling structure on Lisa's property that I thought was a garage. There were trips in flatbed trucks up into southern Colorado, buying and selling and bartering—apples for potatoes, chiles for chickens.

If Rendones owned all this land, then who lived in the house where Angela and I were now?

"That's the house that I grew up in," Joe says, making brief eye contact and then turning away.

"Yup," he says, nodding.

Now there is a long silence. I am living in my neighbor's house. I tell him he should come over.

"One day," he says, "but I'm not ready yet."


GET THE FUCK OUT OF HERE!

Sunday afternoon. For the past hour: screaming and crying, fists pounding on a car hood, screen door slamming, and, in the midst of the battle, the voice of a small boy talking to himself in a make-believe game.

I SAID I WANT YOU OUT OF HERE!

These are my other neighbors.

Rose Garcia and Jose Martinez, a couple, both twenty-three years old. Their boy is perhaps five. She is light-skinned, with long, thick black hair that she teases up in front, old-school Chicana style. She is somewhat pear-shaped, and what's striking about her body is the constant tension of it, every pose tense and blunt as a hammer. She almost always wears T-shirts and pants and flip-flops.

Jose Martinez is short and wiry. He wears his baseball caps backward, XXX-size white T-shirts, and, during the summer, shorts and tennis shoes. I have never seen him without his head covered. What little hair peeks out from beneath the cap is cut very close, a crew cut. I rarely hear his voice, even though the courtyard in front of the house somehow acts as a megaphone so that the southern end of the village can listen in on everything. It is almost always Rose's screams we hear.

The fights occur a couple of times a week.

I'm in the attic. I've made my writing space next to the window that looks out toward Joe Rendón's trailer and the juniper hills beyond the highway. I've taken one of the old heavy doors stored in the garage and propped it up on sawhorses. The door probably hung in one of the original bedrooms downstairs. It is now my writing desk.

YOU TOOK MY MOTA!

She is accusing him of stealing her marijuana.

I DIDN'T TAKE YOUR MOTA, BITCH!

When I hear the screams, I edge up to the window at the other end of the attic, where Angela writes and where I have a direct view of Rose and Jose's. I'm careful to remain in shadow, although I doubt my neighbors can see me, given the angle and distance. In any case, they are too deep in their moment to look across the courtyard and up to the tiny window of their neighbor's attic.

Sometimes, Angela joins me. I kneel by the window and she stands. Or I sit in the rocking chair and she sits on the floor and rests her chin on an arm she supports on the windowsill. We stay for as long as the fight lasts. Until he jumps into his car and drives off in a cloud of dust. (Only rarely does *she* drive off.) Upon his return it'll start up again, muffled shouting from inside the house. A word, then a phrase, louder, closer to the front door, the door opens, now coming at us full volume.

GET THE FUCK OUT OF MY LIFE!

This is her most oft-repeated line. She struts back inside again. The door slams.

Now it is quiet in the courtyard and in the rest of the village. There was a late-season freeze last night, but the sun has warmed the Española Valley. The local weather forecaster wrote that it was going to be a "Chamber of Commerce" day. Flies buzz lazily in the yellow and green and blue of spring. I can hear the rhythmic whir of a few cicadas, the first of the year, coming up from the riverside. The whoosh of cars and trucks up and down the highway. The distant thudding of locals taking target practice on the BLM land across the highway. We are surrounded by millions of acres of public land that once belonged to the ancestors of my neighbors.

And suddenly—

GO TO THAT LITTLE PUTA OF YOURS!

Her voice builds and crests in a shriek, which usually happens on the final word of a phrase, like "life," taking the vowel and bending it in several different directions before her breath runs out. She coughs. She coughs a lot. I hear it early in the morning, late at night. I hear it very clearly when she is sitting on the patio smoking a joint. It is quick and sharp, the throat clenching and tissue grating deep inside her chest.

Every once in a great while, he responds, but he never shouts as loudly as she does.

LOOK AT YOU, YOU'RE PSYCHO, EY!

They are dealing. We have noticed the traffic. Perhaps a dozen cars a day drive through. These customers are men, all Hispanos, young and old, mostly in work trucks. Some will come early in the morning, apparently on their way to a trade job—plumbing, electrical. Others in the early evening, clearly after finishing work. Some in the middle of the day. Some in the wee hours.

It is Rose's house. The Garcias are as prominent in the area as the Rendones. One member of the clan owns the nightclub in the village, another the fruit stand that's never open at the intersection of the highway with Lyden Road. The Garcias, I am told, are an old, connected family. So well connected that our landlady passed on to us the advice she was given by local law enforcement when she suspected that Jose had stolen her lawn mower. We can't do anything to them, the cops told her. But if you want to take action on your own, shoot him, drag him into your house, and make it look like self-defense against breaking and entering.

GET THE FUCK OUT OF HERE, YOU FUCK!

YOU AND YOUR PILLS, YOU THINK I'M FUCKED UP, LOOK IN THE MIRROR!

So Angela and I watch and listen through the screens on the attic windows. The journalist in me thinks: Talk to them. Get close. But we already are. They are our neighbors.

Rose is aware of our presence. During the first fight we witnessed, which occurred just a couple of weeks after our arrival and which included Rose and another woman coming to blows on the patio, she screamed:

I DON'T NEED THIS SHIT, I'VE GOT NEW NEIGHBORS!

Outsiders, I could imagine her calculating, perhaps even thinking of us as gringos—*she drives a Subaru and he never leaves the house before ten in the morning*—because class can trump race, and in New Mexico race does not necessarily mean color. Plenty of Hispanos who claim Spanish lineage back it up with light skin and eyes.

Over a period of months of adjusting to our arrival in Velarde, we come to an agreement, all of us. They won't get in our shit and we won't get in theirs. Which means: We must not feel compassion, or loathing, or fear. We must not feel anything for each other. But still I go to the window in the attic.

When Joe Rendón and I talk across the fence, sometimes we'll dis-

cuss the latest eruption next door. He shakes his head. Joe's young but
he talks like he's old, a man of tradition. He's always reminding me that
the Rendones owned the land all the way from the highway to the river.

"There were orchards and pasture, cows and sheep. And there was
good snow every winter and good rain every summer. Oh yeah, there
were fights, of course, and a lot of drinking, but not cocaine and not
heroin, that's for sure. Now look at us."

The sun dips below the Black Mesa, bringing Velarde's early twilight.
No matter what time of year it is, the sun goes down an hour earlier
than it does anywhere else. Rose explodes one last time:

I CAN'T TAKE IT ANYMORE!

Now she shoots off in her red Chevy SUV. He stays behind with their
son, putters around the yard. She returns in a few minutes, charging
down the road in a dust cloud. She screams some more, goes back inside
the house.

At true dusk, when the last of the sunlight bleeds away from the eastern hills beyond the reach of the mesa's shadow and leaves them in a
blue-gray pallor, I hear her screams again. I'm making dinner, sautéing
Italian sausage and boiling water for pasta. I walk upstairs to the window, where I've spent the better part of the afternoon. I can see the dome
light inside José's small black sedan with the tinted windows. He is sitting inside, listening to music I can't hear. The little boy is gone.

I eat dinner alone. Angela is on the graveyard shift at the clinic. On
Turner Classic Movies, I watch *A Night to Remember* ("Gentlemen, we
are in a precarious position"). I go to the attic to write. I look out the
back window one last time. The dome light in the sedan is off now. A
thin line of light seeps through the crack at the bottom of the front door.

## 4.

Governor José Chacón Medina Salazar y Villaseñor deeded the land on
which the village of Velarde lies to one Sebastián Martín on May 23,
1712, but Martín and his five brothers had occupied and worked the
land since 1703, essentially squatting on territory others had previously
claimed. The region was New Spain's frontier at the time, with bands of
Apaches, Comanches, Navajos, and Utes regularly attacking Hispano
settlements, and Martín is known to have fought the "common enemy"

of the Spanish Crown. The Martín family had deep roots in the region and in conquest. Hernán Martín Serrano had arrived in the area in 1598 with Spanish explorer Juan de Oñate's expedition. "Los linderos," or the territorial limits of the Martín grant, were San Juan Pueblo to the south, the Rio Embudo to the north, Picuris Pueblo to the east, and the Black Mesa to the west. In all, the sprawling claim comprised 50,000 acres that included woods and excellent land for farming on the flood-plain of the Rio Grande.

Martín built his residence and two "torreones"—medieval-style towers to repel Indian attacks—on the east side of the Rio Grande where the present-day community of Los Luceros, a couple of miles from Velarde, is. The compound eventually grew to include some twenty-four rooms, particularly grandiose for the time.

The pop version of these antecedents appears in *Heaven's Window*, a relatively recent coffee-table book capturing an unmistakably colonial point of view that emphasizes the elite Spanish cultural history of Los Luceros, laments its inevitable passing, and celebrates the arrival, in 1918, of Boston Brahmin Mary Cabot Wheelwright. Wheelwright's avo-cation was the study of religion; in northern New Mexico she focused on Navajo traditions, eventually establishing what is today called the Wheelwright Museum of the American Indian. Her arrival coincided with a boom period in the region, a time that resembled the mid-2000s in many ways, turning on a discovery of the West by artists, writers, and bohemian types, which was accompanied by a surge in both artistic representation and real estate values. Indeed, the first is productive of the second. You have to imagine a place before you desire it enough to want it. Wheelwright bought the crumbling Martín estate and trans-formed it into a major destination for the political and artistic elites of the day.

One of the commercial functions of *Heaven's Window*, written by Michael Wallis, an historian of Old West pop, was to draw more tour-ists and home buyers to the region. It is no coincidence that missing from the narrative is the history of usurpation, violent and nonviolent, "legal" and illegal in the area. That history begins with Sebastián Mar-tín himself. Although it is unclear what happened to the previous ten-ants of the tract, Martín was concerned enough about other claims to emphasize in his petition that he and his family alone deserved title to the land, in spite of the fact that he could not procure the tract's original documentation. There is historical record of Martín being capable of fraud: in 1730 he filed suit to secure firm title to Taos Pueblo lands, but his claims were proved false and he was fined for "perjury and misrepresentation."

Fray Francisco Atanasio Domínguez toured the missions of New Mexico in 1776, passing through the string of communities on the Sebastián Martín land grant, including La Joya, which would become Velarde. The Franciscan friar counted about 150 families living in the area at the time. While the grant did not stipulate a commons (the deed made to Martín was considered a private, rather than a community, grant), the uplands between the river and the eastern boundary of the grant functioned as such. Domínguez noted that the acreage was rich in resources—piñon pine for firewood, pasture for cattle, and plentiful water in both the Rio Grande and its tributary streams that drained the Sangre de Cristos. It appears that much of the land was used collectively well into the twentieth century, when the federal government acquired it in a New Deal land-reform strategy called the Vallecitos Federal Sustained Yield Unit, which, rather than realize its stated goal of fostering sustainable rural communities, set the stage for collusion with corporate timber and mineral interests.

A Depression-era study conducted by the Indian Land Research Unit of the Office of Indian Affairs captured the beginning of the transition from a land-based economy to one dependent on migrant labor and federal aid. "Since time immemorial the farmers of Velarde have each spring loaded up their fruit into wagons," the report states, but it also notes that a combination of poverty and increased competition had devastated Velarde's claim as apple king of the Española Valley. In 1935 there were forty-four landholders drawing water from the Rio Grande through the acequia madre (the "big ditch," the main irrigation channel), no one with more than two acres. Some thirty-six of those families were receiving federal aid. The local diet was practically meatless, due to the economy and the tightening on grazing allotments because of overgrazing.

Still, the author of the chapter on Velarde was fairly smitten by the place. "The whole community is beautiful with its orchards and rich fields," he wrote. "The people there think it's the most beautiful of communities and are very glad that as long as the Rio Grande carries water, Velarde will be wonderfully green each summer."

From the point of view of many norteños, the New Deal opened just another chapter in American conquest, in that it disrupted their harsh but sustainable way of life—and, most important, the area's relative independence from federal authority. Hispanos considered federal programs an attack on what is referred to in Spanish as "la querencia"; the term combines the words "querer" (to love) with "herencia" (heritage) for, literally, "love of heritage." The norteño litany encompasses a century and a half's worth of events, beginning with the U.S. Senate's dilution of the Treaty of Guadalupe Hidalgo and the establishment of the Carson and Santa Fe National Forests (in 1908 and 1915, respectively), which steadily whittled away Hispano rights to grazing, timber, hunting, fishing, and water on what had been ejidos, the commons of the land grants under Spanish law. Hispanos, then, saw the arrival of federal programs like the Civilian Conservation Corps, during the Great Depression—which in northern New Mexico helped build tourist infrastructures for the national forests—as replacing norteño autonomy and self-reliance with dependence. The federal presence expanded greatly during World War II with the arrival of the Manhattan Project, which used eminent domain to acquire more Hispano land for Los Alamos National Laboratory. LANL eventually became the Española Valley's major employer (it remains so today), permanently dismantling the traditional land-based economy.

And then there were the nongovernment actors who also took up space and resources. At times in a trickle and at others in fits and starts and on a few occasions in an all-out torrent, over the better part of a century: ranchers, farmers, miners, merchants, speculators and lawyers, builders and tradesmen, writers and artists, consumptives and hippies and spirit seekers of endless varieties, alcoholics and addicts wanting to clean up, families with kids fleeing the drug and gang wars of the cities, families seeking jobs and affordable homes.

The early 1900s were the beginning of what would become a clear division between "old" and "new" Wests. Northern New Mexico played a key role in this process, with the extractive economies of mining and ranching on the one hand, and those based on the representation of culture on the other: the art colonies and tourism, the prototypes of which were established in Santa Fe and Taos. Santa Fe had been the historic

capital through the Spanish, Mexican, and early Anglo-American periods, but when the Atchison, Topeka and Santa Fe Railway bypassed it
in favor of Albuquerque, Santa Fe declined as Albuquerque boomed. At
the turn of the century, a band of bohemians (we could call them pre-
cursors of the "creative class" of the boom and gentrification years in
the first decade of the millennium) arrived and struck a new mother
lode: the past, or at least a romanticized re-creation of it. This venture
included various forms of going native, or "neonative," as the late Western historian Hal Rothman put it—from archaeological digs to appro-
priating Pueblo and Hispano architecture and fiesta traditions. Mary
Austin, one of the most popular writers of the West in the early decades
of the twentieth century, cut the typical figure, fluttering about "wrapped
in a Spanish shawl" and championing Native American and Hispano
causes, even as her imagination colonized the past to fit her desire. The
Taos art colony (founded in 1898 by the visit of painters Ernest Blumenschein and Bert Greer Phillips) invoked similar mythic representations
of "native" cultures, as well as pastoral representations of landscape.
Both colonies—which, to an extent, were competitive—were deeply
rooted in the experience of alienation from the modern and a longing
for what came before, finding meaning in the cultural patterns and the
landscapes of the past, all summed up with the notion of "authenticity."
Often, this idea manifests itself as a clear urban/rural dialectic in which
the modern (urban) subject finds the future in the (rural) past. For more
than one hundred years—and clear across the border of postmodern-
ism's critique of authenticity as inauthentic insomuch as there is no
"original"—this model has worked in different times and places across
the West, reviving dying towns or creating new ones, promoted and
desired for their Western space and light, nature, and native cultural
figures. These days, it's all prepackaged in the ranchette on the range,
the "amenity of rurality."

It makes sense that it was New Mexico that spawned the first Western
art colonies. In many ways, New Mexico was the last frontier of the
West to be opened. Its mining interests were relatively modest, and the
harshness of the climate (frigid winters in the north, heat and aridity in
the south) made it mostly unsuitable for large-scale agriculture and
cattle ranching. New Mexico remained only a territory until 1912, when
it became the forty-seventh state of the Union. The population was

sparse, the land immense, and, for new arrivals from the East Coast, the landscape evoked Romantic awe. Further, the Native American and Hispano populations offered the newcomers the sense that they'd traveled through a time tunnel.

They did not always feel welcome, however. New Mexico has a long history of attempting to keep strangers out, dating back to the Pueblo Revolt of 1680. Achieving solidarity among traditionally competitive pueblos, the Native leader Po'pay of Ohkay Owingeh launched successful raids on the missions, and the Spaniards who survived fled south. After the American occupation in 1848, the Hispano conquerors joined Native Americans as the subjected and as resisters. The Gorras Blancas (named for the white caps they wore) staged guerrilla-like raids on Anglo ranches in the late 1800s. This ideology of resistance was handed down through generations, culminating most famously in the 1960s with the organizer and fire-and-brimstone Pentecostal preacher Reies López Tijerina, who established the Alianza Federal de Mercedes (Federal Land Grant Alliance) and led several takeovers of national forest land that he claimed belonged to heirs of the original Spanish land grantees. An armed raid on the Tierra Amarilla courthouse in 1967 to free prisoners belonging to Tijerina's group brought national and international attention to northern New Mexico.

Curiously, Tijerina was not a norteño, and to this day he is suspect in certain norteño circles as an outsider. A Texas native, he was an itinerant preacher who founded a utopian Christian commune in the Arizona desert before moving to Rio Arriba in the late 1950s. With his electric charisma, he tapped into the powerful Hispano ideal of opposition, the claim for which competes to this day in a "trialectic" with the Anglo conception of the landscape as an American Eden and the Pueblo people's assertion of aboriginal status. The tensions among the three are part of what gives New Mexico its allure: desire here can never be consummated without guilt, which makes it all the more desirable.

## 5.

In a village like Velarde, which has relatively little documented history, the keepers of memory are the elders. At sixty-six years old, Wilfred Gutierrez is a Velarde elder.

He lives not in an adobe but in a single-story, shingle-roofed, wall-to-wall-carpeted house that could blend in seamlessly in any suburb. It stands next to the Iglesia de la Virgen de Guadalupe, which is made of adobe, dates back to the early nineteenth century, and is lovingly maintained by the faithful. The church was built on the site of what was once the village's historic plaza. The stores and trading stalls are long gone. In any case, the Camino de en Medio, more or less Velarde's main street, doesn't even cross the plaza. It is a village square only in memory.

Gutierrez, in addition to being a legendary activist, is one of the few apple farmers left in Velarde.

He answers the door in pajamas and tennis shoes, walking with the assistance of a cane. Kidney disease. He tells me to go to the fridge and get myself a soda. He stands a wiry five foot seven or so, has salt-and-pepper curls, and a thin, taut olive-skinned face with small brown eyes. He reminds me of my "mexicano" grandfather; in New Mexico, mexicano means a recently arrived immigrant from south of the border. Traditional explanations for the nomenclature include the fact that New Mexico was Mexican territory for barely twenty-five years between Spanish and American rule. More recent historical analysis points to an anti-Mexican prejudice in Mary Austin and among the founders of the Spanish Colonial Arts Society in Santa Fe. Austin preferred the "folk" ways of Spain and Native American arts and crafts; if she referred to Mexico, it was usually to praise the indigenous influence there.

"Nothing that could be said of them would be more misrepresentative than that they have 'Mexican souls,'" Austin wrote of Hispanos, adding that their "blood and way of life and mode of thought is predominantly Spanish."

In Wilfred Gutierrez's raspy voice I hear a firsthand account of the better part of the twentieth-century history of northern New Mexico. But the urgent thing he wants to say to me is that he's pissed off at the Our Lady of Guadalupe Church, his next-door neighbor. The new fellowship hall, which dwarfs the church itself and, unfortunately, has none of its charm, has blocked the view Gutierrez had through his living room window of the juniper hills rising toward the Truchas Peaks.

He sits in a chair facing the window, looking out at the back wall of the new building. I sit on a sofa, from where I can see, through a sliding glass door, rows of apple trees and the Black Mesa beyond.

I am now officially middle-aged, but Gutierrez treats me like a young man. That is exactly what I feel like: I don't know much, and norteño elders know that I don't. What do I know of the forest, of the river and its irrigation ditches and water measured in "cubic feet per second," of first and last frosts, of bark beetle infestations? Of land grants and the Santa Fe Ring and masked Hispano night riders sowing terror among gringo speculators?

Gutierrez has been raising hell most of his life, beginning in 1970 as a member of the Acequias del Norte Association, which sought to protect Hispano water rights from the encroachment of incoming ranchers and the thirst of urban expansion. At that time, regional development schemes demanded new sources of water. One plan called for a diversion canal to be built in Velarde to transfer water downstream. Wilfred believed it would have left the Rio Grande dry in the summer. And then what would he have irrigated his apples with? He locked horns with the state engineer of the era, Steve Reynolds, "the water don of New Mexico," as Wilfred refers to him. Norteño resistance stopped the diversion project. The Rio Grande still runs. He still irrigates his apples.

In spite of the endless subdividing and selling of the old land grants, in spite of the new employers across the decades—LANL, Lowe's, Walmart, and the fast food restaurants—and even in spite of the heroin, Wilfred maintains that Velarde is still an agricultural village.

We walk over to the window and look out on the apple trees sloping down toward the river. They are perfectly pruned, branching at identical angles. Between the lines of trees are the irrigation rows, which draw from the acequia madre, which, in turn, draws from the Rio Grande.

It's impossible to overstate the importance of the acequia irrigation system in northern New Mexico. The Pueblos irrigated before contact, but the Spanish system—greatly influenced by Moorish engineering—dramatically expanded agriculture in the region. The system came complete with structure, ritual, and language—the "mayordomo," or ditch boss, who had the final say in allocating water to the "parciantes," farmers with water rights to a given acequia. After the signing of the Treaty of Guadalupe Hidalgo and the Santa Fe Ring's war of speculation, water rights became an essential aspect of land deals. Loss of land meant loss of water, and loss of water meant the loss of a way of life. Over the last 150 years, the struggle over land grants and the acequias on them has grown mythic in the norteño imagination.

That is why Wilfred Gutierrez fought so hard to stop the diversion of the Rio Grande. No water-engineering argument could possibly have gained his support. To him, to most norteños, it was merely the latest attempt to steal historical rights.

It's not just the norteños who invoke a chronicle of loss; Anglos invoke it as well, with lamentations about modernity destroying village life. Indeed, Mary Austin's Spanish folk art revival was based on the notion of a "disappearing" culture, but one that locked norteños into folk caricatures, denying them history, complexity, and a place in the present.

Wilfred, like every good norteño, reveres the past, eulogizes it—reinvents it. In the old days, he'd harvest his apples, then truck them around, selling along the highway to locals and tourists alike, dropping off bushels with brokers in Arizona, Oklahoma, Texas. A broker in California fell in love with his Red Delicious and had half a million boxes shipped out. But Gutierrez's orchard, like other small operations across the country, became unsustainable with the onslaught of corporate farming.

For generations, LANL had been steadily drawing norteños off the land. Wilfred took a job "up the hill" (Los Alamos is in the Jemez Mountains, which overlook the Española Valley). This is where many valley narratives cite the fall. On the one hand, he did very well for himself and his family. But keeping the orchard going as well meant that Wilfred essentially had two full-time jobs. At LANL most norteños, lacking college degrees, qualified for maintenance jobs. Wilfred himself began as a messenger, but during three years in the army he'd taken electronics courses, and he gradually worked his way into more technical jobs in biological labs, cancer research, geothermal work, even inspecting equipment for space flight.

Of course, the story of Hispanos at Los Alamos does not exist in the tourist brochures or in coffee-table books. The historical literature that does exist on the Hispano workforce at LANL—and the many lawsuits filed on behalf of thousands of workers exposed to radiation and toxic chemicals over the decades—is highly specialized material. You have to look for it.

"Right here." Wilfred points out the living room window. "This was la plaza de La Joya," he tells me, invoking the old Hispano name for the strip of land alongside the river—literally, the "jewel," the fertile bottomlands. He claims that the first church on the site was built in 1680 and that it was probably damaged or completely destroyed during the Pueblo Revolt. When he was growing up, the plaza still functioned as a religious and social gathering place. The biggest draw was the Virgen de Guadalupe's feast, December 12. Families would start arriving in their horse-drawn carts two days early. And they'd stay up all night before the feast, singing "Las mañanitas" to the Virgencita till the sun crested the Sangres.

Some of the apple trees in the Valley go back to the turn of the last century, Wilfred says. And the elders still come out to clean the acequia every spring. Just enough apples get picked to make cider and to sell a few bushels.

And who knows, now with the gringos and their organic craze, maybe Velarde will start selling more apples. Maybe some families will actually turn a profit.

## 6.

Miguel Santistevan defies every supposition the elders hold about the younger generation—the "jóvenes."

He lives in a modest adobe surrounded by three-quarters of an acre of farmland on the eastern edge of Taos, the towering Sangres ringing the valley to the east and the north. The first glimpse I catch of Miguel, he is straddling an irrigation ditch and barking orders at two teenagers with shovels struggling to move a large corrugated metal pipe into place.

"You know what's going to happen?" he says in a big, throaty baritone. "The water's going to flow under the pipe. You need a differential of at least a few inches for it to flow through instead of under it."

The kids go back to digging, and it looks like they're having fun.

This is what Miguel Santistevan does: get kids excited about working on the land. At thirty-seven, he is an elder to them, but much younger than his elders. A big goateed punk bear of a man, he stands a thick-chested six feet tall. You can never forget his voice, a gravelly yawp delivering a norteño-punk patois.

"Yup," he is always saying. And "dude." And "you know what?" Sprinkling slightly gringo-accented Spanish vowels across a field of consonant-heavy English, he says that "our people have got to learn from the elders about 'la tierra.'"

The kids are Nicanor and Mike, ninth graders at Taos High, where Miguel teaches earth science. ("There's not a day that goes by when we don't talk about maíz and the acequias," he says.) They wear plain white T-shirts, brilliant in the afternoon sun, Bermudas, slip-on tennis shoes.

Domino's Pizza arrives, and the delivery boy is in a black sedan riding low, blasting hip-hop. Nicanor and Mike query him about the stereo. "Thousand-watt Alpine," says the boy, smiling with pride.

The kids are "animaos," Miguel says, munching on a chicken wing. The formal word in Spanish is animado, as in "motivated"; using a common provincial accent in the Spanish-speaking Americas, Miguel swallows the consonant.

"But they won't take the initiative," he adds. "Their elders have to, like, 'Yo, let me show you how it's done.'"

Nicanor says he's been cleaning acequias since the fifth grade.

"Back in the day," Miguel remarks, "when you were fifteen, sixteen years old, or as tall as a shovel, then it was time for you to clean the acequia and you were considered a man in the community."

After finishing off the chicken wings, pizza, and Dr Pepper, the kids go back to shoveling. The wind rises and clouds gather. It is April and suddenly frigid. (When the warm spring winds began blowing several days ago, Angela and I thought winter was over and stored most of our cold-weather clothes; we will eventually learn to not put them away until well into June.) Miguel and the kids, all in T-shirts, don't seem to mind. I'm in a long-sleeved shirt, and my teeth chatter.

Miguel shows me around his farm, which he christened Sol Feliz for the name of the street his house is on. The land goes back three generations in his family. He's experimenting with dry-farming techniques. He used a swimming pool liner to seal his roof and have it serve as a big rain collector during both winter and the monsoon season, harvesting water in fifty-five-gallon drums placed under the downspouts. Then there's the spiral garden, a pile of rocks on the ground with rock arms spinning out from the center. The rocks heat during the day and release that heat at night, which helps save seedlings from spring frosts; the rocks also collect humidity at night. He calls this "indigenous drip irrigation" and says he got the idea from a "Taos Pueblo dude." He's also dropped perforated clay pots into the ground beneath rock circles, another rustic water-conservation method. The acequia is flowing strong with runoff now, but over the last several years it has dried up by early summer, and the monsoons, which usually help the crops along to harvest, have been disappointing. Miguel is bracing for many more years of unsettled weather patterns. "The drought is Mother Nature teaching us a lesson," he says.

To deal with global warming, he tells me, he will call upon the "memory of the plants" themselves, as well as of the forebears who worked the land.

"I refuse to bring a machine on the land," he says, meaning no rototiller. So he tears it up with a shovel.

Miguel's sensibility is made up of many, sometimes contrary strands. He's a farmer with an activist edge. A survivalist with a patina of indigenous mysticism. A self-proclaimed Chicano who grew up in white Los Alamos.

In New Mexican vernacular, he, like Angela, is a coyote—a caste designation from the colonial era that Hispanos today use as a catchall for "mixed." His dad is a norteño who's struggled with drugs and alcohol. His mom is white. During college, she went on an exchange program to Ecuador while she was pregnant. Because Miguel loves all things indigenous, he believes that by mystical osmosis the spirit of indigenous South America passed to him in the womb. His mother went on to earn a degree in public administration and took a job at LANL. Miguel attended public schools in Los Alamos all the way through graduation, and it was there that his Chicano awareness dawned. In high school a guy named Jeff Hunter called him a dirty Mexican spic. Miguel didn't even know what the word "spic" meant. His mom's boyfriend, Lauro Silva, told Miguel to go back to school the next day and call Jeff Hunter a "dirty piece of white trash and kick his ass."

But not everything in Los Alamos sucked. Among his cohort there was skateboarding, and the glorious rebellion of punk. After his high school graduation ceremony, he and his friends lit their graduation tassels on fire and hung the melted remains on the rearview mirrors of their cars. Then he took classes at the University of New Mexico, but his real passion was music. He was a drummer (with "supersonic beats"), and the band he was in started gigging, for which they needed a name, a punk name. One of the guys liked the term "felch," which, he informed the band, meant a bucket of filth, like the slop you dump in a pigpen. At a gig in Las Cruces, a girl told Miguel what the word actually means: anal sex followed by analingus. The band kept the name.

Lauro Silva, an attorney and land grant activist, had a lasting influence on Miguel. Concerned that the boy needed more indigenous cultural moorings than he could possibly glean from Los Alamos, Lauro introduced him to the loincloths and ankle rattles of Aztec dance. Around the same time, Moisés González, a close friend of Miguel's from UNM, urged him into the Movimiento Estudiantil Chicano de Aztlán. Popularly known by its acronym MEChA, the Chicano campus-based organization has been caricatured by conservative commentators as plotting the "reconquista" of the Southwest. (While it is a nationalist organization in the cultural sense, MEChA is more concerned with scholarship fund-raisers and Aztec dance moves.)

Miguel quit the punk band. One day he found an Andean-style flute at a flea market. He thought of Ecuador as he fumbled around for the notes; eventually he came to play the flute very well. Then Lauro Silva pointed him to the land itself, by inviting Miguel to a meeting of the board that administers the Atrisco land grant, a massive parcel of land bordering Albuquerque. Lauro happened to be a member.

"I didn't even know what a 'board' was," says Miguel.

What would seem tedious to others—administering real estate according to seventeenth-century customs, identifying and organizing thousands of "heirs"—enraptured Miguel. In his imagination, his own family's lore came to life: a great-uncle hanged for resisting the American occupation; his grandfather opening up the acequia on his small plot in Taos. Miguel came to believe that he himself might be an heir to the old Taos land grant, which originally consisted of 38,400 acres. (The Court of Private Land Claims reduced it to 1,817 acres, none of which is held by the heirs today.)

Part of the Atrisco land grant actually lies within the Albuquerque city limits, but most of it is in unincorporated areas of the South Valley, the well-known Hispano barrio where Angela's mother lives; we make the 240-mile round-trip a few times a month. In the early 1990s, when Miguel was introduced to it, the place was mostly undeveloped land rising up to the West Mesa. Developers had long coveted the area, because Albuquerque had already hit the Sandia Mountains in the east. Eventually the developers would get what they wanted—and Angela's mother would get many new neighbors. In the last decade of the twentieth century and the aughts, Albuquerque's developed land area grew by 97.4 percent—111 square miles.

At that first meeting Miguel attended, the board talked about needing a coordinator for the community garden within the grant's commons. Miguel signed up.

He'd never planted anything before. "It was so earth-shattering for me," Miguel says.

He sought out an elder for advice, and the old man told him to plant blue corn—what could be more indigenous than that? It was important to sow the seeds at dawn, the elder said. Miguel dutifully showed up at the garden well before sunrise, expecting a big community affair, like an Amish house-raising, but no one else came that morning. It was just Miguel and the land. The clouds were hanging low over the ruddy stone of the Sandia Mountains.

Rain fell, "a nice drizzle," Miguel says. The sun crested the mountain ridge just below the cloud deck, turning the rain silver. "I saw it out of the corner of my eye and gave a prayer of thanksgiving."

Right then a hawk took off from the branch of a cottonwood and swooped over the field. Seemingly in the wake of its beating black wings, a double rainbow appeared.

"Yup," Miguel says. "I broke down crying, bro."

Miguel's imagination fires on several cylinders at once. His punk sensibility—anarchy, bro, this shit's fucked up!—is inflected with Chicano mysticism: he bows to the four directions on the land of the ancestors. And Chicano righteousness: this land was once Mexican, was once indigenous, and is still. Deep knowledge of current environmental theory, read through a Chicano-indigenist lens—sustainability as indigenous tradition. And a dash of End Days environmentalism: *When the shit comes down, I'm going to be ready for it, dude!*

We've made a complete circle around his land, back to the kids and the culvert. They announce proudly that they're done with the task. Miguel inspects the work. The wind is howling now, dust in our eyes. It is spring, and it will snow in the high country. The seeds and seedlings will have to remember how to survive.

Miguel nods. "Yup," he booms: time to test it out.

He walks a few yards over to the "compuerta" (the sluice gate, in old provincial Spanish) and opens it up. A fist of water charges forward along the ditch. There are some leaves and weeds in the way, and the boys quickly shovel them out so the water can flow freely. It hits the section of pipe they laid and runs into it perfectly, coming out the other end in a few seconds and heading straight for the new seeds.

## 7.

"Leave the Present Behind" reads the billboard on Interstate 40 westbound as you approach Gallup, New Mexico. It should be the state motto. You do not come to New Mexico for the present.

What New Mexico sells is time in a bottle: Indians and Hispanos in adobes, old trucks sinking into weedy earth, the great gorge below Taos showing millions of years of sedimentation, O'Keeffe. You come for the ruins.

The landscape design critic J. B. Jackson's *A Sense of Place, A Sense of Time* is the most evocative elegy. Returning late in life to the New Mexico of his youth (he bounced between prep school in New England and summer vacations on his uncle's farm in Wagon Mound, east of the Sangre de Cristos) he finds only memory: "A flood buried gardens and fields under gravel or sand; a local resource—wood or game or a special crop—lost its market; a railroad ceased operation; the school was closed."

He sighs over prelapsarian New Mexico—the "Spanish-American" golden era of ejidos and acequias, all gone.* It is, he says, as if a neutron bomb had been detonated: "Not a voice is heard; life has withdrawn into

---

* Jackson does ultimately allow for a New Mexican present—the "mobile home on the range." First mimicking the bourgeois critique of trailers—focusing on their aesthetic and functional failures—he then elevates them to "vernacular," and thus deserving of some grudging respect.

the houses behind closed doors, and the windows, with geraniums in tin cans, are obscured by frost."

The progressive proponent of American "vernacular" and landscape architecture critiques those photographers of the early twentieth century who erased from the landscape Hispano and Indian alike, but he does not fully confront his own nostalgic gaze. Dwelling on "decay" and "entropy" (recalling Charles Fletcher Lummis's "land of *poco tiempo*" musings of a century earlier), he himself erases history. Like Lummis, he thinks of himself as a witness to a fading culture, an anthropologist on the verge of archaeology. The driving force of four hundred years of New Mexican history—the symbiotic energy of conquest and resistance, the trialectic of cultures and their contradictory imaginaries—is barely implied.

For Jackson, as for most historians, the three centuries of Spanish history were largely erased by the American defeat of Mexico in 1848. So it is Plymouth Rock, not Española or Santa Fe or Acoma Pueblo, that we regard as the origin of American history. In New Mexico, the guidebooks and interpretive displays that claim foundational status come across more as quaint than authoritative. The Southwest, "Spanish America," is a historical footnote, a failed attempt at empire building.

Comprehensive volumes of American art history acknowledge New Mexico as a foreshadowing of the pioneer European settlements on the East Coast, something of an exercise in alternative history.

What if we stood it all upside down?

If Plymouth Rock were ultimately the footnote and the borderlands were the center of the historical narrative (the zone along the Rio Grande was first a frontier for the Spanish), then perhaps the communalism of New Mexico, as in the ideal of the ejido, would be our ethos instead of hardy individualism. Then maybe New Mexico would be more about sustainability than speculation—not about the past but the future.

## 8.

I feel his beard scratchy on my neck early each morning in Velarde. I have been reading D. H. Lawrence, and we've grown quite close.

*Mornings in Mexico* begins in Mexico in 1922. Lawrence and his wife, Frieda, make the obligatory rounds in the great refracted moment after the revolution, which will come to be thought of as indelibly modern. Out of the moment come the canvases and murals of Los Tres Grandes, the Mexican master painters who depicted the collision of the industrial and the rural, of big capital and the impoverished masses, of earth-brown Indians and light-skinned criollos. Mexico City will emerge out of it as a great metropolis. But Lawrence does not see that. Perhaps he is too early.

Or perhaps he can't see anything other than the "Indian" he's imagined from afar. In this he has been partly instructed by Mabel Dodge Luhan, the cultural lioness of Taos, who summons Lawrence to this new land that is so old, where there are many Indians. She sends him letters imploring him to come, to learn from the Indian an alternative to the industrial grime of Western Europe and the eastern cities of America. She even sends him a care package that includes an Indian headdress. Lawrence is suspicious of Luhan, but he loves the headdress so much that he wears it on the streets of London. He goes native even before he leaves the metropole.

Now he is in Mexico, surrounded by Indians, and he doesn't see what all the fuss is about. He writes of Rosalino, an Indian "mozo," a servant, who "looks up at [him] with his eyes veiled by their own blackness." Lawrence muses that Rosalino occupies a place on the evolutionary plane somewhere between the parrots and the dog of the pensión, where he writes outside under a pleasant winter-morning sun. Rosalino is in "another dimension," belonging more to time than space in a narrowing, dimming tunnel that locks the Indian into what he was before contact with the European.

The Americas are a "wilderness world," and given Lawrence's disdain for what Europe has become, you'd think him a natural to reach into their history and rescue the Indian for the salvation of modernity. But no. Three hundred years after Oñate's conquest, Lawrence indulges the colonial hierarchies. He looks upon half-naked natives, at their "beautiful, suave, rich skins." Only this "richness of the flesh," he writes, contrasts with the "complete absence of what we call 'spirit.'" Good enough stock for mozos, in other words, but not sophisticated enough to enact a revolution, which Lawrence dismisses as illiterates mocking

European democracy. They are a spiritless people whose future will always be deferred, he decides.

"Mañana es otro día," writes Lawrence. "Tomorrow is another day. And even the next five minutes are far enough away, in Mexico, on a Sunday afternoon."

Other new arrivals—Luhan, Charles Lummis, the archaeologist Adolph Bandelier, Mary Austin, the Southwest art and literary world— had taken up indigenous New Mexico because here there was rescue from all the terrible wounds in whiteness: industrialization and the Great War, the Conradian contradictions of empire.

Luhan's arrival in Taos in 1919 was particularly momentous. She was known in New York and across the Atlantic as a patroness and was, above all, a seeker of "authenticity." She was among the pioneers of what would become the first major art colony of the American West (preceding Santa Fe by a few years), laying down a model that would be replicated many times—even and especially a century later, during the boom years.

The Spanish had subjected the Indian with harquebuses, fire, disease—and representations of subjection, beginning with the naming of the Indian as Indian, the Columbian misnomer. Queen Isabella believed she had liberated indigenous America body and soul by abolishing slavery and admitting that the natives could be saved in the Christian sense, but she couldn't do much about how her own Spanish subjects regarded them, nor the complex way that European and Indian would violate, desire, and imagine one another across the centuries.

You can point to the luminaries of the early art colonies of New Mexico and argue their place in American art and political history. There are astonishing portraits of natives by Blumenschein, fellow Taos colony founder E. Irving Couse, and many others—canvases that shimmer with technical brilliance. But what is rarely discussed is the lineage of power in which these artists were complicit or whether their representations of the ennobled "otherness" of the indigenous Southwest fundamentally broke with the history of subjection, left it intact, or even emboldened it. Was the painters' gaze itself an act of brute power— a normalizing of colonization—notwithstanding its aesthetic accomplishment?

The colonies' origins were anything but innocent. After the bloody removal of Indians to the reservations (the Pueblos were among the few to remain on grants originally bestowed by the Spanish), the Atchison, Topeka and Santa Fe Railway completed its route across the Southwest. The region was sparsely populated, and competition with other transcontinental routes was intense. The railroads needed cargo and paying passengers, which could materialize only with widespread regional development. In the late nineteenth century, paintings were the advertising medium of choice. The ATSF and other railroads commissioned artists for works whose sole purpose was to lure migrants westward. The artists came following speculative capital, arriving at a geography haunted by colonial horrors—which, of course, they could not see. (And even if they had, their patrons would not have abided such representations.)

Eminent painters such as Thomas Moran were offered free passage to the Grand Canyon in exchange for a canvas. The ATSF reproduced Moran's rendering with thousands of lithographic copies. The images soon found their way into magazines like *Harper's Weekly* and *McClure's*, and into railroad ticket offices. The Taos colony owes its founding to the ATSF. Ernest Blumenschein was among its stable of artists. He stumbled upon the town when he was exploring the area and a wagon wheel broke; the ensuing encounter with landscape and Indians hooked him. The artists invariably represented Indians or landscape, or Indians on the landscape. At a time of electrification, the advent of motion pictures, and the arrival of the Model T, the most salient advertising trope for tourism in the Southwest was "Leave the present behind."

Mabel Dodge Luhan bought into the promise and enhanced it, helping to lure other spirit seekers. "Oh, I thought, to leave it, to leave it all, the whole world of it and not to be alone. To be with someone real at least, alive at last, unendingly true and untarnished," she rhapsodized in *Edge of Taos Desert*, whose subtitle sums up her projections: *An Escape to Reality.* (The use of "desert" to describe Taos is curious—the valley is abundantly watered by the Sangre de Cristos and is at the edge of a great mixed-conifer forest. But "desert" evokes a much more powerful Western myth.) Little wonder that this "untarnished" reality quickly filled with proto-hippies testing barriers of race, sex, and gender— alternative communities long before the communes of the 1960s. Taos allowed fantastic entrée to the "primitive" subject that so fascinated the modernist mind.

But back to lying in bed with D.H. in Velarde.

I read about his life with Frieda in the little cabin on the mountain—provided by Luhan—and then Angela and I visit the cabin. It is not an adobe. It is made of wood. I am fairly shocked by how small and rickety it looks, how thin, considering the brutal winter. In Velarde we have twenty-four inches of adobe between us and the icy winds blowing down the Black Mesa and still need to fire up all three gas furnaces and the woodstove to keep the entire house warm. (Usually, we run only one of the furnaces; the gas bill would be astronomical otherwise.) To think of a sickly Lawrence surviving a winter in San Cristobal casts him in a martyrly light. In the end, it was his fascination and contact with the other that killed him—he contracted both malaria and the ultimately fatal tuberculosis in Mexico, an inversion of the colonial trajectory of illness.

I find myself liking Lawrence as I read more and more of the voluminous material, most of it hagiographic, written by others about his time in Mexico and New Mexico. I read about him baking bread at the cabin in San Cristobal every day, and soon afterward I am at Walmart buying flour and yeast. I knead dough for the first time in my life. Baking at an altitude of six thousand feet (Lawrence was at about nine thousand) takes much adjusting of recipe ratios, and I never get it perfect; the bread always winds up a bit too dense. But it tastes good. When we entertain guests, I always bake a couple of baguettes and never forget to say that they are homemade.

Along with the vegetable garden I begin to tend, baking my own bread is a sign that I myself am going "native." Except that each step I take closer to norteño culture underscores that I am not, nor will ever be, norteño. Maybe I am like Lawrence in this sense as well; he, too, felt insufferable self-awareness when in contact with difference. For Lawrence, New Mexico was an experience of ambiguity.

After his Mexican verdict of dumb Indians, Indians veiled in their own darkness, he arrives in Taos determined to cut through the mythic crap of the American West: "You've got to de-bunk the Indian, as you've got to de-bunk the Cowboy. When you've de-bunked the Cowboy, there's not much left. But the Indian's bunk is not the Indian's invention. It is ours."

He identifies a range of white relationships to "the Indian," while failing to account for the possibility of ambivalence: "It is almost impossible for white people to approach the Indian without either sentimentality or dislike. The common healthy vulgar white usually feels a certain native dislike of these drumming aboriginals. The highbrow invariably lapses into sentimentalism like the smell of bad eggs."

Lawrence places himself in neither group, neither the common healthy vulgar nor the highbrow. He is actually both. He sentimentalizes, and he dislikes, even as he attempts to take down both representations.

The whites, agitating passionately on behalf of Native Americans and Hispanos, striving to be the "voice of the voiceless," in fact left their cause voiceless.

What a mess. I can imagine the drunken parley at Los Gallos, Mabel's compound in Taos (eighty-four hundred square feet and a big *M* etched on the front door, five guesthouses, separate quarters for servants, stables, corrals; you can take a writing workshop there today).

Mabel, who'd been set on the course of "saving the Indian" by her third of four husbands, the painter Maurice Sterne, would be gushing over her latest discovery at the Pueblo—pottery, blankets, a Tewa feast dance.

The always dramatic Lawrence would be pacing the room, muttering, cackling about how contact with the Indian meant a symbolic death for both Indian and white, and quite possibly the physical death of what was left of the Indians.

And then there was Antonio "Tony" Luhan, Mabel's prize acquisition, her fourth husband, a full-blooded Indian from Taos Pueblo. He is invariably described as "quiet," "almost inarticulate," the very essence of noble, if not savage. He seems quiet in the photograph by Edward Weston: full lips pursed, looking away from the lens—among us but not.

And Frieda seething not so secretly at Mabel, and not so secretly lusting after Tony.

Undeniably progressive in the ideological context of the time, the Taos cohort railed against the American bloodlust of Manifest Destiny, militated for the Indians righteously, and yet consumed them without pity, claiming the indigenous past as the future, the dawn of a new age.

All of which struck Lawrence as sentimentalizing the Indian, which was the same as hating him.

Lawrence instead confronted what critics call the "radical alterity" in the encounter: "He's not coming our way. His whole being is going a different way from ours. And the minute you set your eyes on him you know it." It is such a huge difference, such a vast distance, that an actual meeting is impossible—or, to Lawrence, "fatal."

The fatal line, for Lawrence, is one of language. Europeans have it, Lawrence says, and Indians don't: "The Indian, singing, sings without words or vision. Face lifted and sightless, eyes half closed and visionless, mouth open and speechless, the sounds arise in his chest, from the consciousness in his abdomen." Language comes after the Indian.

One wonders exactly how Po'pay unified the Pueblos of New Mexico in 1680 and conceived his precise military strategy (he handed out calendar sticks to different pueblos for a simultaneous attack) from within a consciousness incapable of representation. Lawrence thinks it is all in the blood, the dark Indian blood that pulls back to the very "centre of the earth," an abyss the white man cannot peer into, even as Lawrence yearns to, seeking the cure for his own Euro-Christian bad faith. This is why Lawrence has come to Taos. Yet he knows that the entire modernist turn toward difference is sentimental. And Lawrence hates sentimentality! So he loathes himself as well as the Indian who drew him in with his "mindless" dancing. Lawrence evinces the ambivalence of a mind limited by notions of "blood," the Victorian consciousness haunted by its tortured desire. This is what draws me to Lawrence.

The great moral failure of Mabel and the Taos scene was the American "I" always at the forefront of the proceedings, which ultimately disallowed the "we" she hoped her breaching of the white Indian divide embodied. You don't read *Lorenzo in Taos*, Mabel's account of that time, to learn about Lorenzo (as she rechristened Lawrence; there's little indication that he resisted). Mabel is an overwhelming presence, with her kooky proto–New Ageisms, her blatant competition with Frieda, and her enthusiasm for the ultimate vanity project: to have Lawrence render her in a novel.

Lawrence never wrote the novel (Mabel blames Frieda and her jealous meddling), but whatever he could not write about New Mexico, he painted. At La Fonda de Taos, a hotel on the plaza dating back to the earliest days of the modernist bohemian rush on northern New Mexico, you can still pay a dollar to see the "Lawrence paintings," the collection of Saki Karavas, the proprietor of La Fonda during its heyday. I walk in one late winter morning when the plaza is empty. I pay at the lobby and am ushered to Karavas's old office.

The paintings hang informally, alongside photographs of famous patrons of the hotel. *A Holy Family* immediately draws me. It is the cleanest of the compositions and features the largest figures. It is, of course, a trinity. At the center is a black-haired, brown-skinned man with almond-shaped eyes and a thick mustache. His blue shirt is open in a V halfway down his chest. A woman sits on his lap. She is white, very white, with blond curls, slightly crossed blue eyes, full red lips. She is topless. Her right arm crosses her body at about the level of her navel; her right hand rests atop his right hand, which cups her left breast, clearly referencing Rembrandt's *The Jewish Bride*. They are both crowned with ruddy-yellow nimbuses. To the left of the couple, seated at a chair before a table, is the child. He must be their child, a boy. He has her blond hair, but it is straight, like his. The boy's eyes split the difference between his father's almost-black brown and the azure of his mother's. His skin is a fraction of a shade darker than his mother's. The composition functions as a series of circles and near circles—heads and nimbuses and bowls and dishes, a curious circular window (revealing a thick house wall that looks like adobe), eyes and breasts. These shapes are separate but echo one another. The most striking face is the father's, which is at the center of the painting. It is one of the most dramatic portraits Lawrence ever painted. The painting is framed tightly on the upper torsos, an intimate family portrait.

Critics have generally commented on the blatant, playful sexuality, but not on the equally obvious nod at miscegenation. Unlike his parents, the boy does not have a nimbus. Could the child of this border-breaking union possibly be liberated of the dead weight of medieval hierarchies? "Holy" in that he is beyond good-and-evil notions of "blood"? (Probably not; as noted, Lawrence himself was steeped in those very ideas.) Yet in all, it is a sophisticated play on race and sex and religion, almost certainly informed by the passion play Lawrence observed at Mabel and Tony's, and far more productive than his own largely ignorant textual studies of Indian dances. In *A Holy Family* he let desire be, let it run where it wanted, let it wander free of history or, in its consummation, rewrite it—all in sharp contrast to his melodramatic ruminations about "fatal" contact between Indian and white.

He leaves the cabin and the great ponderosa shading it—O'Keeffe rendered the tree in a nocturne with sharp stars finding the spaces between the thick, dark clouds of boughs and needle tufts. He swears he will return to Taos. He dies a consumptive in Europe.

To this day, he holds such power over Taos! His ghost and Mabel's preside like the colony's royal couple. We still see the north through the eyes of Mabel and D.H. We are fascinated by and a little scared of the Indians (so quiet, so inscrutable . . . of course we just vote yes for the casino contract). As for the Hispanos, Luhan and Lawrence by and large ignored them. They had yet to be rehabilitated by the Spanish Colonial Arts Society.

Today, Santa Fe and Taos are still filled with galleries featuring Indians riding bareback. The anthropologist Sylvia Rodriguez, of the University of New Mexico, writes of the early bustling days of the colony in Taos and the desperate demand for models. The painter E. Irving Couse contracted Joseph Sandoval, a six-year-old Pueblo, for a sitting. The boy was terrified and ran out of the studio, but was caught and literally chained around the waist to prevent any more escapes. The painting was finished, and Sandoval became a career model.

Generations of artists and writers have kept the representation of both Native and Hispano locked in place. For all the "liberal," "progressive," and even "radical" sentiment expressed by the boho cohort of northern New Mexico over the generations, the art colonies have little to show by way of a fundamental change in their relationship to the other. If anything, the bohemian sensibility has served as an aesthetic cover for the extreme social and economic inequities of the region.

The "gentry"—the artists, writers, photographers, promoters, and tour guides—perpetuate a historical, cultural, political erasure that, in turn, makes them complicit—or, even further, a cause of displacement and poverty and addiction among New Mexico's poor. It is, after all, their representation of an American Western pastoral that lures ever more "migrants" to the area, which fuels speculation, which pushes the native to the margins.

I am not just feeling D.H.'s beard on my neck. I'm wearing it.

## · 2 ·

## HOUSE OF THE MOON

### 1.

Seven years before I moved to Velarde and a little more than seventy years after Lawrence arrived in Taos, I helped write an American desert story of art and speculation. I was part of a new bohemian generation—decidedly more scruffy than the likes of Mabel Dodge Luhan and friends—that moved into San Bernardino County's Morongo Basin, at the western edge of the Mojave Desert (also known as the "high desert," lying north of the lower, hotter Colorado Desert, which hosts Palm Springs). The basin includes three main towns along a twenty-five-mile stretch of Highway 62, the only major route through the area, Yucca Valley, Joshua Tree, and Twentynine Palms. We weren't thinking of founding an art colony in the spirit of Taos, and certainly not of spawning a fierce real estate boom, but that is more or less what happened. And the cradle of this scene was in Joshua Tree, the smallest and most picturesque of the three towns.

The pilgrimage to the desert coincided with the tech swell of the late 1990s and continued through the aughts. People moved: in, out, up, down. The built environment was transformed by the baubles of the boom—hillside chalets laden with such amenities as his-and-her sinks in the bathrooms—and by the clusters of box houses that spread along the dusty yellow flats of the desert, the new Western home on the range for refugees from the gentrified cities. "Nature" changed here, too; that is to say, the way we gazed upon it changed. Land in the Morongo Basin became "landscape," which itself became an amenity to sell the houses staged on it. And wherever the boom struck, it altered history and sense of place. The narratives of the region were rewritten according to the imaginations and desires and prejudices and projections of the new-comers, the speculators—the scruffy artists, the ones with a license to sell real estate, the ones without legal residency in the United States. We had all come to speculate, and not just in the narrow sense of weighing risk and value, but closer to the origins of the word, the Latin verb *speculari*, meaning "to look," which derives from the noun *specula*, "watch-tower." We assessed the land with our disparate desires, united only by the mythic depth of the desert. And everywhere the boom arrived, it erased the stories and people that stood in the way of the representations that sold the new landscape.

This recolonization began in Joshua Tree with a ragged crew of musicians, painters, writers, spirit seekers, and twelve-steppers. We weren't aware of it at the time, but we were reproducing a model of urban gentrification, casting it in the American pastoral of the West, serving as the advance scouts for an invasionary force of investors.

What did we know? That we needed a cheaper place to live, because "urban renewal" was pushing up rents in Los Angeles. (In this sense we were gentrifiers fleeing gentrification.) And we knew Joshua Tree; L.A. considers the area an appendage of itself, a desert diorama two hours from downtown. There had been artists and visionaries in the Mojave before us. In 1914, Job Harriman, a former minister turned radical materialist (he was the vice presidential candidate on Eugene Debs's Social Democratic Party ticket in 1900, and came within a few hundred votes of becoming mayor of Los Angeles in 1913), founded a socialist community on the yucca plains north of the San Gabriel Mountains, which separate the coastal scrubland from the desert. Aldous Huxley arrived a few decades later to sneer at the "Ozymandian" ruins of Harriman's failed commune—and to seek, just as earnestly as Harriman and his followers, another kind of utopia in a spirit quest for the "attributeless Godhead" out amid the "boundlessness and emptiness," of the desert, resorting to everything from *The Tibetan Book of the Dead* to mescaline and LSD.

When we arrived, the desert was already considered cool, a structure of feeling deposited by the several generations of outsiders that had preceded us. In the Mojave, "outsider" had a completely distinct meaning from the violently negative connotation in New Mexico that could get your house firebombed. We were here *because* we were outsiders; to be cool you had to be an outsider. You were outside the mainstream by choice or (just as good) because the gatekeepers hadn't recognized your genius. There was no more authentic a figure in desert cool than Gram Parsons, who had died of an overdose at the age of twenty-six in Room 8 of the Joshua Tree Inn. (It didn't matter that he was the scion of a Southern citrus magnate.)

In my early twenties I worked at the *L.A. Weekly*, and among my elders there was Michael Ventura, a prolific columnist-poet-critic. He wore horn-rimmed glasses and a cowboy hat. Among his favorite musicians was the West Texas singer-songwriter Joe Ely, whose voice and lyrics evoked the dusty desert plains. Ventura, impeccably cool, was a generous mentor. I asked him once to recommend a place to hide away for some writing. He told me to go to Twentynine Palms; specifically, the 29 Palms Inn, a collection of rustic adobes set amid an oasis of palm trees, which had been drawing outsiders and consumptives and cowboys and Native Americans since forever.

There was some rock 'n' roll royalty in the neighborhood. Eric Burdon, the famed singer of the Animals, owned a house in the area. And who could be cooler than Dick Dale, the surf-guitar god, who had a second home up here, too. For decades, bikers and Marines had congregated at the bars of the high desert. Alongside the old-timers with tales of the homesteading days (real cowboys!), there were Native American pictographs on the rocks (real Indians!). And the military base surely hid secrets about alien crash landings.

The early seekers had left enough of an aura to draw succeeding generations and cliques. Thousands of New Agers made the trip to, or tripped in, Joshua Tree for the Harmonic Convergence, a planetary alignment that was to usher in a new era of cosmic peace, an iconic 1980s moment.

Historically, most of the human presence in the region had been transient. Across the twentieth century there had been gold prospecting in the area (but only a handful of modest strikes), and a sprinkling of hardy souls who signed up for the Homestead Act's offer of land in exchange for building at least a modest home (there are abandoned one-room shacks in various states of decomposition across the area). Tourism was relatively light in the decades after the designation of several hundred thousand acres as a national monument, in 1936, mostly because of the area's remoteness and scarce amenities. Yet the new arrivals who began trickling in during the 1990s had little interest in amenities. They were fleeing Los Angeles altogether. Many people were doing so at the time, escaping California-style disasters, both man-made and natural—riots, earthquakes, nativism, floods, recession, wildfires. A-list Hollywood headed for Montana; working-class African-Americans and Latinos, for Lancaster, Las Vegas, Phoenix, Albuquerque, Denver. My parents were among the exodus, finding their retirement Shangri-la in Sedona, Arizona. (The neonativist tide there would eventually send them scurrying back to California.)

If you were a broke artist or musician and wanted the landscape to match your sense of cool, Joshua Tree beckoned.

## 2.

Ted Quinn was as California a kid as they come. Which means that he was born not in California but in La Porte, Indiana, to good American mutt stock—German, Norwegian, Irish. The family came west in 1963, when Ted was about four years old. Both he and his sister, Debbie, were "discovered" after she underwent successful open-heart surgery at the age of five. Talent agents signed the kids up, and Teddy became the "Bayer Aspirin boy." He worked alongside legends—Welles, Hayworth, Mitchum—and retired from film and TV at the age of twelve. In high school he painted and fronted rock bands. Ted was, above all, a child of the 1960s. He'd even seen the Beatles at the Hollywood Bowl; his father had taken him and his sister when they were still in elementary school.

In the final years of the 1970s, while most of America was suffering from a bad case of *Saturday Night Fever*, the really cool kids had gone underground. New York had CBGB, and Los Angeles had its own powerful "new music" scene, centered on several clubs downtown and on the Sunset Strip: the Hong Kong Café, Madame Wong's, the Starwood, and the Legendary Whiskey, where a few years earlier Jim Morrison had writhed profanely. For the edgiest scenesters, living in Hollywood meant being in a band or two or three. It meant shopping for clothes at thrift stores, sharing a one-bedroom apartment in a decaying bungalow court. If you had a day job it meant nothing to you. You got high in all manner of ways, with alcohol or drugs or both or by meditating. You went without meat and followed the Dalai Lama.

Ted is a few years older than I am; I was a youngster on the margins of the scene that he helped to pioneer. What I remember is the astonishing energy—how young people conjured an entire universe of affect, willfully and creatively sculpting every aspect of their lives. We watched punk tear down the pop order and summon up several new ones from the rubble. Ted and his cohort mixed and matched styles—rock, folk, new wave, ambient. They were sixties doves and lovers of melodic pop, but a dose of punk anger leavened their music, and they experimented with the electronica of the early digital age.

It was in this Hollywood that Ted lived, and it was here that he met Fred Drake, the man who would take all of us to the desert.

Fred grew up in Texas and was gay, and early on he understood that he would never be able to reconcile that. He was a rock 'n' roller as well, which further contradicted his gayness—the genre in its mainstream incarnation never having accepted its fundamental homoeroticism (which Todd Haynes beautifully renders with Christian Bale and Ewan McGregor making love on the roof of a London apartment building in *Velvet Goldmine*). Fred was a novice drummer and heard about a class being offered by a member of the Mothers of Invention, the conceptual rocker Frank Zappa's band. The class was in Los Angeles; Fred drove all night. Within forty-eight hours of his arrival, he'd taken the class, auditioned for Ted's band (which sounded, Ted said, like "kids playing on a bunch of broken toys"), and fallen in love with a cute blond-haired, blue-eyed Cuban boy named Tico. Fred would live in California for the rest of his life.

The 1980s dawned with the assassination of John Lennon and the ascension of Ronald Reagan. As the United States supported death squads in Central America disguised as freedom fighters, Fred and Ted and their cohort became fierce poets for peace. The names of their bands—Dream Army, Ministry of Fools—said it all. By the mid-1980s they had established a strong presence in the clubs. There were positive reviews in the *L.A. Weekly*. I was a staff writer then, but I had abandoned rock 'n' roll for Latin American folk (all the better to fight gringo imperialism), and I was completely unaware of their bands even as their biggest critic-fan typed up raves in a cubicle just across from mine in our smoke-filled office. Suits from the industry took note—big labels like Geffen, Atlantic. There were showcases and meetings in posh offices, but no contract was ever offered.

Fred lived in one of Hollywood's many modest Spanish-style buildings of chalk-white plaster and red tile, arches and hardwood floors; they were, above all, affordable. Among his neighbors was Adriene Jenik, a young multimedia artist, and Smokey, the elder of the building, who happened to own a property on the edge of the Big Empty in the Mojave east of Twentynine Palms. Smokey would drive out there in his 1963 Corvette Sting Ray and stay for days or weeks at a time. He was always talking about the desert.

In 1985 the first public HIV-testing program arrived in Southern California. I did not know Fred then, but we could easily have crossed paths—in the music scene, in the gay bars, or on line at the clinic in Long Beach. I tested negative; although because of my risk factors— intravenous drug use, unprotected sex with multiple partners and with men—I was convinced for years afterward that there had been some mistake. Fred tested positive and soon became symptomatic, with a swollen lymph node that required surgical removal. The subsequent loss of movement in his shoulder meant his days as a drummer were over, so he turned to singing, songwriting, and the art of sound engineering. Ted remembers Fred's sound as "dreamy, psychedelic, Beatles-y, Lennon-y."

Serendipity was at work gathering a constellation of personalities. Through Fred, Ted met Adriene, whom years later would introduce him to the performance artist Elia Arce, who I'd met through the Central American solidarity network. Another fixture on the scene was Joe "City" García, who happened to have grown up in Española, New Mexico, come west, and played in several bands with Fred and Ted. Fred was also friends with Debbie Hotchkiss, who married the guitarist and songwriter Tony Mason, who in turn became a collaborator of Ted's. When Ted was lovers with Francesca Lia Block, who would later write the young adult *Weetzie Bat* novels, which conjure a vibrant, multicultural, and omnisexual Los Angeles, one of her best friends was a northern California bookstore manager named Fred Burke, who ended up becoming a dear friend of Fred Drake's.

We all came together in the desert.

Fred was thin and pale and had a bony face, the gauntness partly due to living with HIV for about twelve years by the time I met him. He was brilliant and explosive. Everyone who knew him told stories of Fred "going off" on long-winded and downright mean rants and then just as suddenly slipping back into his smart and charming self. He had a fetish for matadors and cowboys and collected thrift-store hats.

Fred and Ted came to the desert following the narrative trail blazed for them by Smokey's fantastical stories. They ventured out for the Harmonic Convergence in 1987 and then began making regular trips to Joshua Tree, sometimes with pals from the Ministry of Fools cohort. The meeting that set in motion all kinds of changes for the friends and for Joshua Tree itself took place after a few years of these sojourns. In 1993 gay activists planned a march on Washington. AIDS Project Los Angeles promised to sponsor Fred, who by then was a veteran of the activist scene, with a plane ticket. At the last minute APLA bungled the logistics and the trip fell apart, throwing Fred into a dark mood. Now he was determined to get out of L.A.—he couldn't stand the thought of watching the march on TV. His 1962 Ford Falcon wouldn't survive the haul to the desert, but luckily, Francesca Block offered Fred and Ted her Jeep Cherokee.

They drove to Twentynine Palms, a raggedy village on the edge of millions of harsh acres, and checked in to the Harmony Motel, retro with its red neon and casual desert-modern design. Fred was still fuming about missing the march. To distract him, Ted pulled out his acrylics—he always traveled with an art kit—and painted the word GAY in big, bright letters on Fred's T-shirt. Suddenly Fred became obsessed with the idea of getting a Marine haircut; there was no dissuading him. This was Fred in provocative performance mode. Don't Ask, Don't Tell had just gone into effect, pleasing no one and least of all Fred. Tom Hanks would soon unbutton his shirt and show us Kaposi's sarcoma lesions in *Philadelphia*. In Los Angeles, the gay districts of Silver Lake and West Hollywood were losing a generation to AIDS. Fred wanted to make a stand with a glittery, glammy T-shirt and a crew cut, invoking a bit of Bowie and timeless gay camp. The mise-en-scène was perfect: a barbershop where a few hard young men were getting their hair cut by Vietnamese women in the middle of a desert in which the Marines simulated the terrible duty they had only recently fulfilled in Iraq. How would the Marines react to Fred? Was he willing them to fight him or join him out of the closet?

In the end, the performance was better in concept than in execution. Ted remembers feeling nervous, but there was no incident at the barbershop. When they walked back out to the car they realized they'd locked their keys inside. The duo stood glumly by the side of the road in full costume as they waited for the auto club.

The weekend was far from over. To make the most of their adventure, the guys ate mushrooms and drove into what was then called Joshua Tree National Monument (locals called it simply "the Monument," and many do to this day, even though it was upgraded to national park status in 1994). They wound up at Keys View, a popular spot offering a vista of the Coachella Valley, the massive craggy face of Mount San Jacinto looming above Palm Springs, and, on a clear day (that is, when the smog from L.A. doesn't blow in), a glimpse of Mount Signal in Mexico, almost one hundred miles away. With Keys View at a relatively high five thousand feet, the valley many dozens of miles wide, and Mount San Jacinto rising up more than ten thousand feet, there is a Grand Canyon-esque sense of vastness. No doubt all the more so when flying high on mushrooms.

So there they were, sitting on a rock in the golden afternoon, Fred's anger finally dissipating, when they heard voices calling, *Fred! Ted!*

It was Tony Mason and Debbie Hotchkiss, who happened to have driven up to the desert for the weekend, too. They'd seen a segment about Joshua Tree on *California Gold*, a regional PBS travel show hosted by Huell Howser, a golly-gee hawker selling wholesome Americana. Tony and Debbie had just fallen in love, and were newly clean and sober and buzzing with caffeine, nicotine, and the Twelve Steps. Which made Fred and Ted feel rather guilty; the two agreed in whispers to keep their drug trip a secret. The foursome drove to Jeremy's, a modest coffeehouse in Joshua Tree, where they ran into even more friends from L.A. They didn't need the mushrooms to confirm a convergence of harmonic proportions. On their way out of town they noticed a sign advertising a house rental on Hallee Road, at the time the only intersection on Highway 62 with a traffic signal. Fred suggested they check it out. There were actually three small houses for rent, within a few dozen yards of each other. They looked at all of them, and Fred said he wanted to rent the middle house, which happened to be in the worst shape. Ted was shocked, worrying that there would be no decent medical care for Fred. For amenities, there was a Circle K where meth heads brooded by the payphones.

It was like the frontier, Ted said.

## 3.

By winter 1997, Ted and Elia were living in a shack in the desert. So were Tony Mason and Debbie Hotchkiss. Others were trickling in, orbiting around Fred's house on Hallee Road, which he'd converted into a recording studio he baptized Rancho de la Luna.

At the time I was broke, broken, and on drugs. It was my second round with addiction. The first had been in my late teens and early twenties in Venice, California, where I thought I'd found my version of Jack Kerouac's "fellaheen," poor white and poor black and poor Mexican, sublime and scheming street angels. (There is hardly an echo of this cohort on the gentrified beach today.) While I could claim an organic if complicated relationship to these subjects—I grew up middle-class, but only one generation removed from Latin American poverty—in many ways I recognized in myself D.H. and Mabel's fascination with the "authentic" figures they found in their "escape to reality" in Taos. In Venice there was also lots of drugs and sex. It all began innocently enough: an aspiring writer and horny kid looking for experience. Ultimately, I saved myself through politics. The war had broken out in El Salvador, and the twenty-something found a partisan passion that produced a rush not unlike the one from the stimulants he'd been abusing.

The second round began a decade later in Mexico City. There was a semblance of peace in Central America, and I suppose I was looking for a new high. As William Burroughs had discovered, Mexico City afforded the addict relative freedom in the form of hypodermic needles available over the counter and marvelously cheap drugs in the red-light and bohemian districts. Mexico City was another "authentic" place in which to get messed up; I was only dimly aware that I was following in gringo and European footsteps—some revolutionary, some decadent: Bréton, Artaud, Lowry, the Beats. I'd imagined more of a "roots" journey, a "Chicano" pilgrimage to the Aztec capital, communion with my indigenous forebears. It took me a long time to figure out that what I'd actually found were my American roots, and in them an unbridled desire for the other which, at the moment, I seemed able to consummate only through cocaine.

Convinced by Elia that the desert was the only possible salvation for my affliction, I traded one long-standing imaginary for another. In the land that healed the consumptives, Elia put me in touch with Adriene Jenik, a multimedia artist, who had recently bought her old neighbor Smokey's property in Twentynine Palms. On the edge of three vast desert tracts, Twentynine Palms is the gateway to the largest Marine training facility in the country, Joshua Tree National Park, and the open desert beyond the "NEXT SERVICES 100 MILES" sign down the street from Smokey's old place.

"Adriene wants to turn it into a retreat for artists," Elia said. "You would be the first."

I arrived late one afternoon as the sun was falling behind the pinto-colored hills and a frigid, sand-stinging wind rose up.

Adriene showed me around the property, which consisted of several small buildings and sheds. On each structure was a metal sign that warned of "high explosives." It was unclear whether this was a bluff. Smokey had apparently kept a lot of secrets.

"And here's where you'll be staying," Adriene said, pointing to what looked like a metal storage shed.

Which it was. There was a sagging cot, a piece of carpet over bare, stony ground, and a small space heater. Adriene liked lights, and there were many strings of colored bulbs and kitschy fixtures purchased from local thrift stores, all hooked up to a tangle of extension cords that ran to the main house.

It was so cold in the shed that night that my bones ached. When I tried to hook up a second electric heater, the circuit breaker blew. Adriene, an artist prone to artistic mood swings, was not sympathetic.

I lasted only a few days.

Walking around the "neighborhood"—dirt roads that had more street signs than houses—I noticed a place for rent a few blocks away. It was the right price.

Not long after I moved in, I invited Ted and Elia and Tony and Debbie over for a housewarming. Tony presented me with a bundle of sage ("to purify your new place, man"). Out came the guitars and harmonicas. I had just started playing music again after many years, and now I turned to Americana, the style that a lot of people were conjuring in the desert. It seemed the right place to invoke the spirit of Johnny Cash. He might have been from the Deep South, but his music fit perfectly with the landscape.

Meanwhile, Fred Drake was gathering an ever-growing low-rent boho crowd around him at Rancho de la Luna. It was a place of old carpet and couches, coiled audio cables hanging neatly from nails on the walls alongside his cowboy and matador memorabilia. At one end of the living room was an old cast-iron wood-burning stove and at the other a vintage 1970s sixteen-track mixing board with a one-and-a-half-inch reel-to-reel, in open defiance of the digital turn in the recording industry. Fred became known as the "mayor of Joshua Tree" (the village had no official governing body) as more and more friends from Los Angeles made the trip to record, and then friends of friends.

Fred was dying all the while, but he took his time. He refused AZT, calling it "rat poison." He consulted personally with Jonas Salk and participated in an unsuccessful clinical trial for a vaccine. There were bouts with lung cancer, brain tumors, and opportunistic infections, all of which meant frequent trips to the hospital "down below," as locals referred to journeys of necessity on Highway 62 to Palm Springs or other civilized points beyond.

Fred was dying for so long that we thought he was just going on living. Which, in many essential ways, he was. He smoked (first Marlboro
reds, then American Spirit blues, and, of course, pot), enjoyed the occasional shot of fine tequila. He made music, held court, ranted, engi-
neered for the increasing number of bands that booked sessions at the
Rancho. Word had spread. Hanging there were the likes of Daniel
Lanois, who produced U2's *The Joshua Tree*, the band's biggest critical
and commercial success. (The album's only connection to the Mojave
desert was a photo shoot that took place there after recording, which
provided cover art and its title, transforming the lyrics and music into
an iconic desert sound.) The Louisiana native Victoria Williams, a brilliant, idiosyncratic figure in American roots music, bought a place a few
blocks down the road from Fred and recorded one of her finest albums
with him.

The Rancho had become a kind of pop shrine, and Fred a bona fide
"personality," a guru for musicians and assorted scruffy creative types.
And how could we not bow down before him? The gay cowboy rocker
who could sing "Blue Moon" in a sweet croon that was simultaneously
ethereal, earthy, and erotic; who rode his regal Arabian stallion, Kashmir, bareback at sunrise or down to the saloon on Highway 62 (Victoria
Williams immortalized horse and rider in a song); who led us along a
moonlit trail in the Monument, showing us the graves of gunslingers,
crouching low to point out rattlesnakes coiled under rocks.

Ted, Fred, Elia—they spent most of their time in the desert. Me, I
was often hustling "down below." The rest of the world was at the lower
elevations—the cities, the drugs and wrecked relationships and bank-
ruptcies. I commuted to teaching gigs in Claremont, Santa Barbara,
giving one-off performance-lectures across the country. The others left
the desert less and less often, spoke of life down below derisively; Joshua
Tree was Canaan. They had claimed the desert; or, as they would have
it, the desert had claimed them with its mystical power. There were
meditation retreats at the Institute of Mentalphysics, founded by a British journalist who went native in Tibet; there was a Lakota woman who
led the gringos down the Native path.

These were the salad days. We were discovering this new place together,
showing each other what we'd found.

"Hey, Teddy!" I'd gush. "The guy who came over and worked on my swamp cooler is this old blues guitarist who told me about a plane crash during World War II up on Twentynine Palms Mountain. He says the plane was bringing parts for the Manhattan Project to make the bomb. Crazy, huh?"

We'd gather in the Monument often to sit around the campfire like the cowboys and cowgirls we were. The National Park Service helped us imagine the landscape. The exhibits at the visitor center and the interpretive signs along the nature trails played up the colorful history of the pioneers. Bill Keys, Johnny Lang, and the McHaney brothers seemed to have been the typical greedy, ruthless bastards of their time and place. Keys, whose ranch within the park remains private property but is open to the public, shot at least one man dead in a dispute over mining claims (he served time for manslaughter and was pardoned late in life). Today his face peers out from a mural on the wall of a furniture store in Twentynine Palms, mostly white-haired and kindly, but still exuding steely pioneer spirit.

Out in the desert we worked up a new narrative, communing with Indian spirits in sweat lodge rituals and shopping organic at Sue's Health Foods in Joshua Tree when we could afford it. We played acoustic guitars, and if we went electric, it was for twang and reverb, echoing Hank Williams.

Most important in this quest was authenticity. Since none of us actually came from the desert, we needed relationships with people who did, or who at least had been here longer than we had, and in the Mojave that meant that our heroes and heroines were generally working-class. Since we were mostly middle-class, that meant crossing boundaries of caste. (When we arrived there was very little money in this desert, except for the billions in hardware and ordnance on the Marine base.)

I found my local heroes at a bar in Twentynine Palms housed in an old stucco building with a sagging roof a couple of blocks off Highway 62. The sign announced AL's SWINGER in red letters, with a sparkly star dotting the "i." Its founder, Al Ardison, had been recognized as the "first black business owner" in the Morongo Basin. The demographic of residents in the deserts of San Bernardino County is astonishingly white for a community in Southern California (well above 70 percent in most of the tracts in the 2010 census). What "color" exists is provided almost completely by the Marines—Latino and African-American men and women, plus a smattering of Asian wives—and the growing numbers of Latinos and African-Americans priced out of the coast and lured by service-sector jobs in the interior West.

Al's was the only place in the Morongo Basin that brought such a diverse crew together—active duty and retired Marines, Mexicans and Mexican-Americans who worked in civilian jobs on the base, working-class whites and blacks employed in the building trades or semi- or unemployed.

Al was himself a retired Marine who chose to stay in the desert where he had trained. By the time I showed up, he was in failing health and had delegated running the business to Tammy—Tomasa—Castro, a mulata from Panamá who had married into the Marines, lived on the base for many years, divorced, and come to Al looking for work. It was Tammy who served me my first beer at Al's. She was in her fifties, short and pear-shaped, with big, deep-brown eyes that matched the dark tan of her skin. She favored long artificial nails and kept her hair wrapped in scarves, and she spoke a patois of Central American Spanish and English in its black variant, all of it in a booming voice. Tammy sang along to the jukebox, off-key and with great gusto (her favorite was the Latin American bolero standard "Tú, sólo tú," sung by Selena), and always teared up at Satchmo's "What a Wonderful World." She ruled the bar with absolute authority (aided by her equalizer, a long, thick wooden pole that looked like an ax handle, with black electrical tape for gripping at one end). She drank alongside her customers but never got sloppy. And she looked after me and my girlfriend, Ofelia (with whom I shared a chaotic love), like a mother.

## 4.

As I became a regular at Al's, I was furnishing the house in Twentynine Palms with scraps I found on the endless acreage of Bureau of Land Management territory nearby, where there was a lot of illegal dumping. Marine families were the most common perps: a sudden redeployment, family disintegration. In the middle of the night all nonessential belongings would be thrown into the car and driven out to the sandy tracks strewn with spent shotgun shells and glass from broken beer bottles.

The dumping sites looked like houses without walls—as if the walls had been blasted away by a tornado and the belongings somehow left intact. Whenever I stumbled on one of these places—I encountered dozens in the immediate vicinity of my house—I felt I was violating someone's intimate space, but that didn't keep me from rummaging. I poked through board games, wooden spoons, family photographs, porno tapes and sex toys, towels and phone bills and sippy cups and unwashed dishes. One time I found a great pair of dress pants, the kind with a silk lining; they fit perfectly, and I wore them for years. I cooked in pots I discovered half-buried in sandy washes.

The BLM land was adjacent to Joshua Tree National Park, and geologically speaking, they were the same—the border between them was bureaucratic. But the divide in social geography was huge. The vast majority of the million-plus annual visitors to the park were tourists, many of them from overseas, seeking the iconic West: massive boulders piled one atop another in fantastic forms, the Joshua tree itself raising its hairy, crooked arms up to God. The BLM, on the other hand, was a place of four-wheel-drive roads and hardly any of the restrictions of the federal park system. There were no tourists from Japan or Germany or extreme rock climbers or neohippies, because the BLM did not exist in any of the guides. On all but the most technical maps, the BLM was a blank space. It was used almost exclusively by locals, which meant mostly poor whites.

Historically there had been a smattering of affluence in this desert (James Cagney built a mansion on a bluff overlooking the basin in Twenty-nine Palms), and, as in Los Angeles, plenty of the real money leaned liberal, meaning you were green, likely a card-carrying member of the Sierra Club or Defenders of Wildlife. Which in turn meant you were probably appalled by the mixed-use options available on the BLM-administered lands—all-terrain vehicles, plinking, hunting. You could do pretty much anything you wanted on the BLM, and it showed. The area had been exploited for a long time. Abandoned mine shafts dotted the Pinto Mountains. Kids tagged the boulders with spray cans. If a car got stuck in the sand, it was blasted with shotgun pellets and bullets before the tow truck could get to it. You could pick flowers and burn mesquite (strictly prohibited in the park). There were all of seven rangers assigned to the 3.2 million acres of the BLM district this parcel belonged to, and they rarely made it out here. Smoke a j, bury your dog, dig for gold, bring out generators and stage a rave, drive not just off the highway but make your own road in the sand.

And still it was beautiful. The coyotes howled. The tortoises foraged on cactuses, thorns and all, in the dead of summer. The creosote bushes bloomed their tiny luminescent yellow flowers after the monsoon storms.

Some of the things I found at the dumps made me wonder about my neighbors. The empty wooden crates marked "80 MM MORTAR ROUNDS," for example, which I used to store CDs. Shirts with the unmistakable brown stains of dried blood. Balled-up court summonses, restraining orders.

My neighbors: we didn't talk much. There were a lot of young Marines, granted the opportunity to live off the base because they'd decided to stick with the military after their initial enlistment. They'd be gone for days at a time and then return in the middle of the night, screeching down the road in drunken rage. There were bonfires and shouting at three A.M., shots fired, the whir and whine of bullets ricocheting past my windows. The couples would fight loudly and then just as loudly make up.

There were a few encounters. The Marine who lived kitty-corner from me left a pit bull abandoned for days at a time in the summer without food or water. Tired of hearing the animal suffer, I went over and picked him up and brought him to my yard, where Bear and I looked after him. I returned home one day to find my front door knocked off its hinges and the pit bull back in his owner's yard. Maybe there was something about the vastness of desert space that made everyone guard their little piece of it all the more jealously.

I imagined some affinity between my neighbors and me. We had somehow wound up in the desert as a matter of last resort. We were not here because we thought of this place as healing or spiritual. We had not come to build geodesic domes or mud huts or purge our souls in sweat lodges with the ghosts of Indians. We had come not to find ourselves but to get lost from the selves we loathed.

Most of my other cohort, the bohos from L.A., *were* on a spirit quest, sweating in the lodges and building the mud huts. Fred seemed to straddle these two worlds well. He was too cynical to be a New Ager, but I never met anyone in the desert so attuned to place; he seemed to be at home everywhere, with everyone. Yet besides Fred there was hardly any communication between these disparate realms. I struggled to be in both. Cowboy Rube; rock 'n' roll Rube, strumming the guitar around the campfire; Rubén, the brown man, son and grandson of immigrants, hanging with the salt of the earth at Tammy's.

The boho crew kept growing. I could tell by the attendance at Elia's birthday parties. She liked celebrating them at campsites in the Monument, and each year more people showed up. In the desert it's always hot in September, on her birthday. You do not need a jacket or a sweater, even in the wee hours; it is eighty degrees at three A.M.

We would gather in the late afternoon, carloads of new desert denizens and people from the city. Being an immigrant from Costa Rica, Elia's events were much more mixed than the typical desert art scene. But they were still hippie bacchanals, including drum circles (the beat always reached for the tribal). Lots of pot and wine and beer, never hard liquor. A fire in the pit. Never hamburgers or hot dogs, but a lot of fish; Ted would bring his homemade hummus (very chunky), and Adriene would bring her signature mango salsa.

I remember drinking, really drinking. When I arrived in the desert I was still sweating cocaine from Mexico City, but without a connection in the Morongo Basin I drank the desire for coke away, invoking the dictum of "un clavo saca otro clavo," one nail drives out another. Which means that I would have been as loud at these bashes as everybody else. Above the collective chatter would come Elia's laugh, a cackle, an unselfconscious bravura performance. Ted would sing. Elia would sing. I would, too. It didn't matter if I was on or off-key. We glowed in the firelight, and the shadows of our bodies danced on the yellow boulders. There was sand in the salmon. A breeze would kick up now and then, but never a wind. The dogs were with us, off their leashes against park rules: Ted and Elia's Negra, a black-and-brown mutt, frolicked with Bear. Together the dogs would go from person to person, imitating the social dance of the human party. People pitched tents and stayed overnight; since the house I rented was close by, I would weave home with Ofelia and we'd make sloppy love as coyotes howled and Bear howled with them.

## 5.

I would write at night at my perch before the window frame, speculating. I could tell where Highway 62 was—there was a galaxy of light along it. And I could pretty much pinpoint Ted and Elia's house, because it was at the base of a big pinto hill (at the corner, as Ted loved to say, of Sunset and Vine, the names of the dirt roads that intersect in the wash in front of their house). At night the hill was an area of darkness surrounded by twinkling lights, a black hole at the center of a constellation of stars.

I could tell where the daytime horizon line was because of a beacon rhythmically blinking on a Marine base mountaintop. The grunts would be readying an assault, flares shooting up over the dunes, revealing the simulated enemy's position. Below the dunes, a smattering of lights from the houses in North Joshua Tree. There were intermittent bursts of light, different from the house lights, whiter, brighter, waxing and waning—the headlights of vehicles headed down the dirt roads toward Highway 62. This place wasn't as popular with the artists and investors who eventually came, being too close to the base, and too arid. Desert rats wanted to be *out there*, but you could also be too far out (some residences were ten miles or more up washboard dirt roads). North Joshua Tree had a reputation for being a good place to set up a meth lab. There was the occasional razor-wire compound and massive American flag, a little too authentic.


After us came more artists, some of them very well known. They came because we had come.

There is a critical moment in the cycle of gentrification, when what had been informal networking, word of mouth, becomes media buzz, which in the digital age exists in constant dialogue with virtual social networking. Buzz in the one is amplified by the other. And thus the perfect storm of America's latest round in the boom-and-bust cycle: a technological revolution, real estate speculation, a burgeoning service economy luring ever more migrants and, driving it all, imaginaries that manipulate our desire.

The booms of the Old West functioned precisely the same way. The railroads opened the frontier, which drew artists, which drew more art-

ists, which drew speculators, which brought migrants of all social stations. The economic swells of the desert West of the last generation have
lured an increasingly brown cohort, Mexican and Central American
immigrants attracted to new boomtowns with jobs in construction,
hotels, restaurants, landscaping, child care.

At the turn of the new century Joshua Tree was on the verge of a
boom. Once again everyone was speculating, gambling that the wester-
ing way was the future, the better life. And nothing signaled this more
strongly than the arrival of an artist from New York.

Andrea Zittel made her career back East and had achieved enough
critical and commercial success to adopt a bicoastal existence. To her
studio in New York and house in Los Angeles she decided to add a
house in Joshua Tree, one with plenty of acreage for her experiments in
functional art, which consisted of various sorts of pods that served as
living, working, and sleeping spaces.

Her place was south of the highway, backed up against pinto hills,
the boulders strewn about creating a perfect "otherworldly" tableau.
(The Mojave has served as the location for innumerable sci-fi productions.)

"It was the last edge," she told me when I visited, describing what had
attracted her. "When I came here, no one was here." And the place
brought back memories of her grandparents, who'd ranched in the badlands of Imperial County, which occupies the southeastern corner of
California, along the Mexican border. That land was flat and yellow
and hot, and she imagined her grandparents' lives on it as hard but
beautiful.

There were of course many people here, at the last edge, when she
arrived: Tammy and Al, Fred and Ted and Elia, the Marines running up
and down the dunes.

Zittel rehabbed her house, a former homestead shack, into a miniature modernist paradise that she described as "bourgeois Palm Springs
desert." She bought panels of birch for the ceiling. Big windows looked
out over the Morongo Basin, at North Joshua Tree and the base. But in
this view, which was so vast, the landscape swallowed most of the human
narrative; except for the occasional detonation on the base, the mini–
mushroom cloud.

After her, who came after us, came the deluge, a great tornado of speculation: vacation rentals (five hundred dollars a night), investors scouring the desert for homestead shacks to flip, new money buying second or third homes, telecommuters, dot-commers wanting to go off the grid, A-listers catching the buzz and sending their people to scout for that gem-in-the-rough. Then came the galleries and eateries, including a "tea cakes" place with scrumptious scones that I, with my sweet tooth, indulged whenever I could.

Zittel quickly came to miss the old days, when, she said, it was still "like the Wild West," and the pioneers like herself rubbed elbows with the locals. She remembered the soap operas of their lives. "Someone was always getting sick," she said, "someone's house was burning down, someone got in a car wreck."

They still did. Older and poorer, the locals shopped at Stater Bros. and Food 4 Less, and the health care in the desert was negligible. Houses burned down because people smoked in bed or there was a short in the old wiring, and because it was so terrifically dry in the desert. People got in car wrecks because Highway 62 was mostly a two-lane road without a median and seniors had vision problems or someone got drunk or someone was tweaking.

I was sitting on her couch and Zittel was facing me, framed by the window, which showed a tamarisk tree to the right of her, a palo verde to the left. Her face and body were long and thin, and she wore a sleek dress in her signature simple look. She'd once designed a similar dress and had made art out of it by wearing it every day for six months. But that was long ago, when she hosted weekly cocktail parties at her studio in Brooklyn—in Williamsburg, another place that was repioneered by students and artists and became a scene.

At the beginning of Zittel's time here, her ideal was to participate in the local community. In it were ATV riders, meth heads, people who owned guns, us, the pre-Zittel artists, whose class position—our income, what we could afford to pay in the rental or real estate market—was largely indistinguishable from the locals. But Zittel thought she could be a good neighbor, even though her actual neighbor, Marty, was "creepy." She described him as having brown teeth, stalking around his property shooting at snakes with a pistol; he often asked her for a ride into town to buy cigarettes. She decided to rent a commercial space in neighboring Yucca Valley, thinking of starting up a gallery. Yucca Valley is a much larger town, with few of Joshua Tree's hipsters or hippies or its art colony vibe—in fact, it was just the opposite, with big box stores like Walmart and Home Depot, chain restaurants, and many conservative churches. Zittel said she "adored" the people she lived among and hired some local kids to work in her gallery venture.

Zittel paid the kids well, she said, more than they would have made anywhere else in town. In return, she claims, one of the kids stole from her. And the others never showed any motivation, never got art up on the walls. She'd check up on them and, she told me, "there'd be beer cans on the floor."

She had come imagining a life akin to how her grandparents had lived in Imperial, a place so inhospitable that people had to get along to survive. But there was no getting along. She had tried to give something to the locals, but in the end felt used by them. She fired them and abandoned the gallery venture.

Now she concentrated on creating a new space for herself and her friends. Zittel conceived a sporadic art festival that she called High Desert Test Sites, with "sites" across the Morongo Basin, starting out modestly in 2002 with colleagues opening up their studios or creating ephemera in the open desert. As word spread, the event grew to draw artists and audiences from across the country and internationally.

The new scene was a pomo-haute version of an Old Western boom, and it placed my bohemian cohort in an existential bind. Of course we railed against the new arrivals, but in the process we revealed our own tenuous relationship to the place and its people. By asserting ourselves as authentic subjects, we were betraying the locals who'd preceded us, who'd opened their doors and lives to us.

As Zittel showed me around her property, ambivalent voices sounded off in my head. I was jealous: I wanted to own this parcel and its amenity of spectacular landscape. And I wanted to convict the artist for her crimes—for erasing people from that landscape, the working-class people whom I too "adored." (Or patronized?)

We walked slowly through the hot breath of a summer afternoon. Zittel was still trying to figure out how to adjust her art to the desert. She couldn't work much with wood—the elements destroyed it too quickly. Even metal warped in this heat. While she'd been working on some "homestead units," little boxes that in theory could be a person's actual living quarters, a big wind picked one up and tossed it like a toy.

"The desert fucks with your head," she said.

On cue, there was an explosion on the Marine base. First the sound, like a massive boulder dropped on sand, far away. Then the earth and windows shuddering. A coil of oily smoke rose over one of the dunes in the distance.

I thought of grabbing the pair of binoculars I kept in the car, but I knew that even with them, I wouldn't see the Marines scattering along the open sand, looking for cover where there was none.

Usually from my window I had what seemed like hundred-mile views. But one winter day, I could barely make out the Joshua trees in the yard. I looked out the window at two feet of snow draped over rocks and yucca spikes, weighing down boughs of eucalyptus and tamarisk. I had been waiting for the snow for a long time. Weather in the desert—the monsoonal deluges, the dust storms—always seemed to happen when I was away. Ted and Elia and the others were constantly telling me about one great weather event or another. Now I had timed it just right.

I was by myself and unable to drive into town for any kind of human contact, not even if I had wanted to. The dirt roads in the neighborhood were impassable, and even the Monument had shut down. The power went out, and I wondered just how far my experience of the authentic would go. Everything in the house was electric, including the wall heaters and the stove. There was a good supply of firewood stacked outside, gathering snow. I brought a couple of nights' worth of logs and kindling into the house.

I could barely make out the houses a few hundred yards down the road through the vapory wall of pinkish gray. The walls began closing in. And as usual when I am surrounded by nature, I turned paranoid and hypochondriacal. What if my heart went into arrhythmia? The paramedics would never make it out here. They'd find me frozen by the truck. Would the roof collapse? I listened to the radio detail the closures of roads and public facilities. The heaviest snowfall since the record of thirty-six inches in 1979.

When I looked out the window again, there was nothing to see. And with the power gone, there was nothing left to hear, no hum of heater or whir of fridge, nothing but the flow of my blood in my ears.

## 6.

Jennifer lived down the street from Andrea Zittel. She was young and white, plainly pretty, and drifting through her twenties, a hippie decades late. In Seattle she had met a musician and poet named Jema who was also drifting up and down the West Coast. He'd heard about a music scene in Joshua Tree. Jema was on an epic quest for meaning, and this, along with his stage antics, drew Jennifer to him. She followed Jema to the desert and they made something of a life for themselves, but it was all very precarious; sometimes they had a place to sleep and sometimes they slept in her car in the parking lot of the Beatnik Café, long the public home for the scruffy bohos of Joshua Tree.

We sat in the café's back patio, the heat of the day still pulsing from the walls and floor. She chain-smoked, tossed the ash off her cigs with her nail, flick-flick. It was at the Beatnik that she'd heard about a job opportunity at the Marine base. There was an open call for people to perform as civilians on the battlefield (COBs), to provide scenarios in a kind of cultural-sensitivity training program for the Marines. Her relationship with Jema was at a particularly unstable juncture, even though they'd just gotten engaged, and she'd applied for the chance to get away as much as anything.

The simulacrum of an Iraqi village was about a half-hour ride up into the mountains from the main camp at the base, somewhere above the dunes I could see from my window. The buildings were represented by conex boxes, metal storage containers the size and shape of railroad cars. About three hundred actors were brought in for the training exercise. Some were professionals desperate for work, and many were Iraqis (FLSs, foreign language specialists, who earned more than the COBs). The mission lasted eight days. The actors lived in the village day and night, without running water but with an unlimited supply of baby wipes; two cooked meals a day were brought in by truck (a third came in the form of an MRE, the meal-ready-to-eat rations that U.S. military personnel receive in the field).

Each actor was given a conex box house, a broad scenario, and a specific role to play.

They were told: A bomb will go off, you will die. Tell the Marines, "As-salamu alaykum." Tell the Marines, "Bad America!" Be mean to the Marines for the next half hour. You are going to stage a riot.

Jennifer was a mother with a sick baby (a Cabbage Patch doll), then she was a student injured by an IED.

The Marines made a great effort at realism. There were guns firing blanks, explosions that filled the air with smoke, unmanned drones buzzing in the sky, tanks charging up and down the hills, and Chinook helicopters waiting to transport the wounded. In the village, there were garbagemen and taxi drivers; a marketplace had been stocked with plastic fruit. There was even a mosque, made from conex boxes topped by a fiberglass dome.

The main point of the training was to help the Marines discern who was a "friendly" and who was not. They did not always make the right choice. One day three friendlies were shot in the back.

There were rules. No alcohol, no pot, and no sex. Jennifer found it hard to follow the rules.

One day she met an FLS named Mohammed. She noticed him in the marketplace, reading a book. He caught her looking at him. "Shy girl," he called out. Things developed fast. It was wartime, after all.

He told her about life under Saddam. She told him about her engagement to Jema; he said that he didn't want to be a home wrecker and resolved to keep his distance during the rest of the mission.

The resolution didn't last long. Mohammed made sure that the supervisors assigned him to Jennifer's tribe, and he suggested that they play husband and wife.

They made out in a conex box. He made promises.

One night, a flare shot up into the dark of the Iraqi sky. From my window I would watch flares like these slowly descend over the mountains and dunes. On such occasions, I was transfixed: I couldn't move away until the flare was extinguished or fell behind a ridge. Jennifer watched the flare float as its parachute rode the warm updrafts. It finally landed in the very center of the village, striking the dome of the mosque, which immediately burst into flames.

Everyone had been playing their role in the scene, but now they all stopped as the dome lit up the night and eventually imploded in a thousand burning bits of fiberglass.

Jennifer never saw Mohammed again.

Ted and Elia, Jennifer and Jema, the Marine who abandoned his pit bull in the dead of summer, Zittel and the growing cadre of artists with agents: these were my neighbors. Mostly there was space between us, which made each new arrival on the scene stand out like a cactus in silhouette.

One day I heard the unmistakable puttering of an old VW Bug pulling up outside. I looked out the window and saw a middle-aged man, wiry and balding, his tan verging on sunburn. He paced the lot next door, which included a one-room homestead cabin that had been home to nothing but kangaroo rats for a long time. He walked around the property for a good while, toeing rocks, gazing out at the view of the nearby hills (one named Indian Head because it looked like the profile of a chief in a war bonnet) and the blue mountains in the distance.

I didn't see him again for several weeks. When he returned, it was with a small trailer hitched to the Bug and filled with supplies to begin the fix-up.

I introduced myself. My new neighbor was from Germany and spoke halting English. He offered no backstory, even after I prodded him for one. Bear barked loudly whenever he showed up, and unlike with most humans never warmed to him. I imagined the man as a character in a Wenders film, a postwar figure looking to find himself in the wide-open spaces of the American West, à la *Paris, Texas*. He didn't ask me where I was from, which was in keeping with the motif: we'd both been expelled from our pasts and stumbled into a landscape of limbo.

The first or second time I spoke with him, he asked a lot about crime in the area. He was going to be away a lot, he said. I told him what I knew, that there were a fair number of break-ins and with the old homestead cabins there was the particular issue of vandalism—bored teens shooting them up, shitting in them, torching them. The speculators who restored cabins and advertised them as vacation rentals had yet to arrive in our part of the desert.

The cabins were certainly an essential part of the mise-en-scène that had drawn both me and the German. Icons of pioneer life, they had been photographed countless times (for magazine essays, gallery shows, postcards) in their various stages of decrepitude, the California version of New Mexico's old Hispano work trucks sinking into the earth. These images underscored *time*, captured the sensation, or created it, of the tourist or neohomesteader traveling not just through space but also into the past, into a rendition of the West. You were leaving the present behind—your alienated life in the city—and rejoining the pastoral from which your kind had been cast out generations ago. You were now the pioneer.

Indeed, the origin myth of the Joshua Tree boom reaches back to the homesteaders who built these cabins in the early twentieth century, epitomized by the cantankerous prospector Bill Keys. The nameless optimistic souls who followed him left the structures across the desert, the ruins of which were now being put into the service of a new round of prospecting.

In my early days in the desert, Ofelia and I drove east on Highway 62, past the sparsely populated plain of Wonder Valley to the blank spot on the map, the place of NEXT SERVICES 100 MILES. There was the skeleton of a shack on the horizon: no roof, no walls. The prevailing winds from the west, the barbaric summer sun, and the winter freezes had stripped it to its frame. Here I asked Ofelia to take pictures of me. My hair shone with brilliantine. I wore Ray-Ban Wayfarers and a dark blue short-sleeved Dickies shirt, proletarian chic. I crossed my arms, jutted my chin toward the camera. I was ready for my close-up.

The problem with all the imagery was that it was a copy of a copy for which there was no original. Since the time of the first Spanish "entradas," thrusts, the land had been speculated on, bought and sold, the foundation upon which the house of capital was built, physically and culturally and ideologically. In historical, material terms, the abandoned shacks in the desert represented the impermanence of capital, the death of a homesteader's dream, the bust that always followed boom—indeed, that bust made boom possible, a dialectic in perpetual motion.

I'd followed the trail just like the banged-up German had. And now that we were here, alone in the Big Empty, we realized that we had brought with us our city ghosts, intensifying the radical difference of the encounter by filling the desert with scenes from John Ford and urban paranoia (which amounted to the same thing). Coyotes cackling maniacally in the dark, snakes ready to strike from beneath boulders, the heat waiting to suck the life out of you, neo-Nazis, poverty, and the crystal tweakers.

Ted and Elia certainly got a crash course on that desert. The wash next to their house was a popular spot for addicts to score and use. And as a "mixed" couple, they confronted the racial politics of the desert's demographics. Camping in the Monument once, they were surrounded in the middle of the night by drunk Marines who threatened to rape Elia—mentioning her ethnicity—and kill Ted. Among their neighbors was a Latino family who had an eight-foot swastika burned outside their house. In nearby Lancaster and Victorville, there were convictions in homicide cases with racial motivations. Researchers documented an increase in hate crimes across the rural West through the 1990s and the aughts, as black and brown arrived in increasing numbers.

I had no idea how seriously the German would take my rap on the risks to his property. Within a couple of days, he closed in his parcel with a chain-link fence. He covered the windows with plywood shutters, which he secured with industrial-sized latches and padlocks. When he was at home, he would prop up the shutters on two-by-fours, like the cannon ports of a galleon.

A few months into his stay, my neighbor left and never returned. The shack is still there, the shutters sealed tight over the windows, a ship stuck in the sand.

### 7.

"So how did you come to live up here?" I asked Tammy.

"Ay, mi vida," Tammy sighed from behind the bar. It was a summer night, and I was her only customer. The blades of the swamp cooler were clanging above us. "No quieres oir toda la historia porque es tan triste . . . si te la cuento toda, me voy a poner a llorar." If she told me her whole story, she said, she would start to cry.

Above her head a King Cobra sign glowed and buzzed. Next to the
cash register stood a little Satchmo statue and a donation jar for the
NAACP (Al had been a past president of the Morongo Basin chapter).

She had been orphaned in Panamá, Tammy said, then adopted by
a family in Wichita when she was twelve; she had been married twice.
In her description, the first husband, a black Marine who brought her to
Twentynine Palms, seemed like a homosexual, a troubled bisexual, or
just an asshole. He'd admitted to an affair with a much older man and
had kept up a correspondence with him after the physical relationship
ended, but still he'd wanted to stay in the marriage. A woman of conservative Catholic values, Tammy had demanded that he see a priest.
But when the priest had asked Tammy to forgive her husband and start
off fresh, she'd felt that he was taking her husband's side. She'd never
gotten over his affair. After the divorce, she'd married another Marine,
also black. That marriage lasted eighteen years, most of it purgatory.

The abuse, she said, was emotional and physical. One beating put her
in the hospital, and she testified against her husband from a wheelchair.
Tammy thought about leaving town but decided that he should be the
one doing the moving. She would lead her own life. She got an apartment, worked at a restaurant on the base, waiting tables. One night she
and a girlfriend came to check out this hole-in-the-wall place off Highway 62. The first thing Tammy saw upon opening the door was a shriek-
ing drunk holding the bartender in a headlock. Tammy walked right
out, but she returned later.

Al gave her a job in 1980.

"He was a like a father to me," Tammy said, "and I was like his
daughter. He treated me with respect."

Tammy's emotional wounds healed at Al's, but she did not treat her
body kindly, smoking and drinking and eating badly. Now in her early
fifties, she often had severe bronchial infections, a harbinger of the
emphysema to come. "I feel old and tired," she said.

I'd arrived at Al's Swinger well past its heyday, I was told. The building was coming apart. The roof leaked, and the glass in the windows
had been pecked opaque by generations of sandy desert winds. The
countertop of the bar itself was cracked (some of this damage Tammy
had inflicted when she'd slammed down the equalizer to make a point).

The felt on the pool tables was ripped. The floor tiles were separating. The swamp cooler smelled like a swamp. The building was so drafty that it held no cool air in summer and no warm air in winter. No wonder Tammy was always getting sick.

But there was karaoke, a cheap setup on a distorting boom box. Tammy would hog the mike behind the bar, singing "Tú, sólo tú" over and over to an audience that included both young Marines and VFW elders.

One evening Tammy asked me about a miraculous Mongolian mushroom that she'd heard cured just about any ailment. Could I get a hold of one? As it happened, many of my New Age artist friends swore by that mushroom, and I brought her one from Los Angeles, along with instructions on how to cultivate it and use it to make tea. Within weeks Tammy's complexion brightened, she had a burst of energy, she lost weight, and her bronchi cleared. She started stepping out from behind the bar, mike in hand, twirling to a cumbia by Selena, showing off her new figure.

I was healing, too, in fits and starts. I was clean, though not sober. But soon the drug addict made his appearance, scoring (where else?) "down below." Each time I fell I swore I would never do it again, and I didn't, for weeks or months at a time. In the dawn after an all-nighter, I would walk out from my shack in the sand and into a world where every surface vibrated with color. The air was metallic in my lungs, though, and I knew the sight was a simulacrum. The awareness was crushing, because I couldn't bear the thought of relinquishing its terrible beauty.

## 8.

Early on, the migrant flow was barely perceptible because it was so modest and we were concentrated on survival. In any event, my scruffy cohort didn't have the money to put into the upgrades that would become the hallmark of the housing bubble.

My tribe came because it was cheap.

In 1998, I paid $275 a month for my little home in Twentynine Palms; Ted and Elia paid even less for their dilapidated shack above the wash.

We marveled at the prices. We started to look at the real estate ads in the local weeklies, the *Hi-Desert Star* and the *Desert Trail*.

> Cute rustic cabin in Landers. Water available. Spectacular vu of Mt. San Gorgonio. $10,000.

The bohemians started to think of becoming home owners.

A couple of years later, I noticed a small house for sale a few blocks away. It had a slanting roof, burnt-orange plaster trimmed with blue, a yard handsomely landscaped with desert succulents (rather than the more typical sloppy, invasive tamarisks). The lot was a couple of acres and included a large outbuilding of corrugated tin, even larger than the main house. This, I immediately imagined, would be my creative studio. There I would write books and songs, record music. I called the number on the sign and took the tour. The interior was as clean as the exterior. There was a fireplace built of round desert stones. The asking price was $69,000, and the property had been on the market for months. I was told that the seller was "motivated." The agent said she'd give me the keys for a $5,000 down payment (plus closing costs). But, of course, I did not have $5,000. I did not even have $500. I was clipping coupons for London broil at Stater Bros. A year after I saw it, the house sold for well under the asking price.

It went back on the market two years later and sold for close to the asking price of $190,000; it was flipped only a few months later for $280,000. I tortured myself by driving by it repeatedly. Often as not, it was vacant, because it was a country house for city folk. If I'd bought when it was first for sale, I wonder if I would have withstood the temptation to flip.

We could see that there were more and more of us. A dozen became a few dozen; the intimate circle of friends gradually widened and swallowed concentric circles from down below. Visitors became part-time residents, became full-time residents.

But Tammy's crowd didn't hang in Andrea Zittel's desert, and Ted Quinn thought Tammy was cool but never became a regular at Al's.

From the start, the crowd at Al's saw us—Zittel, Ted, myself—for what we were: a new colony. The first time I heard someone use the word "gentrification" was at Al's; a boulangerie had opened in town. "Artsy-fartsy types," I remember someone grumbling.

But a wholesale displacement of the Morongo Basin working class did not arrive with one boulangerie. Some historians refer to the "long boom" of Western development, persistent growth—with slowdowns, of course, some of them precipitous—across not just the last few decades but hundreds or even thousands of years. Most Western cities and towns experienced periods of growth followed by plateaus that eventually led to more growth. There are plenty of ghost towns to visit throughout the West that seem to stand as testament to horrific busts, but these bits of fossilized history are not reflective of the overall regional economic history.

Demographically there have been cataclysmic changes: the death of millions of Native Americans, two mass deportations of Mexican immigrants (the Mexican Repatriation of the 1930s and Operation Wetback in the 1950s). On a whole other scale, locals have been displaced by newcomers during the birth of art colonies and other spates of gentrification, but Native Americans are still here, as are Mexicans and every other variety of westerner. If anything, the West also shows a long, steady arc of becoming ever more demographically complex, Arizona's most recent nativist turn notwithstanding. Which, in the context of desert gentrification, means that integration and segregation are occurring simultaneously. In other words, there is more of everybody out here, but in clusters defined by race and class, not to mention divided by the artistic representations the boom produces, or that help produce the boom.

Twentynine Palms proved quite resistant to change—the boulangerie itself lasted only a short while before it closed its doors. There was the matter of the adjacent Marine base, which wasn't going anywhere. On the contrary: the Marine Corps Air Ground Combat Center had become one of the most important military training facilities on the mainland because it perfectly mirrored the geography and climate of the region that is the current locus of U.S. military operations overseas.

There were only so many artists who would find a close view of

MCAGCC, in addition to neighbors who had just returned from several consecutive tours, conducive to the creative process. This is what made the village of Joshua Tree the most highly prized real estate of the high desert. Mountains and an upsloping mesa north of town largely blocked the view of the Marine base. The larger detonations were still audible, but that was much easier to live with than a full audiovisual representation.

We needed a gathering spot besides the Monument and Fred's Rancho de la Luna; we needed a place where you could have some food, coffee, or a beer. It wasn't Al's and it couldn't be the J. T. Saloon, which in the pre-boom period was mostly reserved for bikers and Marines. So we moved into the Beatnik Café, which saw a succession of owners over the years. The scene was anointed with Ted Quinn's open-mike nights, which attracted an unexpectedly mixed crowd. The gatherings, which took place every Wednesday, were very much Fellini-in-the-desert, with performers and performances by turns brilliant and bad, kitschy and naïve, bold and exasperating and touching. A twenty-year-old Marine just returned from Iraq sang a raw version of Bob Dylan's "Masters of War." A girl from the local high school earnestly covered a Bright Eyes song. A middle-aged man with thick glasses held together by Scotch tape played bizarre lines on his electric bass, unaccompanied, exploring a musical language only he understood. Shawn Mafia, a former undertaker who dressed and sang like Tom Waits, performed numbers about drifters, grifters, and floozies. And there was Ted himself, his voice hitting high, boyish registers on upbeat, melodic numbers (very Beatles-y) about love and peace. But his real strength, it seemed to me, was on the darker pieces, tirades against the Man in one form or another. He delivered these with a low, scary growl that hinted at more than just righteous rage, although he rarely confessed to his own darkness in song. At the Beatnik, people would spontaneously pick up a tambourine or sit in on drums, whether they knew how to play or not. The crew was charismatic, mentally unstable, lonely, AWOL, recently divorced, on the lam. An American carnival.

As the scene grew, Ted began to think of a bigger stage for it, which led to inaugurating a daylong outdoor event he called the Chuckwalla

Music Festival (named for a large desert lizard), consciously staged as an alternative to the increasingly commercial alt-music festival at Coachella in the low desert. He chose a date in May, thinking, like the Coachella organizers, that the temperatures would be mild. By the time my turn came to take the stage, at about three P.M., the temperature was well over one hundred and the modest crowd had sought shade under trees behind the stage, leaving the musicians facing an empty, dusty lot.

A year later, Ted decided to hold the event in Pioneertown, a few miles north of Joshua Tree. He chose the outdoor patio of the venerable Pappy and Harriet's, which seemed to be a classic Old West rustic bar but was originally built, along with all the other buildings on Pioneertown's main drag, as a Hollywood set (for, among many other movies, *The Cisco Kid*). A musician who went by the name of Arjuna played an astoundingly long, segmented Tibetan horn, accompanied by an aging British rocker called Clive on an electric guitar he made sound like a sitar. Throughout the evening a woman dressed in gauzy tie-dye danced with a hula hoop. Accompanied by Raj Mankad, an Indian-American cellist and former creative-writing student of mine from Houston, I fit right in with the circus. Like Arjuna, Raj practiced the Eastern art of Tuvan chanting, a technique that allows the human voice to sound more than one musical note simultaneously. At any other time, I would have judged all of us as silly dilettantes indulging the basest of colonial stereotypes. But we were in the desert, and isn't this what the desert sounded like? The kaleidoscope was in fact a measure of the desert's history, or at least parts of it. Consciously or not, the soundscape we rendered was rooted in the sublimity and the violence of that history— from Oñate at Acoma to the Indian Wars to the hippie communes, from Huxley finding the godhead in the Mojave to a mushroom cloud billowing over the yucca plain in Nevada.

## 9.

I walked into Al's one summer evening and there was no one behind the bar. I turned to find Tammy sitting alone in a corner booth.

Al was dead. "Se murió mi señor," was all she could say, which is difficult to translate, because "señor" can mean so many different things— gentleman, mister, master, savior. Perhaps Al was all those things to

Tammy. The funeral service was held in a sweltering Baptist church in Twentynine Palms, filled with Al's regulars, and there was a big potluck held at the bar afterward. It had been a long time since there had been that many people at Al's Swinger and there never would be again.

Al Ardison's passing let loose the inevitable drama over the future of the bar. Tammy tussled with Al's close friend Andy, another black Marine. Andy's wife was, in keeping with corps tradition, Southeast Asian. He put her to work behind the bar alongside Tammy, and over this Tammy seethed. She wanted to maintain the bar as a shrine to her señor and to continue to wield the only public power she'd ever known, that of the bartender who is the gatekeeper and the keeper of the peace and the conductor of the jukebox and the karaoke mike. Al's son, Darrell, played mediator between Andy and Tammy for a while but made no promises about the future. Tammy did not have the money to buy him out, and she did not know or had too much pride to ask anyone who did have the money.

I imagined that the bar would soon disappear and I did not want it to. So a few weeks after Al's death, Elia was behind the camera, and Tammy in front of it; I was directing a documentary.

It was early evening and Tammy was about to begin her shift.

We began in her house, a one-bedroom bungalow kitty-corner from the bar. She had done her hair up in cornrows and was wearing bifocals with huge round frames, like Sophia Loren. She had just showered and was finishing her makeup.

Elia panned around the apartment. An altar on the living room wall: both ex-husbands, children, grandchildren.

"You've never been in my house, have you?" Tammy asked.

I hadn't. This was great material!

Tammy was in a good mood, ready for her close-up, to present her world to the rest of the world. (We'd told her that the documentary might air on the local PBS station where I had worked before my fall.)

"Now, Tammy, can you walk out the door for us?"

She came out holding a Styrofoam box that contained her dinner. She stopped, looked at the camera.

"Don't look at the camera," I said. "Just keep walking to the bar, you know, like you're going to work."

She frowned. "What is this, some kind of movie? I'm not an actress. Though I do look a bit like Elizabeth Taylor." She laughed loudly.

Watching the video years later, I was shocked by the brilliance of the light, the implacable glow of a Mojave summer afternoon. In the frame, the mountains are beige flecked with mustard and gold, thick blues in their shaded folds, violent browns. You can feel the heat in the shot. The summer light makes the faces and hills resplendent, although it also overexposes, turning things garish. The shadows shift from pastel to jaggedly dark, tearing open the landscape.

Tammy wore black sandals. We heard the rubber soles crunching over the grit on the old potholed asphalt. She crossed swatches of dirt on the road—remnants of monsoon flows or the sand the wind brought from the dunes on the Marine base.

"Whoops," Elia said. She had noticed that our shadows crossed into the frame, looming over Tammy.

We followed her in real time all the way to the bar, only a minute or so by the clock but interminable on the screen.

INT. AL'S SWINGER—EARLY SUMMER EVENING
A two-shot, Rubén and Tammy opposite one another at the bar. He is wearing a white T-shirt and very faded blue jeans, brown motorcycle boots. He is smoking (Camel Lights).

The JUKEBOX PLAYS James and Bobby Purify's "I'm Your Puppet."

*Just pull my string and I'll do anything, I'm your puppet . . .*

Rubén tells Tammy to show us the kitchen where Al used to prepare his famous catfish dinners, which Rubén never tasted because he arrived too late on the scene.

Everything is as Al left it. Salt and flour and spices and fish sauce. Old grease on the black steel burners. Elia lingers on the stove, takes several angles. She finds the pilot light, but resists an extreme close-up. She stays medium, the flame looking fragile.

Tammy enters. Gone is the lighthearted gregariousness. She avoids looking either at me or at the camera. Instead, she stares up into the corners of the ceiling, meekly, as if expecting someone or something to strike her.

Offscreen, Rubén, speaking in Spanish, asks Tammy to tell of the days when Al used to cook.

Tammy delivers a monosyllabic response.

Rubén presses.

Again, she resists.

                         RUBÉN
(Insistent, switching to English)
Let's try that again. One more time.

                         TAMMY
(Exasperated, in her accented English)
This is where he cooked his catfish, okay? He cooked until he got sick and couldn't cook no more "¿Me entiende?"

She stalks out of frame.

Elia, again on the pilot light. It does not waver.

Rubén, the interrogator, dragging his subject toward the point he wanted to make. I saw myself do it again and again on the old tapes as we tried to film Tammy: leading questions, hectoring, coaching, directing.

It was obvious enough what was going on. I was alone in the desert, listening to the rush of my own blood. I wanted Tammy to keep me company. I wanted to keep her company. I wanted to see myself in her story—so badly, that I fed her the lines.

Tammy had not come to life in the frame or in my words because I'd gotten in the way. At the time I thought I had undertaken a righteous deconstruction of frames and gazes that erase, distort, and insult the marginal subject; implicitly I'd identified myself as one, something I had been doing for a long time. It was my gainful employment (that

I profited from my own marginality and that of others is a classic American contradiction). In the cruder manifestations of the occupation, I was a bean counter, scanning the mastheads of newspapers and magazines to tally the dearth of Hispanic names. In its more sophisticated guise—after hanging out in academic cultural studies circles—I performed close readings of texts, looking for evidence of subjection. I found it, of course, everywhere.

The problem is that such a critique does not restore the subject. Cruelly, it continues the erasure.

It is the devil's bargain we enter when we frame a subject—in a book, film, painting, play, song. The frame will always exclude, distort, however we might yearn for the real.

Was there a way to allow the subject to represent itself?

This much was real: Tammy lived. She worked in a place called Al's Swinger, a watering hole for the margins of the margins. It was the first black-owned business in the Morongo Basin. On the best nights, I did not think of Tammy or the crowd at Al's as subjects to represent, or notice the different races commingled. Instead, I thought of how we'd all wound up here. I was so moved by the stories. I thought about what we'd fled down below and how some of us had finally stopped fleeing and made a home.

## 10.

*They come with hats full of feathers across the land*
*They come bearing rainmakers and soldier bands*

This is Fred Drake singing, over a simple two-chord riff, B-flat to A-flat, tonic to seventh, a progression that almost always evokes nostalgia. The song is called "House of the Moon."

*They come in with clouds full of red dust from the earth*
*Dreaming of places of wonder, life, death and birth*

An electric guitar shimmers like the tail of a comet. Fred's vintage 1980s synthesizers evoke fantastic figures in cosmic dust and nebulae. The bass line is a low and slow reggae bounce that barely varies between verse and chorus. The percussion is minimal, slightly syncopated, echoing with reverb. Deep inside the track is a sample of an Armenian duduk horn played by Djivan Gasparian, the same harmonic-minor folk melody he played on Peter Gabriel's sound track for *The Last Temptation of Christ*. In all, it conjures kids on a journey to the mystical desert, children of the sun, free spirits, artists: us.

"House of the Moon" is the first track on *Twice Shy*, Fred's final album. The songs vary from (as Ted said) "Lennon-y" melodic to more ethereal passages. They are all simple but carefully constructed. His vocal delivery is consistent: a breathy plaintiveness belying urgent desire.

As his illnesses became more frequent and more serious, Fred walked a little wilder. He started hanging out at the J. T. Saloon. One night a drunk Marine walked up and greeted Fred with a military salute. It might be difficult to imagine Fred, the gay cowboy rocker, being mistaken for a Marine, but perhaps there was something familiar in the bony angularity of his face and the pale blue eyes. In any event, the young, tight-bodied guy quickly introduced Fred to his cohort, which, we imagine, was made up of other young, tight-bodied guys. Thus began what Fred's friends called the "Marine phase," a period of a few months about a year before his death that Fred described as being in "gay heaven." He never once let on that this was a case of mistaken identity. Soon enough he'd invited some of the men over to Rancho de la Luna for drinks and strip poker. There was no sex involved—at least none that he claimed, but Fred had never been particularly public about his intimate life. Nevertheless, consummated or not, the relationship crossed a rigid border in the high desert.

*They come in bright-colored clothes that show their scars*
*While their bodies are drumming up ghosts in the mountain*

This is Fred pointing at the circus in the desert and at his own body, at what the bright clothes cannot hide.

*And if we rise, and if we fall . . .*
*Carry us swift, carry us all . . .*

Fred died on June 20, 2002, at the Rancho, with a few close friends by his side. A week later there was a ceremony attended by several dozen mourners, including many who came from down below. There was an altar and incense and chimes that rang in the warm wind and a procession around the property that included visiting Kashmir, Fred's Arabian stallion, his perfect black coat gilded in the afternoon light. Nobody sang as we walked. All we could hear was the sound of our footsteps on the sandy, pebbly earth.

Near the end of my time in the Mojave, I was interviewed for a documentary about the desert music scene, *Nowhere Now: The Ballad of Joshua Tree*. Some of the acts who appeared in the film, like Graham Rabbit and The Sibleys, achieved critical and commercial success that brought even more attention to the area. John Pirozzi, who was my housemate in the desert, was the cinematographer. Fred Drake was brought to life through interviews with Ted Quinn and Tony Mason (who talked of the hallucinatory evening when he and his partner, Debbie, ran into Fred and Ted at Keys View). Fred Burke, who arrived in the desert via Francesca Block's relationship with Ted, also rendered eloquent tribute.

I squeezed into the frame, sweaty and drawn. Unbeknownst to my interlocutors, I was recovering from an all-nighter.

"There's a golden moment," I said.

I meant the moment when our community crystallized. After Fred's death, the moment passed. Ted and Elia broke up. And Rancho de la Luna recording studio went through a turbulent period that saw the disintegration of the cohort that had pledged to keep it running, just as the real estate boom rushed across the desert, a reverse Santa Ana wind blowing in from Los Angeles. (On more than one occasion during those years, people knocked on the door of my family's house in L.A., offering $800,000 or more—in cash—thinking that with the quick installation of granite countertops and saltillo floors, a flip would bring a mil.)

The *Los Angeles Times* arrived in the desert to anoint a boom that had already happened.

Headline: "DESERT COOL."

Subhead: "Staking Claim to a New Bohemia."

Deck: "Way beyond Palm Springs' Modernist metroplex, a new tribe of expatriates is pushing into the scrub, boulders and reimagined shacks of the high desert."

The story, written by then staffer Barbara King, was the lead in the Home section on February 10, 2005. The section was a huge moneymaker for the *Times*, brimming with ads from real estate agents. The features had one purpose: to help agents sell houses. There was little journalistic pretense.

The story begins with the desert itself: A cold wind blows. Rabbits and kangaroo rats "scuttle through the scrub brush," and the terrain is "uncompromising." King drives up a "remote twist of uneven, cleft-ridden dirt roads" where "vehicles bump and wobble as if they're mule-drawn wagons." The pioneers are middle-class professionals, the readers of the *Times*—architects, graphics designers, and TV scriptwriters. They have abandoned big-city life for another country, set amid the "serenity, anonymity and the nitty-gritty of the wild." The lengthy roll call includes Eric Burdon, Ann Magnuson, Ed Ruscha, Andrea Zittel. Furniture designers, filmmakers, ceramists. And more are coming. "Rumors circulate that Joni Mitchell, Lucinda Williams and Bob Dylan are house-hunting." Even the Rancho de la Luna gets a mention, cited as a "high-tech local studio," in contradiction to its fame among musicians for its old-school analog equipment. The story proclaims Joshua Tree an artistic mecca, a place to "clear out the psychic cobwebs," where you can buy property cheap (compared to Los Angeles) and make art out of it. Nobody seems to have a job—at least, not a full-time one. Special note is taken that the village is unincorporated. "There are no rules here," King writes. "No historical societies restricting what you can and can't do." The decorating can go anywhere. "They go Mexican, they go Moroccan."

A case in point are James Berg and Frederick Fulmer, a couple from Los Angeles, the former a writer for Hollywood and the latter a painter. They bought an old halfway house, thirty-four hundred "trashed square feet" with thirty bunk beds. A "bottom-to-top renovation," along with furniture collected at local yard sales, made it a "cleverly appointed, comfortable home." Fulmer will create a piece from the springs of the old bunk beds.

The only cautionary note in the *Times*' story comes from Ethan Feltges, the single interview source born and raised in the high desert and the owner of Coyote Corner, an outfitter popular with rock climbers and campers. Feltges laments how fast and far the run-up in real estate has gone—tenfold increases in some cases. He is worried because Joshua Tree's unincorporated status means that its residents do not have much of a say in terms of future development. Technically, there is nothing to stop big box stores from setting up shop, like they've done in Yucca Valley, or major hotel chains, like the ones that have come to Twentynine Palms. What is left unsaid is what happens to the rest of the people who live in the desert. The Marines, people like Tammy and Al, the Mexicans helping clear-cut Joshua trees to make room for a massive Chevrolet dealership and a Home Depot that will both go up in Yucca Valley.

The story in the *Times* makes no mention of the desert working class. Joshua Tree is again referred to as being "in the middle of nowhere," which is another way of saying that no one lives here.

Al's Swinger closed less than a year after Al's death and Tammy retreated to her home in Joshua Tree, with promises from her bar family to stay in touch, to visit. But few of them ever did.

A For Sale sign stayed posted on the inside of the bar's front window for years. The boom centered on Joshua Tree, largely avoiding Twentynine Palms and Al's. The old bar was a "teardown," after all. The signage remained, AL'S SWINGER in chipped red on the façade, "Al's Catfish Dinners" on the side wall facing the highway. Long after I left Joshua Tree, I stopped by the Virginian, another Marine bar in town, run by Alice, a Southeast Asian matron with a big voice and body who resembled Tammy in many ways. She told me that Al's had finally sold and that the building would become an art gallery.

"We don't need another art gallery!" one of her patrons drunkenly boomed. "We need another bar!"

The new owners whitewashed Al's old signs, and I fully expected to see a gallery rise up—slanted roof, floor-to-ceiling windows for the façade, varnished concrete floors, stainless steel in the bathrooms, a big blond desk along a wall, lots of light and space. The speculators were betting that the boom in Joshua Tree would eventually migrate to Twentynine Palms. There had even been talk of Wonder Valley turning—the last community heading east on Highway 62 before the Big Empty. When I first came to the desert it was the butt of dark humor. There were only meth labs and mass murderers out there, people said. The rumors turned out to be not so idle. The gentry indeed arrived in Wonder Valley, and the *Los Angeles Times* was there to mark the occasion.

Then, of course, the boom went bust. Whoever bought Al's did so just as mortgage karma was beginning to topple the house of cards the boom had been all along.

The last time I visited the Mojave, Ted was still living in Joshua Tree, and bands still recorded at the Rancho de la Luna, which was being run by one of Fred's old music buddies. Tammy was ill with emphysema and living down the road from Ted. The teacakes place and the several new art galleries had somehow survived the bust. The old shack that belonged to my German neighbor looked like it hadn't been occupied for years. The tourists still flocked to the Monument, and you could hear and see the live fire exercises on the Marine base. The only overt evidence of hard times was the fact that several realty agencies had closed and there was a profusion of For Sale signs. Home prices, while not down to pre-boom levels, appeared to be less than half of the peak.

The conflict the boom had brought had ended in a kind of stalemate. The Mojave was richer and whiter at the same time as having become poorer and populated with more people of color. I had tried to represent the people I thought had been erased, but I'd come to think that Tammy didn't need me to represent her. What we needed to do was expand the frame around the land and the people who lived on it.

When I drove by Al's, the original building was still standing. There was a Notice of Foreclosure in the window. I noticed that the would-be gallery owners hadn't done a very good job of painting over the old signs. You could still read AL'S SWINGER very clearly on the façade, the red paint emerging through the whitewash.

# IN THE SHADOW OF THE BLACK MESA

## 1.

When I tell people that I live in New Mexico they say, Where? And I say, Velarde, in the north, on the road between Santa Fe and Taos. These two towns—so iconic, so well branded—provide an instant mental snapshot: mesas and buttes in dusty reds and oranges, great skiing, R. C. Gorman prints. Practically everyone responds by exclaiming, Oh! It's so beautiful. And I say, Yes, it's beautiful.

If anyone is interested in more of a conversation, I might add that I live in one of the poorest villages in one of the poorest counties in one of the poorest states and that the region's per capita rate of heroin addiction is higher than anywhere else in the country, rural or urban. To which they will say, I didn't know that. The landscape both reveals and conceals, depending on your point of view.

In the middle of the aughts, the real estate bubble in the West is rapidly inflating. But Velarde is not a hot spot: too many mobile homes, too much negative coverage about the Española Valley and its heroin problem in the *New York Times* and on National Public Radio, two national outlets that make or break many hot spots through the boom years.

Angela and I are among the handful of outsiders in Velarde, and we remain a handful. Because of the saturation coverage of the boom (which is not disinterested, since advertising dollars are attached), the entire region seems engulfed in an upward spiral of speculation—buying, flipping, selling. We see none of that in Velarde, or in most of the villages of Rio Arriba County, for that matter. During the boom years, the poverty rate in Rio Arriba remains roughly the same, even as the housing market that surrounds it expands. In Velarde, things are as they were like before the boom, and Velarde is what most of the West is like.

For this land to be apprehended as beautiful, it first had to be represented as such, because it wasn't always considered so. Early explorers and settlers did not find much beauty in the Española Valley, nor were they looking for it in the pastoral sense. Conquistadors Francisco Vásquez de Coronado, Antonio de Espejo, and Oñate were looking for the beauty of silver and gold, the colonial aesthetic of wealth and power. Desire had conjured the fable of the Cities of Gold (which four hundred years later proved irresistible to planners at Pojoaque Pueblo, who so named their casino). The Spanish had expected to find bars of gold and silver lying on the ground, there for the taking. Mutinies beset the expeditions of Coronado and Oñate; as colonists realized there was no treasure, they "cursed the barren land and cried out bitterly against those who had led them into a worthless wilderness." The Española Valley bottomlands were good for farming—evidenced by the vast stores of surplus maize the Indians had when the early expeditions arrived—but it wasn't easy to farm. There are late freezes in the spring, early freezes in the fall, sudden monsoon deluges in the summer, droughts; present dry spells may be the beginning of a global-warming-induced megadrought, but wet and dry cycles are endemic to the region. Even in places at relatively low elevations, like Velarde (about six thousand feet, within view of peaks at nearly thirteen thousand), winter seems to last six months or longer. The land can be as much a source of suffering as of sustenance.

"Folk art" in New Mexico personifies Catholic themes by rendering images of saints who suffered corporally in their earthly existence and to whom we supplicate on behalf of our own suffering bodies and those of our loved ones. Reference to the land is indirect. Take the Santuario de Chimayó. It lies in a modest valley watered by a stream flowing down from the high country of the Sangre de Cristos. The church rises from earth the same color as its thick adobe walls; the structure, of a continuum with Pueblo architecture, blends seamlessly with the land. Inside the church, however, there is no reference to the natural setting outside the walls. The "retablos," altarpieces that depict human figures, are devoid of peaks, trees, or clouds; the land is taken for granted.

Before the arrival of the Santa Fe and Taos art movements, New Mexico produced no significant indigenous art based on the representation of immanent natural beauty. This is not to say that the land wasn't revered and respected. Its sacred quality lay in how the land worked and produced life. The relation to the land existed fundamentally in the material sense, including the aesthetic dimension— santos and retablos were made of wood from the forest, colored with paints mixed with the sandy earth that rises into mesas and buttes. Similarly, the Hispano poetry of the region hardly mentions the landscape in the way of Romanticism or transcendentalism. No Wordsworthian or Thoreauvian meditations connect the soul to the realm of nature.

This was because living off the land was an all-consuming proposition. And those who did so had a history of having been dispossessed. That was also part of the land—what belonged to your ancestors in deed was no longer yours: it had become the patrimony of a colonial power that had swept through and not only taken the best of the land and what it produced but had reinterpreted its meaning. So what did the New Mexican poets write about? Those featured in Anselmo F. Arellano's definitive collection *Los pobladores nuevo mexicanos y su poesía, 1889–1950* dedicated verse to "la vida dura," the hard life. There are odes to migrant workers dying far from home, such as "A Epimenio Valdéz, quien falleció en Wyoming" ("To Epimenio Valdéz, who died in Wyoming"):

> Sin madre, mujer ni hermanos
> Ni un lamento de ternura
> Desendió a su sepultura
> Ausente de sus paisanos

(Without his mother, wife or brothers / Or even a tender lament / He descended to his grave / Absent from his brethren.)

Poverty itself is often a character, as in these verses by Manuel M. Salazar:

> No hay en el mundo un estado
> Más triste, duro y fatal,

Que el de un pobre desdichado
Que no tiene capital

Le juzgan de bandolero
De vago y de criminal
Que le falta el dinero
Que es lo que hace capital

(There is no state of affairs / More sad, hard and deadly / Than that of the unlucky one / Who has no capital / He who is lacking money / Is judged an outlaw / A vagabond and criminal / That's the way capital works.)

On the rare occasions that the land appears, the material relationship to it is always paramount, as in Higinio González's "The Drought of 1899":

Árida se ve la tierra
Y la lluvia no aparece
La nieve se desvanece . . .
Y se ve la tierra llena
De el polvo que ha levantado,
El valle, el monte y el prado,
El fuego está abrasando . . .
No dudo, sí habrá cosecha,
Pero este año cuando.

(Dry the earth looks / And the rain doesn't come / The snow disappears . . . / And the land is full / Of the dust that rises / The valleys, mountains and plains / Are engulfed by flames . . . / No doubt there will again be a harvest / But not this year.)

Not all is tragedy and lament, a passive Catholic reception of loss. Long before the activism of the Chicano movement in the 1960s, norteños openly organized resistance to what is still perceived by some as colonial occupation. Alejandro Fresquez exhorts:

Despertad, Pueblo Hispano!
Llegó la registración . . .

Despertad, Pueblo Hispano!
De ese sueño paralítico
Y acudid muy político
A la lid como buen hermano
A defender con valor
El derecho y el honor
Que ya se veía arrebatado
Lo que con sangre ganado
Nos "legó" el Conquistador!

(Wake up, Hispano People! / Voter registration is here . . . / Wake up, Hispano People! / From that paralyzed sleep / And with political will go / To the polls like a good brother / To defend with valor / The right and the honor / That seemed to have been lost / That with his bloody victory / The Conqueror "bequeathed" us.)

The Hispano poets themselves embodied the pastoral—not with odes to the spectacular view of the Rio Grande gorge below Taos, but with odes to "pastores," shepherds. Felipe Pacheco:

Vida tan desagradable
Es andar de llano en cerro,
Nunca el trabajo le place
Más que uno tenga buen perro . . .
Todo es una desventura
Nunca no me gustará
Par diez, que es cosa muy dura
Verse en esta soledad

(It's a disagreeable life / Going from the plains to the peaks / The work never pleases / Except when you have a good dog / In all it's a misfortune / That I'll never ever come to like / What's more, it's a very hard thing / To find one's self in this solitude.)

There is a fundamental schism between a "working landscape," to use Raymond Williams's phrase, and one apprehended as inherently beautiful. Perhaps, as Lawrence said about Indians and Europeans, one view is "fatal" to the other. An Hispano logger cannot see the forest through the eyes of the painters of the art colonies.

The kind of New Mexico beauty the Taos and Santa Fe artists produced (and which has been endlessly reproduced) is not Catholic or folk. It is landscape, the archetypal beauty of the American West that is the projection of the Western European imagination. The lineage begins with the tentative landscapes painted by the first American settlers, scenes in which nature overwhelms the new and tenuous built environment. It continues in a more triumphalist vein with what is today instantly recognizable as American Western—Remington and the like, romancing cowboys and Indians firmly from the point of view of the cowboy. The aesthetic blossomed in the modernist moment with the fetishizing of form suffused with Romantic notions of nature and indigenous peoples. Throughout this history there is an erasure of the other—of any Natives who are not plaintive spiritual figures, of Hispanos who don't fit a pastoral that is utterly divorced from their literal experience.

This American beauty is still very much alive. In museums and galleries and bookstores, on websites and billboards, in postcard carousels, in O'Keeffe and Adams, we are directed how to view the land. The projection draws us to a "Land of Enchantment" (the official state nickname), a misty imaginary that erases my neighbors in Velarde and their story of dispossession and addiction.

## 2.

The spring winds arrive. The snow melts and the arroyos run. The cottonwood across the road bursts into green, and the sumac shade trees that ring the house sprout new leaves right alongside last year's brittle bones, which fall slowly through the growing season.

A time to sow. That's what everyone around us is doing. There might be far fewer producing orchards and fields than a generation ago, but bearing out the pronouncements of Wilfred Gutierrez, Velarde's activist farmer, tradition survives just enough for the village to get busy with the start of another growing season. Elders in cowboy hats and overalls roll tractors down the dirt roads. Men and boys shovel out mud and debris from the acequias.

I want to do the same as everyone else does. I take my cue from Miguel Santistevan. I scout the property for the best spot. Unfortunately, there isn't one. All of Velarde is at a disadvantage because the foothills in the east subtract sunlight in the morning and the Black Mesa robs at least an hour of it the afternoon. There are plenty of open spaces around the house, but most of them get even fewer hours of sunlight because of the perimeter wall or the sumac trees or the pump house or the garage and storage buildings. The best candidate is the long, flat stretch just inside the gate, but that is our driveway.

I finally settle on a corner of the outer wall behind the pump house. Six hours of sunlight will have to suffice.

Angela and I make the trip to Lowe's. We aren't the only ones. The garden center is filled with valley residents greeting one another, in many cases for the first time since the interminable winter took hold. We pick up a shovel, a hoe, mesh fencing and stakes (to keep Bear out), steer manure. And seeds: cucumber, cilantro, pinto beans, "calabacitas" (squash), cantaloupe. Miguel would roll his eyes at the packaged seeds, but I'm too shy to ask him for some of his heirloom varieties.

As soon as we get home I head to my corner to turn my first shovelful of earth. I get a teeth-chattering metallic clang as I hit a big oval river stone just beneath the surface. And another, and another. I hurl them over the wall. There are also countless chunks of plaster from when the outer wall was finished. The deeper I go, the more rock I find. I can hear the Rio Grande roar with runoff. I have the river to thank for the stones, of course—four million years of its meandering through the rift valley, perfectly carved to channel mountain streams into a Great River.

Two days later I throw the last big stone over the wall. I have cleared an eight-by-ten-foot space. I take the hoe and start making rows. I am imitating in miniature what is going on around me on plots counted on a scale of acres instead of feet.

The property has no water rights, so there is no ditch bringing water from the acequia madre, which runs through Velarde. But there's the well—and no one will charge me or even know that I'm using it for irrigation. If everyone else without water rights in the valley did the same, the aquifer would quickly be depleted.

And now the big gamble. "Sow after any chance of frost," the seed packages say. We are in mid-May and the temperature still regularly drops to below freezing. You can tell by the ice on the tin roof, which starts to melt and roll off the eaves in silvery drops when the sun crests the hills in the east. The corrugated tin makes popping sounds as it expands.

I sow near the end of May. I've gone back to the land.

A few days later, I bring the garden hose over to the patch. I set it down at the top row and open the valve. A finger of water runs along the earth between two ridges, completing my microdiorama of the Rio Grande Rift Valley. Every now and then the water hits a depression and starts to gather in a little lake and I hoe the obstruction away, my living representation of Hispano spring ditch cleaning. Then I build up a wall of earth at the bottom of the rows. Trapped, the water deepens all along the rows, soaking the berms where the seeds are sown.

A good part of the water, of course, doesn't come anywhere near the seeds. Some of it might make it down to the water table, but most of it evaporates. Many environmentalists have pointed at acequia irrigation as inefficient and wasteful. Hispanos bristle.

I go out every morning to see if the shoots have broken through. The seed packets said a week or so. A week passes, two. The spring fully arrives—no more frosts. And just as I begin to think my thumb is black, up the shoots come. At least some of them do. The pintos, which I sowed in two of the ten rows, are nowhere to be seen. No sign of the melons either. But the cucumbers and calabacita plants grow fast.

I am working the land. I am a farmer!

And then the "chapulines," the grasshoppers, come. All at once, thousands, a veritable plague of locusts. When I walk out to the garden, dozens leap up from the ground with each step I take. They eat the leaves off the cucumbers in a couple of days, and the plants die before any hint of the vegetable appears.

In a panic, I call Miguel. He must know what to do. He has the knowledge of the forebears.

"Yup," he barks into the phone. "Gotta watch out for those chapulines."

It seems that besides watching out there wasn't much else to do. I could never betray Miguel or the memory of César Chávez by bringing in pesticides.

The grasshoppers leave the cilantro alone, but it doesn't matter. The cilantro never gets more than a couple of inches high. It soon turns yellow and dies. Still nothing from the pinto beans, or the cantaloupes.

Only the calabacitas hold on. And thrive. They look more like cucumbers, massive cucumbers, or bedroom toys, twelve inches long. But they are calabacitas. It didn't matter that they only got six hours of sunlight a day or that my irrigation methods were wasteful and inefficient. Or that I didn't have heirloom seeds passed down from the forefathers. I grew them on this old land that had been bringing forth calabacitas "since forever," as the norteños say, and now there is no stopping them. First the burst of yellow flowers and then the green phalluses bulging, ready for harvest only a couple of weeks later, over and over again through the summer.

I snip the first few when they are ripe and bring them inside. A photograph commemorates the moment. My hair is dusty from the dry spring wind off the mesa. I am deeply tanned from the New Mexican sun. The background is the pinkish beige of the adobe wall of the sitting room just off the entryway. I am looking at the camera—that is to say, at Angela—with a slightly embarrassed smile. I hold up three huge calabacitas—more like pumpkin-sized "calabazotas."

The farmer with his harvest.

I have no idea what to do with them, but Angela does. My mother-in-law passed down the recipe that her mother and grandmother used. Wash the vegetables. In a large saucepan, heat a tablespoon or two of olive oil and sauté garlic and onion. Slice the calabacitas in half lengthwise and again into quarters, then chop these into little cubes and toss them into the pan; sauté on medium-low heat until tender (but not squishy). Add yellow corn and green chile. Real norteños have a ready supply of last year's Hatch chile harvest already roasted and bagged in the freezer; not-so-real norteños like us use cans from Walmart. Real norteños would also use fresh corn off the cob; we use canned. Salt and pepper to taste. Serve alongside rice and pinto beans. Open a cold one.

It is summer. In the long Black Mesa dusks our bellies are full of calabacitas, and Bear plays. Joe Rendón barbecues on the patio next door. The Rio Grande no longer roars with the spring runoff. Nor does it make the thin hiss of fall and winter. It sounds full and languorous.

## 3.

A massive dome-topped pink stucco box, the Oñate Monument
Resource and Visitors Center, the only structure built by Rio Arriba
County to host cultural events on the fifty-mile stretch between Española
and Taos, erupts without warning from the grassy plain just off Highway 68. It is a bizarre blend of classical and modern, norteño kitsch. It
sits on a small parcel of county land surrounded by BLM grazing-
plinking-ATV territory—today's commons. It is writ large.

At night the Oñate Center is splashed with amber light, as is the
statue of the building's horse-mounted namesake, Juan de Oñate. The
statue is directly in front of the main entrance and only a few yards off
the asphalt. The lighting gilds the building Las Vegas–style and reveals
Oñate, wearing his battle helmet and his sword sheathed along his right
leg. He holds his horse's reins high, riding hard. His head is turned to
the left, as is his stallion's. Oñate looks relatively puny atop the massive
beast. The wrought muscles of the horse's left front leg are sharply
defined. The hoof alone looks bigger than Oñate's entire spurred riding
boot. But the human figure holds the reins after all, and he is urging his
mount south-southwest, across the highway and straight for the pueblo
at Ohkay Owingeh to unleash the fury of empire. Oñate comes in the
name of the Spanish Crown and the stallion is the power that propels him
to do God's work: subduing natives, mining, farming, ranching, and saving souls (in that very order).

I drive by the statue just about every day during my years in Velarde.
And from the moment I hear the story about how one of its feet went
missing, I can think of nothing else every time I see it.

I first hear the tale from Juan Estevan Arellano, who is at the center
of the narrative because it took place when he was the director of the
Oñate Center. The Arellanos were among our first friends in the north.
They live in Embudo, the village immediately north of Velarde on 68.
There is plenty of poverty and addiction in Embudo, but somehow,
unlike in Velarde, the bucolic mise-en-scène hides it better. There is no
hiding it in Velarde, beginning with the big sign for Hoy Recovery, the
drug rehabilitation clinic where Angela works, at the very entrance to
the village. In Embudo there are more adobes than mobile homes, and
during the boom years the village sees an outright invasion of outsiders.

In cinematic terms, Embudo is an elegant period piece; Velarde, gritty documentary-style realism.

Estevan is a complicated norteño figure. You can count on him for a biting comment about the crunchy, Subaru-driving, Birkenstock-wearing, organic-farming gringos who have steadily invaded Embudo. He calls them outsiders, "gabachos" (akin to "gringo," but with even more of a pejorative edge) or "pendejos" (much worse). On the other hand he is no essentialist when it comes to "Hispano" culture. What exactly are Hispanos? he asks rhetorically. Who is it that arrived here in 1598? When he says "here," he means *here*: along the Black Mesa, where his family has held land for generations, next to the pueblos up and down the Rio Grande. Here as in "el norte de Nuevo México." There is not a single square inch of this land upon which Pueblos or Hispanos or Anglos have not stood, driven cattle or sheep, farmed, spilled blood. Estevan delights in complicating the subject that is Hispano history, a practice that always leaves one group or another insulted. For example, he takes the long view on Juan de Oñate. The expedition leader might have been a full-blooded Spaniard, but he was born in the New World and on that basis alone should probably be regarded as at least partly "indigenous," Estevan argues, a claim that goads Native American activists.

Then there is the motley crew who accompanied Oñate on the journey north from Mexico City. Estevan points out that between the "full-blooded" Spaniards (who'd mixed for six centuries with the Moors), and the Native Americans there were a plethora of mixed peoples—or "coyotes" (like Arellano himself with his striking blue eyes and light olive skin, or Angela, with her light skin, emerald eyes, and thick black hair). The diversity does not end there. There were also Frenchmen in Oñate's crew, and natives of the Canary Islands. In a classic New Mexico contradiction, "blood" meant everything—with it you claimed birthright, your tenure on a land grant or in a pueblo—but it was also meaningless, because every line had been crossed.

Estevan and I are easy colleagues because he is first and foremost a writer and for a long time he has been contemplating the subjects I am now grappling with. He is my elder by a decade, and I naturally look to him, and to several other graying norteños engaged in similar pursuits, for knowledge.

The first time he received me in his house, we sat in the dark, roomy kitchen and noshed on olives and hummus. "The Moorish legacy," Estevan made sure to note. Later he would start a restaurant called La Charola, "the tray" in Spanish, just a few hundred yards up the road from his house. The menu features Pueblo, Moorish, Mexican, and Spanish dishes with nouvelle twists conjured up by his eldest son, Javier, the chef.

But Estevan's multiculturalist stance is not entirely expansive—he stops with the gringos, at least with most of them. This is a matter of politics and history, and perhaps literature. What better foil for tension, contradiction, righteous indignation? As a multifaceted writer (essays, journalism, fiction), Estevan feels called upon to battle with the twisted imaginaries imposed by Anglo settlers, from Mary Austin to the nearby New Buffalo Commune (founded by hippies in the 1960s and alluring to icons of the era, like Dennis Hopper), from Mabel Dodge Luhan to the most recent artist from New York. It was the "outsiders" who'd founded the Spanish Colonial Arts Society, the legacy of which still resonates through the annual Traditional Spanish Market in the Santa Fe Plaza, which struck Estevan as patronizing if not downright racist, collapsing his beloved multidimensional norteño identity into an Iberophile fantasy. It was the gabachos who said they wanted to learn from the locals but wound up telling them that their methods were inefficient—*unsustainable*—and always insisted there was a better technology, for irrigation, for building, for cooking. It was the pendejos who sought spiritual enlightenment or absolution or sex from the Indians.

No, he didn't hate all gringos. There was for example his friend Chellis Glendinning, an outsider who'd thrown her lot in with the "tecatos," the heroin addicts in the village of Chimayó and written an influential essay titled "Inhabited Wilderness," a manifesto lambasting the mainstream environmental movement for its biases of race and class. Gringos who attempted reverse-assimilation like Chellis met with Estevan's approval, sometimes. But there was Stanley Crawford, a well-regarded author (at least in the gringo world) who'd lived thirty years in Embudo and written a memoir about becoming mayordomo of the local acequia. Estevan liked to make jokes at his expense, as when the irrigation canal crumbled and flooded Crawford's land. Estevan believed Crawford was taking over the reins of representation on the land that Estevan considered his birthright.

For a full century, northern New Mexico had been a de rigueur destination for serious artists. Among them were Robert Creeley, Godfrey Reggio, John Nichols. Some stayed, most left. All were drawn by the idea of New Mexico. Many claimed that the land itself spoke to them, but if it did, it drew them through the words and images of travelers who'd seen it before them. Estevan argued that the gringos had de-Mexicanized New Mexico, de-Moorified it, shrunk it down to flamenco-strumming Spaniards and powwowing Indians.

Estevan felt it was his mission, as director of the Oñate Center, to push back against these tropes. And then someone, under cover of darkness, chopped off Juan de Oñate's foot.

It was 1998. Hispano New Mexico had geared up to celebrate the four hundredth anniversary of the arrival of Juan de Oñate and his fellow settlers in the Española Valley to establish the first capital of Nuevo México. The statue was not at the front of the building at that time, but in the back patio. All the better for the vandals to have at it.

The phone rang early one morning as Estevan arrived at his desk. It was a reporter from Albuquerque, who asked, "Is it true?"

"Is what true?" Estevan replied.

"That someone cut off Oñate's foot?"

"I don't know," Estevan said, because he didn't. He put the phone down and rushed out the back door to take a look. It was true. Right foot amputated at the ankle, sawed clean off. The news spread fast. No one claimed responsibility for the act, although the perpetrators left a note. It said, "Fair is fair." That was all. Later, an unsigned communiqué was delivered to the press: "We took the liberty of removing Oñate's right foot on behalf of our brothers and sisters of Acoma Pueblo," read the statement, which was accompanied by a snapshot of the hostage foot. "We see no glory in celebrating Oñate's fourth centennial, and we do not want our faces rubbed in it."

There were no arrests in the case and it became one of New Mexico's great mysteries. There are many theories. The most obvious being that an activist from Acoma Pueblo had taken revenge. The pueblo has harbored a centuries-long grudge against Oñate for the barbaric quashing of the Acoma rebellion in 1599, in which every Pueblo male over twenty-five years old lost one foot and those aged twelve to twenty-five were sentenced to twenty years of personal servitude. Although the communiqué stated that the act was committed "on behalf of" Acoma, seemingly pointing to non-Indian actors, it could have been a feint to throw people off the trail.

Estevan discounts the theory of Acoma perps. One time he told me that it must have been a wacky gringo environmentalist from Santa Fe.

"How could it have been an Hispano or an Indian?" he said. "In the middle of the night? We're all drunk or asleep at that hour."

Furthermore, Estevan maintained, the vandals needed a grinder with a diamond bit to cut through the thick bronze. We, he said— meaning Hispanos and Indians—don't have that kind of equipment. (Maybe he did essentialize a bit, after all.)

Or perhaps it was an activist from another pueblo—there are eight in the north and nineteen overall in New Mexico. Maybe it was an His- pano activist—maybe Estevan himself was involved and he'd been throwing everyone off the trail for years with his denials steeped in stereo- type. But that scenario didn't make sense either. Estevan did not see in Oñate a figure of pure evil but a complicated man who undeniably played a major role in the formation of New Mexican society. Then again, there was something of the "pícaro" in Estevan, and maybe he just wanted to stir the historical pot, get everyone arguing over New Mexi- co's identity crisis. The Land of Enchantment is often represented as a land of three cultures in a sexy ménage, but it is a rare day when His- panos, Native Americans, and gringos sit down for a friendly beer at the casino. They hardly ever sit together anywhere.

Since the 1960s, long before taking over the Oñate Center, Estevan has been involved in several art-meets-activism projects, many of them with his close friend Tomás Atencio, also an Embudo native and a soci- ologist at the University of New Mexico. Atencio received a fair amount of notoriety in the 1980s, by helping to introduce the concept of the New Mexican "crypto-Jew," a controversial claim of Sephardic heritage among some of the region's Hispanos, where there is family lore of Shabbat-like rituals—lighting candles on Friday night, for example. Research has as yet failed to conclusively back the claim that "Jewish- ness" somehow survived the Inquisition, the Expulsion, passage to the New World, and four hundred years of secrecy in the mountains of New

Mexico. Nevertheless, the notion of Sephardic roots spread rapidly over the past generation, and generally coincided with the reassertion of Hispano claims of authenticity, which in the context of northern New Mexico amounts to another kind of indigeneity.

As young activists, Arellano and Atencio were fundamental in the region's reformulation of Hispano identity, a rebuke of the Iberophilia imposed by the Spanish Colonial Arts Society. Together they started up several literary journals and oral history projects. They developed the concept of the "resolana," a pedagogy based on the local custom of town elders gathering alongside a sunbathed patio wall (resolana) in the mornings to shake off the chill of the night and share coffee, tobacco, and conversation.

The new conversation was about recognizing that the acequia irrigation system was Moorish in origin and that the Virgen de Guadalupe, Mexico's Catholic patroness, was a composite of Spanish and Moorish and Amerindian deities. That Oñate himself, revered by New Mexico's Iberophiles as a founding father of the state, married a mixed-blood descendant of Moctezuma.

Atencio and Arellano tried to tear down the stereotypes, but tourists still came asking for santo carvings, for woven blankets, literally knocking on Estevan's door at odd hours, looking for folkloric curios. His house happened to be situated on a slight rise just east of 68 along the Rio Embudo, practically on a pedestal for tourists to admire. From the road it was the very picture of New Mexican pastoral.

As for the Oñate foot story, it had legs, as it were, climbing the media ladder all the way to the *New York Times*. As the director of the Oñate Center, Estevan now stepped up to defend Oñate, after all those years of bending the myth this way and that. He was cited in the *Times* article. "Give me a break—it was 400 years ago. It's okay to hold a grudge, but for 400 years?" The juicy quote got him enmity from some and accolades from others, the typical reception for publicly discussing norteño history.

## 4.

La Charola Restaurant opened in the late winter of 2005. It was the only such place among the cluster of villages lining the 68, since the closest actual sit-down restaurant was at least a dozen miles away, in Española.

The Arellanos ran the business with a small crew of investors organized by Estevan's wife, Elena, who had a day job as a librarian at Ohkay Owingeh. It was their second restaurant venture in the village; they ran the first out of a trailer. La Charola was housed in the biggest adobe in the area, a two-story in an excellent location, just across the bridge over the Rio Embudo where the 68 meets Route 75, which runs east through Picuris Pueblo and Peñasco, then intersects with Highway 518, a.k.a. the High Road to Taos. These are considered among the most scenic routes in all of northern New Mexico and draw plenty of tourist traffic from spring to fall.

The idea was to feed the tourists, but the restaurant also acknowledged the demographic shift in the area. Parts of Embudo and especially its close neighbor Dixon (whose Anglo name, reputedly of a Civil War deserter, is disputed by Hispano elders like Estevan) had become "amenity villages" in recent years, markers of rural gentrification. Newcomers had started up galleries, wineries, gourmet chocolate boutiques; taken over old orchards; and established a food co-op. Almost all were run by Anglos. By the 2000 Census, Hispanos had become the minority. To succeed, La Charola had to bring in the local population with disposable income, and Hispanos did not typically fit the profile. Which meant from the start that the venture was a complicated one for an activist like Estevan.

La Charola was not the first restaurant in the building, which had a long and checkered past. The Chili Line, a narrow-gauge railway, ran through the area until 1941, and there was a station and restaurant at Embudo, perfectly positioned between Santa Fe and Taos. The celebs of the day drank and ate there; Baby-Face Nelson made a legendary appearance. After the Chili Line was dismantled, the property passed through several owners, gringos and Hispanos and mixed Hispano-gringo couples. Lore has it that the place saw many bar fights over the years, a few stabbings, and at least one death. According to Estevan, who grew up within a few hundred yards of the building, the latter part of the century is when the place really declined. This coincided with the arrival of hard drugs into the area—a development that Estevan linked to the hippie wave of the late 1960s as well as to Hispano veterans returning from Vietnam. In addition to alcohol, Hispanos and Indians could now kill themselves with heroin, cocaine, and methamphetamine. Estevan pointed out that fast food arrived at around the same time in Española—Riverside Drive was lined with McDonald's, Burger King, Pizza Hut, KFC, and more—and coincided with the opening of the Indian casinos: two in Española, one in Taos, two on the road to Santa Fe, another between Santa Fe and Albuquerque, plus the monumental sites in the Albuquerque area, Sandia and Isleta. The casinos were watering holes as well as places to lose a month's pay or your Social Security check.

In this way, in little over a generation, an epidemic of addiction and disease came to flow along the Rio Grande, the riparian trail that watered the people and beasts of the Oñate expedition, the Camino Real that for centuries conducted trade across the vastness of New Spain, the same route the gringos undertook with the cavalry and in hippie bus caravans and tourist expeditions.

After reaching a deal to lease the property, which included the building and a few acres, Estevan and his family began a massive cleanup—both inside and out. A farmer like Estevan took invasive species personally, and they were everywhere—Russian olives and shiny elms elbowing out the native junipers and cottonwoods. During the cleanup, Estevan found used syringes all over the land.


Estevan had big plans for La Charola. It had been almost a decade since he was unceremoniously fired from his post at the Oñate Center, when he ran afoul of the Rio Arriba County officials he worked for; he says they demanded a more traditional—a more folkloric, more essentialist—representation of local culture and history and he refused to comply. He was then in his late fifties and looking for another strike—another platform to focus his political and cultural energy, from which to agitate about land and water and history.

La Charola, Estevan said, was going to be a "slow food" place, an antidote to the corporate poison peddled on Riverside Drive. At La Charola, Spaniard and Moor and Native American would meet in the pots and pans on the stove. And for once Estevan would even indulge some of the local gringo growers in the area (of which there were an ever-increasing number), cooking up their fresh organic produce.

Estevan's three children helped out. Javier, the eldest and an aspiring filmmaker, wore the chef's uniform. His daughter Única Paloma, on her way to college, hosted; his youngest son, Carlos, still in high school, played shortstop. The menu embodied Estevan's expansive norteño vision. The "enchiladas de quelites" (a spinach-like Indo-Hispano staple) spoke of Native and Mexican roots; the "capirotada" and "arroz con leche" puddings paid tribute to the Moorish presence on the Iberian Peninsula. Lard-averse gringos loved the pinto beans cooked in olive oil. And there was also a nod to nouvelle cuisine, in the signature dish, "pollo embudeño": apricot sauce–rubbed chicken breast topped with green chile, white cheese, and sliced almonds, served on a bed of mushroom-and-herb rice.

But Estevan wanted more than a restaurant. He wanted a cultural center—to draw back the crowds he'd gathered for music and spoken word at the Oñate Center. He hung art on the walls, paintings and photographs (including several aerial shots of the Embudo area, which showed the thin swirl of cultivation along the river and the more arid immensity of the juniper and piñon hills). Farmer-activist Miguel Santistevan could hold workshops on Hispano and Native agricultural traditions. Land grant and acequia organizers could plot their next political move.

The prospect of such a place excited me—there was nothing like it anywhere in northern New Mexico. There were plenty of traditional Hispano joints of cheap and tasty fare, but how many times could you order the "carne adovada" plate or answer for every other item on the menu, the all-important chile question: "red or green?" There were high-end places in Taos and Santa Fe and even across the Black Mesa from Velarde at the Rancho de San Juan (a Relais & Châteaux resort), where white folks dressed up New Mexican cuisine or avoided it altogether and charged exorbitant prices for smart presentation and minuscule portions. There was nothing in between the populist and the haute.

At La Charola, the three cultures would come together, across lines of race and class, and break bread over an honest political conversation. It would be a momentous meeting, like Mabel Dodge and Tony Luhan at Taos Pueblo.

It would never work.

La Charola closed less than a year after it opened. There was simply not enough business, and the Arellanos couldn't make the rent. Was it because Estevan's position toward the gringos was just too contradictory? Did the gringos want a more folkloric, less nuanced performance, on the plate and off it? The problem certainly wasn't the food, which was excellent.

As for the Oñate Center, there have been only a handful of community events there in the years since Estevan was fired. Most of the building is empty; there are no exhibitions of local artists or spoken-word gigs. You walk in, hear your footsteps echo, wind up on the back patio, and take in the great view of the Truchas Peaks.

The only reason now to visit the Oñate Center is to gaze up at its namesake (his new foot blends in seamlessly) astride his ferocious mount, the father of New Mexico looking toward Ohkay Owingeh and trouble on the horizon.

## 5.

One spring morning, Estevan takes me on a tour of his acequia, from the main compuerta, or sluice gate, along the Rio Embudo to where the ditch crosses onto his property. There has been a heavy runoff, and the ditch has sprung many leaks. Since Estevan is the mayordomo the parciantes focus their ire on him. The acequia is lined with a porous black material that was supposed to keep its walls from crumbling, but the spring came on hot and fast and ditches all over the north are straining under the heavy flows. The liner was a state engineer's idea.

"Pendejos," Estevan mutters. "Engineers always think they know more than we do, when they should be learning from *us*."

Something flutters upstream. At first I think it's a white bird floating down the water, but as it comes closer I see it's just a plastic bag from Walmart.

We run into Harvey and Gale, Estevan's neighbors. Estevan is neither gruff nor particularly pleasant, but he does strike up a conversation, which surprises me. Soon I see that he's trying to make a point. They have to sell off some of their seven acres of land.

"How much do you want for the whole thing?" Estevan asks.

"Fifty thousand dollars an acre," says Harvey. This sounds insane, but it's close to the going rate in the area.

"How much for the whole thing?" Estevan insists.

He wants Harvey to say it out loud, so that I hear him.

Harvey sighs and goes along. "Seven hundred and fifty thousand dollars."

"Sell it all together," Estevan says acidly. "So I won't get stuck with too many neighbors."

Now Estevan stands on a tall aluminum ladder propped high against the trunk of an old cherry tree on his property.

The "borregas," his sheep, are kneeling and bleating under a weeping willow close by. Yesterday one of them died, a breech birth. Estevan had to pull the lamb out; it also died. He'd thought that at least the mother would survive, but she'd bled too much.

I stand at the foot of the tree, which is about twenty feet high. It's an old one, like most everything in the orchard. It's brimming with perfectly ripe dark red cherries. If they're not picked now, the birds will finish them off or they'll rot on the tree.

"El cerezo está muy trabajoso," Estevan says. Cherries are a lot of work. We always speak first in Spanish, switching to English deeper in the conversation, a typical Hispano mode of conversation. He shows me how to twist the berry's stem where it joins the twig, how to slowly pull a branch down close enough to pick off the fruit. Yank too hard and you break the branch. Estevan picked cherries on neighboring farms when he was a kid, filling a ten-pound bucket for ten cents.

The sun breaks through the branches and illuminates his more-salt-than-pepper hair, a halo upon San Estevan, patron of stonemasons—and of Acoma Pueblo, a place where "since forever" runs far deeper (and bloodier) than for any Hispano.

"When you grow up eating tree-ripened fruit," he says, "and then buy it in a store because you think it looks good and shiny ... well, there's just no comparison."

I try a cherry. Soft and sweet. The morning warms to midday and Estevan lets me climb the ladder and pick some while he keeps up the story of how things used to be.

Once there were four hundred varieties of apples in northern New Mexico. Now there are only twenty-eight heirlooms left. When he was a kid, he used to go out to the road—it was a road, not a highway—and sit in the middle, waiting for a car to pass. You could count on two hands the number of cars that came through on any given day. His grandfather lived next door to the adobe Harvey and Gale live in now. His aunts and uncles were all nearby. They had told young Estevan about how things used to be in their day, and about what they in turn had heard from their ancestors, who had fought in the Mexican-American War in a battle at Embudo, part of the failed Taos Revolt of 1847. The land Estevan farms today is part of the Embudo grant, 25,000 acres deeded in 1725—all of which were denied by the Court of Private Land Claims. The Hispano families that remained essentially had to buy back land that was already theirs.

Estevan holds on to it all: to his parcel, to the water rights that go with it, to the heirloom apricots and apples, and to the house that he and his family built with their own hands, on the land of their forebears.

I ask my next-door neighbor Joe Rendón about hiking on the Black Mesa.

"It's all private land," he says; he's never been up there. "A guy named Richard Cook owns a good part of it." Joe has a dim memory of his grandfather talking about having grazed cattle on the mesa decades ago.

I'm shocked that the area is off-limits. There are only a handful of homes at the lower elevations and no water sources on the tabletop. Building on it would be financial suicide. So besides grazing (not much, because of all the basalt), what possible value could the land have?

"Gravel," says Joe. Richard Cook's gravel operations are near the base of the mesa. This does not explain why he would limit access to the tabletop.

On my next drive north toward Velarde, I notice the gravel mines for the first time, deep yellow gouges in the mesa. I hear Cook's name often during our years in Velarde. In addition to the gravel operations—which bring dust contamination to the village and big trucks to the narrow roads—he owns 110 acres alongside Riverside Drive, and more than 7,000 in rural Rio Arriba County. He is often in court, sometimes being sued by community groups but more often suing them or the local government when they stand in the way of his business. Activist Hispanos and environmental gringos are typically at odds in northern New Mexico politics, but they line up together against Richard Cook, the classic outsized Western landholder.

The more I hear about Cook, the more I want to hike the Black Mesa.

I buy detailed topographical maps. Huge swaths of public land surround Velarde, delineated in patches of green (the Carson and Santa Fe National Forests), blue (state land), and yellow (BLM). The Black Mesa is almost entirely white—private land, just as Joe Rendón said. My consolation is that there is one yellow area close to Velarde, opposite the mesa to the east of 68, and I soon discover an entrance. It's only about a quarter mile from our house, but to take Bear there, I have to pack him in my truck because of the prickers that lodge in his paws. I pull up to the intersection of Lyden Road and Highway 68, one of several deadly points along the road to Taos. The intersection is perilous, day or night, for anyone who misjudges the distance and speed of oncoming traffic while making a turn. It's made all the more dangerous by patrons who depart Club Lumina, Velarde's only bar, just up the road, weaving their way home. There are several "descansos" in the vicinity, the Hispano-Catholic roadside shrines that for tourists are a colorful, folkloric sight and for locals markers of family tragedies. That is how Joe Rendón's father died—hit by a drunk driver from Club Lumina.

During this time my eyesight worsens considerably and I begin to wear glasses. The consensus is that I have central serous retinopathy, a condition in which tiny vessels in the retinas bleed and form scar tissue, creating permanent clouds in one's vision. The deterioration began in Mexico City and during my first few years in the desert, which correlates with my drug use. There is no medical literature that links the two, but abusing stimulants like cocaine could have exacerbated the condition. In all likelihood, I was snorting myself blind.

Sometimes when I pull up to the stop sign at 68 to make the right turn toward Española, I stay there several minutes until the highway is empty. I don't trust my eyes.

Crossing all four lanes to get to the BLM gate is even worse, but after a typically long wait I charge over the intersection and roll off the asphalt. The ranch-style gate is barely held shut by a bit of bent fence wire. A large "descanso" of sooty plastic flowers hangs on the fence just a few paces away. A sign warns that charges will be pressed if anyone leaves the gate open, allowing cattle to wander onto the highway.

I drive up the dirt road, taking care to avoid the several places where runoff has carved out axle-breaking gulches. On the maps the road parallels what is called the Truchas River, but on the ground it's a dry wash that runs only during the wettest of storms.

The hilly land is furrowed by parallel sandy barrancas, little gorges carved by runoff. There are a few modest mesas and arroyos dotted with bunchgrass. The part of me that desires to be in the "wilderness"—the amenity of nature for the newcomer—soon confronts the reality that there is no place that hasn't been refined by a human presence. A fat tire mark here, old barbed wire fencing there, rocks set under wire netting to avoid more erosion in a gully, expended shotgun shells, the occasional windmill alongside a stock pond filled with mossy water. All sharing space with green or dying or dead piñon, with ancient wavy branches of juniper, with grassy pellets of rabbit scat and coyote scat embedded with juniper berries. And everywhere, the land is moved by wind and water and gravity—the mini-buttes along the barrancas inexorably being ground to dust, the Sangre de Cristos crumbling and being carted off by the Rio Grande.

This is where I walk Bear, sharing the land with kids riding ATVs, a few horseback riders, cows and cow pies, the occasional hunter or plinker, heroin addicts shooting up, a crew of balloon enthusiasts floating by. I never see a ranger, and most of the time I am here alone with my dog, so much so that encountering another truck on the road or hearing a voice carried on the wind from far away startles me.

I am walking the old commons of the Sebastián Martín land grant, which served that purpose from the early 1700s on—piñon for firewood, grass for pasture, small-game hunting, plentiful native trout in the Rio Grande.

The Sebastián Martín grant survived the Mexican-American War but not the adjudication process that followed, when lawyers representing the claimants ultimately took the vast majority of the grant for themselves, which they then sold to speculators, including the aptly named Rocky Mountain Exploitation Company. The fertile bottomlands along the river, encompassing present-day Velarde and its neighboring villages (about 2,800 acres), are still largely Hispano-owned, although the acreage has been steadily eroded throughout the twentieth century by several waves of outsiders (including Lisa Salcido, our landlady, who bought from the Rendones) and constant subdividing among

Hispanos. The Sebastián Martín land grant no longer exists, but map-makers continue to delineate its boundaries, inscribing it with the name of the man who received the original deed, a textual ghost.

To me, this piece of public land seems to serve the communal pur-pose it was intended to: witness the multiple constituencies it provides space for. But Joe Rendón relieves me of my romance.

"I can't just go up there with a chain saw and get my wood," he tells me one evening across the fence. "I can't just shoot animals up there. I can't even pick up a rock if I want to. I need a permit for this, that, every-thing. That's not a commons. That's a place owned by someone else."

As for the Black Mesa that dominates the view from our attic win-dow, rising suddenly and steeply from the bottomlands of the Rio Grande just a few hundred yards away, I can't figure out from the maps if there's a way to hike it without trespassing. Every chance I get I drive around it, looking for a gap in a fence, an open gate. It is a long time before I find one.

## 6.

Velarde is the first time we've lived together. Getting to sleep at night is extremely hard for Angela—as it becomes for me as well. Close the cur-tains on the big picture window in our bedroom. Get up to make sure the doors are locked. Turn on the noise maker, a small fan. No matter how quiet Angela tries to be getting out of bed, I always wake up and I always ask her where she's going. To sleep in the living room, she says, or to the bathroom. Either way, I know she is going to take pills. She has a tin box filled with old scripts. She refers to it, with terrible humor, as the "suicide box." It is under the bed, where, for the moment, my own addiction metaphorically resides. Sometimes she takes more than the prescribed dosage. I am afraid. As soon as I wake up, I give her a nudge. She groans and wants to sleep more.

The *DSM-IV* lists "hypervigilance" as one of the criteria of posttrau-matic stress disorder. She is terrified of what might come in from the dark. This is not the vestige of some childhood fear. Something did come in from the dark, a few years before I met Angela. The adult trauma makes her as vulnerable as a child.

I'm here, I try to reassure her, but sometimes the Velarde night haunts me, too. On weekends, Club Lumina, perhaps two hundred yards away, features live music. We hear the bass, usually playing an up-tempo Mexican number. At first I enjoy the sound—it reminds me of Los Angeles, the reverberation of the immigrant city celebrating the end of the workweek. But now it becomes the sound track to Angela's stories about the graveyard shift at the clinic and to the screams from our neighbors. Trucks charge up and down the dirt road in the wee hours, pulling in and out of Rose and Jose's place.

In one two-week period, two people from the village die of over-doses. One is a fourteen-year-old boy who grew up in Velarde and got into so much trouble that he was sent to his father's home in southern New Mexico. The boy had been there only two months when his father found him barely breathing; he died later at the hospital. And there was Albert Garcia-Martinez, twenty years old and also an addict. One Saturday he overdosed and was revived at Española Hospital, which has the only emergency room in all 5,986 square miles of Rio Arriba County. Because of slow rural emergency response times, many people choose instead to drive those in distress to the hospital themselves. That was the case with Albert, and he survived. Except that the following day, he overdosed once more. His family put him in the car again and sped south down 68, trying to revive him. The fourteen-mile distance was too great. Albert had stopped breathing. He had turned blue. Five blocks from the hospital, the car ran out of gas. The family called 9-1-1, and even tried pushing the car, but Albert was dead on arrival.

All that is outside our bedroom window. The music from the club stops sounding celebratory; it seems ominous.

Still, there are nights when Angela agrees to leave the curtains open and the fan off. With my head on the pillow, I can look straight out the window. A cone of amber light from a single streetlamp about seventy-five feet away illuminates some of Joe Rendón's yard and much of the yard of his neighbors, whom we haven't met and never will. They live on a small parcel in what looks like a tidy trailer. The view includes Joe's trailer and the wooden porch he added on, his neighbor's trailer and, in the center of the tableau, the streetlamp, under which there are two animal pens where a white mare stands still as a statue and a lonely lamb stares into the night, bleating occasionally. Within the cone of light, moths swarm in summer and snow whirls in the winter. When I have trouble sleeping, I concentrate on the amber light, the horse, and the lamb.

We are married at La Iglesia de la Santa Cruz de la Cañada, a church founded in 1695, three years after Diego de Vargas's "reconquista" of New Mexico. It takes some time and effort to convince the Franciscans to let our Jesuit friend, Fr. David Ungerleider, officiate at the altar, but Christian spirit prevails.

The wedding takes place on a relatively warm and perfectly clear December day. Our families meet at the church, named for the Santa Cruz River, which flows down to Española from the Sangre de Cristos. The church building has two steeples and thick walls of deep-brown adobe. It is in all the tourist guides. Sitting atop a rise on the road to the Santuario de Chimayó, the first step of the foothills of the Sangres, it looks out on a grand view across the valley to the Jemez Mountains rising over Los Alamos. We walk to the altar surrounded by saints who intercede for the fallen. Joe Garcia, my musical compadre of many years, plays guitar and harmonica for the liturgy.

Because there are few venues in the Española Valley that my family would consider respectable, the reception is at a restaurant in Santa Fe, slightly cheesy, where the menu is split between New Mexican (calabacita squash, pozole, sopaipillas) and Old Mexican (pollo en mole, tacos de carne asada). The only real drama at the reception is provided by Angela's teenage brother and nephew, suddenly my in-laws, who decide to explore the streets of Santa Fe and promptly get lost, or at least pretend to. We don't hear from them for hours and finally call the police. After much hand-wringing among the wedding party, we learn that they are picked up by Santa Fe's finest as they wander the empty boutique streets of the plaza.

We stumble to our hotel room and make mad love, and there is nothing in the night to keep us from sleeping.

## 7.

After the gray bitter winter, the warm winds of spring blast at last year's leaves from the sumac jungle around the house. The cottonwoods along the river bring the sharp green of their new leaves and the aspens and the grasses of the alpine meadows revive in the high country. The arroyo that bisects Velarde runs strong, carrying melt from thirty miles up in the Sangre de Cristos down to the Rio Grande. In late June the monsoon brings a second spring and the cottonwoods let loose their snow, big tufts of cotton swirling in the roads and gathering in doorways. Black-eyed Susans dance alongside the highway, rabbitbrush blossoms paint the hills mustard yellow. At the end of August the last of the rains have fallen. In early September the apples are heavy on the trees and the evenings begin to cool. The Hatch chile harvest comes in, and the roasters are rolled out. In Española, families buy boxes of chiles at Walmart and cart them straight to the roasters in the parking lot. At home you peel the outer skin away, seed the chiles, bag them, and avoid rubbing your eyes for days. A few bags go to the fridge for immediate use; the rest wind up in the freezer to be parceled out over the next several months. Another year in Velarde, and everyone does as they've done since forever, prepare for winter.

I notice neat stacks of firewood rising up in the carports and patios of the houses around us. One of Joe Rendón's neighbors has a wood splitter and the blond pile next to it gets bigger every day. It is that time when guys go up into the mountains in a pickup truck with a chain saw and a case of beer. The Forest Service sells "dead and down" permits, $40 for ten cords per household for the season.

"It's messed up," Joe Rendón says. "Why should I have to buy a permit for something that my great-grandparents got for free, that they owned? It's not right."

It sounds like a good deal to me. If you massage the system a bit and get several permits (having different family members buy them separately), you can conceivably make several hundred dollars selling the wood—a good Christmas bonus.

"But *it's not right*," Joe says.

Still, it looks like people are doing just that. In the Walmart parking lot and on vacant lots along 68, pickup trucks park with their beds loaded with a cord of wood, handwritten signs advertising the merchandise: "Piñon $140," "Pine $100." Guys snooze in the cabs, waiting for takers.

I don't know what kind of wood to buy, so I ask Joe across the fence.

"Oh, I'll go get you some," he says.

A few weeks go by and no wood, but Joe assures me that he'll go up into the mountains. I want to go with him, but he doesn't invite me.

One Saturday afternoon I come back from hiking on the BLM commons to find a mass of wood half inside and half outside the wire fence that encloses the front yard. Joe comes over and points to the pile.

"There's a lot of piñon," he says, "and cedar and some pine. A bit of ocote. I love ocote, it's great for a fire starter, you know what I mean?"

We haven't talked about price.

"A hundred and eighty," he says.

I've never seen a sign advertising a cord for that much money, but I feel I'm no position to bargain; Joe is my neighbor. I notice that most of the logs in the pile are too big to fit into the woodstove. Some of them look like wide-diameter ponderosa trunks, the kind foresters call "old growth" that serve as habitat for all kinds of animals and organisms, even when the trees are dead.

Joe offers to borrow a splitter from some relatives, but I decline. I want to do it myself, with an ax. Joe gives me a quizzical look and shrugs his shoulders.

Only someone born and raised in the city could possibly think it would be fun to split a cord of wood with an ax.

I go to Walmart and buy a double-bladed model, reasoning that two blades are better than one. I also buy a sharpening stone and oil—vague memories from my Boy Scout days. One day after the sun dips below the mesa—by December it is twilight in Velarde at three in the afternoon—and a genuine autumnal breeze shivers through the turning leaves of the cottonwood across the dirt road, I take the ax out and approach the wood pile.

I try to think of the last time I saw anyone split wood. I can't even conjure a TV or film memory.

I place the first log on the dirt in front of the pump house. I tell myself this is like hitting a baseball, which I had been very good at in high school. Bear watches me warily from a distance.

I swing the ax up high and come down—on dirt and rock. I try again. Miss. Then I almost cut my foot off.

A couple of days later, Joe finds me, with ax in hand, staring glumly at the wood pile.

"You see those big stumps I brought you?" he says. "Roll one over, and set the log you want to split on top of it. That'll be easier."

I immediately realize that this way I won't have to worry about accidental amputations.

I swing the ax up high and come down, and the log goes flying, barely missing Bear's head. From now on, Bear hides whenever he sees me with ax in hand.

I swing again. Out of sheer luck, or guided by the invisible hand of a forest duende, I come down on the sweet spot and the piñon splits perfectly in two.

But like in baseball, I hit the sweet spot only once out of every several attempts. Back to Walmart. I tell a kid in the hardware section that I am having trouble splitting wood with the ax I'd bought. (I think it is the ax's fault.) He recommends a heavier ax. He shows me a model with a red plastic handle and a single blade, the back side of which is blunt and even more sinister-looking than the sharp edge.

Back home, I swing it high (*grunt*) and come down, on a spot that is not sweet and whose resistance I feel in every bone in my body, like a cartoon character meeting a frying pan.

Again, Joe to the rescue.

"The knot," he says. "Line up your ax with the knot."

This is a true revelation. From now on, I hit the sweet spot nine out of ten times. But it is not easy. I am sweating like a monsoon shower and out of breath after fifteen minutes on the pile.

One evening I come in from splitting and decide to take a shower. As I undress, Angela points at the backs of my thighs.

"What's that?" she says.

I have to stand with my back to the mirror and contort to get a look. There are purple blotches all over my thighs.

"Oh my God, what is that?"

"I don't know. It's probably nothing, it doesn't hurt, does it?"

"Well, I noticed that my legs have been a bit sore since . . . I've been splitting wood."

The hypochondriac in me is so beset with worry about hemorrhaging—my diagnosis from studying a med school web page: the potentially fatal Henoch Schonlein purpura (HSP), a form of leukocytoclastic vasculitis—that I convince Angela to take me to the ER at the hospital in Española.

During the fifteen-minute ride, I start imagining that the purpura has turned inward and is invading my vital organs.

Once at the ER, we pass through the same entrance that admits the heroin overdoses.

The nurse-practitioner examines me and confirms that the marks on my legs are bruises, the result of my wood-splitting activities.

"Sounds like you've been swinging the ax too hard," she says. "My daddy always said that you should let the ax do the work. If you line up the log right, the weight of the blade itself is enough to split it. It should feel like slicing through ice cream."

The next time I swing the ax—through a furry piece of cedar—that's exactly how it feels.

The first night that it is cold enough, I start a fire with a pitchy piece of ocote. It burns slow and thick, like an oil lamp—beneath my perfectly laddered chunks of piñon.

I leave the stove door open just a hair to get a good draft (as per instructions from the Internet). Within minutes the fire is roaring, and the iron of the stove starts to ring as it expands with the heat. I close the heavy glass door and the flames roil like a furiously boiling soup.

Angela and I sit on the couch and watch the fire like it is TV.

## 8.

Heading north on Highway 285 through Ojo Caliente, I realize that I'm early for my interview. To kill time I pull off the highway at a Forest Service road entrance. The car behind me on 285 pulls in as well, and immediately I turn paranoid—it is relatively rare for two cars to coincide at a Forest Service gate. The driver is invisible behind the tinted windows of a late-model silver SUV, which rolls past me slowly, as if the driver is checking me out. A hunter, some kind of drug transaction? Maybe someone just scored and is looking for a place to fix.

I'd done the same thing at one time in my life. I ran with a handsome, crazed gringo named Joey on Venice Beach. He liked shooting cocaine amid nature scenes. One of his favorite spots was a shaded creek in

Topanga Canyon. He fixed me, into the soft flesh on the underside of my elbow. The sound of the creek swelled and rolled.

The SUV dips below the horizon. I step out of the truck to look at the view and there is a metallic glint in my peripheral vision. From my vantage point I can see only metal poles joining at a forty-five-degree angle above the juniper. I walk toward it. It is a child's swing set, in perfect working condition. I will never know why that swing set was sitting out there on that lonely stretch of land. Did someone think of the place as their land grant commons?

Bill and Claudia Page live in the village of La Madera, just north of Ojo Caliente at the base of the Tusas Mountains. La Madera is not a big tourist draw, though the mineral springs at Ojo Caliente are. The geography and climate here are harsher than Velarde's, but there is hardly an ugly landscape in northern New Mexico, at least not to the eyes of the outsider.

I get no answer when I knock on the door, and I wonder if I'm at the wrong house—there are three in the compound, one of them occupied by Bill and Claudia and the other two by Claudia's siblings. I walk over to the next building. They're all about the same size, comfortable looking, not overdone like the few massive outsider adobes in the area. The exteriors are of gray pumice like the long, tall frontage wall, and all the roofs are New Mexican–style pitched Pro-Panels. Approaching the door of the second house, I set the dogs off. I retreat to the first house and another dog comes toward me barking, and behind it Bill and Claudia.

They hadn't heard me because they were on the back porch, cleaning garlic freshly harvested from their farm. Clean bunches hang from clotheslines strung above them on the support beams.

From the porch we can see a good part of the farm's ten acres. Pears and apples and plums, wheat, honeybee boxes. There's a riparian stand at the northern end of the property, where the Rio Ojo Caliente flows. On the other side of the river a mountain rises steeply from the valley, a rocky face dotted with piñon, mesa-topped. The property has some history. Reies Tijerina, the legendary leader of the 1967 Tierra Amarilla courthouse raid, is said to have lived in an old adobe on it. Down the road once lived a relative of Mabel Dodge Luhan's.

Bill and Claudia sit at a wooden table, a lit citronella candle between them, dirty garlic to their right, clean bunches to their left. An old dial radio plays jazz on KUNM, the public station out of Albuquerque. They are both light-eyed; his are slightly milky. Bill looks older, with his deeply creased, ruggedly handsome face. Claudia has a plain prettiness. Her hair is back in a bun, a few long strands falling over her forehead. They are intelligent and talkative. They have divergent styles and sometimes disagree, but you can sense tenderness between them.

The two Americans striving for a good Jeffersonian life had been described to me by an Hispano elder as "outsiders." The connotation was white and of means. While both of these terms describe them to an extent, Claudia is not an outsider in the literal sense. Born in northern New Mexico, she grew up in El Rancho, next to San Ildefonso Pueblo; her father, a physicist, arrived at Los Alamos in 1953, when the labs were less than a decade old. Claudia and her three siblings went to local schools. Her mother bought the old mercantile building in El Rancho, fixed it up, and ran a store out of it. When Claudia was in high school, her family traded that building for another, in Ojo Caliente. After graduating, Claudia went to Reed College in Portland for two years, and then to Portland State, where she studied sculpture and art before returning home.

Bill is more the outsider, although still very much a Westerner, a native of Denver. He comes from a family of the left; his mother, in particular, was enough of a progressive activist to make Richard Nixon's "enemies list." After college, he developed a career as a commodities broker. His mother moved to New Mexico and she met Claudia's mom in El Rancho; the mothers introduced the future couple.

Bill and Claudia were married in 1985. The way they acquired the land in La Madera was also a family affair. Claudia's youngest sister, Sarah, bought the acreage, but the siblings rotated the mortgage payments among them to make the land affordable. Dividing the plot, Sarah took seven acres for herself, leaving ten for the remaining three siblings, who decided to live next to one another in separate houses and farm the bottomland. Forming a commune of sorts, they wanted to get off the grid as much as possible.

"We're simple people with simple tastes," says Bill. They like wine, tobacco, and bread. They decided to grow grapes, tobacco, and wheat.

The siblings put up a small adobe by the river and lived in it for a year while they built their real houses. Each one took a separate loan and the bank, which considered them high risks, gave them six months to complete the houses. Construction was a family affair, too. Bill's two sons from an earlier marriage came out to help. The know-how came from Claudia's brother, Nick Wimett, who is a builder, and her brother Darrel, a carpenter. They all scraped together enough money to hire two Hispanos from the area.

Bill and Claudia think that locals saw the houses going up really fast and thought the family had "all the money in the world." Since they knew few people in the community, they had no way to dispel the illusion. Lacking local connections is, of course, an essential definition of being an outsider. That the siblings had half a century's worth of history in El Rancho, which is less than fifty miles from La Madera, made little difference to many of the local Hispanos. What mattered were the Anglo surnames and the light skin and eyes. (In a great contradiction, light skin and eyes on Hispanos themselves are often held up as proof of their Spanish roots and a way to distinguish themselves from Mexicans; and of course Hispanos were once light-skinned outsiders themselves when they made contact with the Pueblos.)

Quickly, the family realized there was one big problem in their plan. They could not farm the land without water. Bill took one look at the acequia, which draws from the nearby Vallecitos River, and knew that it hadn't flowed in years. The property was at the end of the acequia, which meant that no water would reach them without the cooperation of their neighbors.

Bill went to the state engineer's office and looked up water law. He read books about the tradition of the communal spring cleanup and the bylaws governing the acequias. He went and knocked at the property next door and then at the one after that. The Hispano elders invoked the crusty chorus that no one wanted to work the land anymore and that in any case there was no money for repairs to the irrigation works. Bill came to the realization that they could avoid all these problems by simply digging a dedicated agricultural well, and Nick Wimett knew how to drill. They applied for a permit for the well, which would draw water from the regional aquifer, through the bureaucratic channels, and published, as per the law, three consecutive notices in the *Rio*

*Grande Sun.* The old-timers of La Madera were avid readers of the public notices section. A group of them arrived on the Wimett property with a letter detailing the reasons why the community supposedly objected to the plan. The argument was that drawing from the aquifer rather than the river would affect domestic wells across the valley, an assertion Bill thought was bogus. It seemed to Bill a backhanded way of getting the newcomers to invest in repairing the acequia. But the opposition was real—even a bit scary. The Hispano contingent that showed up to deliver the news, Bill said, behaved in a "very threatening way."

So Bill abandoned the idea of the well and decided to organize and revive the acequia. The bylaws called for annual meeetings, and on a cold December evening at Dora's Hall, the building used for village assemblies, Bill and Claudia met the men from the mountains.

Everything was contentious. There was debate over whether the meeting should follow Robert's Rules of Order. And there was an argument over whether it should be conducted in Spanish or in English—perhaps a few anti-gringo elders thought they could isolate the family linguistically. But the nationalists were bested on that count, because Bill speaks Spanish very well, enough to eventually become a Spanish teacher at the local high school. Everything that the family thought would work in their favor—quasi-native status, knowledge of language and customs, willingness to learn more—in fact only fanned the resentment among locals.

"There's an inherent distrust of someone with a piece of paper in his hand," Bill says. "It's a very anarchic part of the world."

Claudia worried that her family would become the pioneers of a new boom, a cycle of gentrification. From her childhood she remembered the hippies of the 1960s picking up the trail blazed by the likes of Mabel Dodge Luhan and Georgia O'Keeffe, reenchanting the land. The "intentional communities" of the late 1960s and early 1970s occupied the same space as the utopian outposts of the early part of the twentieth century. Ken Kesey's Merry Pranksters rolled through and communes appeared all over northern New Mexico. New Buffalo Commune and the Lama Foundation were among the most famous; others included the Hog Farm (which was featured in a memorable scene in *Easy Rider*), Reality Construction Company, Tree Frog, Morning Star, and the Family. From the east and the north and from west of the West arrived barefoot kids who were penniless or had trust funds, and not a few rock 'n' roll celebrities (the photographer Lisa Law framed Janis Joplin sitting with her back against a crumbling adobe wall). These outsiders wanted to live on and from the land and proclaimed free love and stoned freedom. Most of the communes were in the vicinity of one of the northern Hispano villages, so there was constant contact across the borders of ethnicity and culture; most of it was tense, some of it violent. Claudia remembers how most of the newcomers left after "someone shot their dog or burned their house down."

This new other, and those who followed, offered Hispanos and Native Americans the opportunity to define or redefine themselves as they attempted to resist economic and cultural encroachment. In the resistance, essentialized culture was the weapon of choice. I recall a group of Hispano land grant activists arriving at the Santa Fe Roundhouse, the capitol building, for a protest; the first speaker was an elder singing an ancient penitente prayer. Such resistance occasionally paid political and economic dividends—the Native American casino economy, the survival of a few hundred thousand acres of land grants, and a political class of Hispanos serving in statewide office—but overall, the New Mexican caste system, with its poverty and addiction, remained intact.

Bill and Claudia's place in this scheme was preassigned. Because of what they believed about their personal antecedents in the West, they did not regard themselves as outsiders, but they stepped into an aura of the past that ensured they would be viewed as invaders to be resisted.

As the family built the three houses on their patch of earth between the highway and the river, some locals welcomed them with taunts.

"They'd drive by and fire off a clip from an automatic," says Bill.

"They'd yell, 'We're going to burn you out,'" says Claudia. "And, 'Give us a job!'"

One time the family was out repairing the perimeter fence along the highway, the men wearing tool belts and unspooling barbed wire, when a truck drove by and the norteños inside yelled out some epithets. Nick Wimett snapped a mental picture of the truck, its dents, and because there's only one road going through La Madera, sure enough a short while later it drove back and the Wimett men came out to confront the offenders. They had been drinking. One of them worked as a cop in

Española, and as words were exchanged he got out of the car, unzipped, and urinated at the Wimett men's feet.

One week before Timothy McVeigh parked a Ryder rental truck outside the Murrah Federal Building in Oklahoma City, Bill and Claudia were in Denver, wrapping up their lives there. The only thing left to do to the houses in La Madera was to finish up the stairs. No one was in any of the units when a bomb—forty pounds of ammonium nitrate and diesel fuel—went off.

Some people thought that Timothy McVeigh and Terry Nichols had come through the area en route to Oklahoma City and rehearsed with a miniature bomb. The blast destroyed only one wall, a modest $14,000 worth of damage, which was covered by insurance. But if someone had been home there could easily have been serious injury or death. There was considerable local press, but nothing beyond Santa Fe and Albuquerque. (It is extremely rare for New Mexican stories to make national headlines. Acequia controversies, land grant minutiae, three cultures at one another's throats, four hundred years of history—these stories do not sound the least bit sexy to national editors.)

"Those articles made me sound racist," Bill says. He even got calls from neo-Nazi groups offering paramilitary training.

The family approached Bill Richardson, who was the congressman for northern New Mexico at the time, about getting the FBI involved. But that never happened because the bombing only could be considered a federal offense if it was a hate crime.

"This could not be considered a hate crime," Bill spits out sarcastically, because "white people can't be considered minorities." No one was ever arrested.

A dozen years later Bill and Claudia are still here. I have heard about many firebombings in the north, a few times by norteños who are proud of the deed. But I've never heard of victims of firebombings who stayed and rebuilt.

"We never considered selling," Claudia says, handing me a cookie made of grain from their fields. How could they sell? Who would consider buying? There are not too many Hispanos with disposable cash for a prime riverfront property with water rights. No sane gringo would go for it.

Most people in the area thought the bombing was a terrible act. Hispana elders came by with pozole, the pork-and-hominy comfort stew, and condolences, like those for a death in the family. The women told them to stay, saying, Don't let a few hotheads get under your collar.

The problem, Bill and Claudia tell me, is that the people who were once closest to the land are now estranged from it. The old-timers just keep chopping it up, Bill says, subdividing the subdivisions, and now there are more trailers than adobes in the mountains. "No one works the land anymore," he says, which is an exaggeration but reflects the trend. If you are an Hispano in northern New Mexico, you are more likely to get up at four in the morning and drive to Los Alamos in the dark, practically in your sleep, than get up at dawn to prune your orchard.

Bill and Claudia believe they're bringing the land back from its Hispano tenure, when it was overgrazed. They will be applying for organic certification soon. And fifty percent of the bread they now eat comes from the field. They see themselves as assimilating into a culture that was assimilated by the culture Bill and Claudia have left behind. They are the authentic subjects now.

"You see," Bill says, "the Hispanos, they bought into the other tradition." He means the Anglo. "When I'm the most qualified Spanish teacher around, they've lost their tradition."

Claudia redoubles the point: "Why do young Hispanics want to buy so much stuff? If you grew up on TV, you're dead."

And here it comes, seemingly straight from the gut, filled with guilt and guilty pleasure and power and anger and fear and desire: "I'm not really the back to the earth type," says Bill. "The bottom line, it was cheap land. It was a gentrification opportunity. It was the last best place."

We take a walk. A 1949 Case combine stands at the edge of the wheat field. The relic has a significant provenance—it used to work on Ghost Ranch, when O'Keeffe was there.

I am standing behind Claudia, trying to see what she sees. She is looking past the grain of the field and the cottonwoods along the river, at the mountain rising sharp and alien from the refined space of the valley at its feet.

I smell the wet fields. Bill and Claudia glow ruddy and golden in the late afternoon light after the rain.

"We'll do a better job at protecting this place than the norteños," Bill says. He and Claudia have covenants written into the deed about what can and can't be done with their land when it passes from their hands. There shall be no mobile homes and no commercial development.

As for the acequia, it was finally fixed, and the water runs all the way down to their farm today. Bill is now the mayordomo.

# 9.

Bear was born in the Mojave Desert, on the edge of the Marine Corps Air Ground Combat Center in Twentynine Palms. An Akita mix, he has the curl on his tail characteristic of his breed, but his ears droop a bit and his face leans toward German shepherd or chow. Bear took me out on walks and got me writing again and helped me mostly stay away from the addictions that had brought me to that lonely house on the edge of the big nothing.

When we arrived in Velarde, Lisa warned us: "Don't let him out," she said. "They shoot dogs around here."

Still, Angela wanted her own dog. We went to the shelter in Española, which is next door to a stinking sewage treatment plant. I picked out the puppy. He was from a litter that had been found abandoned along the 68 below Taos. A mutt, his short coat was a great tan that accented the browns and yellows of the land around us. We named him Chino, the blanket term in Latin America for Asian—it suited his almond-shaped golden eyes. I'd always thought of it as a benign name, until the day Angela and I and the dogs went out hiking and called to Chino just as we were passing a Chinese couple. From the look they shot me, they clearly did not consider the name a term of endearment. By then Chino was almost a year old and although we felt guilty, we never did change his name.

Bear and Chino were inseparable. Bear looked after Chino with the love of an older brother, and Chino, in return, seemed to keep Bear young and playful. Remembering Lisa's admonition about trigger-happy, dog-hating Velardians, I tried to keep them inside the wire fence. But they would always find a way out, no matter how many times I mended it and filled in the holes they dug. I even tried bricks, which they nosed aside with ease. When we'd leave for the day I'd inspect the fence and convince myself it was impenetrable. We'd come back to find the dogs lounging on the dirt road, waiting for us. There was nothing to be done. They roamed the neighborhood freely, and I hoped for the best.

About six months after we got Chino, Joe Rendón came home with three puppies, which he kept like norteño dogs—in a doghouse outside, never letting them inside the human dwelling. Only two of the puppies survived the first winter. They were both mutts many times over. One was a large, goofy blond long-hair Joe named Güero, Spanish for light-skinned or -haired. The other was a small spunky boy who looked like he was wearing a black-and-white cow-print vest and seemed to smile whenever he wanted affection or you gave it to him. Kimba.

Joe's fence was as permeable as mine, and soon all four dogs were running together. Bear, the undisputed alpha, led by example rather than by force. He would take the pack on expeditions along what became well-worn trails; to the pasture next door, where they roamed amicably with the cows; to greet the horse and the lamb; all the way up to the county road; to the acequia to cool off their paws and bellies in the summer. There were many threats besides armed ranchers: coyotes, poisons in the water and the soil, trucks barreling down the road.

Sometimes Bear would wake in the wee hours and whine to be let out. I'd groggily open the door for him, and Chino would go, too. I'd lie back down in bed and look out the window into the cone of golden light and watch Bear lead the foursome on a nocturnal tour. Together, they were invincible.


After LANL, Walmart is the largest employer in northern New Mexico. It is also the county's social hub, serving the function of the old Hispano plazas or Pueblo kivas. Because the rural north lacks both serious street life (except for occasional lowrider cruising in Española) and pedestrian-friendly routes, Walmart is also the only place besides church where you're going to run into people.

There's Joe Rendón, charging up the aisle with his son Little Joe riding in the basket. There's Elena Arellano, Estevan's wife and the Ohkay
Owingeh librarian, looking for the least toxic products to augment the
locally grown veggies and fruits that make up the bulk of the Arellano
diet. There's one of Angela's former clients from Hoy Recovery—wearing
a blue Walmart "How May I Help You?" vest. If the statistics hold, she
will probably relapse within a few weeks or months.

After the arrival of Lowe's, rumors circulate that more serious money
and store chains are Española-bound, that speculators are considering a
full charge on the erstwhile Hispano capital. Among the most-often mentioned possibilities are a Starbucks and an Office Depot.

The months go by. No Starbucks, no Office Depot.

Then we notice a new construction site between Lowe's and Walmart.
Every time we drive by, the work has leapt forward, from clearing the
footprint to pouring the cement for the foundation to erecting the gird-
ers to the rising of the stone façade, piece by piece. Finally a crane low-
ers a big red pod with a green stem into place above the entryway.

*Chili's.*

That is the extent of Española's transformation. No army of specula-
tors comes to rehab crumbling Hispano houses and produce a reality
TV show ("Flip This Adobe") to advertise them. The town remains the
Hispano working-class commercial hub of the rural north.

But immigrants do come and Española does grow. They are not new
gilded age New Yorkers or back-to-the-land Californians. They are
Mexicans, from Mexico. Decades ago there had been a smattering of
migrant workers in the area. They'd left their names carved on the pale
bark of aspens in the high country where they herded sheep. They'd
helped bring in the apple harvest in Velarde. They'd troweled plaster in
new home subdivisions on the outskirts of Albuquerque. They'd cooked,
washed dishes, and generally wiped up gringo messes in Santa Fe. But
unlike Texas and California, which began a "re-Mexicanization" of the
population after decades of Anglo demographic, economic, and social
ascendancy, New Mexico, lacking major agriculture and industry, drew
only modest numbers from across the border, the majority from the
neighboring Mexican state of Chihuahua.

However, the latest wave of immigrants to Española is bigger than anything the elders remember. In 1990 immigrants made up 5.3 percent of the state population. That number will nearly double by 2010, the vast majority from Mexico. Like Mexican immigrants across the country, they are overrepresented compared to the overall population in low-wage jobs concentrated in the service and construction sectors. And with their increasing presence come increasing tensions—not with Anglos, as one might expect, but with Hispanos.

Soon after arriving in Velarde, I start noticing the immigrant ma-and-pa stores. Bargain clothing at a storefront called Tencha's. At Tortas Rainbow you can get a real Mexican torta—a sandwich of bean paste, mayonnaise, avocado, onion, tomato, cheese, and your choice of meat. At Los Compadres genuine carne asada is rolled up in soft corn tortillas, not Taco Bell hard shells with ground beef and cheddar cheese. Corn tortillas roll fresh off the conveyor belt at Tortillería Temosachic. (Many norteños prefer white flour ones from Walmart.) There is a Western Union outlet for migrants to send money orders back home, the clearest sign that the Mexicans have reached a demographic critical mass.

One day I see a small tractor digging alongside the 68 on the north end of Velarde near the Conoco station. The work crew is Mexican, and mostly very young. I ask one man what they're building. He refers me to the "patrón," middle-aged and paunchy, wearing the big "hebilla" belt buckle typical of provincial paisanos, who tells me that he is going to start up a "frutería," a fruit stand, on the highway.

This is big news in Velarde. A Mexican—not a New Mexican, but a Mexican—is starting up a business on old Hispano land. No one can recall this ever having happened before. Outsiders, yes: various gringos over the years, such as the family that opened Black Mesa Winery, which offers gourmet chocolate and Cabs, Chards, and Rieslings. Up the road in Dixon/Embudo there are plenty of gringo organic growers and even a farmers' market. But fruit stands in Velarde have been Hispano-owned since forever. The Hispanos are used to the gringos and their relentless desire; the Hispano relation to Mexico and Mexicans is altogether different.

Those unfamiliar with New Mexican history might have expected Hispanos to welcome Mexicans. After all, Mexico and New Mexico do share a history of three hundred years as Nueva España. We might expect some solidarity because the Rio Grande that flows between the Sangres and the Jemez became the international border downriver at El Paso only because of imperialist aggression. But the core Hispano mythos relies on the ideal of an unbroken Spanish history. The story can be complicated, like the multidimensional tale told by Estevan Arellano and others, but its imaginary remains firmly Iberian.

New Mexico is unique in this regard. In every other formerly Mexican or Spanish territory, the Hispanic mythos was deconstructed by Chicano activists and artists who shifted the nationalist emphasis from Spain to Mexico (often to a romanticized indigenous Mexico). Hispanos do not see Mexicans as long-lost brothers. They see them as Mexicans.

## 10.

During the early winter cold snap, the news goes around that a Mexican owner of a migrant business has been murdered—gunned down, execution style. Two weeks later, there's a second homicide, also of a Mexican, who also runs a small store, also by gunshot. There are no immediate leads, but it doesn't take long for two full-blown theories to develop.

If you are Hispano, you almost certainly believe that the murders are related to the drug trade, which in the Española Valley is dominated by heroin and cocaine, the former by far the most destructive. In just over one year there were seventy overdose deaths in the valley, whose population is approximately thirty thousand; that ratio is over twice the national average. Almost all the heroin comes from Chihuahua, where the poppy fields of the Sierra Madre produce the variety known as "black tar." From the Mexican mountains it is smuggled across the border and comes up I-25 with drop-off points for local consumption; the rest continues on to the major hub at Denver and from there fans out across the country. Despite the absence of any hard evidence, popular imagination holds that local dealing is concentrated among Mexicans, consumption and addiction among Hispanos.

According to the rumors, at least one of the murder victims did business with Mexican dealers. To Hispanos, the second murder is related or just a freakish coincidence. And the fact that there have been no arrests only confirms that there is a connection to drugs. Threats have been made; no one will snitch; it's all very narco-professional.

If you are Mexican, you probably believe that the murders are related to Hispano hatred. If you are Mexican, you have probably experienced discrimination. Perhaps something innocuous, like an epithet tossed at you from a car, or a more serious affront, like getting punched at Española High School, where Hispano-Mexican tensions are frequent. Complaints about the Mexican presence are common public discourse. People say Mexicans—by and large synonymous with "illegals"—are taking away jobs. They say Mexicans work for lower wages, driving down Hispano pay. If you are Mexican, the fact that there have been no arrests confirms your conviction that the Hispanos have it in for you. Of course the police won't lift a finger. They're probably involved in the crime—at the very least covering up, if not perpetrators themselves.

If you are a white, reactionary reader of the *Santa Fe New Mexican*, you will post your typical comments on the paper's website.

*Española is not just the "lowrider capital of the world," it's the LOW-LIFE capital of the world!*

*Hand out automatic weapons to both sides and let them wipe each other out.*

*Deport them all!*


The story makes headlines for a couple of weeks in the *Rio Grande Sun* and the *New Mexican* before fading away, but for the Mexicans in the Valley, the wound hardly heals. They feel as if they are on a death list.

I am reminded of a central, devastating scene in Michael Cimino's *Heaven's Gate*, the Western that in most quarters is regarded as the film that bankrupted United Artists. In the movie, small-town sheriff Jeff Bridges discovers just such a death list, put together by a band of regulators on behalf of big cattlemen. The list targets small-time farmers who depend on communal rangeland and water and who also happen to be Eastern European immigrants whose political sympathies clearly run red. At a town meeting, Bridges slowly reads every single name out loud; the utterance of each brings shouts and cries from the family of the target.

Cimino loosely based his narrative on the Johnson County War in 1892 Wyoming, a classic Western clash between rich cattlemen and small farmers and ranchers. The death list was intended to wipe out the farmers and clear the land for large-scale ranching. There were many immigrants in Wyoming at the time, but not many Eastern Europeans, and there is no reference whatever of these among the historical characters in the Johnson County War. With them Cimino had added his own touch, his sympathy for hard-bitten, against-the-odds immigrant America.

The Mexicans I spoke to after the shootings were shocked and terrified in the way that Cimino had imagined his immigrants would have been in Wyoming in 1892. Unlike in the Old West of *Heaven's Gate*, however, the victims and victimizers in New Mexico at the beginning of the new millennium were fundamentally on the same socioeconomic plane. The people in the role of the regulators were farmers or former farmers with a tenuous hold on not much more than subsistence employment and the ghost geography of the land grants. The people in the role of the impertinent, ambitious merchant class were barely making rent by selling piñatas and pirated DVDs—and there didn't seem to be a sympathetic lawman in town willing to listen to them.

Francisco Torres, forty-two years old, was the owner of Novedades Tere, a Mexican shop on Paseo de Oñate just west of the bridge over the Rio Grande. From the ceiling hung bright, ruffled dresses for little girls. There was Mexican popular music and B-movies. It was the classic old-world shop in the new. Torres was from Jalisco, and had come to the States twelve years earlier. He'd opened the store in 2002, tailoring his wares to the steady stream of Mexican migrants arriving in the Española Valley.

The morning of December 3 was frigid. Torres was alone in his shop at around nine A.M. From the crime scene, it looks like Torres and his assailant exchanged words, either inside the shop or just outside the front door. When the assailant pulled his gun, Torres ran a few paces east on the sidewalk and ducked into the alley alongside the shop. The first two shots hit him in the back. He fell facedown onto the frozen ground strewn with river stones and broken glass. Torres then apparently turned over to look into the eyes of his murderer, or perhaps the gunman turned him over so that the last thing the victim would see were the eyes of his killer. The coup de grâce was fired into Torres's chest at nearly point-blank range. An electrician found him about forty-five minutes later, still warm to the touch but dead. He was facedown. It seems that he turned to the ground again to die.

Evidence suggested not only that the murder was premeditated but that the assailant had been preparing it since at least the night before. Torres had called the police a little after eleven P.M. to report that his electric meter had been stolen. Patrol officers responded to the call and took down the report. At two-fifteen in the morning, an officer driving by saw Torres marching back and forth in front of the store with a rifle. The temperature was near zero at the time. The officer told him it was illegal to carry a loaded rifle on the street, so Torres went back inside the store, where he spent the night with a friend, convinced that a burglary was imminent. They left the store around dawn, and Torres returned a couple of hours later. At eight-thirty a Jemez Mountains Electric Cooperative crewman arrived; he told Torres that before he could replace the meter some work had to be done to bring the store up to code. The murder occurred in the hour or so between the departure of the crewman and the arrival of the electrician Torres hired to do the work and who discovered Torres's body in the alley.

La Mexicanita on Los Alamos Highway was in every way like Novedades Tere, if even more modest. The business was housed in a cramped storefront next door to an accountant's office. Arturo Plácido Rodríguez, thirty-nine, and his wife, Gloria Chávez Hanrahan, did the best they could with what they had. They tried to call attention to the store by hanging big piñatas from the eaves of the building.

On Sunday, December 18, two weeks after the murder at Novedades Tere, Arturo was at the store by himself. He spoke to his wife by phone at eleven-thirty A.M. There was no indication of trouble at that time, according to the statement Gloria Chávez gave police. At one-thirty P.M., a customer called 911 on her cell phone. She was outside La Mexicanita, having come to pick up a pair of shoes she'd ordered, and could see a body on the floor inside. The informant left before police arrived. Officers found the front door locked and Rodríguez lying in a pool of blood, a coat hanger clutched in one hand. A small-caliber bullet had entered his skull at the back of his head.

The similarities between the two murders were many and immediately obvious. Both victims were owners of small stores catering to the Mexicans of the Española Valley. They were roughly the same age, both married with children. The stores were within two blocks of each other and had even swapped locations—Rodríguez and his wife had originally occupied the Novedades Tere storefront. Both men were shot from behind, during the weekend, in broad daylight. In both cases family members appeared to have solid alibis. Robbery did not seem to be the main motive, although Torres's wife did report that money was missing. Both of the dead were regarded as amicable and hardworking. Hispano stereotyping notwithstanding, neither of the men were the focus of Mexican talk involving narcotics trafficking. From the Mexican point of view, that left only one possible motive.

With Rodríguez's murder, the Mexicans were convinced of conspiracy. Word spread rapidly. Mexicans in the valley knew about Rodríguez's death long before the street vendors hawked the weekly edition of the *Rio Grande Sun* along Riverside Drive on Wednesday afternoon. Rumors produced more rumors that had nothing to do with the facts.

The owner of Tencha's, yet another Mexican novelty shop, was shot a couple of days after Rodríguez's murder. (Rumor.)

Mariscos La Playa, a Mexican seafood restaurant, received a death threat by phone. (Rumor.)

A man walked into El Paisano Mart brandishing a gun and threatened the clerk behind the counter. Fact: a man did enter the store with a gun in his waistband but he left without threatening anyone.

There was a death list with the names of all the valley's Mexican business owners on it. (Rumor.)

Beyond dispute was the profound Mexican conviction that the two murders (and surely there were more to come) were the culmination of a long season of anti-immigrant sentiment, not just in the Española Valley, and not just in New Mexico but throughout the United States. This latest season of xenophobia was at least as virulent as the mood of the early 1990s (when California voters passed Proposition 187, the anti-immigrant ballot initiative), and probably more on the order of the political atmosphere that produced the systematic deportation raids of the 1930s and 1950s. As one of the biggest economic expansions in American history was nearing its peak, the political moment increasingly belonged to racist retirees who called themselves Minutemen and hunted immigrants in the Arizona desert, to nativists demanding that the Great Wall of America be built on the U.S.-Mexico line, to Republicans conflating Al Qaeda operatives with undocumented nannies and busboys, to opportunistic local officials feeding off the frenzy by promoting ordinances that would turn landlords and schoolteachers and hospital attendants into de facto immigration guards.

An economic boom coinciding with anti-immigrant activism seems counterintuitive, since nativist reaction typically accompanies economic downturns. But the boom in fact fostered migration—low-wage labor was subsidizing the hottest sector of the economy: construction. And, critically, the boom was not "raising all boats," to use the supply-side cliché. The middle and lower rungs of the economy were trapped in "median wage stagnation," with salaries flat or declining through the aughts even as the real estate bubble was rapidly inflating. Economic insecurity was just beneath the glossy surface, while the productive side of the economy drew migrants and resulted in at least the appearance if not the fact of the displacement of "native" workers—fertile ground for hostility across all kinds of borders of class and ethnicity. Northern New Mexico experienced all the changes of the new economy from within a context of long-standing inequity and intergroup tensions.

Against this background, the Española police failed to turn up an actual death list, but the bullets in the bodies of Arturo Rodríguez and Francisco Torres conjured one as real for Mexicans as if they had.

About a week after the second murder, I stop by Tortas Rainbow, where since arriving in the valley I have regularly been eating the best chicken torta this side of Juárez. At a little after one in the afternoon, there are three people behind the counter, and I am the only customer. The woman at the cash register is light-skinned and orange-haired, pleasant but nervous. I know that she owns the place with her husband, but she denies this at first. She thinks she's on the death list. Finally I convince her that I'm really a writer.

Her husband works in construction in Santa Fe. The hours are long and so is the commute, which has slowed because of endless improvement projects on Highway 84-285, between Santa Fe and Española.

Since the murders, she's been closing early. If there are no customers after six—well, after dark in December—she locks up.

She's heard all the rumors I have and more. Like the police believing that the same weapon was used in both killings. (Unsubstantiated.) Yes, she believes that the assassin or assassins are trying to send a message to the Mexicans. She's been here for eighteen years, and for most of that time her family has lived in peace, but she's felt the sting of discrimination. She spent four years working at Big Rock Casino, a few hundred yards south on Riverside Drive, and in that "diverse" workplace (Native Americans, Hispanos, Mexicans) she often heard the stock epithets. You're taking away jobs . . . Go back to Mexico . . .

"Tengo miedo," she says. She's afraid. She says that the police should give Mexican business owners some sort of protection from the Chicanos (not the "Hispanos"—no Latin American uses the term except when referring to Spanish-language speakers, *hispanoparlantes*). "Hispano" is a norteño invention, part of the Spanish mythos, adopted by norteños to distinguish themselves from Mexicans. Not so much because they hated Mexicans—back then, during the days of the Spanish Colonial Arts Society, there weren't enough of them to hate—but because the gringos did. The Mexican was a symbol of backwardness, dirtiness, the vanquished Aztec empire.

Of course the owner of Tortas Rainbow knew the dead. "Todos los conocíamos," she says. "We all knew them." She'd bought clothes at Tere, candy at La Mexicanita. "What a way to spend Christmas," she says. She never thought anything like this would happen here. In Phoenix, sure, that's where that racist sheriff, Joe Arpaio, "America's toughest cop," rounds up Mexicans. But here, in the mountains that remind her of her pueblo in Chihuahua? Here, among "la raza," who could have imagined such a thing?

Tencha's, a sister store to La Mexicanita and Tere, is in a prominent Riverside Drive location. It is closed, at four in the afternoon a few days before Christmas. A handwritten sign on the window says that Tencha's offers piñatas, wire transfers, "cobijas coreanas" (bedspreads with huge images in screaming colors—roses, lions, a Native American in full headdress), phone cards, shoes, jewelry, women's fashions, ceramics.

Another sign announces that Tencha's is Española's "transportes" hub, with regularly scheduled van trips from Española, Santa Fe, Albuquerque, Los Lunas, and Belén to destinations on the other side of the border in Chihuahua—Palomas, Ascención, Janos, Nuevo Casas Grandes, San Buenaventura, Zaragoza, Gómez Farías, Cuauhtémoc. The route was once the Camino Real. Now it is the royal road of immigrants and drugs and free trade.

Next to the transportes sign is another one, hastily scribbled. It is the only one in English. In big bubble letters:

MOVING SALE. EVERYTHING MUST GO.

Tencha herself—her name is the diminutive of Hortensia—is an attractive woman in her early forties, wearing pin-striped slacks and a brown blouse with gold trim, looking very much the businesswoman. Her three teenage children are helping to pack up the store.

As soon as I introduce myself and my intentions, she bursts into tears. No, the move isn't directly related to the murders, she says. She has a new location picked out, just a couple of blocks north on Riverside. But since the murders, her children are begging her not to reopen the store. Someone called her this morning to say they'd heard that she, Tencha herself, had been murdered. What if she was next on the list?

"We're all so nervous, all the paisanos," she says. "Of course I know the widows, they are fine, friendly people."

The tears come again. "Twenty-six years I've been here. And now, who knows where we'll be next year?"

The worst thing, she says, is the police have no evidence. "They have no suspects. They have arrested no one." It is "un misterio enorme," a great mystery.

One plausible theory is put forward by Rodolfo Valdez, the accountant whose office is next door to La Mexicanita. He is an elderly man, about five-four, wearing wire-rimmed glasses, a brown fedora with a leather band, a tweed suit with creased trousers, and worn leather shoes. But for the computers, the office looks like it hasn't changed since 1950, which is when Valdez arrived in Española from Raton, a small town near the Colorado border.

"Arturo was the nicest guy you'd want to meet," he says. When business was slow at La Mexicanita—as it often was—Arturo would come to Valdez's office and invent odd jobs for himself. He'd fix the furnace or the air conditioner. Things that Valdez thought of throwing away became projects. One time Arturo fixed a broken paper shredder. When a transient walked into the office and terrified Valdez's secretary, Arturo was there in a matter of seconds to chase the man away.

Valdez says he saw in Arturo the values he grew up with: work hard, save your money, do right by your family. Values, Valdez says, that have eroded over the course of his lifetime. He invokes the conservative norteño litany, which apportions blame to gringos and Hispanos in equal measure. The gringos stole the land, but the Hispanos grew complacent. Valdez says that after FDR's Works Progress Administration showed up in the region and Los Alamos went nuclear, "we learned to look to the government for jobs and, worse yet, for handouts. Damn lazy is what people became. And you see the results. You can't get decent help around here—except for the Mexicans."

All this is to say that there was no Hispano-Mexican divide between him and Arturo. "Eramos de la misma raza," Valdez says. We were of the same blood.

Valdez's theory is that a drug addict desperate for a fix killed Arturo and stole the money, knowing that everyone would think of the crime in relation to the murder of Francisco Torres. This is very plausible, I think to myself. The next building south on Los Alamos Highway is a methadone clinic.

I hear the muffled sound of a phone ringing.

"That's Arturo's phone next door," Rodolfo says. We listen to it ring for a good while.


Every story on the murders in the *Rio Grande Sun* quotes Lieutenant Manuel Trujillo of the Española police department.

Of the two available chairs in his office, one is stacked with boxes of live ammo and the other has two shotguns and a semi-automatic rifle leaning against it.

"Here, let me get that out of the way for you," he offers.

Trujillo, who is in his late thirties and has a lot of gel in what is left of his hair, says that he hasn't had time to clean up the office with all that's going on. I assume he means the holidays, the murders, and two of Española's finest getting royally wasted while off-duty and attempting to score coke in the Dandy Burger parking lot, a story that makes a big splash in Santa Fe and ultimately goes national.

"There might be a break in the case," he says. "This guy calls up and tells me that he saw two men with the second victim before the murder."

The two men are Mexican nationals. He's going to check out the lead today.

The investigation has been frustrating, Trujillo admits. "The Mexicans"—that's what he calls them—"they don't talk, they stick to themselves." They don't inform on each other. It's usually the norteños who roll over on the Mexicans when copping a plea.

"They don't get along," he says. "You see, there's two gangs. The Norteños and 13 Street."

You mean the Norteños and Sur XIII, I tell him. There is no "13 Street."

"Yeah, well, they hate each other."

There have been several shootings, a few injuries, but no deaths. Sounds like sparring over territory.

"But I can tell you this," he says. "I can tell you that there is no drug connection we know of with the first victim. And we still aren't sure the second crime is related to the first. Oh, and one other thing. There's never been a hate crime in Española."

After leaving Trujillo, I drive north up Riverside Drive. I notice several police cars in the McDonald's parking lot. A bust is going down in the middle of the lunch rush. A battered 1980s Toyota sedan is being towed away. One of the cops tells me that the car had broken down in the lot and when he checked on the occupants he saw a syringe full of heroin "ready to go" on the dash.

"I've made too many busts in this parking lot," the officer says.

I ask him about the rumors of a drug connection in the Mexican murders.

"I know both of those families," he says. "Never heard of drugs around either of them."

The lunch rush continues unchecked. The kids shriek in the plastic playground. The drive-through line is ten cars long. Happy Meals and heroin to go.

. . .

A few weeks later, Manuel Trujillo is dead, a sudden collapse. No cause of death in the *Sun* obit. There is no comment from the Española PD when I ask.

## 11.

Arturo Rodríguez's widow, Gloria Chávez, reopens La Mexicanita two weeks after burying her husband in Mexico.

I tell her who I am, and she curtly responds that she has nothing to say. But she keeps talking, and I keep standing on the very spot where Arturo Rodríguez died.

"Arturo and I arrived in Española ten years ago," she says. She wears a suit jacket and pin-striped slacks, dressed almost exactly as the owner of Tencha's. "Not even Walmart was open yet. We were the first Mexicans to open up a business."

The store is tiny. There are piñatas, sports caps and jerseys, a few religious icons, candies near the cash register. Some of the jerseys feature the number 13 prominently; these, it is presumed, are bought by Sur XIII gang members and wannabes.

Gloria rode the Camino Real from Chihuahua to Santa Fe and worked three jobs at first. At six A.M. she started maintenance at the capitol building. From five to eleven in the evening she worked at Furr's cafeteria. On weekends she cleaned rooms at the Best Western Lamplighter Inn.

She and her husband saved diligently, bought a bit of land in Alcalde, and eventually put a trailer on it. Then they moved to Española and started up La Mexicanita.

And now?

She will stay on. "I can't go back to Mexico," she says.

Why?

Because of her grade-school-age sons. "They are Americans. What would they do in Mexico?"

One darkening afternoon just before the holidays, I am driving north on Riverside Drive, headed back to Velarde. I glance, as I always do, at the vegetable stand across the street from Walmart. There is nothing for sale in the middle of winter, but I pull in, remembering the Mexican family that works the last remaining plot of agricultural land on Española's main drag.

I had spent a pleasant afternoon with the Corona family several months back. In the fields rose four varieties of squash, three of cucumber, three of onion, and four of chile. There was also okra, sunflowers, apples, tomatoes, corn, and green peas, and a cluster of cherry trees. Dolores, the matriarch, presided over the vegetable stand, near the street, while her husband, Salvador, and their teenage sons worked the rows. Salvador had been a migrant "solo," as they say in Spanish, roaming the States alone, looking for work and a place to settle and bring his family. A stint in South Carolina soured him on the American South; later, while he was on his way to Chicago, a fellow migrant convinced him to go to Santa Fe, where he took a job at a dish factory. By chance one day he met the man who owned the agricultural land across from Walmart. Joseph Merhege was in his seventies, and had not worked his land in years. They struck a deal, Merhege offering the family living quarters in return for reviving his farm.

I'd assumed Salvador and his family, natives of rural Guanajuato, were campesinos, but they were "gente de tabique," brickmakers. Merhege taught them to farm. I interviewed the family as they worked in the fields one summer day. They'd been living and working at the place they called El Ranchito for several years already. Months before the murders put the Mexican community on edge, Salvador spoke to me of anti-immigrant attitudes among Hispanos. He was having problems with the mayordomo of the acequia, who never let him irrigate, forcing Salvador to open the compuerta on the sly. Salvador said the Hispanos saw the Mexicans as "una invasión ilegal," that his sons had been called "mojados," wetbacks, at school. Still, the Coronas considered their life in Española a good one. They loved the land they worked, even if Walmart obstructed their view of the Jemez range, and they loved the old man they worked for, whom Salvador referred to as "un señor árabe," an Arab gentleman.

It is the old man I want to talk to now. His house is set back from the street and adjacent to the fields. I ring the doorbell, but there is no answer. I walk around back and run into Salvador Corona, who calls Merhege on his cell phone. The old man hadn't heard the doorbell. He would receive me now.

With the fading light, it is dim inside the house, but Merhege doesn't turn on any lamps. He is tall and thin, green-eyed, wearing a red-and-black flannel shirt and tennis shoes. Merhege's parents arrived here shortly after the turn of the century, from Lebanon via New York City. New Mexico was a popular Western destination by then, the beginning of the boom that brought artists and speculators to Taos and Santa Fe. The Merheges bounced around the northern part of the state. They worked apple orchards, opened a dry goods store, grazed sheep on the Black Mesa.

"We were discriminated against, very much so," says Merhege. "They called us "árabes puercos"—Arab pigs. They were told to "go back home."

They stayed on, and literally integrated into the community. Merhege's brothers married Hispanas; one of his sisters married an Anglo.

"We're all closer than our prejudices," he tells me.

Yes, Merhege has heard about the murders. He doesn't know who the perpetrators, are, but, he says, he does know that the Mexicans endure today what his own family once did. At the kitchen table where we sit his face is in silhouette against the windows that look out upon his land. The Coronas don't just work for him, Merhege says. They are also his neighbors.

When I leave the old man, Salvador Corona walks me to my car.

"We've made our home here," he says. Night has fallen but his face glows in the light from Walmart. "We aren't going anywhere."


A couple of weeks before he died, I called Trujillo to ask him if there was any news on the case. He said no.

What about the informant who said there were two Mexicans with Rodríguez before he died?

"Not relevant," he said.

To this day, there have been no arrests. Es un misterio enorme.

# WATER IN THE DESERT

## 1.

The Mexican body figures prominently in the Western. The Mexican body sneers, flirts, knifes, leers and lures, dances, sells and is sold, is drunk and dying or dead, a head in a sack with flies buzzing around. But there is another Mexican body: out on the land, in the desert, looking for water. This, too, is a Western.

I have been coming to Arizona for a long time. The requisite childhood trip to the Grand Canyon; to the red rocks of Sedona; to the searing urban flats of Phoenix; to the old Mexican barrio in Tucson; to the O'odham reservation that sprawls across the southwestern part of the state. And, of course, to Monument Valley, which John Ford presented to me in *The Searchers* long before I saw the actual mesas and buttes up close.

In Ford's movies, the desert plays as it does in the Old Testament: the enormity of the place serves to build human archetypes, and these in turn project their power back onto the landscape, infusing its forms. In *The Searchers*, the vengeful hearts of the vanquished—Confederate soldiers and Indians—mold the buttes (which in lesser, more reactionary Westerns can stand as triumphalist symbols) into brooding sentinels that seem to sink into the land as much as rise from it. My father was eleven years old when he saw John Ford's classic for the first time, in Mexico City. I imagine that the Spanish dubbing was probably brash, because that is how Mexicans imagine Americans, missing entirely how John Wayne brilliantly suppressed Ethan Edwards's voice, rage sucking the words inward like a black hole swallowing light. In contrast to the idyllic vision of the diorama in my grandparents' living room in Los

Angeles, this was the darker desert my father bequeathed me. The ideas and emotions that my father cannot say he always imparts to me through films: with John Ford, Pop told me that the ghosts of conquest haunt every frame of our lives. We both identified with Jeffrey Hunter's Martin Pawley, a "half-breed" who suffers at his Uncle Ethan's hand. Martin reminds Ethan that conquest is itself desire, that both winner and loser are irrevocably changed by its violent dance. (Hunter, a white actor, plays a half-breed in brownface.)

It was John Ford's celluloid ghosts that lured Pop to the desert as a young bachelor (racing an MG convertible up I-15 for all-nighters in Vegas), as a father (on our shoestring family vacations in the early 1970s), and, finally, as a retiree. In the late 1990s, my parents joined the exodus from coastal California to the interior West and moved to Sedona, which looks like Monument Valley in miniature and draws gaggles of New Age tourists. The full-time residents are mostly elderly, mostly Republican, and mostly white. The Mexicans and the smattering of Central Americans that showed up for the boom in construction and service jobs as the town grew rapidly through the mid-aughts were priced out of living in Sedona proper and relegated to the more modest rents, mortgages, and red-rock views of Cottonwood, about twenty miles to the southwest.

Southern Arizona is defined by its proximity to the border, which used to be largely invisible. At one time, you looked across the frontier and it was just a desert vista, no real demarcation between one side or the other. Now it is a real line, a martial one, and if you cross it you'll be hearing from a Border Patrol agent or a Minuteman or Phoenix lawman Joe Arpaio himself. Washington sent the engineers and contractors and construction workers to build the great wall—twelve-foot-high fences of rusty steel, concrete-filled bollards riding the land to the horizon, stadium lighting, one-hundred-foot-high digital sureveillance towers—to placate Arizonans apoplectic about immigration.

The political momentum for SB 1070, which would require local law enforcement to check on citizenship status during even the most inocuous traffic stop, began with Proposition 200, the ballot initiative approved by voters in 2004 that sought to deny most state services to immigrants without papers. Like local anti-immigrant movements that sprang up after 9/11 in dozens of states across the country, proponents claimed they sought to protect working-class Americans from unfair job competition and uphold the law of the land. Nevertheless, practically all these movements received support from crackpot nativist organizations like Population-Environment Balance, which publishes monographs with titles such as *Why Excess Immigration Is Increasingly Threatening Public Health and Quality of Life.* As a result of the nativist legislative drive, by the beginning of 2008 there were sure signs of a brown exodus, including spikes in apartment vacancies in heavily immigrant neighborhoods. Because many Latino families include both legal and illegal members (parents born in Mexico, children born in the United States), the evacuation included both.

Arizona's anti-immigrant posse claimed it had finally beaten back the "illegal invasion." What it didn't foresee was that Proposition 200 would coincide exactly with and aggravate the deepening economic recession. Illegal immigration had been a key component of productivity (higher output at lower cost), and had served as a hedge against downturns. Suddenly, there was panic not just in the immigrant barrios but also in the Phoenix statehouse, where emergency proposals called for a "temporary worker" program and pleaded for the federal government to make it easier for agricultural workers to obtain visas to work in the state.

My father looked through his living-room window in Sedona at the spectacular view of Thunder Mountain, a corrugated behemoth of pale yellows and dusty pinks with coyotes howling on cue, and sighed: his Western retirement fantasy had turned out as dark as *The Searchers.* Ultimately, my parents fled Arizona, horrified by the nativist resurgence and its public policy toward the Mexican other. Pop had had enough of playing Jeffrey Hunter to the John Waynes who surrounded him.

## 2.

Despite the brown exodus from Arizona, migrants continued to cross its border with the Mexican state of Sonora to reach destinations more hospitable to brown labor. The migrant flow had been shunted into Arizona from California back in the 1990s by the Clinton administration's Operation Gatekeeper, which fortified what was then the busiest illegal crossing at San Diego–Tijuana. But there is one big difference between the two entry points: in Arizona the border is in the middle of the Sonoran desert, where there are only a handful of water sources. As it has always been in the desert, water is a matter of life and death.

I have been thinking about water in the desert for a long time. When I first arrived in Twentynine Palms, I hiked with Bear in Joshua Tree National Park, seeking remote springs, seeps, old livestock "guzzlers." After a long, soaking winter rain or a brief summer monsoon deluge, I'd go out looking for running washes, and experience deep gratification if I found even a trickle coursing over the sand. When it was more than a trickle, I'd dunk my head into the cold froth and come up with an exhilarated whoop.

I was not in a particularly reflective mode back then, so I couldn't have said what I was doing or why. Nor would I have been able to explain why for most of my life I'd been similarly obsessed with weather and climate—to a degree with the technical minutiae but mostly with the sensual experience of it: the crisp smell of Santa Ana winds rushing across the Los Angeles basin, the thunderhead swelling over the desert plain.

Later, I found the origins of this desire in my imagination. A Ford Western my father showed me early in my childhood was *Three God-fathers*, which follows John Wayne again on an odyssey through a deadly desert, now with a baby in his arms, trying to fulfill a promise to a dying mother. The message is simple: faith flows from the spirit and fills the body, urging it onward not for its own sake but for the body and spirit of the child; in the desert we are purified. Still, John Wayne had to make it out of the desert alive to save the child and walk into a bar and order "milk for the baby and a beer for me." One of the "godfathers" in the film is played by Pedro Armendáriz, a legend in golden era Mexican cinema, here reduced to a greaser lackey who succumbs to the elements and becomes a ghost urging Wayne onward. Down to the hierarchy of race, the old tropes remain largely intact in the West.

On average, at least one migrant dies every day in the borderlands, usually of exposure (notwithstanding narco-noir representations), often in Arizona. The deaths are so common as to hardly warrant any notice in the national press. There is regular coverage in regional newspapers, of course, dispatches leading with language like: "The bodies of three more illegal entrants were recovered in Pima and Cochise counties, raising the weekend's death toll to eight with nearly 40 people rescued, officials said." Such stories rarely name the dead, because these migrants are usually found without proper identification and there is hardly ever a follow-up story to remedy the elision. Occasionally there is a "special feature," in which a newspaper or magazine sends a reporter to a dead migrant's hometown for the pathos-driven backstory.

And then there are documentary projects, such as in the pages of *National Geographic Adventure*, where photo spreads feature the desert with deeply filtered skies, all the better to contrast with the brilliant bleached skull of an unknown migrant resting on burning sand. The narratives are typically long on physical detail (the symptoms of hyperthermia: muscle cramps and nausea), with scarcely any political analysis, even less ethical discernment. The main character is the desert, inevitably referred to as "remote" or "otherworldy." This distancing, in conjunction with an emphasis on Mexican difference, makes impossible any intimate representation of the subject. In the end, the Mexicans disappear. What remains is the landscape.

Over the years, the political economy of the weather in the desert became clear to me. A perennial spring or a wash running for just a few hours could make the difference between a migrant surviving or not. It is no longer possible for me to walk in the desert today without imagining the bodies in it.

## 3.

Mike Wilson brings water to where the migrants need it the most: one of the hottest, driest corridors of the Sonoran Desert, the Baboquivari Valley, on the eastern flank of the Tohono O'odham reservation. Each weekend Mike, a member of the reservation and a former Presbyterian seminarian, fills the bed of his pickup truck with a white plastic one-hundred-gallon tank of water and two coiled hoses, one yellow and one green; fifty translucent one-gallon jugs; five blue ten-gallon containers; a wheelbarrow, work gloves, plastic bags filled with emergency food rations, a rake, an ax, and a shovel.

To bring the water, Mike crosses several borders—between reservation and nonreservation, between the United States and Mexico, and between the political and moral camps that define American immigration politics. As the aughts wore on, more and more migrants died on the Tohono O'odham reservation for lack of water. At the same time, more and more people did not want Mike Wilson to bring water to the migrants.

The first time I visited Mike I got lost looking for his house in the Tucson suburbs. There seemed to be road-improvement projects everywhere; chewed-up asphalt, detours, signs flashing caution on the interstate and local roads. The city's streetlamps weren't very bright to begin with, and where Mike lives there weren't many of them. My main signpost was the Casino del Sol, a Mediterranean-themed resort on a slice of Indian reservation at the edge of the city, anchored by a colossal dome that glowed bright amber at night, seeming to float above the modest subdivisions surrounding it. The casino is owned and operated by the Pascua Yaqui, a tribe whose name might remind baby boomers of the time when they followed the adventures of Carlos Castaneda as he tripped on peyote in the desert with the "sorcerer" Don Juan. I headed ever farther west and could tell that I was close to my destination by street names, which had switched from English to Iberian Spanish (Aragon, Sevilla), but then it got so dark—a rusty blackness—that I couldn't read the street signs at all, even when I got out of my car and stared up at them. I rang Mike. It was four forty-five A.M., and he was awake. After his years as an army Special Forces master sergeant, the clock in his head never let him sleep late. I was only a couple of blocks away, he said. He guided me in.

In the immediate vicinity of Mike's house were Far West Tucson subdivisions built by companies with names like Sonoran Ranch Villages and Richmond American Homes, where you could buy paradise for the "high 100s." The houses always offered some variation of an open floor plan downstairs and a clutch of bedrooms upstairs. Sometimes there was a neighborhood park, a tiny tuft of thick green grass with a jungle gym. The homes were salmon-toned boxes with metal-framed windows and mini chandeliers with small torpedo-tip bulbs hanging in the entryway. In the dead of summer there was hardly any movement in these neighborhoods, day or night. Most everyone was indoors, or trying to get there. If you took a stroll in the heat, all you heard was the collective whir of swamp coolers or the grinding noise of air conditioners.

These houses were an integral part of the boom, and can be found in the suburban rings of any American city. They were also a fundamental migrant magnet. At the peak of the housing bubble in January 2006, when the annual pace of new home construction hit a blistering 2.29 million units, an estimated 14 percent of laborers in the construction sector were undocumented immigrants, including 20 percent of carpet, floor, and tile installers, 28 percent of drywallers, and 36 percent of insulation workers. In September 2007, housing starts were down almost 50 percent, prices had tumbled, and tens of thousands of migrants had lost their jobs. By the end of the decade, an estimated one million undocumented immigrants had returned to their home countries. But even as they did, others were heading north into the desert.

Mike's place was the last house on a street that abuts what's left of open desert in the Tuscon area. An older home for the neighborhood, 1970s vintage, it had a traditional pinkish mud-brick exterior. In the front yard a huge angel's trumpet bush was in full blossom. It gave Mike great pleasure. He never pruned it, even as the bush crept ever closer to blocking his front door.

Inside, I saw white walls and white tile floors and not much else. The rooms were large and Mike had very little furniture in them. There was a coffeemaker in the kitchen, and a big can of Folger's for the watery morning coffee. The fridge was nearly empty.

"I don't cook," he told me. "Mickey D's is right up the road."

It was a clean, minimal space, offering the barest of comfort.

Mike is fifty-eight years old but could easily pass for forty-five. With his broad chest and sinewy arms, he looks every inch the soldier he once was. His shiny black hair is streaked with white, trailing halfway down his back in a ponytail, which is held in place by a metal ring etched with the O'odham "maze of life," a labyrinth with a human figure standing at the opening. (I cannot tell whether the figure is entering or exiting the maze; every time I try to trace the path I wind up at a dead end.) He likes to wear guayaberas, the embroidered short-sleeved shirt of the Latin American tropics, which also work quite well in desert climes. A four-inch-long wooden crucifix hangs from his neck. When walking in the desert, he wears khakis, work boots, and a military-style boonie hat with a chin strap. His handsome face is bronzed and blunt; his lips thin; his almond-shaped eyes dark brown; his eyebrows slight. He speaks slowly and deliberately. He has a penchant for logistical details and is also given to intricate political analysis. When he is relaxed he laughs a lot, and, with his gleeful falsetto cascade, he reminds me of my maternal grandfather.

Sunrise: the first of several I will see at Mike's house. Whenever I accompany him on a trip to the reservation, I will have either spent the night or show up, per his instructions, well before dawn. Daybreak here always inspires the same swell of emotion. On this summer morning the sky is a patchwork of altocumulus, countless cottony crests very high up, dabbed pink and white and gray and gold, the enormous distance between land and clouds creating a sky cathedral. The cloud cover is evidence of monsoonal moisture bulging up from Mexico; it may or may not produce thunderheads later in the day; may or may not bless the land and what lives on it with rain and momentarily cooler temperatures.

When the sun breaks over his neighbor's roof, Mike loads up his truck, a metallic-green Dodge four-by-four with a good ding in the right front fender and a long horizontal crack along the windshield that glints when he's driving into the sun.

We head west on Highway 86, a two-lane road. The basin abruptly gives way to the Baboquivari Mountains, which run north from the border and end with Kitt Peak, a "sky island" that sustains oaks and pines at its highest elevations, in radical contrast with the saguaros, creosote bushes, and ocotillo that dominate the valley floor.

The first of Mike's water stations is underneath an arroyo bridge on the highway. There are three such stations in the immediate vicinity; he has named them Father, Son, and Holy Ghost. Father is at a characteristic stop on the migrant path—the bridge offers deep shade from the heat as well as cover from the Border Patrol. These are the stations of desperation. If the migrants reach them it means they've walked the entire length of the Baboquivari Trail—thirty miles or more over three or four, maybe five days. They would be suffering at least the first stage of dehydration. The lucky ones would have picked up water a couple of days earlier at one of Mike's stations off of Fresnal Canyon Road, closer to the border. The unlucky ones would have run out of water a day or more earlier.

Mike gets out of the truck carrying a clipboard with a sheet divided into columns for date, location, and number of gallons dispensed. At nine in the morning the temperature is already into the high eighties, but under the bridge the concrete-scented cool of night lingers. Only five of the one hundred gallons he placed here (in straight rows of ten) have been used since his last visit, a week ago.

"That's good news," Mike says, bringing over five fresh jugs from the truck. The containers haven't been confiscated by tribal authorities (in which case all of them vanish at once) or slashed by vandals—both of which have happened on more than one occasion. Recently he'd placed one hundred gallons at mile marker 12 of the Ajo Highway, which transverses the reservation, and someone had run over every single one with a car or truck.

Mike was on his way toward ordination as a Presbyterian minister before dropping out of seminary school. The water stations have become his ministry. He says that scripture would have him do nothing less.

"We must offer hospitality in the desert," he says, "because that is what the God of the desert calls us to do."

But many of the secular authorities in the area don't follow his clean moral logic. Indeed, the question of whether to give migrants water has torn the Tohono O'odham Nation apart. Since Mike began his mission in 2002, tribal officials have passed resolutions forbidding him to set up or maintain the water stations. He has disregarded them. After confiscations or sabotage, he simply replaces or fixes the containers. When he's not refilling tanks and jugs, he is often in the desert leading search parties for missing migrants. As his water operations have grown over the years, so has the number of families that come to look for the bodies of their dead.

The number of immigrants entering through southern Arizona increased steadily after the inauguration of Operation Gatekeeper. That barrier was followed by others, at the crossing between El Paso and Juárez, between Arizona's Nogales and Mexico's Nogales, and between Douglas and Agua Prieta. If the desired effect really was to deter illegal immigration (and not only to placate the nativist right), the walls were an utter failure, since they succeeded only in funneling the smugglers and their human cargo farther east into Arizona, into the more isolated and rugged border deserts. To the wicked terrain of the Cabeza Prieta National Wildlife Refuge and the adjacent Barry M. Goldwater Range, for example, where there are live fire exercises and the distance migrants must travel on foot—up to seventy-five miles—ensures that whatever water they bring with them will run out long before they get picked up by smugglers along Interstate 8. Or into the Huachuca Mountains north of Naco, where sky-island peaks rise up to nine thousand feet above sea level—a region previously only traveled by the hardiest of narco smugglers. Or to the O'odham reservation.

The new corridor has resulted in a rising death toll. In 1993, there were 180 crossing-related deaths; in 2005, there were more than 500, a trend that correlates with the long upswing in the American economy, as well as with the implementation of the North American Free Trade Agreement, which precipitated wide-scale economic dislocation in Mexico, particularly in rural areas.

Through the 1990s, the new barriers not only altered the migrant stream but also brought more Border Patrol infrastructure directly onto the reservation, along with more migrant deaths, more swaths of desert torn up by smugglers blazing new roads with the BP in pursuit, more drugs, and more reservation residents smuggling and using drugs. Over the past decade, O'odham land—one of the vastest stretches of desert in the United States with the fewest natural water sources—became the deadliest corridor and the focal point of the political and moral disaster of the border.

Ironically, for the O'odham, whose very name means "people of the desert," the border had historically been more of an idea than a fact. I was drawn to the reservation precisely because the border here had been particularly unreal. Most O'odham live in the United States, but there are also several villages and ceremonial sites in Mexico. Tribal boundaries and pilgrimage routes were not much affected by the Spanish conquest or even the Mexican-American War; the Treaty of Guadalupe Hidalgo left O'odham territory entirely in Mexico. The land was split only in 1854, by the speculation deal named after the southern railroad tycoon James Gadsden. Although decades of trouble ensued over property lines and water and mineral rights, the border had no significant impact on most O'odham lives until it became a late-twentieth-century symbol of a failed war on drugs and a brown invasion. Then, after 9/11, the frontier was transformed into a line of defense in the war on terror. Homeland Security rendered the line on the reservation real with the introduction of agents in helicopters and fixed-wing aircraft, riding four-wheel-drive SUVs, ATVs, and horses; a surfeit of surveillance technology; and even a temporary detention center that immigrant rights activists dubbed "the cage" for its open-air chain-link design. A good part of the border on the reservation is now also literally represented with "vehicle barriers" made of railroad ties; the barriers are meant to prevent smuggling vans from cutting new roads through the desert (although these are relatively easily overcome by coyotes with ramps) but do not prevent the passage of people on foot.

Still, many O'odham insist on living as if their world remains borderless, breaching the line on feast days for celebrations on one or the other side.

At the Father Station, the only evidence of recent migrant passage is a peace sign, about a yard in diameter, shaped with stones. I imagine a Mexico City "rockero" kid taking the time and effort to make it. Delirium? What kind of peace did he want to communicate? Peace of mind to other migrants undergoing the same devastating journey? Peace to the Border Patrol? Peace to Mike, thanking him for the water he left in the shade of the arroyo bridge?

In the early days of his mission, the BP would often pull Mike over for questioning. He'd respond to their abrasive attitude with his own, saying things like "This doesn't pertain to you, does it?" But he found that the best tack was to play the Indian card: "This is tribal business, so we won't go there, will we?" And they didn't.

We arrive at the Son station. Not a single gallon has been used. Mike does not stop at the Holy Ghost. "Every gallon I've ever put out there has been slashed," he says.

Next come the stations he named for the Gospels: Matthew, Mark, Luke, and John, all along Fresnal Canyon Road, which bisects the Baboquivari Trail about seventeen miles north of the border. Once, he found eighty-four gallons shredded and emptied, but not by human hands; Mike could tell by the claw marks that badgers had done the damage. As usual when he faces a setback, Mike approached the incident as a strategic challenge. To baffle the badgers, he restocked the gospel stations with fifty-gallon barrels that rested sideways on yard-high metal stands. He also filled a fifty-gallon drum with empty jugs for migrants who'd lost theirs or wanted to carry more water.

When we arrive at John, one of the barrels is lying on the ground, empty. After careful study Mike discounts the possibility of sabotage. Recent monsoon rains made a muddy mess here, and he thinks that the metal stand kept sinking from the weight of the barrel, until it simply turned over.

Mike places the barrel on a drier patch of earth and goes to work with his system: Lower the Dodge's tailgate. Back up to within an inch of the barrel. Begin emptying the ten-gallon bottles from the truck directly into the fifty-gallon barrel, one at a time, while refilling the freshly emptied containers with the green and yellow hoses that siphon water from the one-hundred-gallon tank in the pickup bed. After years of trial and error Mike has learned that this is the fastest way. The quicker he refills a barrel, the quicker he can get to the next station.

John Station is in the sun-dappled shade of a mesquite thicket, and with all the splashing from the ten-gallon containers and the hoses, soon there are diamonds of light glinting on every surface, drops of water whose brilliance disappears within seconds as the blazing air sucks the moisture away.

## 4.

Mike grew up in Ajo, where his dad worked in the massive pit of the copper mine. It was a company town then, and segregated. Native Americans lived mostly in a section called the "Village," and the Mexicans in "Mexican Town." When his dad was fired from the mine, the family moved from the village to the town. There was little obvious difference between Indians and Mexicans. They had plenty of borderlands culture in common—popular music and food and religion. But there was the distinction of language, of O'odham and Spanish. Mike Wilson grew up hearing more Spanish than O'odham. Today, he speaks Spanish with a bit of an accent—or, rather, he speaks it like he speaks his O'odham-inflected English: melodically and with slightly clipped vowels.

His first wife was Mexican, and the marriage horrified his in-laws—anti-Indian prejudice runs deep among Mexican mestizos, in spite of the irony that many have more Indian "blood" than Indians. Then there is the anti-Mexican sentiment among the O'odham, a pretzel of a contradiction when one considers that a significant number of elders born on tribal lands in Mexico (or on the U.S. side, but without a proper birth certificate) have long lobbied the American government to be recognized as citizens even as they would deny other Mexicans safe passage across the borders of the reservation.

As a young man in the 1980s, Mike enlisted in the army. With his excellent Spanish, he wound up where his language skills were most needed at the time: Central America. He served as a so-called technical adviser to the Salvadoran armed forces, who made international headlines with their torture and death squads. He was there during the "final offensive" by the anti-government guerrillas of the FMLN in 1989, at the same time that the Tucson-based Sanctuary movement was helping smuggle refugees from the conflict across the border. He does not say whether he saw action; as a technical adviser he was not supposed to. He does not speak much about the experience, and yet what happened in El Salvador seems to have been the beginning of a great moral and political awakening for him.

After returning home, Mike attended San Francisco Theological Seminary in the northern California pastoral of Marin County, green hills and oaks and mission architecture. Each of the stained glass panels in the seminary's Stewart Chapel honored a Presbyterian who served on the frontier. In one panel, a missionary held a cross over a cowering native shaman, who tried to shield himself with outstretched hands—except that he did not have hands but claws and the shaman's face was not human but that of a horned devil. When Mike saw the panel, he confronted the elders. Is this what you think of Native American spirituality? he asked. The Presbyterians had not noticed the depiction, had not seen it, until Mike Wilson saw it for them. The window was removed.

Angry and disillusioned, Mike returned to Arizona. He still wanted to minister so he approached the Presbyterian session, as the local body of elders is called in the faith, when he heard that they were looking for a new pastor. He got the job and began preaching at the Presbyterian church in Sells, the O'odham Nation's capital, as well as regularly visiting three rural parishes on the reservation. A couple of weeks after 9/11, he stopped in one of the villages and heard about migrants passing through, begging for food and water. There was talk of break-ins, armed drug smugglers, and Indians—those other Indians, from Mexico and Guatemala—carrying burlap sacks stuffed with marijuana, cocaine, heroin, meth. "Mulas," the smugglers were called, mules. And he was told about the bodies.

He knew Reverend John Fife, the pastor of Southside Presbyterian, a well-known activist church in Tucson, and a founder of the Sanctuary movement. Mike heard him preach about migrants and the desert, about the moral and political imperatives Fife believed they signified. It is a matter of hospitality, Fife said; it is a matter of our privilege and their need. It is a matter of the laws of God versus human laws. Later Mike saw one of the first "death maps" made by Reverend Robin Hoover, another longtime activist and the pastor of Tucson's First Christian Church; red dots marked the locations where bodies were found, forming striking clusters throughout southern Arizona. On the reservation, there were two major clusters. One began at the San Miguel Gate on the border, an informal crossing that the BP had long allowed the O'odham to use without having to prove citizenship or declare customs; the red dots were heaviest along Highway 86, several miles northeast of the gate. With the increase in trafficking, the BP established a more substantial presence at the gate, and many O'odham complained of harassment when crossing. The second cluster was at the far west end of the nation's territory; it followed a paved reservation road north from the border. The majority of the deaths on the reservation have occurred within about thirty miles of the line, a distance that a healthy person could cover in about two days with enough water and food, and if they hiked mostly at night in the summer to avoid hyperthermia, or by day in the winter to protect against nocturnal hypothermia. There were other red dots scattered across the nation, diminishing in frequency farther north from the border, and beyond O'odham territory, near the towns of Eloy and Casa Grande and on the Gila River Indian reservation. The final dots were well over one hundred miles from the U.S.-Mexico line.

In 2003, Robin Hoover founded a group called Humane Borders. For its logo he chose the drinking gourd, the symbol of the Underground Railroad for black slaves.

*When the sun comes back and the first quail calls,*
*Follow the Drinking Gourd.*
*For the old man is waiting to carry you to freedom,*
*If you follow the Drinking Gourd.*

Humane Borders started placing water stations along the deadliest routes in southern Arizona, but tribal authorities refused to grant the activists access to O'odham territory, citing, among other reasons, the fear that water stations would attract even more migrants. Hoover made the argument public with an opinion piece in Tucson's *Arizona Daily Star,* noting "Migrants do not die near water stations, and migrants choose where to cross the border not because of water station locations but because of where the Border Patrol is working and where supporting infrastructure exists."

Then–tribal chairwoman Vivian Juan-Saunders pleaded the nation's case, citing the heavy toll on tribal health and law enforcement resources, as well as on O'odham residents living along migrant routes. In an open letter to the United Nations Secretariat of the Permanent Forum on Indigenous Issues, she and then–vice chairman Ned Norris Jr. wrote, "Our tribal members live in fear for the safety of their families and property. Oftentimes, members have been assaulted, their homes have been broken into by those desperate for food, water and shelter, and our beautiful Sonoran landscapes are tarnished by the deluge of trash that is left behind."

This language employed the tropes typically invoked by the anti-immigrant movement: the environmental image of migrants "trashing" the desert, as well as the portrayal of migrants-as-criminals (or, by Homeland Security, as possible terrorists). Hoover responded with Christian ethics. "What is needed is a concerted effort by all concerned parties to the immediate crisis that is killing people."

In the nation's official view of the story, there is no place for an innocent migrant; in Hoover's, there is no place for inhumanity.

The argument opened a deep rift in the local activist community. Tucson has a long history on the issue of migration, dating back to the sanctuary offered by Southside Presbyterian and other churches to Central American refugees. Back then, Fife and other movement leaders were convicted of breaking federal immigration laws and sentenced to probation. Their example inspired widespread defiance of those laws throughout the Reagan and Bush years, with churches, universities, and local and even state governments declaring themselves sanctuaries.

The debate over water stations on O'odham lands exacerbated standing political tensions between Hoover's First Christian Church–based Humane Borders and groups affiliated with Southside Presbyterian— the Samaritan Patrol and No More Deaths, who carried out medical evacuations of migrants suffering from exposure. Hoover generally supported a new guest-worker program, which was anathema to the more radical activists at Southside, who considered any such move the institutionalized exploitation of labor. And more specifically, Southside Presbyterian accepted the nation's opposition to opening its borders to humanitarian aid as a matter of Native American sovereignty, while Hoover had no patience for such pieties. But by making the debate public, he practically guaranteed that the nation would never allow Humane Borders on the reservation.

## 5.

Mike Wilson stood between the activists and the nation, between his religious mentors and his people, but the moral dimension of the migrants' situation moved him profoundly: he felt compelled to try to prevent deaths he believed were preventable. Water in the desert kept people alive; the moral imperative was to bring water to the desert. Mike therefore sided with Hoover and against the official policy of his own tribal government. So he went out into the desert on his own. He sought out smuggling trails, which were not difficult to find. All he had to do was look for the translucent water jugs, which, by sheer contrast, stood out at the base of a creosote bush or mesquite tree. There was nothing else in the desert that remotely resembled that shape or color.

What Mike saw directly inspired his strategy and tactics. Sometimes, a trail would fall into disuse; he could tell because the water bottles he left were untouched; in such cases, he packed up and moved on to fresher paths.

In the beginning, he made no public announcements about what he was doing. He was acting on moral impulse and hadn't thought very far ahead. It started as a small-scale operation, maintaining about twenty-five gallon jugs at a handful of locations. But Mike didn't hide his work, either. On the water trips he parked his truck openly along Fresnal Canyon Road, the major vehicle route along the Baboquivari Trail; passersby could easily see him pushing a wheelbarrow full of jugs. As word got around, though, he decided to inform the Presbyterian session. Soon enough, O'odham tribal officials took up the matter as part of the heated debate over how the nation should handle the increasing numbers of migrants crossing its land. Ultimately, both the session and the tribe decided to censure him. The Baboquivari District Council acted first by unanimously passing a resolution stating that the water stations

> encourage illegal entry through the District, heighten criminal activity, including transporting drugs and illegal immigrants, breaking and entering of homes to steal food, clothing, blankets and the misuse of communication systems ... barbwire fences being cut for passage which then leave the cattle to roam through the desert and the clothing, water bottles and trash that is left behind by the illegal entrants.

The session's own resolution went even further, expressly prohibiting Mike from keeping stations not just in the Baboquivari District but anywhere on the entire reservation. In response, Mike quit his post of lay pastor and continued putting out water. It became the central activity of his life, going out at least one day each summer weekend, from before sunup to late afternoon.

He decided to go public like his spiritual and political mentors, Fife and Hoover, and, like theirs, his name began to appear frequently in media accounts of the border. He understood that the water stations served both physical and symbolic purposes; they could save lives and also stand as ethical arguments in the media debate, which could, in turn, have an influence on policy.

But not all Mike's media appearances offered a simple message. In the documentary *Crossing Arizona*, a film crew accompanied him on a tour of the water stations. The crew, riding with Mike in the Dodge, captured him in an encounter with a lone, lost migrant on the Baboquivari Trail. It was early morning, a cloudless summer day, the truck casting a long shadow westward along Fresnal Canyon Road. Mike, in profile, was at the wheel. The camera jostled; the filmmakers were waiting for this moment. It provided the film's main publicity image: a medium shot of a migrant, in a red T-shirt and light blue pants, walking away from the camera, down an empty dirt road in the desert.

The migrant approached Mike's window. Mike asked him if he had water. Very little, the migrant said. He didn't know where he was or where he was headed. He had spent the night under a mesquite tree. He was from Hidalgo, one of thirty in his migrant crew. The "migra" chased them, and they scattered. The red T-shirt read, "Intramural Community Recreation Basketball."

"How far is it to Phoenix?" the man asked.

"Days or miles?" Mike asked back.

"I mean, how many hours?"

"Days, my brother," said Mike. "Days."

This hits the man hard—he recoiled as if a fist caught him on the chin. No, he cannot do it. He had been out here for two days already. In his eyes were exhaustion and hunger and, most of all, fear. The better part of his face, from his eyebrows to his mouth, was fixed in a pucker, like he was trying to swallow himself. He accepted Mike, who offered him water and spoke Spanish, but he was trying to avoid the stare of the camera.

"I can't take you," Mike said, "because if the Border Patrol passes and sees you in my truck, I can go to prison. What I suggest you do is, walk down this road toward the highway. The migra will drive by. Go to them. Don't be afraid. The only thing I can do is give you water and the little food that I have."

Mike gave the man a fresh jug of water and took the empty. (It went into the back of the pickup to be filled at home and brought back out the following weekend.)

The nameless migrant turned and faced west on the road, away from Baboquivari Peak, the most iconic and sacred feature of the O'odham landscape, which rose in a dusty gray cone on the horizon. The camera continued rolling. Was it because of the camera that he chose this moment—his departure—to begin the soliloquy? That he began tearing up, speaking of his wife and her medical bills, of his young children, of the job he wanted for them, for them only? Or was he hoping that Mike would relent and give him a ride to Phoenix? He did not realize that the camera probably sealed his fate. It would be one thing for Mike to "aid and abet" a migrant by giving him a ride to Phoenix. It would be quite another to do so before a camera, a prosecutor's unquestionable evidence of guilt.

And yet, here was a man alone in the desert who wanted not just water but to find a job and provide for his family. "What part of Scripture don't you understand?" Mike often asked his critics rhetorically, referring specifically to the Gospel of Matthew: "For I was hungry and you gave me food, I was thirsty and you gave me drink, I was a stranger and you welcomed me . . ." Mike was able to give the migrant water but forced to deny him the rest.

The Tohono O'odham Nation's policy regarding migrant aid or, rather, its policy against having a migrant aid policy was easy to criticize. But in practical terms, how was an O'odham living along the Baboquivari Trail to respond upon having fifty migrants cross his land, tear up his fencing, leave his cattle gates open, break into his house and use it as one big bathroom?

But the nation's stance was also perhaps rooted in corruption. Several relatives of former tribal chairwoman Vivian Juan-Saunders had been arrested and convicted of drug smuggling before and during her administration. Saunders's opposition to providing humanitarian aid conceivably fulfilled two purposes: taking a populist stand with aggrieved community members, and deflecting attention from tribal members complicit in trafficking drugs and people. The involvement of some O'odham as mules, lookouts, and sources for drop houses was likely among the reasons the Baboquivari Trail became a major—and deadly—migrant thoroughfare.

The nation's representation of itself could not admit responsibility for Indians gone bad—the tribe was heavily invested, like many, in cultivating its gaming brand (Desert Diamond Casino), which was best served by the idea that support for Native gaming essentially helped Indians be Indians. The story of the Shadow Wolves supported the cause. An elite counter-narcotics smuggling unit, it was formed in 1972 under what was then the Customs Service. After the creation of the Department of Homeland Security, the unit was transferred to the Border Patrol. Dressed in boonie hats and desert cammies, carrying semi-automatic M4 rifles and Glock 9mm sidearms, every member of the unit was O'odham, expert trackers all, relying on "skills that have been handed down from generation to generation for centuries," recalling tracker-characters in countless Hollywood Westerns and fulfilling several stereotypes: Indian with animal instincts, Indian close to the land, Indian turncoat. Under the Border Patrol, the Shadow Wolves complained of an increasingly marginal role—indeed, their numbers dwindled to sixteen full-time members. With the billions Homeland security funneled to the militarization of the border, the unit, which sometimes worked on horseback, seemed a quaint relic given the federal government's use of crude physical barriers and panoptical digital technology (not without infamous glitches, such as Boeing-built surveillance towers that couldn't tell the difference between a cow and a human being). But the Shadow Wolves were not likely to disappear anytime soon, hauling in as they did thousands of pounds of drugs, and playing a strong symbolic role for both the O'odham and Homeland Security: Indians being Indians.

## 6.

Humane Borders received permission from the Mexican government to place a water station just across the border from the reservation. It is on Mike's route.

At the San Miguel Gate crossing there is no actual gate, at least not the kind I'd imagined, like a big corrugated side of aluminum that swings open wide. It is simply a gap in some modest strands of barbed wire. The gap is bisected by a deeply rutted dirt track. There is no checkpoint on either side, no bridge, no dogs, no video surveillance that I can see. The border here is represented by nothing. Such places have become quite rare along the two-thousand-mile-long frontier. Here, bodies still cross back and forth, in vehicles and on foot, along a two-way path— here, the border becomes just land again. But no matter how much I want the place to resonate with political or even spiritual symbolism, it is not a romantic landscape. It is flat. The sand is brownish-gray, as if singed by the Sonoran sun. There is the occasional mesquite tree, but by and large this is a creosote plain, which generally signifies the harshest of environments, since the creosote is the plant of last resort, a master of storing water deep within itself to withstand the hellish redundancy of desert drought. As we get closer to the gate, beer cans and bottles appear in greater numbers by the side of the road. The sale of alcohol is prohibited on O'odham Nation land.

We cross and soon spot the blue flag marking the new water station. It is a simple triangular banner, flapping atop a thirty-foot aluminum pole that bends slightly in the hot breeze of midday. We hear shouts and whoops: a crew of American O'odham has crossed the line before us, bought beer, and is now partying around a cluster of pickup trucks. There is no shade anywhere. The revelers are just standing in the middle of the desert, drinking under the sun. All around them, to the east and to the west, dozens, perhaps hundreds, of migrants are being pushed by their smugglers across the border. Some have already hiked several miles even before they cross. The Humane Borders water tanks, sky-blue barrels, sit just a few feet from the fence. They have been tagged up by kids with Sharpie-like pens: "LOKO" . . . "RATA" . . . "GUATEMALA." A yellow sign hangs on the Mexican side of the fence: "PELIGRO, TEMPER-ATURAS EXTREMAS." Placed there by the Instituto Nacional de Migración, as ineffectual a bureaucracy as there is in the Mexican government, it delivers a warning that stops no one.

We top off the tanks and head back. About a hundred yards into America, a Border Patrol agent stops us. Mike tells him that he is a member of the nation. The agent looks at me. "And he's with you?" Mike nods. And that's it—Mike and I drive up San Miguel Road.

There is one other water station to check, under an arroyo bridge on Topawa Road not far from Sells. When we arrive, it looks like a flash flood has swept through. Mike had placed the gallon jugs in cardboard boxes; several of these are overturned with the jugs leaking amid swirls of dried mud and debris. Mike makes the tally. There are only thirty-six left out of the ninety-eight he counted last weekend. The question is, Where did the rest of the jugs wind up? Washed downstream by the muddy torrent? Or picked up by a large crew of migrants?

Mike gets back in the truck believing that the migrants got there first.

"Can't play the intellectual game of 'What if?'" he says. "You just put the water out there."

He used to agonize over whether the water would reach the migrants, but now he says he realizes that he has no control over how it finds its way to someone in need.

"You did what the Lord required you to do," he says. "You put water in the desert, and I find comfort in that."

He finalizes the numbers on the clipboard. Two hundred gallons dispensed today. "That's a good day's work," Mike says.

## 7.

Lucas Montejo, a Guatemalan immigrant who lives and works in San Diego, has enlisted Mike Wilson to search the desert for his cousin, Sergio. A teenager from a Guatemalan village in the Mayan highlands, Sergio had crossed onto the reservation about a week earlier. According to witnesses, he collapsed and died two days into the journey, but his body has not turned up. Now a three-car search party is out looking for his body in the desert—and documenting the quest.

The party includes the symbolic leader, Sergio's uncle Lucas; several cousins; and even a few neighbors from the family's village in Guatemala. They all look to be well off, dressed comfortably in casual American wear. Several journalists are here also—two Italians, a Mexican, and me. Mike, the media-savvy activist, often bundles journalists on his missions to the reservation. Rounding out the crew is David Garcia, a former O'odham legislative council member who has become Mike's key ally in the ongoing political battle over the water stations. The two have gone out into the desert before, searching together for the dead. David looks the elder, lean and bronzed, his long, mostly silver hair wrapped by a blue bandanna.

We head west on Highway 86 toward the Tohono O'odham Nation; the green mass of Kitt Peak, crowned by the chalk-white domes of its famous observatory, grows steadily as we approach. We make the requisite pit stop at the gas station and general store at Three Points, where several Border Patrol vehicles are idling in the lot—jeeps, SUVs, and trucks with ATVs in tow. There are also a couple of full-sized buses with bars across the passenger windows, the same kind used to transport prisoners between correctional facilities.

"There are billions to be made through DHS," Mike says, gesturing at the scene.

Indeed. The total budget in 2010 for Customs and Border Protection was $11.5 billion; the Border Patrol's slice was rougly one-third of that, representing a 714 percent increase since 1992. The buses are emblazoned with the logo of the Wackenhut Corporation, a subsidiary of G4S, a U.K.–based security-systems giant with half a million employees in more than one hundred countries. The suits in London use natives to quell native unrest. Its CEO, Nick Buckles ("generally an affable, open sort of gent," according to the *Independent*), makes about $2.3 million a year; G4S security guards in Malawi make $30 a month.

Migrants apprehended anywhere in the vicinity—that is, from the hundreds of square miles of open desert on the reservation—are brought here, loaded onto the buses, and eventually deposited at the gleaming new BP Tucson Sector headquarters (built at a cost of $34 million) next to Davis-Monthan Air Force Base. The sound track of a visit to HQ is the earsplitting propulsion of A-10 Thunderbolt jets taking off and landing.

The Three Points general store is dim and labyrinthine, every surface coated brownish gray from the Western wind blowing in bits of desert. There's always a strange, tense mix of customers here: O'odham, poor white, Border Patrol cyborgs in mirrored sunglasses, the occasional nervous tourist family thinking they've taken a wrong turn. Every few minutes another crew of the detained migrants is dropped off and herded to a corner of the large dirt lot that surrounds the store. There they wait to be processed and placed on the Wackenhut buses, whose engines and air conditioners never cease their rhythmic growling.

Back in the Dodge, Lucas Montejo tells me about his nephew. Sergio is—was—nineteen years old, even though he carried with him an "acta," a fake Mexican birth certificate, stating that he was twenty-one. This is common for migrants from Central America, who have long been led to believe by unscrupulous traffickers that impersonating a Mexican will keep them from being deported the two thousand miles back home rather than merely across the border to Mexico. With a short interrogation, U.S.

authorities can usually determine whether the migrants are indeed
Mexican or, in BP lingo, OTM, "other than Mexican." Fake IDs discovered on bodies in the desert cause American coroners plenty of problems. There may be long delays in notifying surviving family members.
If the bodies remain unidentified and unclaimed, they are ultimately
buried in county cemeteries in unmarked graves.

Sergio was overweight, Lucas says. He'd led a troubled youth. He had
a girlfriend and a year-old baby. And he left the village without telling
his mother, Lucas's sister. He was "soberbio," young and full of himself.
He worked as a bus driver and wanted a taste of something bigger, so he
went to the local loan sharks and bought a transportation route—that
is, the rights to one, which meant every bus driver who worked it had to
pay him a tithe. He borrowed half a million quetzales to do it, about
$64,000 in U.S. dollars. He'd been slow in paying it back, and the sharks
had started threatening him. That's why he'd come north. Not to avoid
the debt (he knew the sharks could easily find him in the States) but to
make good on it by working for American cash. Maybe he was starting
to grow up, after all.

When Sergio arrived in Nogales, he called his family back home to
say that he was fine. The coyotes had told him that from Nogales their
crew would travel to Altar, a provincial town that had been transformed
into a major staging area and was about an hour's ride on a washboard
road up from the border.

That was the last anyone heard from him. An acquaintance from a
neighboring village who had traveled in Sergio's migrant crew phoned
his own family, who contacted Sergio's family; they, in turn, called
Lucas in San Diego. The news was slightly ambiguous. The traveling
companion said that Sergio had started having trouble breathing and
had fallen behind the group, eventually collapsing at the foot of a tree,
where he'd died. The friend added that he'd left Sergio a gallon of water
in case he "revived," and the gesture suggested that perhaps Sergio
hadn't really died.

"For me," Lucas says, "he's not dead until I see the body."

Family members began working the phones. Lucas called the Guatemalan consul in Phoenix (there are now enough Guatemalans, living
and dead, in Arizona to warrant one), who met with him and said he
would do what he could.

The strongest lead came when Lucas contacted the coyote who'd led Sergio's group into the desert and had reportedly been with him when he'd died. Don't worry, Lucas told him, we're not going to snitch on you; we just want to know where you left Sergio. There'll be no vendetta, no vengeance, as long as you tell us where we can find him.

The coyote told Lucas that Sergio was at the foot of a tree in a "zanjón," a dry wash, next to an old cemetery, near the turnoff to Arizona City, past the Comobabi Mountains.

As Lucas tells me this, I notice Mike glancing into the rearview mirror and shaking his head slightly, but he doesn't say anything.

We enter the reservation and drive along the base of Kitt Peak. We pass by Mike's Father, Son, and Holy Ghost water stations; we don't stop. He says there's been little water consumed here in the past few weeks, but it wasn't long ago that he was replacing dozens of gallon jugs weekly.

The highway curls around the westernmost edge of Kitt Peak, and the Baboquivari Valley opens up before us. From this point on, the flatlands are broken by only a few modest ranges until the Ajo Mountains, at the Western border of the reservation, more than seventy miles away.

Baboquivari Peak will watch over us for most of the rest of the journey. Depending on the view, it can look like a heart or a fist or a John Ford butte or someone sitting with a blanket gathered around his shoulders. An aesthetic magnet that draws in the surrounding landscape, "Babo," as some locals call it, can seem menacing when backlit by the moon. According to mountaineering websites, the peak "requires technical climbing to reach the summit." (I once stood below its rocky face and thought I would climb it but got lost on a cow path.) It is the home of Elder Brother, a central figure of the O'odham creation story, who Mike thinks he saw one haunted night when he was stranded high up on the mountain. And like any wondrous landscape feature in the desert West, Baboquivari also sells real estate: "Wraparound patios with an incredible view of Baboquivari Peak to the West."

We leave Kitt Peak behind and drive deeper into the O'odham desert. Bunches of blond thorns hang from crooked cholla arms. Columned saguaro hold up the sky. The brilliant green of tiny creosote leaves contrasts with the ash gray of the thin, knobby branches. And everywhere there is mesquite, sometimes in stands tall and thick enough to make their own barbed sky and claustrophobic horizon. Among the many border ironies is that the O'odham survived here for generations precisely because they were so adept at manipulating what little water there was—with wells, irrigation canals, and flood-plain farming.

Since he was a child, Lucas says, he's loved to work on the land, a campesino. And so when he came north it was natural that he would work on it here, too, not in "los files," the picking fields, but in the city, in the fine gardens of the San Diegan middle class that, when it was not paying immigrants meager cash to trim their lawns and fold their laundry, fulminated against them. For three years, he worked for a landscaping company owned by an elderly Japanese man. Inspired by other paisanos who started up their own businesses, he saved and did the same. Soon, in the boom times, he was making $700 a week.

As hard as he worked, he partied. It's a wonder he didn't get AIDS, he tells me. He hardly saw his children and he could not have said back then that he loved his wife, even though he did. He paid the price, of course, but in America you pay it more poignantly or absurdly than back home. Here, in the land of opportunity, two of his children from his first marriage became heroin addicts.

"Lo ganas todo para perderlo," he says. You gain everything to lose it all. And then, eight years ago, he found God, who Lucas trusts will lead us to Sergio.

We arrive at the village of Quijotoa, which consists of the modest Gu Achi Trading Post and a few widely scattered houses. The store sign features the O'odham maze of life symbol. We stop here because this is where Highway 86 meets the road to Arizona City. Lucas looks at his notes from the conversation with the coyote. Yes, he confirms, this is it.

After taking a turn, we drive for a mile and a half and stop at a dirt road. Mike says this is the road to the Presbyterian church at Santa Rosa where he'd been a lay pastor. Our caravan pulls over in a cloud of dust, and we all get out.

The Guatemalans have a journalist among them from Jupiter, Florida. His name is Enrique Díaz, and he owns a radio station that broadcasts locally as well as to, as his business card tells it, "70 percent of Guatemala" via satellite. Back in Guatemala, he was neighbors with Lucas Montejo. When he heard about the tragedy, he didn't hesitate to offer his help and quickly organized a solidarity crew in Jupiter. They have brought plenty of documentary equipment—cell phones, digital cameras, laptops—all to record what we cannot see.

Lucas confers with Mike and we are told to spread out in a line, leaving about twenty yards between searchers, and to scour the area heading south from the dirt road back toward the highway. Within a couple of minutes the group splinters and the line is no longer. David Garcia goes off on his own—as he will do at every place we search today. There is little obvious sign of migrant passage here. No water bottles or discarded food tins or wrappers, no footprints. There are only animal trails and cow pies.

It doesn't take us long to arrive back at the trading post, everyone except David. We debate whether to send a search party for him but ultimately decide to wait. The desert is David's home, after all; he must know where he's going. We sit at a table beneath a giant palo verde tree, drinking ice-cold water out of bottles from the big coolers in the back of Mike's truck. Enrique Díaz interviews Mike Wilson and then each of the journalists, using his cell phone, which is patched in live to his radio station in Florida and, via satellite, to the audience in Guatemala. When it's my turn he asks me what I, as an American, can tell the listeners back in the old country. I'm usually never at a loss for words in such circumstances, but suddenly I find it difficult to form a coherent sentence. I imagine the Guatemalans listening to the guy with the funny Spanish accent (is he Mexican? Central American? Gringo?) talk about the deadly desert. What can I possibly say to them that they don't already know?

Enrique gives no indication that he is disappointed with my sound bite. He thanks me with the florid formality of a Latin American deejay and snaps the cell phone shut. Then he takes a panning look around the desert. He stops and stares in the direction of a particularly tall saguaro across the highway.

"I passed through here," he says.

No one says anything for several seconds. Flies buzz. The slightest breeze sighs through the palo verde.

"I did, too," says another of the Guatemalans, a young man with a crew cut that is as shiny black as his eyes, and with smooth skin a perfect shade of copper. I thought he was a teenager, but he says he's twenty-four.

"I came through here seven years ago," the young man says, "with gallons of water and a stack of tortillas"—he separates his hands vertically about a foot—"this thick." On the fifth day, they were hiding in the mesquite when they saw the van that would take them to Phoenix idling by the side of a paved road; maybe it was on this very highway. And right then the Border Patrol showed up. Improbably, he outran the migra and it took him another day and a half to get out of this desert.

More silence. Two other compatriots nod gently, seemingly remembering their own treks. Because they all came through somewhere like here. It could have been near Douglas, a hundred and fifty miles away, or eastern San Diego County, or the Rio Grande in the Big Bend region of Texas, but it was here, in the desert, in the West.

Now the Mexican journalist strikes up a conversation with me. Pedro Ultreras wears a T-shirt that says "Ecoturixtlan," the name of a company that offers eco-friendly adventures in Oaxaca. For several years he worked as a cameraman in Arizona, for one of the Spanish-language TV networks. He came out to the desert dozens of times to report the news of the border. He'd seen "the cage"—the temporary detention center prior to deportation. He'd seen the bodies; he'd seen it all. Now he is making a movie about migrants crossing the desert. He has connections in Mexico City; an actor with a bit of a name (a supporting role in *Amores Perros*) signed on. The film is called *7 soles*, "Seven Suns." "Cuando crees que el futuro está del otro lado," is the publicity trailer's tagline: When you think the future is on the other side.

The Guatemalans listen carefully but make no comments and ask no questions. At this point the group begins to break along a clear line: the Guatemalans gather together on the steps of the trading post, and the rest of us remain at the table beneath the palo verde. The split will persist through the rest of the day.

It is past noon, and we have searched less than one square mile of desert. The O'odham reservation, the largest of the nation's parcels, comprises some 2.7 million acres. Mike has made a point of allowing the Guatemalans to call the shots so far, but now he feels the need to intervene.

"Sometimes," he says in his clear and precise Spanish, "we see things more with our heart than with our head." He proceeds to tell the Guatemalans that their search map is nearly worthless. "You were told that the body was left at the foot of a tree in a wash next to the highway to Arizona City, near a cemetery. Do you know how many places that could be?"

The Guatemalans shoot each other looks. They huddle and begin working their cell phones intensely, speaking in their indigenous language. One points his finger north, another east. They draw up new maps. Word comes to look for a trailer near the highway. Someone says that he noticed one crowning the hill just west of the trading post.

David Garcia finally shows up; he didn't find anything. He hiked for over an hour in the desert at midday without any water and has hardly broken a sweat. He calls a friend who works as a nurse at the reservation hospital in Sells to ask her whether any migrants have shown up DOA in the last few days. She doesn't recall any, but it's hard to keep track, she tells him. So many come in all summer long.

We watch the Guatemalans; they watch us. Mike shakes his head.

"False positives," he says. "You gotta watch out for those."

"How far is Eloy from here?" Lucas asks Mike. Now it seems they've been told the body could be along the highway near that town.

That would be along Interstate 10, about fifty miles from where we stand.

After much deliberation, the Guatemalans decide to stick with the original coordinates: dry wash, cemetery, the turnoff to Arizona City. They ask the clerk in the general store if there are any cemeteries close by. Yes, he says. We only have to drive a mile to find it. There is a dry wash next to it. We are within a mile of the turnoff to Arizona City. We sweep the area with our scraggly search line. Now and again, an empty gallon jug, a scrap of clothing fluttering on a cactus thorn, an empty backpack half-buried in the sand of the wash.

A Guatemalan whistles a discovery: several burlap sacks half-hidden at the foot of a mesquite tree. Mike takes a look.

"Drugs," he says matter-of-factly. "Don't touch them."

We drive farther west and park next to an old Catholic church just as the priest is pulling up. A pink-faced man with a Hemingway beard, he tells us that there are two more cemeteries in the area, and yes, he believes there are washes next to both of them. I start to suspect that every cemetery on the reservation is in the vicinity of a dry wash.

It is getting on to the hottest part of the afternoon. The sun bears down on the monsoonal moisture in the atmosphere, and a massive thunderhead billows up in the east, domed by a wisp of silvery cirrus. It is raining out there—twenty-five miles away, fifty, impossible to tell. It will not rain here. It is about ninety-five degrees, cool by local standards, and I've been drinking water all day; even so, I've got a headache and feel sluggish, the first signs of dehydration. With each search sweep, the group becomes more disorganized; I fear that there will be more than one person to look for before the day is through.

In my own aimless roaming through a thicket of mesquite the wall of a house suddenly appears. Noticing that the front door is off its hinges, I approach cautiously. Then the stench hits me. The living room and kitchen look normal enough. There is a dining table, utensils in the drawers, children's toys that do not appear to have been exposed to the elements very long. But in the two back rooms I find a pile of clothes about two feet high, wall to wall. This is where the smell—of human excrement and urine—comes from. I'm in a drop house, one that appears to have been used several times recently. The owners might not be aware of what has happened—they may be away for the summer or for just a couple of weeks. This is a typical smuggler's tactic, a good way to provide migrants with rest and keep them out of sight.

We regroup next to the cars. Next to the church is a basketball court with cracked gray backboards but new, pearly-white nets. The discussion begins again. Now we wonder about the sequence of the signposts the coyote gave. It all depends, we realize, on which way the migrants were traveling. What came first, the cemetery or the highway junction?

Mike says that if the body was in a wash, it could have been swept for miles in a flash flood from the recent torrential rains. David looks at an ocotillo. Hasn't rained here, he says; there are no leaves covering the thorns. Doesn't have to rain right here, Mike responds tersely; a flash flood can travel tens of miles. I realize that the friends are bickering.

There is time only for one more quick search. We arrive at Mountain Village, a place that lives up to its picturesque name, in the hills south of the highway. We sweep both sides of the road for about half a mile. Even before we start everyone knows we are not going to find Sergio Montejo.

When we return to the cars, the desert is aglow. The sun slants west and south, verging on the autumnal equinox. Several more storm cells have developed along the horizon. Thunder rumbles in the distance.

The wind rises, bringing us the creosote-scented breath of the rain. There is still the silvery dome atop the biggest storm cell, but it fades fast—I look away for just a few moments, and when I turn back it's gone.

It is a magical photographic image, and there is a flurry of picture-taking. Mike is telling one of the Italian journalists about the O'odham maze of life symbol. We'd seen it at the trading post, on the altar at the old stone church, and on Mike's silver ponytail holder—a man at the entrance to the maze, about to enter, or just having left.

Lucas Montejo sleeps next to me in Mike's Dodge for the entire drive back to Tucson. On the eastern edge of the reservation the tires hiss along wet asphalt. On KOHN, "Voice of the Tohono O'odham Nation," the Emergency Alert System tells of flash flooding and power outages, urges listeners to move food from the fridge to the freezer, avoid low-water crossings, and check on elders. As the storm breaks up, I look south along the great valley for Baboquivari Peak. The top half of the mountain is hidden in mist.

I open the window of the Dodge and wet creosote breath fills my lungs. I wonder whether the rain is falling on Sergio Montejo's cracked and blackened skin, whether the storm is filling his eyes with tears.


Everyone has chapped lips and reddened skin; we are all tired and hungry. The Casino del Sol, on the Pascua Yaqui Reservation, beckons on the horizon. On the outskirts of Tucson, it is as good a place as any to eat.

The building's exterior is made up of amber-lit arches, domes, slotted windows, and minarets. Inside, we head directly to Moby's, a "beach-themed diner" whose decor includes aquamarine Formica-and-stainless-steel tables and a wood-paneled, white-walled station wagon riding along a wooden "pier," waves curling along the walls. We are too big a group to sit together, so the Guatemalans wind up at one table and the rest of us at another. We order burgers and club sandwiches and tuna melts; fries and Cokes and milk shakes. The desert is distant even though we're in the middle of it. I cannot hear what the Guatemalans are saying, but they look relaxed, too.

After the meal the visitors want to see the casino, so we walk around.

The main gaming room sits under a massive cupola painted a perfect Mediterranean blue. An extraordinarily realistic sky—it looks like mid-afternoon—is accented by the slightest wisps of cirrus; the constant horizon is an Italian-style villa of red tile and windows with wooden shutters. The cupola peaks at about fifty feet; the mural encompasses some forty-six thousand square feet. The massive room swallows bodies, gaming machines (thirteen hundred slots), and time itself. It is as if the energy of the slots—their collective humming and punctuations tuned to C-major (to avoid dark aural themes)—rises to hold the heavens in place.

There is a god in this heaven, and his name is Drew Carey. A digital edition of the comedian is the host of the casino's biggest jackpot, announced by a twenty-five-foot-tall column crowned by his crew cut, horn rims, and showbiz smile. The pot is currently at $298,120 and ticking up every few seconds.

The Guatemalans are awed and giddy and far from the desert of Sergio Montejo. They flip open their cell phones and take pictures. Most of all, they want to pose with Mike and David—the Indians of El Norte— and then there is the obligatory group picture, which we ask a stranger to take: the Guatemalans and the rest of us, all smiles.


The day after the failed search, I have morning coffee with Mike at his house. He'd offered the Guatemalans his floor, but they'd opted for motel rooms. I think about how middle-class they are, Lucas with his gray Dockers and one of the younger kids from Jupiter with brand-new Timberland hiking boots. They'd worked hard in America and made it.

Mike tells me about something the Italian journalist had confided in him. She'd had a dream about him two nights before she met him. Yes, she saw him in the dream, even though she'd never even been near a picture of him. She'd known that she was destined to meet him here, in the desert, she said, "in this spiritual place."

I groan mentally. Another white person's projection on to people of color, especially Indians. I tend to judge people who think and talk like this harshly, thinking the impulse ignorantly colonial. I expect Mike will say something in this vein.

Instead, he says: "I go to church on Sunday, but the desert is my spiritual home." He received the journalist in it; because the desert was his home, it was hers as well.

I had always thought of hospitality in terms of providing shelter to the traveler in need. Mike is telling me that the only true hospitality is one that welcomes all of the others, especially those who inhabit the most prejudiced places of our imagination.

That, I think, is a worthy ideal, but almost impossible to practice here, where our imaginations are so profoundly prejudiced, where each of us has at least one other to fear or to loathe.

## 8.

The tiny border town of Sasabe is at the eastern edge of the O'odham reservation. From many places in Sasabe you get a postcard view of Baboquivari Peak, and that is what Melissa Owen and her husband, Troy, both on the young side of middle age, saw when they were searching for their desert paradise. She holds a PhD in anthropology, and Troy is a radiologist. She lives in Sasabe full-time; he spends the workweek in Tucson and the weekends on the ranch. Their property, just a few miles north of the border, comprises 640 acres of stunning Sonoran desert— hills and ravines and cacti and the sight of Baboquivari from the front porch of their handsome house, 1920s vintage with Moroccan arches, tall ceilings, and an exquisitely tiled kitchen.

They bought it in 2002—before the real estate market went into overdrive, and before the Minutemen, the vigilantes of the border, started patrolling with their American flags and sidearms. But soon, the iconic Sonoran Desert, the venerable real estate brand that had drawn outsiders of all social strata almost since forever, was in the midst of a war on drugs and a war on terror. That is what Melissa and Troy found they had bought into.

When I visit the ranch, Melissa invites me to sit on the porch for lemonade. She is a tall woman, everything about her lean and long. Two dogs lounge at our feet in the late-afternoon heat. The sun has fallen behind the rise of land to the west. We see an air force C-130 cargo plane, massive and forest green, barely a few hundred feet in the air, make a steep turn over that hill. Melissa is unfazed; it happens all the time. Neither is she bothered by the big black wasps that float all around us. "They're pretty benign," she says.

She's a "land person," she tells me, but there are so many people on this land. She wants me to be sure to understand her: she is most certainly not a Minutewoman, and no "racist." She is, all in all, a liberal. But Melissa and Troy did not come to the desert to hear migrants rustling through the "matorrales," the scrub, at night.

I hear a hissing sound coming from the direction of a large eucalyptus tree beyond the driveway. So does one of the dogs, Luna, a black short-haired hound, who rushes out to investigate.

Melissa and I follow. We know what it is before we see it. The closer we get, the less we hear a hiss and more the sound of a rattle. The snake is coiled up near the trunk of the eucalyptus, a mature Western diamondback, at its thickest point approaching the diameter of my forearm. Its neck is bent like a coupling on a sink pipe; its rattle rises perfectly straight and vibrates so rapidly it blurs, like a hummingbird's wings.

Just a couple of weeks ago, Melissa's other dog, Ruffian, had been bitten and it had taken a "ridiculous amount" at the vet to save him. Still, she wants to give the snake a chance to live. She bought special pincers made just for snake handling. I'm directed to one of the outbuildings to fetch them, along with a big paint bucket with a lid to transport the snake to another habitat. Melissa stays behind to make sure the dogs don't get bitten.

I spend a few minutes looking for the pincer but cannot find it and return to Melissa with only the paint bucket. Now she goes off to look for it. She is gone for several minutes. It is just me and the dogs and the snake under the tree. A sudden gust of hot wind sighs through the eucalyptus. The dogs, sensing that the snake is not going anywhere, lie on their stomachs and seem to lose interest. Me, I can't stop looking at it: the sublime symmetry of the diamond patterns, the flat head with its tiny eyes and slit pupils communicating implacability. I test it to see how sensitive it is to my movements. When I step forward, it rattles incessantly. When I step back, it quiets down. I raise a hand, it rattles. The slightest movement of my head: rattle. The only thing it doesn't seem to find threatening is the blinking of my eyes.

Melissa comes back with the pincer and a single-barrel shotgun. She seems to have lost her compassion.

"I'm really sorry about this," she says to the snake. She aims and pulls the trigger.

The blast sends up a big puff of dust and a confetti of dead yellow grass. The snake leaps up a few feet as well, then flops back down in two big pieces and begins its death writhing.

Melissa allows me the honor of using the pincer to pick up the pieces and place them in the paint bucket. I do this, trying mightily to keep my face from turning away from the dying-dead thing.

Dinner is tamales, white wine, and a classy salad made with a variety of lettuce I cannot name. We make small talk in the kitchen as she brings the meal together, beneath a Virgen de Guadalupe mural on the wall. Jazz plays softly on the stereo. Two exotic cats, looking like company for an Egyptian ruler's tomb, watch us. In an illuminated display case, there are small toy animals, enacting what looks like a pastoral from East Africa: several jackals surround a fallen zebra.

"It's good that you are here," she says. "Maybe I'll get a little sleep tonight."

She describes her nights on the ranch like working the graveyard shift. Especially when she is alone, when Troy is seventy miles away, in the city.

At night the desert comes alive. The cobalt of deep dusk fades to black, and the coyotes howl. The Border Patrol trucks and SUVs begin charging up and down the highway. In clinical terms, Melissa becomes hypervigilant. She imagines the migrant crew stumbling through the matorrales. It is a moonless night. The drug runners, campesino kids dressed in black, rushing down well-worn paths. She visualizes them coming down the saddle between the two hills behind the ranch house. Walking up to the house, up to the bedroom window, peering in at her.

"You must understand, Rubén. These are not Juan and María." They are, she says, like "feral dogs."

I tense. There is a great contradiction between us, in the way we imagine who is on the land. Who is the figure crossing the desert? Is there evil walking across the land tonight?

I want to believe that it is Juan and María out there because those are the people I have rendered in language, a representation of the bodies and souls I traveled alongside during the years I worked as a journalist. I know that they are out there, even now. But Melissa has in mind narco shoot-outs in the border towns on the Mexican side, the murders of hundreds of young women in Juárez, executions of everyday migrants by

Mexican narcos, by gringo vigilantes. And she is the one who lives here, not me.

She keeps her shotgun against the wall next to her bed. It is for rattle-snakes, she says, and for other animals in the night. She takes a bite of her tamal and gestures with her head in the direction of the darkness in the window.

If Luna barks, she gets the shotgun. Or she lies still in bed, shuts her eyes, trying to block out the thought that someone is in the house. On a typical night she will fall asleep at three or four in the morning. By that time, she knows, most of the migrants will have moved past the ranch, northward. After crossing her property, they pass through or circumvent another big parcel in the area, Rancho de la Osa, a high-end guest ranch dating from the 1920s, visited by two presidents (FDR and LBJ) and generations of Hollywood A-listers. Talk recently has been that the current owners want to sell. But who would want to buy the place, even if it is one of the "last great Spanish haciendas still standing in America," given the macabre diorama surrounding it?

When Melissa wakes in the morning, she goes out to the vineyard she and Troy recently planted, the vines only a foot high. In the light, it all looks like a spread in *Sunset* magazine. As she makes the rounds, she searches for signs of migrant passage—the swirls in the sandy dirt of the washes, the empty water bottle.

## 9.

I've been drawn to the line my entire life, beginning with childhood family jaunts to Tijuana and back, a leap from the monochrome grid of Southern California to the Technicolor swirl of urban Baja California. My parents and grandparents crossed the line before me. The line does and does not exist. It is a sieve and a brick wall and not even linear. It is a historical, political, economic, and cultural fact. It is a laughable, puny, meaningless thing. It is a matter of life and death.

It is also a very productive trope in both American and Mexican pop culture. The cowboy crosses the line to evade the law, because he imagines there is no law in the South. The immigrant crosses the line to embrace the future, because he imagines there is no past in the North like the one he is seeking to escape. In novels and films and songs, it is most often evoked by the river: the Rio Grande, if you're standing in the United States, the Río Bravo, if you're in Mexico. It can be Lethe or Styx or Jordan or just a place to raft the rapids. The artists who've drawn from it come from both sides: Cormac McCarthy and Carlos Fuentes, Marty Robbins and Los Tigres del Norte, Emilio "El Indio" Fernández and Sam Peckinpah, Gloria Anzaldúa and Charles Bowden, to name just a few.

In the Western, the moment of the crossing—the lawless gang heading south, fleeing the lawmen, their horses' hooves muddying the muddy waters all the more—is heralded by a stirring musical figure, brassy and percussive, leaping several tonal steps with each note. Once they're safely on the other side, the melodic strings of Mexico take over. The swaggering American has his way with a Mexican señorita. Postcolonial revisions of borderlands representations—produced by Mexicans and Americans alike—have yet to soften the edges of the trope. The whorehouse across the river is still there, even so that a spurned Jake Gyllenhaal can find solace with smooth-skinned brown boys in *Brokeback Mountain*. Americans fictional and real fantasize about remaining in that racy, lazy South, but business or vengeance or a respectable marriage usually call the cowboy back home. The return, if it is represented at all, is less meaningful and quieter; the party is over, and you don't want to wake up the law.

The Mexican or Chicano production is an inverted mirror of the same. The climax of Cheech Marin's *Born in East L.A.* (and dozens of Mexican B-movies) fulfills every migrant's fantasy of a rush of brown humanity breaching a hapless Border Patrol, which occurs many times a day on the line (albeit, for most migrants, in harrowing fashion) and feeds the nativist's paranoid vision of a reconquista. (A handful of crackpot Chicano nationalists notwithstanding, this has been largely invented by the nativists themselves, white men with some justifiable economic complaints unfortunately marinated in traditional borderlands racism.)

Every step across the line ends up being a breach of one code or another—some on the books, some never written down—and the continual breaching creates a structure of feeling that draws more people to it (migrants, politicians, journalists, artists).

Among those who've been pulled in by the energy of the line are the

volunteers of the Samaritan Patrol, a group organized through Southside Presbyterian Church, who search the migrant corridors seeking to
aid migrants in distress. What struck me most about the Samaritans
when I rode along with them was the intensity of their desire, which
their moral impulse didn't quite fully explain. They longed to see the
migrants in the flesh, with their stinking feet and bloody noses, dried
saliva crusty around their mouths. They wanted to swab the blisters and
lift a water bottle to cracked lips. They longed to touch those suffering
bodies in the desert. They were doing the right thing, and at the same
time enacting archetypes from Judeo-Christian mythology. They were
sheltering strangers, personifying the Samaritan who slakes Jesus's
thirst in the Passion, invoking the laws of God against the laws of Men,
looking out for the neighbor. They were also trying to breach the border
of incommensurability: they would never walk a mile in the shoes of
migrants, but they very much wanted to.

The group I had joined drove along the east side of the Baboquivari
range, from Three Points to Sasabe, and then across the grasslands
of the Buenos Aires National Wildlife Refuge—so incongruous to the
severity of the surrounding desert—to the tiny town of Arivaca. Seven
of us caravanned in two cars, the demographic leaning heavily toward
white, upper-middle-class middle-aged women. We spent hours scanning the sides of the road, turning our heads left to right, like fans
watching a tennis match, for sign of migrants. I could not suppress the
thought of a safari, or a wild animal park. We looked for buzzards
circling over migrant carrion. And we kept an eye out for the Border
Patrol, as if we ourselves were somehow the game. We stopped on a few
occasions to hike along well-known trails, carrying bottles of water and
food rations. We "cut sign," in the lingo of trackers, searching for broken twigs, footprints, flattened grass—affecting the authentic Western
experience. Back in the car I saw my group's adrenaline flow—and felt
my own—when two migrants appeared from the mesquite and flagged
us down. The doctor, myself, and a couple of others got out while the
rest of our party drove both our vehicles down the road about a hundred yards to allow us time to discern just what the situation was—in
other words, to give us the opportunity to hide from the Border Patrol
if they appeared and in the event that the migrants didn't want to be
turned in. I sensed disappointment among the activists when the

migrants said they did want to be handed over to the Border Patrol; they wanted nothing more to do with the migrant trail, Samaritans or no.

We continued on into the bush. "¡Tenemos agua, tenemos comida!" we called out as we hiked into the mesquite. "¡No somos migra!" We have water, we have food. We are not the Border Patrol.

I was on the line for the same reasons that the Samaritans were: I wanted to see migrants in the midst of their crossing, which is truly unknowable, since no one but the migrants live it. Crossing is political and juridical, but also extraordinarily private—an extreme relationship between the body and the land, between the body and the desert, between the subjectivity of the migrants and a landscape sculpted by the scriptures of Judaism, Christianity, Islam, and Hollywood.

My own desire was, among other things, ethnographic: the crossing has taken on mythic and political proportions over many decades and for that reason, the physical, emotional, and spiritual experience of the migrants themselves has been largely erased, no matter how many die in the process.

The mass of bodies is mostly invisible in American media and only slightly more visible in Mexico. I wanted to write the migrant body back into existence. Ultimately, I wanted to see the migrants up close, for myself, without the mediation of the Samaritans or the Minutemen or anyone else. I had no idea that language would be of no use to me, or the migrants, when I finally walked into the desert of the border on my own.

## 10.

It is a late August afternoon on the Buenos Aires National Wildlife Refuge, a day that will not make headlines because there are no Minutemen patrols out hunting migrants, and no Samaritans out seeking to save them. Nor are there, for the moment, any Border Patrol officers in the immediate vicinity. The land is as its public designation intended: 118,000 acres of Sonoran Desert habitat traversed by grasslands that are home to hundreds of rare species, including the endangered pronghorn antelope; it is also a world-class birding location. But there are no birders in the dead of summer. The birders, and the Minutemen, have no wish to be out in temperatures that often rise over 110 degrees.

I park at the Arivaca Creek trailhead. The interpretive sign tells of the possibility of hearing the "snap of vermilion flycatchers snatching insects on the wing." And it mentions another species, a relative newcomer to this "riparian ribbon": "Visitors to BANWR are advised to remain alert for illegal activity associated with the presence of undocumented aliens (UDAs). There is also increased law enforcement activity by several agencies & organizations."

The bulleted guidelines advise visitors not to let "UDAs approach you or your vehicle"—a variant of "Do not feed the wildlife."

The sign also notes that "cell phones may not work near the international border." I hesitate. I've always done most of my hiking alone and have grown more cautious with age, coming to regard a cell phone signal as just as important as water in the desert. My hand reaches into my backpack, for the phone, but I tell myself that I'll take just a short walk; it's getting late, and I don't want to get caught by darkness.

The humidity from the recent monsoonal deluges in the area is stifling, making one hundred degrees feel much hotter and wetter. The ocotillos have sprouted their lime-green leaves, hiding their terrifically sharp thorns. Moss flourishes on arroyo stones. Mosquitoes zip and whine through the thick air. The desert jungle.

The trail climbs up from the creek bed, which is dominated by mammoth cottonwood trees, and south into hills of red dirt, a path used by birders and UDAs alike. I can imagine an Audubon guide leading a gaggle of khaki-clad tourists, who look through their binoculars first at a vermilion flycatcher and then at a Mexican rushing through a mesquite thicket, *Profugus mexicanus.* These encounters between contraries are a defining characteristic these days, not just of the borderlands, but of the desert West: gentry and day laborers, trailer-bound seniors and snowbirds in adobe chalets, artists and addicts, "natives" like my neighbors in Velarde and outsiders like me, peering in. The pairings resemble not so much parallel universes but more saw-toothed eruptions, the crumpled metal of a collision.

In the microcosm of the BANWR, birders meet migrants, the Samaritans the Minutemen. Hunters encounter stoners; there is at least one Big Pharma magnate in the vicinity, along with ranchers, retirees of modest means, hellfire Protestants, Catholic penitents, and New Age vortex seekers. Living here or passing through are Americans and Native Americans and Mexicans and Mexican-Americans and Mexican Indians, all of varying shades and accents; undocumented Iranians and Guatemalans and occasionally Chinese. This kind of situation was once affectionately referred to as the melting pot. But now, it is more like speaking in tongues, speaking in Babel.

I climb into the red hills as the sun nears the horizon. The sky at the zenith is a stunning true blue. Reaching a saddle, I stumble onto a large migrant encampment—water jugs and backpacks and soiled underwear and tubes of toothpaste and a brand-new denim jacket finely embroidered with the name of a car club in Bell Gardens, California, and opened cans of refried beans, bottles of men's cologne, Tampax, tortillas curled hard in the heat. The place marks eleven miles into the approximately fifty-mile hike to smuggling rendezvous points in the Tucson area and this must have been the migrants' first full camp, several hours of rest. They had probably begun to realize the weight of the things they carried and had resolved to travel lighter. If something went wrong and they got lost, hyperthermic and delirious, migrants have been known to strip the clothes off their backs.

It is possible that they've just left; it is possible that they saw me coming and are hiding behind one of the saddle's humps.

"No soy migra," I call out, the phrase I learned from the Samaritans. It is a good line in the borderlands; I can't think of anything better to say. The real problem is, what am I going to respond if someone actually answers? The journalist's lame introduction? Of course, they would have no reason to stop and speak to me—just the opposite. Indeed, why would they believe that I am not migra? And what if the smugglers are hauling a load of narcotics instead of humans? What if they are carrying weapons? This is not idle paranoia: the desert is armed with the assault rifles of the brigades on all sides. In any event, I have nothing to offer the trekkers; they most likely have not run out of water yet (by tomorrow, after fifteen or twenty miles, they well might).

Picking through their things, I am suddenly ashamed, as if I've intruded on a tremendously intimate moment. I feel like I've come upon a couple in erotic embrace, their bodies vulnerable to the harshness of the land and to my gaze, to the laws that proscribe their very weight on this earth.

The sun sets, a funnel of gold that joins the cerulean canopy to the bloodred earth. For a moment the land is completely still. I hold my breath. I realize that I want the migrants to appear. I want to join them on the journey, the migrants staggering through the desert, and I after them.

"¡No soy migra!" I shout again.

Silence. I sweat profusely, soaking through my T-shirt. Even my jeans hang heavy with perspiration. Swatting mosquitoes, I retrace my footsteps until I arrive back at my truck. I had placed water jugs on top of the hood; they are still there.

I drive west in the dimming light. I pass not a single car.

Suddenly, a flutter in my peripheral vision. A man crawls from the brush and waves to me from the left side of the road. I stop the truck and roll down my window. He is plaintive-looking, in his thirties, with thick black curls and a sweaty, smudged moon of a face. His large brown irises are ringed by reddened whites. He is wearing a black T-shirt, blue jeans, and white tennis shoes. He carries a small blue vinyl bag. He says his name is Victor Jiménez.

"¿Qué pasó?" I ask.

With the first syllables of his response, I can tell that he is from El Salvador. The accent splits the difference between the typically muted tones of the Latin American provinces and the urgent desire of urban speech. It is the accent of my mother and her family; it is the Spanish accent I associate most with my childhood. Victor had hiked about twelve miles into U.S. territory and could not make it any farther. His migrant crew had traveled all night and started up again late in the afternoon— just a couple of hours ago—but he'd become extremely fatigued and his vision had begun to blur.

"Soy diabético," says Victor Jiménez.

Immediately I grab my mobile to dial 911. It chirps a complaint: there is no signal. I think: Hypoglycemia; he needs something sweet. I think this because of the plotlines in dozens of TV dramas I've watched since I was a kid. In the backseat I have enough supplies to keep a dozen hikers going for at least a day in the desert: energy bars, fruit cups, tins of Vienna sausages, peanut butter crackers, bags of trail mix, several bottles of Gatorade, and gallon jugs of drinking water. I expect him to tear ravenously into the strawberry-flavored bar I give him, but he eats it very slowly, taking modest sips of water between bites.

I flip open the cell phone again. Still no signal. The particulars of the problem begin to form in my mind. Although I am not a medical expert, it is apparent enough that Victor Jiménez needs urgent attention. But there is no way to contact medical personnel. The only option is to drive Victor to the nearest town, which is Arivaca, about ten miles away. I grow aware that if I do so, both Victor and I will be risking apprehension by the Border Patrol. More than one border denizen has told me that merely giving a migrant a ride can place a citizen in a tenuous legal situation. Indeed, United States Code (Title 8, Chapter 12, Subchapter II, Part VIII, Section 1324) stipulates that an American citizen breaks the law when "knowing or in reckless disregard of the fact that an alien has come to, entered, or remains in the United States in violation of law, transports, or moves or attempts to transport or move such alien within the United States by means of transportation or otherwise, in furtherance of such violation of law."

But the ethical calculation is simple enough. The law might contradict my moral impulse, but the right thing to do is obvious. I am aware of a pending federal court case against two young activists, Shanti Sellz and Daniel Strauss, who attempted to conduct a medical evacuation by taking two apparently distressed migrants directly to a hospital rather than handing them over to the BP. Federal prosecutors decided that the activists were indeed transporting the migrants "in furtherance" of their illegal presence in the United States, and indicted the pair on several felony charges. The activists and their supporters say that the ethical imperative of offering aid in the context of a medical emergency supersedes the letter of immigration law—a moral argument without juridical precedent on the border. (Ultimately, all charges in the case were dropped; the judge agreed with the defense that the activists had made all reasonable efforts to avoid breaking the law and that the singular ethical circumstances of a medical emergency in effect transform the context within which the law is applied.) Finally, I also tell myself that in the event of apprehension by the Border Patrol, the truth of the situation will suffice. I am a Samaritan after all, not a coyote.

The truth will suffice for *me*, that is. I will go free. Victor will be deported.

I tell Victor to get in the truck.

The night falls fast. Soon the only things we can see through the bug-splattered windshield are the grainy blacktop ahead and the tangle of mesquites lining the road. I keep expecting more migrants to appear in the headlights and wave us down. At any given moment, on this stretch of borderland, there may be hundreds of migrants attempting passage.

It is a winding road and I'm a conservative driver, so there's time for small talk. Victor is much more animated now. He says he is feeling better.

He is from Soyapango, a working-class suburb of San Salvador that I remember well from my time in the country during the civil war, when it had the reputation of being a rebel stronghold. Right now, Victor is some eighteen hundred miles from Soyapango.

"¿Y a que se dedica usted?" He asks what I do for a living.

I reply that I am a writer, and then there is silence for about a quarter of a mile.

The Border Patrol will appear any moment now, I think to myself.

Victor's large, round eyes glisten, reflecting the light from my dashboard. More questions. What's the name of the town we're heading to? How far is Phoenix? How far is Los Angeles? Phoenix: where the coyote told him he'd be dropped off at a safe house. Los Angeles: where his sister lives. He has memorized a phone number. It begins with the area code 818, which is in the San Fernando Valley.

Yes, he is feeling quite fine now, Victor says, and he realizes that I can't drive him all the way to Los Angeles. But Phoenix is only 170 miles away.

There is still no Border Patrol in sight. This does not make any sense to me. Hundreds of agents should be on duty right now in what is called the Tucson Sector, the busiest and deadliest crossing along the U.S.-Mexico line.

Now, I realize, the problem has changed. Victor is apparently no longer experiencing a medical emergency, although I cannot be absolutely certain of this. If the law is ambiguous on the matter of Samaritan aid, it is not at all amibiguous about what Victor is now asking me to do. If I drive him to Phoenix and put him in touch with his sister, I will clearly have provided transportation "in furtherance" of his illegal presence in the United States.

The air-conditioning chills the sweat on the wet rag that my T-shirt has become. It seems that there are now several possibilities, several problems, many right and wrong things to do. The scenarios tumble through my mind. Risk the trip to Phoenix. (Where is that BP checkpoint on I-19, is it north or south of Arivaca Junction?) What if Victor is actually still sick and on the verge of a seizure—shouldn't I turn him over to the Border Patrol? (But will the BP give him the medical care he needs?) And not least, what of Victor's human right to escape the living hell of poor, crime-ridden Soyapango? If Victor does indeed have that essential human right to seek a better life for himself and his family, what is my moral duty when he literally stumbles into me on the border? Am I willing to risk federal charges to fulfill an ethical responsibility that I decide trumps the laws of my country?

I slow to a crawl as we near the outskirts of Arivaca, a town famed for a 1960s-era commune and the weed-growing hippies who hung on long past the Summer of Love. Word these days is that the hippies aren't quite as peace-loving as they used to be. Apparently, not all of their crop is solely for personal consumption, and the increase in migrant traffic—which, in turn, has brought an increase in law enforcement traffic—has been very upsetting to some of them, who blame the situation on the migrants.

It will all end here in Arivaca, I tell myself. The BP trucks will be lined up outside the one small grocery store in town, or maybe up at the Grubstake, the only restaurant, presided over by a gregarious Mexican who waits on the embittered hippies and the handful of outsider artists who arrived years ago, thinking they'd found the grail of Western living.

But when I pull up to the store, there are only a few local kids—white, shaved heads—standing by a pay phone beneath a flickering streetlamp that's gathering a swarm of moths. Now it occurs to me that there is a possible solution to this mess. In the rush of events, I've forgotten the activist encampment about four miles east of town. A faith-based organization, the group, No More Deaths, baptized the place the Ark of the Covenant. Like the Samaritans, No More Deaths recruited student activists from around the country—among them Strauss and Sellz, the pair who were indicted—to come to southern Arizona and walk the lethal desert trails seeking out migrants in need of aid. No More Deaths has a protocol for dealing with migrants experiencing medical emergencies involving a ride to a hospital in Tucson where no one asks the migrants for papers. Once the migrants are treated, they are simply released. They walk out the door and into America. The fact that migrants might ultimately remain in the country is not the goal of the evacuation, the activists say. Now all I need are directions to the Ark of the Covenant.

I tell Victor to stay inside the truck, and I walk into the store. The clerk behind the counter is reading a newspaper, head cupped in her hands and elbows leaning on the food scale next to the cash register.

I briefly blurt out my story.

She asks me where Victor is. In the truck, I say. Immediately she tells me that the BP can impound my vehicle, that charges can be filed against me. She tells me that she can call the Border Patrol for me. She seems to know exactly what the right thing to do is. She places her hand on the phone.

A few seconds later I'm back in the heat of the night, and I turn to the first passerby, a young blond woman who says her name is Charity, for directions to the encampment. She draws a map for me on a page of my reporter's notebook. She says, Here there is a hill. She says, Here there is a llama ranch. A quarter of a mile, then a couple of miles, then three-quarters of mile and left and right and across. Good luck, she says. I notice that it is a moonless night.

I climb back into the truck and key the ignition. I give Victor the notebook with the map. In a minute we're out of town and on the first dirt road of the route. Still no BP. The map is accurate. I pass by the llama ranch, barely catching the sign in the dark.

For several minutes I ride on impulse—no thoughts at all. But as I turn left just where Charity told me to, a thought powerful enough to take my foot off the gas seizes me.

I can't ride into the Ark of the Covenant with Victor in the truck. I now remember hearing that before and since the arrests of Sellz and Strauss, there had been constant BP surveillance of the camp. The government thought that medical evacuation was a cover for activists to offer migrants a ride on the midnight train. Here I am, bringing someone with no apparent signs of distress into the camp, and I am not even a member of No More Deaths. If the BP sees me dropping Victor off, will they, can they use this as evidence of the organization running a de facto smuggling operation? What if there is a conviction? What if a judge orders the Ark of the Covenant closed?

I weigh Victor's singular rights and desire against the goals and strategy of an activist movement that has helped dozens of migrants in distress and that continues to help many more.

The problem is that my cell phone is dead. The problem is my desire to run into a migrant. The problem is that I have placed myself on the line without being ready for what it is asking of me.

I slow down, and the dust kicked up by the tires envelops the truck. Victor Jiménez and I turn to each other.

Fifteen minutes later, we pull up, for the second time, at the convenience store in Arivaca. The clerk is still reading the paper. I tell her that Victor Jiménez has diabetes and symptoms of hypoglycemia. I tell her to call the Border Patrol.

She picks up the phone. "We've got a diabetic UDA," she says matter-of-factly.

I walk out to Victor, who is standing next to my truck, staring into the black desert night. He asks me again how far it is to Tucson. I tell him that if he tries hiking it, he will die.

# A WALK IN THE WOODS

## 1.

My mother-in-law, Wilma Garcia, grew up Hispana-Apache in Albuquerque, and she loves the land, the landscape. She bought a piece of it on what was once the edge of town, in the South Valley, at the foot of the West Mesa. The one-acre parcel is within a mile of the Rio Grande. The view across the valley to the Sandia and Manzano Mountains is vast and intimate, otherworldly and so very familiar: basin-and-range country.

Fifteen years after she bought, Wilma no longer lives on the outskirts. The area is now real estate, in the fastest growing part of the Albuquerque metro area. Angela and I visit a few times every month, often spending the night in Wilma's trailer, which she moved into when it was the last residence before the open desert. Now she is surrounded on all sides by cookie-cutter subdivisions and trailer parks—the affordable housing of the boom years.

Wilma's property sits on what until late 2007 was the Atrisco land grant, also known as the Westland Development Corporation, in which heirs of the original Hispano grantees held stock. After living on, working on, and holding the land since 1768, the heirs joined the age of speculation and sold to SunCal Corporation for $250 million, profits from which were distributed among some six thousand shareholders. SunCal, according to its virtual brochure, now owned an urban development site "twice the size of Boston." Ultimately, SunCal's development dreams were clouded by the crash of the housing market, and the land was sold again, at a substantial loss.

The lion's share of Atrisco, like all land grants, was used as an ejido, a commons. Lying just west of the Rio Grande, it was the last big swath of undeveloped land in the region. The commons—a good part of which remained much as it had been since the eighteenth century—ceased to exist the moment the heirs sold to SunCal. The Treaty of Guadalupe Hidalgo notwithstanding, the ejido had finally been assimilated into the market of private property. One more loss of communal land on a landscape of losses.

The sense of mourning is the desert West's eternal refrain. Every subdivision invokes an elegy, and there is still plenty of open space on the horizon to mourn in the future. Indeed, the desert is so big that much of it appears as land unto itself, even though anyone with a cursory knowledge of environmental history recognizes the toll of invasive species, unreclaimed mining, overgrazing livestock, all manner of unsustainable human practices. But the lamentation accompanying the transformation of a desert landscape into rows of a subdivision's hastily built stucco boxes is itself an aura that imbues undeveloped land with nostalgia, which is, in turn, part of the brand that sells the West. As long as there is a prelapsarian view of Sandia Peak, the ruddy behemoth overlooking the valley, the metro area will grow.

Alongside the recent development there are still vestiges of Atrisco—working farmland, acequia ditches. The South Valley has a complicated personality. Here, messily bordering each other, are a pastoral living museum, an old urban Chicano barrio, iconic open space (the flanks of the West Mesa), the development of the boom. (Soon there will be the stalled construction of the bust—roads that go nowhere, half-built houses vandalized by bored teens.)

Jimmy Santiago Baca, poet laureate of the South Valley, writes:

Things change.
Pseudo Spanish-style apartments
now loom on the east mesa.
Used to be land grant tierra.
Now retired Texan ranchers park
their Revcon travel-homes,
pampering them like prize bulls.

And there is a devastating emptiness in the lives staged on the land:

> In the distance
> I could hear someone chopping wood,
> and smell the heat wavering off stones,
> and sense the loneliness that brimmed
> from adobe houses at dusk—
>
> a loneliness
> no one could see, that I sensed
> in a horse's tail,
> a cow's glum, dumb look, or in the lizard's
> blinding scurry into weeds.

The land is there to remind you that it is no longer yours. It has become a landscape for others.

When Angela first invited me to visit Wilma, she was married to Clark, a man almost twenty years younger than her. She had always shown an iconoclastic streak in choosing her romantic partners; her first husband was Alex, the son of Greek and German immigrants, an aspiring academic who took Wilma and their "coyote" children on a peripatetic tour of rural college towns. After the marriage ended, she came back home and drifted for a while until she met Clark, himself a coyote, a social worker, and a talented musician. Together they bought the trailer and the acre at the foot of the mesa.

Pretty much all of the homes in the immediate vicinity were trailers, most of them herded in the nearby trailer parks. A few yards from Wilma's house, a large culvert helped drain the flood-prone South Valley, one of the few infrastructure improvements in the area. Within view was the Rio Grande bosque, the line of cottonwoods parallel to the river that sustained Albuquerque and the string of towns southward— Los Lunas, Belén, Socorro, all the way to El Paso, where the river became border. It was a home on a hard and beautiful landscape.

Clark wasn't a big home-improvement enthusiast, but he began a flurry of activity as he and Wilma were splitting up. By the time of their separation, he'd added two rooms and redone the kitchen. After he left, Wilma plastered about half of the outside of the trailer with earth-toned stucco. This kind of transformation was popular in New Mexico, as it was inexpensive. You made your trailer look like an adobe, right down to the big fireplace in the living room—the next phase of development of what critic J. B. Jackson called the "mobile home on the range." Unlike a new adobe, however, an old trailer can't hold heat in the winter or swamp-cooled air in the summer. The heating and cooling costs are excessive, which is why whenever we spend the night at Wilma's there is a tug-of-war between Angela and her mother over keeping the heater or swamp cooler on through the night.

If Wilma was hoping her new son-in-law would step up to the task of completing the renovations, she was disappointed. Angela and I visited often, usually displacing either my nephew Noah, who sometimes spent long stretches with his grandmother, or Zak, Wilma's youngest child. But I never wore the tool belt or shopped at Home Depot. I was always more interested in exploring the land around her house, looking for the best view of messy immensity. I goaded the kids to take me on tours of the mesa. They led me to desiccated coyotes in the washes or to the latest fort they'd built out of construction scraps from the subdivisions sprouting up all around us. At night I'd smoke on the front porch, where Wilma fought a losing battle with the sand that blew in off the mesa, and look across the valley of amber city lights to the sudden area of darkness created by the Sandias, which gave way to starry desert sky.

There was much of the "Western" or, rather, the New Western, at Wilma's. She was on the edge of the big empty that fills our imaginations, where the monsoon storms would rake the sky and leave it naked, startlingly close. Great high-tension towers stood watch over the sage plain. There were Indian pueblos on the horizon, their casinos glaring in the night. A strong wave of Mexican migration had arrived in the old barrio just down the street—their labor raised the houses of the boom— creating a familiar set of tensions between Hispanos and Mexicans.

Wilma was the granddaughter of a woman who was born on the Apache reservation, the daughter of mining people from the Silver City area (where *Salt of the Earth*, the great banned labor film, was made; some of her distant relatives might have been among the extras). She was taught in schools at a time when children were severely punished in the heavy consonants of English for pronouncing Spanish vowels, years before anyone called themselves "Chicano" or took public pride in speaking Spanish or Spanglish; and the shadow of the Bomb, built up north in Los Alamos and tested down south in Alamogordo, hung over it all. Wilma took off as soon as she could and came back when her first marriage ended, almost twenty years later. This land was home to her people, and here she put together a philosophy to defend herself against the world that willed against Mexicans and Indians and women and people who lived in trailers. She read a lot. She took extension courses. She watched public television. She picked up a bit from Carlos Castaneda, a bit from Gloria Steinem, and some from Sandra Cisneros and Ana Castillo. She read *A Course in Miracles* and loved *The Da Vinci Code* and went to a church that Angela thought smacked of Scientology but Wilma insisted it wasn't, and what if it was?

Life was tough after Clark left—she hadn't worked in years and was on the mature side of middle age. She found a job at a print shop near the airport: collating and stapling, part-time with no benefits. She loved it and started dating one of the pressmen. He had long hair and a beard and freckles and wore bandannas. Keith looked like Willie Nelson and loved to talk, talk, talk—about the article he'd just read in the *Nation* and working on strike crews in the burning hills of San Diego County when he was young and about his hobby of fixing up cars, fixing anything at home. Of course he was married, but soon enough he wasn't and Keith and Wilma looked to be set. Then she hesitated. Other men appeared. Older guys, Hispanos. There was Paul, handsome and bronzed; he had all the construction know-how to finish off the trailer or knock it down and start anew. There was John, a Harley-riding former federal agent who carried himself more like an outlaw, ate only one meal a day, and drank the rest of the time—but he never dropped his bike. And there were others who would show up for short stints, one-off dates or a couple of weeks—Anglos, Indians, African-Americans—all of them middle-aged, all of them respectable and respectful of her. They'd worked their whole lives, hard, were strong and calm on the outside and, I imagined, broken on the inside. There were Saturday afternoons at Wilma's when she'd invite all the suitors and they'd all actually show up and pretend to get along with one another and each would make sure to spend a few minutes with her one-on-one in a quiet corner. Her children and in-laws all had opinions about who she should choose—that is, we all thought that she *should* choose one and thought we knew which one was right for her. She, on the other hand liked things just the way they were. Didn't we realize that she'd spent over a quarter century of her life married, and now she felt good alone? There were times, more and more lately, when it just felt good coming home and pouring herself a gin and tonic and lighting up a Camel and watching MacNeil (or was it Lehrer? She could never remember which one left) and just be in her body, in her house, out on the land at the foot of the mesa.

## 2.

The great boom of the first decade of the 2000s is on, and with our modest income—Angela is still a graduate student and I teach part-time—we have been priced out of the coastal cities. At the same time, a flood of migrants is headed into the West—the high rollers looking for their country houses and the lower middle and working classes, the refugees of gentrification, just looking for something they can afford.

Angela and I fall between the two, into that vast, fuzzy region known as the middle class. We are not refugees—we live in Velarde by choice. Angela is chasing the ghosts of her family, trying to understand the political, historical, and cultural geographies in which addiction occurs. I came following her, into the West that was already a powerful object of my desire, bringing the ghost of my addictions with me.

Is desire for the land itself a kind of addiction? The dictionary lists definitions of addiction as "devotion to," "dedication to," "obsession with," "infatuation with," "passion for," "love of," "mania for," "enslavement to."

What is the genealogy of this desire? Surely the tree-sitting environmentalist had in her consciousness residue from the Romantics? And what was in the Romantics' imagination of the desert metaphors in the Bible—the exiles, the fasting, the demons and temptations, Moses approaching both the burning bush and the "thick darkness" where God dwelled in the wilderness. Indeed, the longest lasting of the tropes was the mystical desert: monastics across millennia pondering, experiencing its nothingness and fullness, the end of language and its point of origin, at least in the Judeo-Christian tradition. Did Fred Drake and his boho cohort in Joshua Tree sense something of the aura of Meister Eckhart, the High Middle Age theologian who conceived of a perfect spiritual "oneness" in the desert, a vision powerful enough to carry across the centuries to lead Aldous Huxley to the Mojave? What remnants of the human relationship to the desert remain from prehistory, melding with narratives of conquest and refuge, underlying our own aesthetic and spiritual experience of it?

I desired this place. I had come back to the land, the only Eden this city boy had never known. Eden with poverty, Eden with drugs, Eden with class warfare, but the landscape camouflaged the contradictions very well. Angela's desire wasn't as strong as mine, but she had settled into the desert, too. She did not share my crunchiness about it, the obsession with acequias and organic farming. But this was the land of her mother's people (or at least was within about a hundred miles of it), and she had her *Little House on the Prairie* fantasies from childhood.

Between the two of us, then, there was enough desire that—in spite of our modest income and shaky credit (my fault; Angela's was perfect), the IRS levying our savings only a few months before our wedding (my fault again), hardly any cash to speak of other than meager retirement accounts from previous jobs, and my strong aversion to the idea of owning real estate—we started looking to buy a house in northern New Mexico, among the very norteños who'd been fighting off outsiders since forever.

## 3.

The Española Valley is surrounded on three sides by mountains dominated by coniferous forest. Everybody calls it "the woods."

There is a social geography in the forest every bit as complicated as the human history at the lower elevations. There are very few human physical structures in the forest, but there are people spread across it, a cohort as motley as the migrants who'd been drawn to the West in the last generation. And even when those people weren't physically in the woods, they gazed upon and imagined them from the houses in the towns and cities nearby. The forests of northern New Mexico are a repository of conflicting longings and claims, which themselves reveal

the divisions of race, class, and culture in the region. The Hispano
hunter, the environmentalist from Santa Fe, the multinational logging
firm, the seekers of spiritual solace—they bump into each other deep
in the shadows under the ponderosas and spruces and firs, in meetings
that tend toward the awkward if not overtly contentious. When you
think of the Forest Service, for example, do you think first of Smokey
the Bear? Or do you regard it as an occupying army, a shill for corporate
loggers, a numbingly dumb bureaucracy? When you look across the
hills of piñon, do you think of hiking or grazing or riding your ATV?

The longer I live in Velarde, the higher up I go into the forest, walking into the woods with the others.


Elizabeth Robechek is a landscape architect who lives down the road
from Velarde in Santa Fe. I'd heard the word "mystical" used to describe
her, and I am interested in the connection between the mystical and
this land of enchantment. She is among the most recent generation of
migrants drawn to the West by the amenities imagined to be plentiful
here: cleaner air, more nature, perhaps even spirit.

Elizabeth offers to take me on a walk in the woods. She chooses Bear
Canyon, on the edge of Santa Fe. We meet in the parking lot of the Ran-
dall Davey Audubon Center. A fit middle-aged woman, she is dressed in
a blouse with thin black and white stripes, tight on her torso, and black
pants, also of skin-hugging material. She wears sandals with Velcro
straps. Her sandy blond hair is thick and electric. She has a silver brace-
let on her right wrist, with a faintly Native motif. Pale blue eyes, flecked
with white, a bit of makeup.

Originally from upstate New York, Elizabeth first visited the West
because of "health issues" in the early 1990s and fantasized escaping to
it ever since. After a divorce, she moved to Vail in Colorado, and then,
six years ago, to New Mexico. With a successful career—a project of
hers was recently featured in *Sunset*, the ultimate Western magazine—
she has no plans to leave.

Although it is a weekend, the parking lot is not very crowded. There
is no real workweek for the gentry of Santa Fe. Because of the wonders
of the home office and telecommuting, the hiking paths in the area can
just as easily be jammed on a Tuesday morning as on a Saturday.

At the trailhead, Elizabeth asks me to think of a question and thus give myself what she calls a "frame of reference" for the journey.

"It could be personal," she says, "or like 'What's my role in something political?' For me, it could be maybe a design project. Think of something in your life, put it out there and let it rest as things in the canyon attract you."

The hike is modest, and so is the canyon, which is pretty and quiet. There are piñon and ponderosa pines, the latter mostly young with a few verging on old growth, a slight yellow cast on their great cracked barks. There is plenty of space between trees, and with the pines only modestly branched and needled, a fair amount of sunshine dapples the ground, unlike in the much denser forest at the higher elevations. Many piñon here have survived the bark beetle that is ravaging drought-enfeebled trees across the West, and there is even a good number of seedlings. A stream runs intermittently along the trail, and grasses flourish next to it.

"Some of them have become friends," Elizabeth says of the ponderosas. "Some of them I think of as uncles."

This year the area got a good amount of snow and the stream ran strong. In the spring Elizabeth came here and, she says, "I danced with the river, crossing back and forth over it."

Butterflies float by. Lizards scurry across the rocks. She has seen "evidence" (hunters would say "scat" or "sign") of black bears and mountain lions. In all these, she senses a kind of language.

"Maybe," she says, "this form of life has clues for what I'm pondering."

I note an immediate and sharp contrast with the BLM lands up north around Velarde: no Walmart bags. But untouched nature it's not. Barely an eighth of a mile into the hike, we find that someone has built a little enclosure of fallen branches, in the shape and size of a pup tent. On the other side of the stream, there is a large cairn built from the same. "Oh, I love this," she says, embracing the whole scene.

Now she talks about feng shui and vastu. "You can't just be in service to humans," she says. "I'm not just looking to heal the person, but the place as well. Looking at the relationship of rocks to humans. It's all relationship and communication."

We come upon an old-growth ponderosa.

"This," she says, looking up, "is Uncle." She wraps her arms around its belly, buries her nose in a crack of the bark, and says it smells like vanilla.

Elizabeth practices and teaches a breathing technique that, she tells me, "allows the border between the tree and the self to soften. You breathe the tree's essence in, and when you breathe out, you are giving of your essence to the tree." Then, she says, "the tree's soul is in you, and your soul's in the tree."

We can learn a "new way to approach inquiry" from the tree. "It's not so different from massaging your foot and thanking it for carrying you around all day."

A dragonfly levitates over the stream. We stop and look at its perfectly, intricately striped abdomen. In the shade, its wings are invisible. It zips back and forth before us, seemingly just for us.

A sign?

Elizabeth has found a "new way to speak" here, one that her friends and family back home "don't get." In her language and philosophy, she is a child of the California of Krishnamurti and Huxley, Esalen, the Monterey Pop Festival, the be-ins of Golden Gate Park, macrobiotics, gurus here, there, and everywhere, Timothy Leary. But today New Mexico is the stronger magnet for those who wish their spirits to be cleansed, made new.

Initially it is hard to keep my cynicism in check around Elizabeth, but the higher up the trail we go the more I begin to acknowledge our similarities. I too arrived in the West with "health issues," after all. My desire to live on this land flows from an urge to get and stay clean. If I regard Elizabeth in contrast to Rose Garcia and more like myself, then perhaps I need to reexamine my representation of poor Hispano addicts, since I live next door to Rose Garcia, not Elizabeth Robechek. But the gulf is even wider because the imaginaries that Elizabeth and I followed into the forest are the very ones that have erased lives like Rose's.

We stand beneath a tall ponderosa. "This is Grandmother," Elizabeth says. I look up and my mind flashes to the O'Keeffe painting of Lawrence's pine in San Cristobal. This one's belly is glowing pumpkin-yellow, a sign of great age. Grandmother has a beehive in her side. Grandmother is dying. Her lowest large branch has broken, is now only barely attached to the trunk. A beetle with blue dots on its back eats lichen embedded in her bark.

"At first it looks like devastation and destruction, but I was getting that the tree was actually freed up," Elizabeth says and then adds quickly, "although I shouldn't paraphrase." She means that she doesn't want to paraphrase what the tree communicated to her, which was not in the language of words, but through non-verbal, sensory, or spiritual communication. She did not *hear* the tree. She *got* the tree.

On the other side of Grandmother there is another large tree with a natural niche formed by a trunk split into several large branches. This is a special place for Elizabeth. She has left apples there, as offerings. One time, she returned and found a quarter where she'd placed an apple.

Perhaps because we are in her special place, Elizabeth begins to speak to me intimately about her human relationships. Her voice catches, and she tears up. On a recent trip to Ohio, where she lived before coming west, she saw an old love and she realized that it was not going to work out.

"A lot of people just aren't going to go into this new consciousness," she says.

It sounds like he judged her.

"And I can't go back," she says.

It sounds like she judged him, too.

We move on to an area she calls the Place of the Lost Boys, a rocky patch where the vegetation is thicker and there is more shade—more forest. It is a place where kids could easily hide from one another or their parents.

She says that when she was a little girl, she spoke to the stones, and they spoke to her. "And they still do."

There is a rock shaped like a love seat, old moss gray and crunchy where the rain once collected and stood long enough to become the soup of life. The rock, she says, "is the protector of this space."

Near the Place of the Lost Boys Elizabeth wants to be quiet, which means she wants me to be quiet. We are on a large outcropping that rises up from the center of the canyon and climbs westward. She sits in the shade near the canyon bottom, facing north. I sit higher up, in full sun, facing east. There is a breeze, the air cooled slightly by the ponderosas.

A hawk screeches from the top of a tree about thirty yards away toward the west. I have no idea what the hawk is telling me, but something is happening to me here, I begin to feel close to Elizabeth, who left a past steeped in pain and found a land where she felt alive again. That is how I arrived in the desert after Mexico City.

On the way back to the car, I ask about her landscaping practice. She says that her clients seem to be in more of a "Zen minimalist" mood these days, as in "lots of space between objects." Or lots of similar objects held apart to give the illusion of space.

"Very Zurich," she says. "It's cleaner, not bound to plants needing water."

It is summer, and there's plenty of work for Elizabeth, lots of backyard projects. She shows me a modest portfolio. In *Sunset*, a photograph of one of her designs is captioned "Stylish Courtyard." There is a swimming pool—not much conservation there—and a small stand of aspen, stamped concrete. Another backyard project is a swath of gravel, a brushstroke of Mexican beach pebbles, a mound of river rock, and a slender waterfall that falls in a perfect V (to minimize evaporation), with a bit of ornamental grass at the base.

We talk about the others, Hispanos, Pueblos. She was hired for some landscaping work at the Museum of Indian Arts and Culture, where she tried to engage the elders, but they weren't much interested. It is the same with the Hispanos, she says. She has done her share of study. She tells me that she believes in the commons, the regional legacy of the Hispano land grants.

"But," Elizabeth asks, "how do we get to have a commons with different viewpoints, when we're all on the same land at the same time?"

When we say good-bye, she gives me a white rock, quartzite, shaped like a heart. It is the size of a three-year-old's hand.

## 4.

Angela and I are insiders and outsiders, here and not quite here. We are outsiders because we have not lived in northern New Mexico since forever, because we earn our income elsewhere, because I have come from afar to write about the north and the people in it, in a long tradition of artists who came, dazzled by difference. But we do live in Velarde. The clerks at the post office know us by our first names. Joe Rendón, our neighbor, watches our house when we go away. We speak Spanish and English and Spanglish, grow squash and eat it slathered with green chile accompanied by flour tortillas from Walmart; we know the most intimate details of Rose and Jose's disintegrating lives; and there is a connection unspoken as it is profound: drugs. Addiction unites us with our neighbors across time and space, generations and social class.

After living in the north for two years, I realize that the outsider-native dichotomy is as simplistic and convenient for me as it is for my neighbors. At this point, I, too, am a neighbor, and with that comes a sense of responsibility that baffles me. What, exactly, is the neighborly thing to do in Velarde, given the landscape of addiction and loss?

Next door to Jose and Rose's adobe is a trailer where another couple live, Lena and Jose. We referred to this Jose by his nickname, Cuchi. They are in their early forties. Lena is Joe Rendón's cousin and her trailer is just a few paces away from an empty patch of earth that had reportedly been the site of one of the early adobes of Los Rendones, back when the family owned all the land from the highway to the river. Cuchi is from Los Angeles, which gives me someone to bond with—the two guys from L.A. who married authentic Hispanas.

Lena and Cuchi's grown children visit now and then; I occasionally see at least one grandson, playing in the carport. Lena stopped by our house soon after we moved in and welcomed us cheerfully. But after several months of smiles and waves and brief neighborly chats, the couple seem to disappear into the trailer. Then Cuchi's car is gone for days or weeks at a time and the children visit less. One night as I am writing, the attic suddenly fills with red flashes from a paramedic's truck. I watch through the window as Lena is taken away. Joe Rendón tells me that she overdosed. She survives.

I begin to understand that clinging to the distinction of outsider has relieved me of my ethical responsibility as a neighbor. And the native who brands me outsider is denying both my presence and their ethical responsibility to me. Buying a house, I decide, is both the brash outsider's move—our economy is not integrated with the village's, so we have means that most locals do not—and the only way to become more fully neighbors.

And to do that, we have to look at the practical modes of the real estate market. There has been a lot of subdividing of the old agricultural holdings in Velarde, down to the legal limit of three-quarters of an acre. The land grants had comprised hundreds of thousands of unbroken acres, but the old norteño families sold outright or divvied up the land among the children, some of whom sold and some of whom stayed. If you stayed, you put a trailer on your three-quarter-acre parcel. The radical subdividing and the trailers keep most of the gringos away from Velarde; they want adobe to accent the view of the Rio Grande bosque and the Black Mesa, not rusting single-wides leveled on cinder blocks.

We don't mind the trailers, but we also want an adobe, and adobes are affordable in Velarde—to us at least—precisely because there are so many trailers.

The ad is in the *Rio Grande Sun*, in the Coldwell Banker box that runs every week in the classifieds.

Charming, remodeled adobe home with tile floors, large kiva fireplace, hot water baseboard heat, upstairs bedroom with office/studio space below, two bathrooms, one with a clawfoot bathtub, one with a tile shower, all on 2.46 irrigated acres with fruit trees. Community water, private well, and irrigation rights to the mother ditch that flows between the house and the orchard. Quiet and peaceful setting in the beautiful Velarde Valley.

The ad is a classic of the form, run-on sentence and all. "Adobe" grabs you early, and its two modifiers tell us that it is old ("charming" means authentic) and habitable ("remodeled" means that it's not a fixer). The tile floors are a letdown for the buyer seeking the original wood, but what the hell, they're easy to clean. The "kiva" fireplace brings us aboriginal culture; you might imagine hanging a Navajo rug next to it, or a framed Gorman print. The baseboard heat will be familiar to house hunters from back East, and "office/studio" is a smart contraction nodding at both telecommuters and painters (or telecommuting painters). The clawfoot bathtub is a shout-out to subscribers of *Sunset* or *Dwell*, just as the irrigated acreage is aimed at city slickers pining to get back to the land, like Lawrence reading Mabel Dodge's letters in London.

The "quiet and peaceful setting" is, of course, an outright lie.

### 5.

The day he takes me up into the woods, Sam Hitt stretches his arms out wide and literally hugs a ponderosa. He buries his nose in one of the jigsaw cracks of the big pine's bark. Sam says it's an old tree. You couldn't nearly encompass it with your embrace. A "yellow belly," as foresters say, maturity bringing a pumpkin tinge to the trunk.

He takes a deep whiff.

"It smells like vanilla," he says, exactly as Elizabeth Robechek had. "Try it."

I spread my arms. The bark scratches my nose. I breathe in. It smells like vanilla.

Sam is approaching sixty; he's tall, with thinning hair, has a plain face, and wears wire-rimmed spectacles. He dresses simply and speaks softly, which belies his legendary status in the north. In certain circles, Sam is loathed as the very caricature of an environmentalist—the white guy who cares more about a worm than a human being. In others, he is lauded as a brave movement purist. For the better part of the 1990s, he appeared regularly in media reports about the forests, perhaps the most contested space of all in northern New Mexico.

In these segregated forests, Sam has something of an alter ego: Ike (pronounced "Ikie") de Vargas, one of the best-known Hispano activists of the north. Sam and Ike are about the same age; Sam an outsider, Ike a native. Where Sam sees "wilderness," Ike sees a "working landscape." Regarding the same dense stand of ponderosa pines, Sam sees old-growth trees that should be preserved at all costs, while Ike sees the ideal site for the thinning projects that provide jobs for Hispano loggers. And they are both obsessed with a legendary place high up in the mountains known as La Manga, a region of old-growth trees that each claims for his respective vision.

Sam is a longtime proponent of "zero-cut" forestry. Even dead trees, called snags, are sacred to him. More than anything, he wants to protect what he considers to be pristine nature. Sam's means to that end landed him in a high-profile controversy and gained him the enmity of de Vargas and most of the Hispano activist cohort in the forest. As the executive director of Forest Guardians, a Santa Fe–based advocacy group, Sam filed a lawsuit against the U.S. Forest Service, urging action to protect the endangered Mexican spotted owl, whose habitat includes the Carson National Forest, which surrounds the Española Valley and was the commons for several Hispano land grants. As a result, a federal judge handed down an injunction banning the gathering of firewood, which communities in the north use for woodstoves, the main source of heat in many village homes. A decade later, mention of Sam Hitt's name still raises hackles among many norteños. Passions ran so strong over the firewood injunction (which was largely symbolic—lasting only one season and never strictly enforced) that Hitt and some of his fellow environmentalists were hung in effigy at norteño demonstrations. It was Ike de Vargas who tightened the noose.

This is not how Sam Hitt had imagined his life in northern New Mexico.

He first arrived from Michigan as an undergraduate at St. John's College in Santa Fe and explored the northern villages in the late 1960s along with the hippie hordes. He spent a year at Christ in the Desert, a Catholic monastery set on a remote, remarkable landscape of stratified mesas and piñon pine along the Rio Chama. He lived for a while in Dulce, in far northern New Mexico Navajo country, where he roomed with an Indian. He tended bar in Lumberton ("at the end of the world"), getting drunk Indians drunker, something he still feels guilty about. He visited all the communes, too, including the smallest secluded ones, not just the rock star sites like New Buffalo, where Dennis Hopper and Peter Fonda hung out.

He was searching for beauty, which for him was in the isolated, the untouched, the natural. His father was a forester, so from early on Sam knew the woods well. And where better to explore them than in northern New Mexico? Between them, the Carson and Santa Fe National Forests contained some three million acres, from the piñon-juniper lowlands to peaks above the timberline.

He had a long-distance lover named Wendy in Denver. He hitchhiked back and forth between New Mexico and Colorado and told Wendy about the wonders he'd seen, ultimately convincing her to join him. Horrified, her parents cut her off. That first winter, they had no chain saw, and no wood splitter. He chopped wood for months. It was, he says, the best year of his life.

Early in his move to New Mexico, Sam felt as much fervor about being among the people of the north as living on the land. He settled in La Puente, a village near Tierra Amarilla, only a few years after Reies López Tijerina, the fiery land grant activist, staged his audacious raid on the courthouse there in 1967. Sam says he had "sympathy" for the Hispanos, though this did not help him in La Puente. Nobody in the village spoke to the couple during their first year there. But after they survived the first winter (including spells of twenty and thirty degrees below zero), Sam and Wendy planted a garden. The harvest included some broccoli, which many locals had never seen before. He passed it around the neighborhood, and people liked it. It was a good icebreaker.

Sam started to meet the movers and shakers in the community, especially through La Clínica del Pueblo, a rural health center that was one of the more tangible positive outcomes of the norteño activism that blossomed after the Courthouse Raid. He was hired by Maria Varela, a well-known community organizer who helped open the center, to build solar greenhouses.

As Sam got older, the romance began to wear thin. This happens to many outsiders who attempt to live in norteño villages. He saw alcoholism and domestic abuse among the lives of his neighbors. He and Wendy now had children and they agonized over whether to send them to the local public schools—the dilemma of the American middle class. All the while, Sam was learning more about the land and how the people he thought were living in harmony with it were actually living unsustainably. Take the adobe, the classic rustic norteño dwelling steadily being supplanted by the trailer, and the object of desire of those seeking authentic Western living. The structures that were seventy-five or a hundred years old were far from airtight, allowing in winter chill and summer heat. The adobes typically had single-pane windows, many of which were cracked. The old woodstoves looked great but were terribly inefficient, didn't draw air well, and didn't radiate enough heat. Too much wood was burned for too little warmth. And by extracting excessive wood from the mountains—that is, beyond the rate at which trees replenish themselves naturally—the community destroyed wildlife habitat and threatened species and even the forest itself with extinction.

"I never had stars in my eyes" about the norteños, says Sam, but maybe he did. When he talks about his time in Dulce, at Christ in the Desert, and at La Puente, he speaks of a young man's great adventure, his eyes opening to the world, to the beauty of difference. Once he arrived in the forest, he was surrounded by activists of one sort or another. He decided that he would be one, too, and bring his knowledge of the forest to the community. Everyone would become even closer to the land they all loved.

. . .

Sam offers to guide me on a hike in the woods. We start in Española, at the Community Bank parking lot. It is early June, just after dawn. The forecast calls for a warm, clear day, no mention of rain. The monsoon hasn't started yet.

We hop into his Toyota pickup, which looks to be at least a decade old, powder blue, no frills. We head north on Highway 84 toward Abiquiu, O'Keeffe country. Here, she bought a house on Ghost Ranch and painted the forms of the land (like *Pedernal,* in 1942, a portrait of the most famous volcanic feature of northern New Mexico, a majestic, flat-topped mountain) and, occasionally, the built environment on it (the church at Ranchos de Taos, with its overwhelming apse) but never the people. As absorbing as O'Keeffe's works are, they have had the effect of aiding in the elision of the human figure in the north.

Whenever I look at the yellow-magenta bluffs dotted by juniper, cumuli mushrooming over distant mountains, I feel a swell of emotion—but I can't tell if it's a genuinely sublime moment or a conditioned projection onto the landscape.

Sam has no such doubts. The landscape, he says, is "fucking beautiful." He brought me out here to show me pristine nature. We are going to La Manga, high in the Tusas Range, north of Abiquiu. The road climbs above the valley cut by the Rio Chama. When you crest the ridge headed north, a big basin opens up, and Ghost Ranch is in the middle of it. The mesa stone passes through shades of white, yellow, pink, red, brown. To the west is O'Keeffe's Cerro Pedernal. She literally said it was hers: "mine—God said that if I painted it enough, he'd give it to me." The boast was borne out. I cannot look at the mountain without thinking of O'Keeffe.

The road continues to climb. There is the turnoff to the village of Canjilon, which Tijerina used as a base of operations and where one of his disciples, Moisés Morales, agitates to this day (constantly running for one elected office or another, occasionally winning). At the turnoff to Tierra Amarilla, the location of the Courthouse Raid, a historical marker offers a thumbnail history of the town. The final sentence reads: "In 1967 it was the focus of conflicts between National Guardsmen and land rights activist—" Tijerina's name has been crudely scratched out.

"I don't know why I get so sad when I come up here," Sam says, as we drive by his old adobe in La Puente. The village is the very image of rural decay, as if the wilds are reclaiming it. What Sam lived for back in the 1970s—idealism, integration—stayed in the 1970s, it seems. There is only a faint echo of the communes, of the moment when the Taos Pueblo elder "Little Joe" led white kids on a magical mystery tour into indigenous mysticism. A generation later, Little Joe is long gone, and you can't get beyond the visitors' plaza in Taos Pueblo, where tourists are treated to the spectacle of a handful of naïve American families supposedly leading "traditional" lives without electricity or running water.

We roll past the adobe where Maria Varela once lived. "And this is where the store used to be," he says, pointing to a tiny mud-brick place shuttered, seemingly, for a hundred years. We roll by an adobe painted pale blue. The Martinezes, Sam says. They had eleven children, only a few of which survived into adulthood. There are several For Sale signs, some of which lean toward the earth as if they've been through more than one winter.

Now there is not even a store or a gas station in La Puente. The old rural economy vanished, and most of the village with it. Back then, Sam says, time went by very slowly. Sometimes you'd pick up a book in the morning and wind up spending the whole day reading. No TV, no Internet, just Sam and Wendy and their babies, trying to grow their own food, trying to make a living. They bought the house from a Communist doctor for $5,000. The whole place smelled of cat piss. Sam insulated the old adobe and built a greenhouse. Wendy, especially, never shook off the feeling of being a "foreign invader," but after a time they made some friends. A Hispana neighbor taught Wendy how to make sopaipillas (the Hispano version of fry bread, dipped in honey to cool the tongue from the fire of the inevitable green or red chile smothering the main course of lamb or pork or enchiladas). Wendy returned the favor with her recipe for bagels. They even had some parties, where the back-to-the-land Anglos mixed with some Hispano activists. Tijerina protégé Moisés Morales came by once, and so did Ike de Vargas.

"He was kind of scary," says Sam. "You know, how the Vietnam vets looked back then. I liked him. He was intelligent, articulate . . ."

His voice trails off. It was a moment. Ike was organizing for the Chicano nationalist Raza Unida Party, which was established by activists throughout the Southwest to channel the energy generated by the Courthouse Raid, while Sam mostly hung with the back-to-nature crowd. When a uranium mine was proposed near Canjilon, there was a big Chicano-hippie fiesta of organizing, powerful enough to stop the mine.

And then the moment passed. Sam didn't want to leave. Wendy pushed; she decided the kids couldn't go to school here.

We pull into Los Ojos, which on many maps is still named Park View, the site of a naming war between Hispanos and Anglos. We stop by Tierra Wools, a woman's cooperative that was born from the wave of activism in the wake of Tijerina's uprising. The front of the space is a classy modern gallery for rugs featuring Native designs (even though the weavers appear to be all Hispanas), and in back you can watch the women work the big looms. The rugs are expensive—a miniature a few inches square can run to $100, one big enough for a living room several thousand dollars.

Sam and Wendy left for Santa Fe in 1980 and have lived there ever since, but Sam's professional life has remained focused on the norteño forests surrounding the village of his youthful dreams.

By the early 1990s, the Forest Guardians had become an important player in the region, wielding the environmentalist's sword of litigation. The other players completing the political triangle were the Forest Service and the Hispano villagers. All sides believed there was a crisis, that not only principles but the very life of the forest, a way of life in it, were at stake. The Hispanos believed their historic claims to the forest (land grants and their ejidos) trumped both government bureaucracy and the environmental movement's claim to scientific (or even spiritual) authority. They had also seen corporate-scale and even small logging operations sustain dramatic reductions over the decades, which meant that the timber-based village life was on the verge of extinction. Environmentalists looked at the forest and saw the ecological disaster that had resulted from centuries of unsustainable logging and grazing practices. Caught in between the two was the Forest Service, charged with protecting the land and accommodating these and yet other constituencies—

OHV riders, skiers, hikers, equestrian groups, and so-called "wise-use" corporate logging interests (their prospects brightened during George W. Bush's tenure and its Healthy Forests Initiative). Among and between all of them, there were internal factions and ideological disputes and debates over science and history and place. Even attempts at compromise— such as the Vallecitos Sustained Yield Unit, a 73,400-acre parcel that included La Manga and was designated by the federal government in 1948 in part to address norteño grievances about the eroding timber economy—were fractious and ultimately failed to appease anybody.

The two great political collisions that occurred in the forest in 1999 were over logging and firewood. The media looked for personality more than community, symbol more than context. Thus the Forest Service came to be represented by the Camino Real Ranger District's lead ranger, Crockett Dumas, a crusty cowboy with a handlebar mustache and an independent streak in a bureaucratic institution that generally abides little idiosyncrasy. Ike de Vargas was the media magnet representing norteño forest activists, with his strategic brilliance, striking helmet and beard of yellow-white hair, and exceptional oratorical skills. In addition to his Hispano cohort, Ike motivated other activist-minded gringos, like those who'd arrived in northern New Mexico along with the back-to-the-land movement and stayed on after the party was over. Among them were Mark Schiller and Kay Matthews, a couple who built their own house in the forest and published *La Jicarita News*, the only substantial political newsletter of the north. Their movement stood for what came to be called "environmental justice," the marriage of social justice activism, traditionally associated with racial and ethnic minorities, and environmentalism, long the domain of the white middle class. While the movement is often harnessed by poor urban communities of color confronting environmental hazards like toxic waste dumps, in northern New Mexico the battleground was the forest.

There was decidedly less diversity among the radical environmentalists, who had rarely operated in tandem with the social justice groups that flowed from the civil rights movement. Sam Hitt embodied the environmental radicals, cutting, with his long, thin-lipped face, a much less sexy figure than either Dumas or Ike, but he spoke with great self-assurance and claimed the objectivity of science.

All parties knew that political battles turned on public representations, the performance of politics. There were dozens of demonstrations
over the 1990s, some of them fine pieces of political theater, much of it
centered on La Manga, where Sam and I had gone to hike. Environmentalists attempted to block Hispano loggers from the section of forest set
aside for community-based timber projects. On one occasion, Forest
Guardians and norteño loggers set up rival camps in La Manga. There
were more effigy burnings led by Ike de Vargas. Meanwhile Crockett
Dumas made sure to offer the media opportunities to photograph him
riding a horse—illustrating how the Forest Service wasn't an uncaring
establishment but was capable of working with the rural villages, reaching out with "horseback diplomacy," even as Sam Hitt and Forest
Guardians secured court injunctions against logging that threatened to
ignite the kind of norteño rage not seen since the Tijerina days.

In the end, all of the sides lost something. Dumas took institutional
heat for giving the appearance of being too accommodating to Hispanos
and ultimately left the Forest Service. Ike de Vargas won the battle but
seemingly lost the war: the injunctions on La Manga were lifted, but the
local companies that could do the logging and fulfill the decades-long
promise of the Vallecitos Federal Sustained Yield Unit collapsed amid
financing problems and factional disputes.

If Ike lost the war, it could be argued that Sam and the Forest Guardians won it. After all, there are only a handful of permitted logging "pre-
scriptions" (as sanctioned logging zones are called) in the norteño
forests today, and it is illegal to fell a standing snag. But Sam also lost
the world he knew in La Puente, when for a moment brown and white
and middle-class and poor lived side by side, partied together, stopped a
uranium mine together.

Few people who live in the north dream of integration today, other
than perhaps a handful of tourists who've read about the three cultures
of New Mexico or the latest generation of crunchy kids who arrive
believing that the Pueblo spirit world will open up to them, that the
earth itself will pull them close and still their inquietude.

Sam and I begin our hike to La Manga at the Vallecitos Mountain Refuge, which he describes as a retreat for "burned-out enviros." It offers

workshops in various disciplines, such as Aztec dance and Buddhist meditation. The building is massive and opulent. It was homesteaded in the 1890s and became a hunting lodge in the 1950s before being reclaimed by activists. When we arrive, several workers are finishing up the spring cleaning in anticipation of the year's first workshop. The meadow surrounding the lodge is thick and brilliant with golden banner, delphinium, and dandelion.

Our destination is a stand of forest above the meadow that Sam says is pristine. The higher we go, the more radical he turns. He says that domestic livestock don't belong on this land, period. There has long been a divide between conservationists and norteños with small ranching operations and grazing permits on public lands. Permitees dwindled through the twentieth century, due to restrictions on grazing imposed by the Forest Service, and the subsequent attrition stoked resentment among traditional Hispano ranchers. Sam believes that recognizing the petitions of land grant heirs would only redouble injustice. Just how do you determine title and tenancy? How many generations make an authentic claim? And he believes that forest-thinning projects—sometimes cited as necessary for the prevention of devastating wildfires—are just a ruse to get multinationals back to massive exploitation.

Sam confers with the ranch manager about crossing the creek adjacent to the ranch house. He says that it's higher than anyone can remember having seen it but that there's a log not far downstream, the only way to get to the other side. Sure enough, a ponderosa has fallen clean across the creek, bridging about twenty-five feet of water, many of its branches still in place, like spokes on a wheel. Sam practically skips across it without the least hesitation, then quickly disappears into the forest on the other side. My turn. I place one foot on the old pine and peer down into a white roar as loud as a freight train's. I judge the risk of drowning extremely high. It takes me a good five minutes to crawl across the fallen trunk and another few to catch up to Sam. Beneath his khaki shorts, his calves are thick with muscle. Sam climbs the incline as fast and quiet as a bighorn sheep. The altitude gets to me. I can feel each heartbeat thud through my entire body.

"Look at that yellow-belly!" Sam cries at the foot of a venerable ponderosa. "The trees here are ancient." He tells me that they turn yellow at 180 years, then "pumpkin" at 300 to 400 years. When the tree dies, the snag remains full of life. It becomes like a high-rise apartment building. Holes form where branches break off and woodpeckers start boring in. On the branches still attached perch Mexican spotted owls. The snag also provides a habitat for the endangered northern goshawk. Ike de Vargas claims that the norteño forest has never been a major habitat for either. But Sam believes—no, *knows*—that it is, in spite of the fact that he's never seen a spotted owl here. (He swears he's heard one.) As for the goshawk: yes, he's seen it. Fearsome yellow eyes, immense wingspan, swooping low over him . . . The exhilaration he felt!

"Here"—he points to erosion—"there's been grazing."

"Here"—he sweeps a hand against a hill interspersed with stumps and anemic understory—"there's been logging."

"Here"—touching the cleft, charred trunk of an otherwise healthy ponderosa—"lightning struck."

We crest the ridge. Sam is looking for an elusive trail. We'll spend most of the day "blasting," as he says, our own. Eventually, we come upon an old logging road. There are stumps on either side, and hardly anything grows on the track itself because of the radically compacted soil. Eventually, the forest will take over—baby aspens are already creeping toward it. "But that will be long after we're gone," Sam says.

After several hours, my eyes start to see what Sam sees. The forest is no longer abstract bioscience or a New Age communion with nature. The cultural metaphors fall away. The pliable aspens bend in the steady breeze. A pinecone falls from a Douglas fir. Tears of sap sparkle on bark where bears have scratched. Everywhere there is movement and memory, stillness and anticipation. The forest is, simply, alive.

We break for lunch but I have brought no food. I had no idea that Sam had planned a daylong hike. At first he offers me nothing from his cache of fruit and nuts, and I do not ask. But eventually I do receive: he gives me half an apple, for which I am grateful. I am running low on water, too. But the old Boy Scout I am never leaves home without his Swiss Army knife and GPS. Sam does not use a GPS, preferring a compass, which he presently consults as he looks at a topo map of the area. He says he's famous for getting lost. We follow the old logging road west for about a mile but eventually have to backtrack.

We are still trying to find that place, that pristine place, the one that's never been logged. Suddenly a large outcropping rises from the forest floor of pine needles and dark earth. This is it.

Ponderosas and firs and aspens growing in clumps here, clearings there. There are no sawed-off stumps anywhere, no signs of logging roads or even footpaths.

"Here," Sam says, "you are looking at the forest the way the first Americans saw it a hundred and fifty years ago, the way the first Hispanos saw it four hundred years ago, the way the Indians saw it before contact. The way it was unseen before human eyes could see."

I am exhausted. It is now late afternoon and all I've eaten since breakfast is half an apple. We've been hiking for hours. Perhaps it is the exhaustion that allows me tears. Or seeing some of what Sam sees. The land without us. At some level I am still aware that in this construct the forest is still a metaphor—one for transcendence. But the sensation that fills me as I see this scene the way Sam wants me to is moving enough to momentarily overpower the critic.

The storm starts right there.

From the outcropping there is a view—we've been able to see beyond the treetops only a couple of times today—and sheets of white hang from gray bellies all around us. First the growl of cloud-to-cloud lightning and then the bolts hurled at the earth. Here comes the wind. The rain, then freezing rain, now thick, wet snow. June in northern New Mexico.

We run down the mountain toward the creek, lightning on our tails. All day I've been falling behind Sam, but now that I've got some real incentive, we're side by side. I shout a question to him about people getting hit by lightning.

"Yeah!" he shouts back. "Happens all the time up here!"

At the creek he floats across the log like a ballet dancer, and I dash on all fours like a bear. My hands are wet and cold. I'm within a yard of the bank when I slip and fall into freezing water up to my thighs.

A bolt strikes so close I hear the electricity rip the air open before the thunderclap. I look over my shoulder, expecting to see a ponderosa split open and aflame; I see nothing but the forest closing in on itself as I run from it.

## 6.

The house is on the county road at the northern end of the village, just west of where the Mexicans are building their fruit stand, one cinder block at a time.

We meet the Coldwell agent there, Mickey Coker, native of Mississippi; he's wearing tan cowboy boots and a black long-sleeved shirt, with his silver hair in a ponytail. Very Santa Fe, except for the drawl.

There is a lockbox hanging on the gate, but it holds no key for the gate itself, so we clamber over a low adobe wall and go to what seems to be the front door—it faces the road—but the key doesn't open it. We go around the side of the house, where a large, pretty patio has been painted bright New Mexican blue, a shade ubiquitous among Hispano houses and chapels. Here the key opens the back door.

It is freezing inside, winter locked in by the adobe walls. Several windows have blinds that have been pulled down, and it takes a few moments for my eyes to adjust to the dark. Even when we open the blinds, there is still a general air of dimness; most of the windows are small and face north or south. There is plenty of space—2,119 square feet according to the listing. The back door leads into an open area that functions as foyer, with a small room to the left (counted as a bedroom) and the kitchen to the right. The kitchen is not as airy as Angela would like.

At the end of the foyer, we come to another, very large room, with an inset bookshelf. Dining, sitting, den? It has a woodstove in the corner. To the right is the master bedroom, the darkest room in the house. It has only one small window. The bathroom is wainscoted, and there is the clawfoot tub mentioned in the ad.

I open the bathroom window and hear the sound of rushing water. Just a few yards away I see the acequia, running full and pungent and murky green, with runoff that gravity has pulled thirty miles from the Truchas Peaks. I am astonished by the sight. This is not a diversion but the actual Acequia Madre, Velarde's main, concrete-lined ditch. I've never seen it so close to a house before. My first reaction is excitement: that's practically a river running alongside your bedroom! And then I think about the ditch flooding that often accompanies the spring thaw.

In the living room is the kiva fireplace, awkwardly rendered, a bulging mass of lathery plaster, an improvement gone awry. This room is the brightest in the house, owing to an adjacent solarium of slanting glass panels facing east, clearly a recent addition. To the left is the entrance to the third bedroom, which has a three-quarter bath. A staircase leads to the "office/studio" space above. It is not nearly as big as the attic space we have in our rental, but it's big enough for one of us, and with plenty of light, a row of tall windows looking south over the apple orchard next door.

And then there is the land, those 2.46 acres with water rights.

A small bridge over the ditch leads to the outbuildings and the orchard. The latticed wood of the bridge is old and gray and a few planks are missing. I make my way across it carefully, imagining myself tumbling into the frigid runoff. A large chicken coop. A barn with old horse manure. Dozens of apple trees. Jumbles of branches jut skyward; they haven't been pruned for the season, or maybe it's been years. But the trees look very much alive in their old thick gray-white bark, a reminder of Velarde's heyday as the apple capital of New Mexico. Beyond the orchard, there's a large space for alfalfa or vegetables. It is my tiny gardening plot multiplied dozens of times.

I leave Angela chatting with Mickey and walk all the way out to the western boundary. The sky opens its arms, becomes a vast blue plain held up by the tan foothills of the Sangres in the east and in the west by the juniper green–dabbed basalt of the Black Mesa. To the north, the gorge the old Hispanos call "la boca del cañon" yawns steep and craggy; to the south the Española Valley is flanked by the heavy bulk of the Jemez. I walk through the grass, my boots sinking into muddy earth and splashing through standing water; it seems that the neighbors are irrigating. That, or a diversion ditch has crumbled and started to flood.

Angela takes pictures with the digital camera she bought to document her research, although since both her university and the clinic demand the strictest anonymity for her addict subjects, she has mostly used it for landscapes. Mickey is turning the survey plat over in his hands, trying to decipher its bearings.

I stand out there by myself for a few minutes. The water begins seeping into my boots. I feel as immense as the land—I *am* the land.

I rejoin the others and we come back across the footbridge and inspect the northern end of the property. There is a small pump house and a stand-alone one-room adobe, perhaps fifteen feet by fifteen, that wasn't mentioned in the listing. It is a classic norteño structure; perhaps it was a storeroom for fruit and vegetables, or maybe a chapel. Hanging on trellises nearby are wine grapes and various berries. It is all pastoral perfect.

The plat names the owner as Pedro Ortega (he is a relative of Eulogio Ortega, Velarde's most famous wood-carver, who lives about half a mile southwest). It was drawn in 1992, when Ortega made minor adjustments to the boundary lines. The plat describes the property as "lying and being situated in the Village of Velarde, within [tract] 5 in the Sebastián Martín Grant," as if the old grant and commons still existed. The street, which is physically signed as County Road 52, appears as "Camino de la Cochia" on the plat—probably a misspelling of "cochina," Spanish for a female pig. Perhaps there was a hog farm once. The ditch is named "Acequia del Medio," and every feature is noted, including all the outbuildings, a rock wall next to the road, and the footbridge over the water.

We stand in the late spring sun and talk. I smoke a cigarette. Mickey adjusts his black, long-sleeved shirt—he's starting to sweat in the heat. He admits that the layout of the house is a bit strange, at least to a modern American middle-class sensibility; the house was built to serve other purposes in another time, for another people. (It would have begun as a small norteño adobe with a couple of small bedrooms and a large kitchen and pantry; the attic would have been used for hanging chiles and jerky.) The Ortegas probably held the land for a few generations, maybe since forever—the family may have arrived in the area along with de Vargas's reconquista. Mickey does not have the complete chain of title, but we know that the current owner is one Tim Woodward, who, Mickey says, bought the house in around 2000, occupied it for a couple of years, and then moved to Washington State. It has since been on the market twice without selling and leased once. Woodward made plenty of improvements, adding the solarium and the saltillo floors, large smooth tiles that suggest Mexican style rather than New Mexican and that are an aesthetic hallmark of the boom years. He redid the roof, and is almost surely the one who attempted the kiva, and undertook practical upgrades, like copper plumbing, varnishing the vigas, and adding a new layer of stucco.

Of course, the fact that Woodward has not been able to sell should be a warning to any buyer. There are For Sale signs on properties like this one all over the area. While speculation is driving up prices elsewhere up and down the Rio Grande—Embudo, Taos, Bernalillo, Santa Fe, Rio Rancho, Albuquerque, and even Truth or Consequences, in the dusty badlands of the south—Velarde remains depressed, like its more urban neighbor Española.

A place like this in Velarde would be attractive only to village natives (but beyond the means of many; one-fourth of the population lives below the poverty line), to a gringo who's fallen in love with the view of la boca del cañon and is ignorant of the social and economic context— or to us.

Thus far I've been the driving force in the house hunt, but now Angela is inspired, too. I can tell because she starts imagining our own upgrades. She says we could punch a hole in the master bedroom ceiling for a sky-light. She doesn't like the floor tiles; we'll install wood. We'll have to paint—shades of yellow and beige, to brighten the place up—and put in a new kitchen sink, oven, and range.

"There's nothing about the condition of the house that would prevent you from moving in right away," Mickey says. "Then you can do your own remodel over time. As money permits, of course."

With the tour done, we walk back to Mickey's pickup. He pulls out some more listings. There's a house in El Valle (a village off the High Road to Taos that Angela feels is too isolated), and a cheap place in Truchas (which I nix because it has no land). Truchas, Mickey sighs. He's constantly having to go up there and restake his real estate signs. The locals keep pulling them up or burning them.

Angela and I get in the Subaru, and in five minutes we're home, Bear and Chino bounding out to greet us, their paws muddy and wet from dancing in the acequia.

A warm wind rushes down from the Black Mesa and rattles the fresh cottonwood leaves. It is time to make a decision.

## 7.

Every norteño tells me that I must speak to Ike de Vargas—activist, logger, organizer, hunter, land grant heir, descendent of Don Diego de Vargas, el reconquistador de Nuevo México, local historian, environmentalist hated by environmentalists, Hispano who holds court with

Anglos and Indians, Vietnam veteran, man you want to be lost in the
forest with during a blizzard because he will get you out.

And everyone has an opinion on Ike de Vargas. Regarded as a has-
been or a would-be, he is loved and loathed, dismissed and desired,
suspected and respected, pitied and feared.

I meet him early on during my time in New Mexico, and together we
keep going deeper into the forest, higher into the mountains. He lives
in Servilleta Plaza, a village much smaller than Velarde, a hamlet of
about twenty families in adobes and trailers, surrounded on all sides by
the Carson National Forest. The first trip to Ike's feels like a major expedition. As with any destination west of Velarde, first I have to circum-
navigate the Black Mesa (there is not now, nor will there ever be, a road
across it). The land on the other side of the mesa is drier and yellower.
The Rio Chama flows here, eventually joining the Rio Grande just north
of Española, but it is a trickle compared to the Great River and offers little in the way of a greenbelt. I head north to Ojo Caliente, a small town
built around a popular hot springs, and then into the foothills that rise
from the valley, passing through the village of La Madera, home to Bill
and Claudia Page, the couple who stayed on after the bombing that was
meant to scare them away.

A steep, winding road climbs into the Tusas Mountains. Then you
round a curve and a little plateau opens up. I pull over and get out to
take in the view, which looks west for dozens of miles across soft-
domed hills and more sharply defined peaks. Piñon gives way to ponderosa to aspen to fir and spruce, the forest ladder that ends in the
alpine meadows where the headwaters gather. The gray of dead piñon
nearby shifts at the higher elevations to the many greens of what to my
eyes looks like an immense and eternal forest. Both loggers and environmentalists would disagree, of course. The environmentalist sees the
lingering effects of rapacious logging, and wants the old roads closed to
leave nature to recover. The logger sees land mismanaged by the Forest
Service, a land grant commons that sustained generations stolen by the
government.

But right now what I sense is space. The forest often hems you in—
Angela has an aversion to it, feels claustrophobic—so that when you
gain a view above the trees, you feel an inevitable swell of emotion and

the romance is unavoidable. This is a view Oñate might've seen. And Po'pay. And Joe Rendón's grandfather.

I take a step, and my boot kicks something. At my feet is a crumpled can of Bud Light.


Ike's trailer sits not more than fifty yards from the Tusas River. There is a big pile of split firewood on the other side of the entry gate. Two mastiffs trot out to sniff my truck, followed, comically, by a Chihuahua. Wisps of smoke rise from the chimney.

He opens the door just as I'm about to knock. He is a beautiful man. The famous shell of white hair with a slight yellow tint sits above two deep furrows on his forehead. He stands about five-seven and is built lean and tough. He wears a sleeveless black T-shirt, blue-gray khakis, white socks and tennis shoes. A tuft of silvery beard is set in a perfect tan oval of a face. It is difficult to look into the hard beauty of Ike's eyes. Their color changes depending on the light; right now they are a brilliant, almost sky blue, set amid yellowy, bloodshot whites—a disconcerting combination.

"Come in," he says in an effusive rasp. "Have a seat."

A fire is roaring in the woodstove. On the wall are framed family photographs going back three generations, as well as a Virgen de Guadalupe, a large United Farm Workers flag, a hunting rifle, and a calendar featuring the iconic visage of Che Guevara (Ike says a friend brought it back from Cuba).

He takes down one of the framed photographs: his Marine unit in Vietnam, Special Ops. He asks me to guess which one he is. I point to the skinny kid with black hair, front row left, looking like a young Santana—wiry and wired. Yes, it's him, eighteen years old, from northern New Mexico into the jungles of Vietnam; he enlisted in 1964, when he was seventeen. He spent a good part of his childhood in the mountains with his grandparents. When his grandfather died and his grandmother took ill, he was sent to live with his parents in Española, and he quickly figured out that he didn't want to be there.

"There's no forest," Ike says, "only a thousand ways to get into trouble. You can get into trouble twenty-four/seven without wanting it in España."

He uses the popular diminutive for Española, which, in turn, was the name Cristóbal Colón, a.k.a. Christopher Columbus, gave to the land he first touched in the New World; it literally meant "Spanish Island." "España" may sound innocent, but when a northern villager says it, the name carries the symbolism of a colonial settler in a remote land referring to the metropole.

The Marines left their mark on Ike's body. He has a fading skull-and-crossbones tattoo on his right shoulder, the only visible memento of his two tours with the Marines in Vietnam. Inside he carries more. The VA doctors botched a liver biopsy, perforating his gallbladder; he almost died on the table. He has a prescription for oxycodone. He still drinks and smokes (American Spirit blues).

Although he is more than willing to pontificate about politics—norteño, American, and global—he insists that he is retired as an activist. He spends his days tending the vegetable garden and his animals (at different times, goats, chickens, ducks, sheep, and the rattlesnakes, which he refuses to kill because he likes to let them be) and going up into the forest as often as he can, as often as the pain lets him. There are days when he can't leave the house, and he has frequent appointments at the VA.

His political career spanned some of the most tumultuous moments in norteño history. He missed Tijerina's courthouse raid because he was in Vietnam, but he returned to find the villages buzzing with political energy: agitation over land grants, water rights, rural gentrification, and access to quality health care and education. In the aftermath of the courthouse raid, the Raza Unida Party set about organizing northern New Mexico, which proved particularly fertile and dangerous ground. The Hispano political machine, run by Emilio Naranjo, a legendary norteño boss, perceived young upstarts like Ike as a threat and spent years trying to undermine them, up to and including, Ike says, putting out contracts. The RU, like all civil rights era organizations on the left, was infiltrated. Drugs were planted on activists, Ike says; snipers staked out rallies. By the early 1980s, external pressure and ideological intrigue had taken their toll, and the movement faded. A new order of accommodation was symbolized by both Adolph Coors Brewing Company and *Time* magazine declaring the eighties the "Decade of the Hispanic."

But Ike was to live for another political day; in the 1990s, he came face to face with Sam Hitt, fighting over gathering firewood and logging—whether or not there could be a sustainable way to conduct either—and over the very meaning of the forest and its history. The two were on opposite sides of a bitter struggle over public lands management, a divide that opened everywhere between those who called themselves environmentalists and those who called themselves advocates for social justice.

Ike might no longer be actively organizing, but nevertheless he cares deeply about the norteño political legacy and his place in it. In the modest world of journalists and academics who write about the region, Ike is totemic, and he spends plenty of time speaking patiently with those who seek him out.

When Ike makes a trip into the woods, he piles into the back of his white Chevy Silverado 2500 HD a chain saw, cans of oil and gas, an ax—not for chopping down trees but good for delimbing ones already fallen—and a shovel. You never know when you're going to get stuck and need to move dirt or mud from around the tires. Also a .22-250 rifle with scope, in case he runs into a bull elk. Piñon nuts, the perfect energy snack, and a six-pack of Budweiser. He tunes the radio to KANW, the only one on the dial to play "New Mexico Spanish music," one of the last great regional music stations in the country that features what is essentially Tex-Mex, performed by local acts, such as Al Hurricane, the patron saint of norteño music.

I get in the truck, in my ill-fitting Wrangler jeans and carrying my daypack. Inside it, there's everything I'd need were I to get lost in the backcountry: GPS, matches, jerky, knife, water, nuts, cell phone, as well as my reporter's notebook. I sit in the passenger seat, the business end of the .22-250 sticking in my left calf. Ike is at the wheel, drinking his first Bud of the day, smoking his American Spirits and occasionally a joint.

It takes only a minute to blow through Servilleta. There was once an actual plaza, Ike says, but it no longer exists. (It met the same fate as Velarde's and those of many other northern communities.) We head north to Petaca, another tiny village completely surrounded by public land. Here we take a Forest Service road west, up onto Jarita Mesa, a much beloved spot among norteños, famous for its herds of wild horses and infamous for several sections that were nearly clear-cut by logging in the early twentieth century. The work was performed by the Hallack and Howard Lumber Company and, later, by Duke City Lumber, which operated a mill in nearby Vallecitos.

We crest a dome-shaped rise and come upon the devastation: the forest suddenly disappears except for yard-high stumps and occasional ponderosa seedlings, none over six feet high. Ike says that these could well be fifteen years old, their growth inhibited by drought. The trees may not reach old-growth diameter for generations, or ever. It is overcast and flurrying as we drive through, making the scene look like nuclear winter.

Ike's eyes constantly scan the land, darting back and forth. Now and then he pokes his head out of the window and looks down. He likes to hunt when there's snow on the ground—the tracks are in perfect relief. Deer and elk drag their feet, leaving long channels as if a snow sled had come through. Coyotes and cats lift their paws and make distinct impressions. Snowshoe hares leave big splayed toe marks that give the appearance of something much bigger tramping through. And in the snow, "if an animal's shot and wounded," Ike says, "the blood will lead us right to him."

The morning goes by languorously, and then midday leaps to late afternoon, when time seems to stop altogether.

The shift from subject to subject in our constant conversation is as slippery as time. The land, forest, animals, Vietnam, the pain in Ike's body, norteño history—it all blends into one vast yet intimate subject. "Asina, bro," Ike likes to say, using an emphatic bilingualism that captures it all: Asina is a norteño archaism of the basic Spanish "así," meaning "like that." Asina el elk appeared in a clearing. Asina los jodi'os—those assholes, he says, swallowing the final *d* in the manner of rural Spanish—planted the drugs on him. ¡Asina ve! Look! he shouts, pointing to a burl bulging from a ponderosa trunk. "Asina" is a word Oñate would have used in 1598, wondering about how to climb the mesa in his assault on Acoma. "Asina," he would have told his captains, pointing to fissures in the cliff face. That way.

"Asina nos vendemos," Ike says. That's the way we sell out. Asina, bro. That's the way it is.

. . .

I wouldn't have seen the horses if Ike hadn't pointed them out. Standing perfectly still in a small clearing about fifty yards away, a black stallion faces us. He is protecting the mares—four of them, one clearly pregnant—and two yearlings. Ike stops the truck. We look at them, and they look at us. The midmorning sun is behind them and shines directly on the stallion, adding shimmer to his shiny coat, a collection of lazy flies his corona. He turns to the mares and takes a step toward them, all the urging they need to head deeper into the forest and away from us. Then he comes back around and faces us again—the movement very slow and deliberate, the minimal display making his point all the more powerfully. He is telling us to move on.

Ike says that he had a young mare in a corral on his property. A wild stallion came down from the mesa, broke down the fence, and stole her away.

The horses animate for me every Western fantasy I was weaned on—including the notion that these herds are direct descendents from the mounts of the early Spanish conquistadores, the progeny of the very horses that Espejo, Coronado, and Oñate rode. The horses also are a serious problem for local ranchers because they compete with cattle and sheep on grazing allotments. (And unlike sheep and cattle, the horses forage year-round in the mountains.) At the ranchers' insistence, the Forest Service contracted a wrangling outfit from Texas to trim the herds. The agreement called for one hundred horses to be removed. The wranglers got only three, defaulted on the contract, and left with several broken arms and legs.

"Asina, los jodi'os learned their lesson," says Ike. "It's easier said than done to get those caballos off this land."


When we started out the snow was deeply rutted with the tracks from other trucks. Now, at a higher elevation, there is denser forest, deeper snow, and only animal tracks.

Ike stops suddenly.

"Asina ve, that's the track of a bull elk. Looks like he's by himself."

He was a hunter in Vietnam, too. He took his reconnaissance training in Okinawa. Drills wouldn't commence without at least a small-craft-warning level of wind and waves. A typical exercise would include five-man teams in rubber boats, at night, ordered to rendezvous with a submarine in the dark. Ike says he's spent the last forty years trying to forget about it all.

He says that norteños served with Teddy Roosevelt's Rough Riders (their Spanish-speaking skills were welcomed). And even further back. The Indian Wars: Hispanos knew the natives well—they'd been living with them, and often fighting them, for three hundred years before the gringos showed up. World War I, World War II, Korea, Vietnam, the first Persian Gulf, and back again to Iraq and Afghanistan. His nephew was in Iraq in 1991, returned home, and is losing his eyesight and hearing. Ike thinks it's from the depleted uranium rounds they were using for ammo.

When we come upon a crossing or a fork, Ike downshifts, slows almost to a stop. He looks one way, the other, pops the truck into neutral, and then, at the very last possible moment, makes a decision. I see him nod his head just a bit, his memory of the land and his desire leading him on.

He pokes his head out his window and down at the snow again.

"Nice-sized buck," he says. "We're getting closer."

Ike has been hunting since childhood. Every part of the animal is used for something. The teeth, antlers, meat, skin. He killed his first deer when he was ten years old. He was in the mountains with his father and they spotted it near the road. Ike asked his father if he could shoot it. His father said, No, you're too young. Ike insisted and took a shot. I think you hit it, his father said, "vamos a ver." They found the deer a short distance away. Ike looked into its vacant eyes and at a reflection of himself.

Hunting, Ike says, is five percent shooting talent, five percent tracking ability, and ninety percent luck.

"You see it?" he whispers suddenly. "You see it?"

To the left of the road, in a clearing about twenty-five yards away, the bull stands motionless, his head turned slightly, staring straight at us. In the few seconds it takes Ike to brake, turn off the engine, pick up the rifle, open the door, and step out of the truck, the elk has disappeared into the forest.

By the time I get out of the truck, Ike is at least ten paces ahead of me. I feel like I'm on a dance floor and don't know the moves; I try to follow his. He steps forward slowly, boots coming down soft on the snow, slightly crouched, holding the rifle with both hands except when he has to move a branch out of the way. Somehow, he avoids twigs and branches on the ground without looking down. I snap several.

I lost sight of the bull immediately after he bounded into the trees, but Ike sees him for a while longer, and tracks him a few dozen yards before stopping.

To me, the bull looked magnificent, wildlife royalty.

"Just an old rag bull," Ike says, an elk banished from his herd. "Now you see them, now you don't. They're like apparitions sometimes. Asina, bro."

We climb up into the aspen country. Which means graffiti, messages carved into the bark with pocketknives by "borregueros"—shepherds—leaving their mark. The older the carvings, the more difficult it is to discern the name or the figure, due to the stretching of the bark as the tree grows. The borregueros have been mostly Mexican immigrants for a long while now. If *Brokeback Mountain* were set in the present, the protagonists would be a couple of young guys from Guanajuato.

"The Hispanos," Ike says, "don't want to work the land no more." The elder's lament. A young Hispano activist like Miguel Santistevan would say: *You need to take the kids out to the forest with you—you can't expect them to follow if you don't lead*. But Miguel is down below, where you can grow crops. There are only a few young mountain activists, it seems, not many young Hispano borregueros, only a handful of junior loggers. The young have gone away, to España and its twenty-four/seven trouble, to LANL and its steady wages and benefits, to Santa Fe or Albuquerque or Southern California.

Ike says he has a firewood permit and a Christmas tree permit from the Forest Service. (He once proclaimed to me that he never bought a permit for anything.) "La floresta," he says, using the norteño term for the Forest Service, "is asking you to pay them for the work *they* should be doing." That is, thinning what Ike believes is a terribly overgrown forest.

"La floresta should be paying *me* for helping thin the forest," he says. "Why should they pull me over? Am I the Osama bin Laden, the Saddam Hussein of the forest? Está jodi'o."

I sense a flash of the Ike that led norteños in crusades against the Forest Service and "enviros." Thirty years of organizing, of conference talks and strategy meetings and factional intrigue, of being surveilled and framed and calling your lawyer and giving depositions, talking to reporters and writing letters to the editor. That'll turn your hair as white as the top of a thunderhead.

He worked hard, partied hard, and won some battles, including overturning Sam Hitt and the Forest Guardians' injunction against gathering firewood. Pressure from community activists galvanized by Ike de Vargas was at least partly responsible for the exit of Duke City Lumber, a large corporation that Ike claims routinely overcut its pre-scriptions in the Vallecitos Sustained Yield Unit, where it had been the designated operator. Duke City's departure—the result of years of His-pano organizing—opened the doors to the possibility of community-based sustainable logging and regional autonomy, the embodiment of la querencia, the communal ethos Miguel Santistevan talked to me about when I first arrived in the north, a philosophy rooted in both Hispano and Native American tradition. But instead of presenting a united front to take over the mill abandoned by Duke City, at least two Hispano fac-tions emerged and claimed rights to the timber of the VYSU, includ-ing the La Manga section, prized by Ike and Sam Hitt alike. Ike led one of the factions, establishing a firm called La Compañía Ocho, claiming that his outfit was the only one with the expertise necessary to run the mill. On the cusp of beginning the new Hispano-run venture, a series of setbacks: a new wave of lawsuits from environmentalists, more bureau-cratic obstacles from the Forest Service, feckless mediation from then-congressman Bill Richardson, and the devastating Cerro Grande Fire of 2000. The mill remains silent today.

Ike's forest is the land in which his distant forebear Diego de Vargas walked, hunted, sowed, and spilled Indian blood. Not that Ike invokes de Vargas as a relative very often. He might have the blue eyes of the conquistador, but Ike believes his blood is as mixed as a mutt's. He likes to emphasize the blending of Pueblo and Hispano, the Greeks and Poles and Irish and Arabs who arrived in the north with the Chili Line and the Hallack and Howard Lumber Company, the motley stream of migrants that came after reading the breathless dispatches of Charles Fletcher Lummis. No one has a pure claim to the land, Ike believes, and surviving land grants—or those that might one day be reclaimed—should not remain the exclusive preserve of the direct descendants of the original grantees. New Mexican history is such a tangle that claims dating to the sixteenth century can have no meaningful validity in the narrow sense, he says. The grants should remain a matter of international law—the Treaty of Guadalupe Hidalgo—but must admit the demographic of present-day New Mexico. Just as rights to the acequias pass with the deed of property to new owners, no matter their race or connection to the families of the original deed, the commons—the heart of the land grant—should be for all who live on it today. This pits Ike against other norteño elders, who would rather the gringos were gone, period. Both positions—cultural nationalist on the one hand and Marxist-tinged internationalist on the other—are intensely idealistic, because both imagine a world other than the one that exists.

On one road trip, Ike tells me about how you can get in trouble in the forest. A guy was struck by lightning and survived to tell the tale—only to die when he was struck a second time. Once, Ike himself got turned around in a heavy fog and couldn't find his way back to the truck for hours. And there was a time with Antonio junior, his only son, when the boy was about ten years old, that they took a snowmobile trip on a day when a blizzard swept in. About eight or nine miles from the truck, they hit a snowbank several feet deep, which pinned the snowmobile. Ike gave little Antonio, teeth chattering, his jacket, and got on his hands and knees to flatten the snow as much as he could. It was so cold that even the snowmobile's skis were frozen stuck. After several unsuccessful attempts to jump the vehicle out, he noticed a tall pine snag up the hill. He'd empty the snowmobile of gas and torch the tree—as a rescue signal and for warmth. He decided one last time to try to get the snowmobile out. He told Antonio to fire up the engine, throttle it all the way and if he got free to just keep on going—not to stop, not to worry about his dad, he'd catch up. Antonio fired the engine and blasted out of the snowbank.

But there came a time when Ike could not save his son, now a man, tall at six-foot-four. He never got in any real trouble, just occasionally driving around drunk; not a mean bone in his body, says Ike. Antonio junior lived in Albuquerque and worked as a mason setting the coping around swimming pools. On one job, he got caught in the crossfire between a coke-dealing, check-stealing coworker and someone's irate boyfriend. While Antonio was waiting in the passenger seat of the coworker's truck, the boyfriend fired a shotgun. Part of the shell went in one side of Antonio's skull and out the other.

"That's the thing," Ike says. "He didn't know what hit him. He didn't suffer."

At the trial, the defendant copped to involuntary manslaughter—maximum sentence eighteen months. Ike addressed the court before sentencing. He began by saying that the court was in contempt for even considering the proceedings to be just. He did not ask for the maximum sentence, because, he said, the sentence would be meaningless. Turn him loose, Ike told the judge. Turn this cokehead loose on the streets. His own kind would make sure he got what he deserved.


Ike calls the last decade of his life his "unlucky streak." His son was murdered. Ike was in a head-on car crash, and the VA hospital's doctors almost killed him. His dream of a norteño-run lumber mill failed. Both his parents died.

Now I understand him better when he says he's retired. He drags hard, keeps the smoke in, shifts gears with the hand holding the joint, exhales, and continues talking. Then the cough comes. It's an almost metallic raking sound from far back in his throat. There's a rhythmic hacking in sets of about six, followed by a quick, wheezing gasp for air. Ike's head rocks back and forth with each cough, his shoulders hunch together, his right hand balls into a fist on his mouth, like a singer bringing the microphone close.

If it's a really bad fit, he'll slow the truck to a stop. An attack can last for a few minutes. I look ahead, at the snowy-mud ruts in the road, at the cracked bark of a yellow-belly, down at my notes, but I cannot look at Ike, even if what I feel like doing is putting my hand on his shoulder to bring him close, to rock back and forth with him to the rhythm of the spasms.

When it ends, there are tears in his eyes, which are now more blood-shot than before.

He opens a new can of Bud, puts the truck in gear, and drives higher up the mountain.

## 8.

The asking price for the house is $249,000. You can buy an acre and a mobile home for much less than half that in the vicinity. When I ask Wilfred Gutierrez, Velarde's activist elder, if he can come by to look at the apple trees, he wants to know the price. I fudge it and say $200,000, the same as when I talk to my writer friend Estevan Arellano, who grouses about gringos in Embudo paying up to $70,000 an acre for undeveloped land. But the embarrassment does not keep us from mov-ing forward.

We offer $210,000.

They counter with $235,000.

We counter with $225,000.

They say 229,000.

I am not around when their last counteroffer comes in—I am in the mountains with Ike, beyond a cell phone signal—and a response is required by the end of the day. Angela must make the decision for both of us.

She thinks I've gone slightly mad with my longing for the land, that I have fallen for the same tropes I criticize. But Angela has her own imaginaries, ones that revolve mostly around idealized homes—which she did not have growing up. Her love for *Little House on the Prairie* is not because of the setting but because the Ingalls tribe survived hard-ship and tragedy through the strength of family ties. (During the years she watched the show, Angela's family was disintegrating.)

This adobe could be our little house, Angela thinks. But she is also a practical woman, clear-eyed and strict with matters of finance, a trait forged by the frequent poverty of her childhood and in which her mother still lives. She runs the numbers. We won't have a cent to spare, but we can come up with the down payment. As for the mortgage, it will be tight until she finishes her degree and gets a job. The question of where that job will be is another matter. Living in Velarde will limit her options to teaching at the University of New Mexico, which hardly recognizes her field, medical anthropology (and is, incidentally, a 240-mile round-trip commute along the Camino Real). There probably should be jobs for someone with her expertise at LANL, so the institution could study its own devastating role in job-related illnesses that disproportionately affect Hispano maintenance workers. But of course there aren't.

The counteroffer deadline is five P.M. Angela is ambivalent. Hoping for illumination, she gets in the Subaru and drives the five minutes to the house. The gate is locked, so she can't pull into the driveway. She parks right there, in the middle of the narrow asphalt strip, and turns off the ignition. She just sits in the car and stares at the house, at its atypically relaxed A-frame roof, at the sumac shoots coming back up after having been whacked down probably only a few months before.

She thinks she's made up her mind—why not?—when the neighbor appears. We hadn't noticed the adjoining house to the north because it was hidden by a sumac jungle, from which the neighbor has just emerged.

He is short, big-bellied, in his late forties or early fifties. He wears a sleeveless T-shirt. The top of his head is bald, with unruly salt-and-pepper curls at the sides. His eyes reddened.

She expects the worst, and of course he gives it.

WHAT THE FUCK ARE YOU DOING HERE?

He is at her window now, which she'd opened earlier to let in the summer breeze.

GET THE FUCK OUT OF HERE! He jabs his finger, bits of foamy saliva flying.

Then come the "whores" and the "cunts" and the "bitches," in English and in Spanish.

Angela does not say a word. She starts up the car and drives away.


We stop looking at real estate.

Time slows in the northern New Mexican winter. I chop wood. Angela knits. We eat lamb stews. I walk on the BLM land in the icy mornings, puffing mist, imagining myself a poblador in the Oñate days or a Pueblo rebel during the revolt of 1680. Angela dotes on Chino, whom she calls "honeybuns" and "Cheeny-bopper" and "Cheenster" and just "Cheeny." He is a strange, perfectly lovable creature, but it's impossible to tell his breed—he's the ultimate coyote. His bark is loud and piercing and fits right into the neighborhood, providing a perfect harmony to his older brother Bear's baritone.

The river is quieter, a distant hiss, the water near the banks turning to ice on the coldest nights, which Joe Rendón's dogs somehow survive. Rose and Jose are quieter, too. Everything turns inward for the season.

The first snow settles on the Black Mesa, looking like a blanket of white that cannot completely hide the tombstones in a cemetery. It is a time of melancholy, or even greater melancholy, in a place suffused with it.

In the north Hispanos mourned the loss of land, landscape, and the means to make a living on it. Displacement began with the Mexican-American War and accelerated during and after the Great Depression. Hispano families emigrated in large numbers because of increasingly limited employment opportunities and the end of the old land-based and subsistence economies. Colonial domination displaced the very structures of identity: connection to place, modes of production and representation, the spiritual life. Depression here is both economic and existential, exacerbated by the dimming of prospects for a better life or even maintaining the life of one's forebears. Thus the stage is set for gentrification: the arrival of outsiders of means is made possible by the differential economic positions of newcomers and natives. Depressed real estate values means an "opportunity" for elites, a "steal." Gentrification needs the dispossession and displacement of an old economic and social order, while it also intensifies those very processes. When the elites arrive they experience a forgotten place with a history to be unearthed, an archaeological adventure, as if the remaining Hispano and Native American populations exist only to offer a window into the past. The land that sustained norteños for four hundred years and Pueblos for much longer is no longer material, but ghostly, a representation of loss, even as for the strangers it is pretty as a postcard.

Angela has spent more than a year working at the detox clinic, at the heart of Hispano loss and depression. Now she seems to internalize this affect. She was never a big outdoors type, but early on she would regularly accompany me on modest hikes. These days I am always alone with the dogs on the commons. When she sleeps late, I ask her if she took pills the night before. At first she always says no, but eventually she confesses.

The people Angela spends the most time with are addicts and their caretakers. Sooner or later, her male subjects, particularly the ones in positions of relative power, proposition her. They note my long absences from home and say that's "no way to treat a woman." We do not have much of a social life. Angela has no real friends in the north. I know several people and call a few of them friends, but they are not intimates. Now the season isolates us even further as the norteños cloister themsevles for the winter.

In this dark place, we somehow decide that Angela will undergo fertility treatment, because we've tried to have children for two years and nothing's happened. During our preparations to conceive life, I find out about what came into my body along with the drugs I abused.

We are in Taos, in the parking lot at Cid's, about to buy some outrageously priced food, when my cell phone rings. The nurse from the fertility clinic tells me that the routine blood panel shows the hepatitis C virus, seven million copies of which course through my veins.

"Really?" I say, loudly, in a strange enough tone that Angela blurts out a concerned "What?"

The nurse passes a message from the doctor: my illness will in no way affect the doctor's ability to use my sperm to fertilize Angela's eggs and implant them in her uterus. She gives me the name of a specialist. "Good luck," she says.

I snap the phone shut and tell Angela. We sit in the car for a long while.

Later, the specialist tells me that I must never drink alcohol. Not even a glass of wine now and then, with dinner? I ask, the addict immediately opening negotiations. None.

A close friend of Angela's who studies epidemiology at Columbia says go ahead and have a glass now and then.

Which I do, "now and then" being just about every day, worrying about my liver each time I take a sip.

On a cold but bright January morning Chino bounds into our bedroom, jumps up on the bed, and kisses Angela awake. Then he props his front paws on the sill of the picture window. He wants out.

I open the side door. It is still below freezing—the frost holds onto the tin roof instead of melting in silvery drops. Knowing that Chino will find a way out of the wire fence, I open the gate at the end of the patio for him.

That morning there is no breeze off the Black Mesa carrying the sound of the river; I hear instead the hollow whoosh of morning traffic on 68, almost all of it heading south—the norteños commuting to Española or Santa Fe or Los Alamos or even Albuquerque.

Chino runs into the yard beyond the gate, pees on the hard stony ground, and takes off in the direction of the garage, the usual starting point of his morning rounds. I go back inside and brew coffee.

At around three o'clock that afternoon, I realize I haven't seen Chino since the morning. I walk out to the dirt road, toward the old cottonwood, look down at the acequia, dry and full of leaves this time of year. I whistle. I call out his name. I look up the road toward the camino de en medio, and call once more.

As I walk back inside the gate something catches my eye in the space between the perimeter wall and the chain-link fence around the house. It is Chino. Even at a distance of twenty yards I know immediately that he is dead.

He had collapsed near a fast-maturing shoot of sumac, at a spot along the fence that had given me headaches since he was old enough to attempt escape—I could never secure it. His head lies between his front paws, which are awkwardly splayed. His eyes are open, seemingly staring straight ahead. It looks like he'd collapsed in mid-step. There is no obvious trauma; we will never know how he died.

Oh Chino, I whisper. I touch his forehead. It is cold, and he is stiff. He probably died shortly after I let him out. Then I realize that I have the terrible task of telling Angela. I could write the cheap psychology of

Chino as surrogate child, of how pure he was when everything around us seemed so corrupted, but what's important is that she loves Chino as part of our family. The season makes it all the crueler. The long winter has brought us closer together for warmth, and it's from this close place that he has been taken.

Angela holds on to me for support as I walk her out to him. She kneels down and kisses his forehead, and as she does so, his eyes close.


These are the darkest days. I don't see the neighbors much. Joe Rendón hardly putters around the yard, and Rose and Jose don't appear for what seems like weeks at a time.

One day I notice a car in the driveway of Lena's trailer. It belongs to Cuchi, Lena's husband. Our relationship centers on talking about growing up in Los Angeles; he tells me that coming to New Mexico saved him from the gang life. I ask him about the kids tagging up the old adobes in Velarde; he dismisses them as "wannabes," no comparison to the vatos of L.A.

I ask Cuchi where he's been.

"I guess you didn't hear that me and Lena split up," he says.

I hadn't, and say I am sorry.

He tells me that after he moved out, Lena sold off everything in the house for drugs. There was nothing left, not even the stove or refrigerator. The news shocks me. Since her overdose, things have been very quiet at the trailer. We live within yards of each other, yet I had no idea what had been going on inside.

Now the trailer is his. "I don't think I'm going to live in it, though," says Cuchi. "How do you get rid of the memories?"


Toward the end of the winter, UPS drops off boxes of fertility drugs and the dozens of syringes to use to deliver them. The last time I had such easy access to clean "works" (as addicts refer to needles) was when my grandfather was dying of cancer. On one of his visits from El Salvador he brought a vitamin cocktail his doctor had prescribed, to be administered by injection. I was working as a journalist then, only a couple of years removed from shooting meth and coke. I stole one of the syringes.

No one ever noticed that it was gone, and my grandfather never missed a dose, but the guilt remained with me, as well as awe at the power of addiction to push an addict to cross any moral border. Armed with my fresh works, I went back to one of my old connections, scored, and brought the drugs home. In the wee hours I got high—too high. I woke up my girlfriend of the time to keep vigil with me until I fell asleep, just as I have done, before and since, with fellow users. I told her to throw away the syringe, swearing, as I'd done many times before, that this was the last time.

Now I am in possession of this box of syringes—big ones, small ones, all in their sterile packaging, an IV drug abuser's dream cache. I think of knocking on Rose and Jose's door. I rehearse the conversation in my mind. I know he would sell me cocaine.

Angela never knows how close I come to doing it.

The cottonwood across the dirt road comes back to life. The old-timers clean the acequias. The pilgrims make their way to Chimayó. I get stuck behind growling tractors on the camino de en medio. The lowriders come out of hibernation, too, cruising the Sonic Burger across from the Walmart in Española. Some apple trees get pruned, and others grow wild. The Rio Grande roars.

We sleep over at Wilma's the night before my appointment at the clinic.

At seven in the morning, while Angela is asleep, I am stuck in rush-hour traffic on I-25. I am nervous. I should have gone to the bathroom before leaving the house. I can't hold it in anymore. I swerve off the highway at the exit for the airport, park, run down an embankment of yellow dirt and sage, squat next to a small juniper bush, and let go. I make it to the appointment on time.

A few hours later, five of my sperm fertilize five of Angela's eggs.

We are at home when the clinic calls with the news. You are pregnant, very.

The first ultrasound is ambiguous. "Triplets," the young Texan endocrine doc says. "And you see that shadow there? Maybe quads." At the next appointment, he says it's definitely triplets. The appointment after that, twins. It stays that way.

Two months later, we snap a picture of Angela's growing belly in front of an adobe wall in Velarde.

Three months later, I get high.


Angela and I begin talking about the future. I think of life in Velarde as open-ended, an eternal present. I am a figure on the land that I love, a contradicted figure on a contradicted land, but on it. Each step I take—hiking in the BLM, trudging up a mountainside with Sam Hitt—makes me feel closer to it.

Angela has other ideas. We are going to raise a family, so we need stability and security. And Angela needs a job; she will soon write and defend her dissertation on heroin addiction in the Española Valley. More important, she had come here to confront the ghosts of her family's addictions, and she has done that—she does not want to live among the ghosts for the rest of her life. And what about our kids—the twins we will name Ruby Graciela and Lucia Simone? The public schools in northern New Mexico are as troubled as any public urban district—gang, drugs, low academic achievement.

In response, I quixotically attempt a back-to-the-land argument. We will live in the high country like D.H. and Frieda (who never had children). I even mention homeschooling. But I can hardly convince myself. It is not 1969 or 1922, and the results of those experiments are clear. Almost all the communes and other modes of alternative living were shortlived and those that have survived are elite, cultish clubs.

I know now that we will be leaving New Mexico.

## 9.

At every chance I get, I go up into the BLM land and into the Carson and Santa Fe National Forests, pushing myself harder and farther. Steeper flanks, ever more remote hikes. I get stuck on mesa cliffs. I dodge lightning in monsoon storms on the sage plain. I roam burnt forests where the wind fells charred snags behind me.

One morning I decide it's time to climb the Black Mesa, a hike I've put off for three years, in part, because I have no idea where and how to approach it. No one I know has been up there, and I've heard rumors of gates locked by Richard Cook, the gravel-mining baron who owns much of the tabletop land.

But one day, while driving toward Servilleta to visit Ike I see and make a mental note of an open gate that appears to approach the mesa from the west side. The topo maps are confusing, with their patchwork of private and public land administered by several different agencies in the area, but I assume it is a public portal precisely because it is open.

I drive over the cattle guard and climb a narrow road barely wide enough for my truck. The road ends in a stand of blooming cholla cactus, the base of the Black Mesa before me.

I scramble up the basalt boulders, meet many dead ends, get stuck with thorns, wax paranoid about snakes, and sweat profusely. It is not a big vertical climb—maybe eight hundred feet—but the chaos of the jagged broken lava makes it difficult.

Concentrating only on my feet and hands for well over an hour, I never once look back over my shoulder during the ascent. So when I crest the final boulder and turn around to the view, I am astonished by its vastness. The mesa squats in the middle of two wide valleys; likely they'd been one before the lava flow. On the western horizon, the fire-scarred girth of the Jemez; to the east, the Sangres, still snowcapped in midsummer. To the north, I can see as far as the mountains of the San Luis Valley in Colorado, about a hundred miles away. The mesa tabletop itself, which I've never seen, is shockingly green with bunchgrasses and junipers.

I cannot see Velarde; I cannot see any of the villages of the north, for that matter. The natural geography hides the human. From here, the north looks completely uninhabited, although the juniper and piñon that dot the valleys almost appear as a huge crowd gathered at the foot of the mesa, like the audience at an outdoor rock festival. I am on the stage, at the center of a universe swirling with cloud and sky, stone and dirt.

There are no gates, no neighbors, no land grants, no Oñate, no Acoma and no Kit Carson, no since forever, no heroin and coke, no LANL, no tourists. The land is not Ike's or Sam's or Richard Cook's. There are no grazing permits because there are no sheep.

I have climbed to a place that seems to be before history. I do not want to return.

But, of course, I do, back down into history, into the forever of my remaining days in Velarde.


We leave in less than two weeks. It is a cold October morning, in the twenties. The cottonwood across the road from the house has burst into yellow. I have been making fires every night and will continue to do so until our last. I've been splitting wood again. The piñon smells sweet and spicy. On windless nights and through calm dawns, the smoke rising from the chimneys of the adobes and trailers becomes a halo over the village.

It is the season of piñon fires and piñon nuts, of "carne seca" (this weekend is the first rifle shoot for deer and elk), of fresh batches of green chile, of magpies combing the recently picked fields for leftovers, of bears coming down to the valleys for their final meals, of elk spooked by the arrival of hunters in the mountains, of first frosts and first snows and the first icicles hanging over the banks of the rivers and streams.

I visit Ike one more time.

The roads are mostly empty. The tourist season is over; the population surge that comes with Albuquerque's world-famous Balloon Fiesta has gone home.

When Ike appears in the doorway of the trailer, I am struck by how his body seems to have shrunk. The taut lightweight fighter's body now looks fragile, especially his legs, which are twiglike.

"Se me aflojan las piernas," he tells me—his legs go rubbery on him and he's been feeling an overall lethargy. Could be his liver, or the aftereffects of his botched surgery. He's been going for weekly phlebotomy sessions. The level of iron in his blood is too high; draining a pint out of him forces his body to produce fresh blood and reduce the iron. It all sounds very medieval.

As usual, Ike and I exchange modest gifts. I give him a copy of a book I bought recently and skimmed, *The New West Atlas*. He hands me a musty, worn manila envelope stuffed with old documents—land grant papers and clippings from the local press. These are from the days of Ike the young firebrand.

"I was going to throw them away," he says of the papers, reminding me that he considers himself retired from "la política." Now he is just a man of the forest.

Our original plan is to go out to gather wood for latillas, but on the spur of the moment, Ike decides he wants to go fishing. He digs up some worms in the wet, dark earth beneath the shade trees. Just a few paces away is a grave marker of carved wood. This is where Antonio junior is buried.

Our destination is the Rio Vallecitos. We head west from La Madera, past the village of Cañon Plaza, past a rusting lumber mill, and finally off the paved road and into the mountains. Ponderosa country. It is late morning, but the chill of the night is still in the air. There are still signs of the monsoon, tufts of green bunchgrass, a few wildflowers—but these are overwhelmed by the turning of the season, the rattling of dead leaves in the wind, the graying of the land.

The road we are on becomes faint, almost completely overgrown, an old logging route descending toward the gorge. We park alongside an "ojito," a stream that feeds the Vallecitos. We see plenty of elk sign and some cow pies, but we are the only humans. As we follow the ojito down to the river, Ike drinks a Bud and tosses the can. I wince.

The Vallecitos is running with a moderate late-season flow of glassy swells over smooth, round boulders. The steep walls of the gorge are thickly wooded, so we can't even see the ridgelines. I follow Ike, who is following a game trail along the riverside.

I have been fishing only a couple of times in my life, and I have no idea what I'm doing. He threads the line for me, attaches sinker and hook, and then pierces the worm.

"Asina," he says, "into la corriente. Just watch me."

He pulls some slack with his finger low on the pole and then flicks his wrist, letting the slack go. The hook and sinker hit water, the current twirling the line just a bit before it starts pulling it downriver.

I try to imitate Ike. Sometimes the line hits more or less where I want it to; most of the time it lands where it wants to. He makes the first catch, and the second and third, before I make my first. A sudden tension, a quick jerking—it is easy to visualize the fish snapping its head back and forth. Instinctively I pull the line up and over to the shore and the fish flops onto the rocks. I shout to Ike, "I've got one!"

A silvery brown trout, a few dark freckles, unblinking eye looking straight at me, or so it feels, gasping for water. Ike fashions a fish tote out of a branch. This is the only fish I will catch. A grand total of four between us in three hours.

At times I lose sight of Ike, and I worry that he's slipped on a rock and hit his head. He does slip several times, but he never goes down; I slip too, and get increasingly nervous leaping across the wet stones. As bad as he says he feels, as fragile as he looks, I can't replicate some of my elder's agile moves.

After about an hour, we take a break, eat some carne seca, and smoke a couple of cigarettes.

"They're not biting today," he says finally.

It doesn't matter.

We're in the truck again, rolling across the land, and Cerro Pedernal comes into view, brooding in the late afternoon light of autumn, in sharp contrast to the airiness of O'Keeffe's rendering.

I ask Ike a question I'd been meaning to for a long while. What is behind the gulf between the different gazes upon the land? I have fallen for this landscape like the city slickers, I tell him, the Easterners, the midwesterners who upon arriving are smitten—there is no other way of describing it—by Western space, by its distance and elevation, by the shapes that are icons: the mesas and buttes and stands of yellow-bellied ponderosa. And by the characters that are icons: the Indian and the Mexican and the gringo frontiersman, scheming or valiant, mystical or dumb, noble or ruthless. By the bigness of the narrative and the symbolism, the desire of empire, the trauma of it, the guilt of it, the resistance against it, the adventure of it.

I'm rambling. "Do you know what I mean?" I ask him.

"I know exactly what you mean," he says. "Mira, it's not just the outsiders that fall for it. It's the locals, too, the ones who've gone away and come back."

Ike's cousin, for example, who has lived in Pomona, California, for forty years. Now he's retired, and he and his wife come out to visit every other month or so. They are among the people who complain that the locals don't appreciate what they have and accuse them of abusing it, what with their tossing cans of Bud out of their cars, carving up the land with ATV tracks, dumping refrigerators into the gorge.

Ike tells his cousin that he's become one of those tree-hugging gringos.

But why is it okay for Ike to toss a can into the forest?

"They stole this land from us!" Ike says, reaching the heart of his Hispano rage. "Now we can't make a living off of it. We have to get permits from the people who stole it from us to do what our forefathers did for generation after generation, not with permits but with legal deeds that according to the Treaty of Guadalupe Hidalgo were to be respected by the United States government."

So, he's saying that tossing a can of Bud is a kind of resistance?

"That's exactly what I'm saying. Asina, bro. They come here and they see it, they fall in love with it, they want to save it like a damsel in distress. But they're pulling the same power trip that the old logging companies did. Same as the Santa Fe Ring. It doesn't matter that they're trying to save the spotted owl or old-growth yellow-bellies. The forest isn't theirs to save. They go crazy. Están locos.

"They love it so much," Ike says, "that they can't leave it alone." They love it so much, that they want to buy it. That they think they can tell people who were born here how to treat it.

"So let them," he says acidly, "pick up my Bud cans."

A little while later Ike's bitterness gives way to an expansive, inclusive vision: Declare the mountains a "semiautonomous region" in which land grant heirs and recent arrivals decide not just how to use the land but even how it should be seen. Rewrite the history that was rewritten. Rebaptize the places that were renamed. Dismantle the Forest Service bureaucracy, reinhabit history like Miguel Santistevan and his cohort on the farms down below. Start up new projects based on the old Depression-era Civil Conservation Corps model. Jobs for locals thinning the forest, restoring the watershed . . .

Stirred by the vision, I almost ask Ike if Sam Hitt could serve on the new regional council.

We are back at the trailer. Ike guts the trout in a tub of water, bags them in a ziplock and hands them to me.

"Nothing like fresh fish," Ike says.

. . .

Several months after the neighbor chased Angela away, I drive by the house we almost bought, which has finally been sold. There is a white Subaru in the driveway, but nobody seems to be home. I am wondering how the new arrivals are getting on when I peer through the sumac thicket next door. It looks as if there has been an explosion; the house is turned inside out. Scattered around the yard are a rotting mattress, a half-burnt couch, a refrigerator lying on its side. Someone has tried to board up the windows, but the local kids must have pried the plywood off and left their graffiti tags.

At the house we almost bought, the apple trees have been pruned. I want to know whether a young family lives there or gringo retirees or a neo-hippie back-to-the-land couple. I wonder what they've seen, what they've heard of their neighbors.


Angela is in Albuquerque for the weekend. I'm supposed to be getting some writing done. I'd scored in Los Angeles a year before. The addict knows how to stash.

I greet the dawn high, exhausted, and guilty, sitting at my desk in the attic.

Later in the morning I hear Rose cough outside her house. I come to the window and perch the way Angela does when we spy on the neighbors, on the floor, knees drawn up, chin atop an arm draped over the sill. I watch Rose resting there in the sun for a long time.

Rose did not know that I talked to her that morning. She never knew how close I was.

# WHERE THE RIVER BENDS

### 1.

Often as not, artist colonies host writers' retreats. The Lannan Foundation, which awarded me a generous fellowship, has one in the town of Marfa, Texas, which achieved fame as a creative enclave during the boom years. The Lannan residency program, established in 2000, is itself a sign of the town's transformation. The foundation bought five houses and a storefront in Marfa, keeping the exteriors quaint and rustic while renovating the interiors with modernist precision: white walls, blond cabinetry, stainless steel appliances. I wrote a good part of this book during my stay.

By the time of my residency, I had already visited Marfa and the Big Bend region several times, drawn by the fantastic light and space of West Texas, and by its proximity to the border. Like most of the art colonies in the region, its roots were in the Old Western economy (cattle ranching, oil). Hollywood had put the town on the map when it came calling in the 1950s to shoot *Giant*, the cast and crew moving into the Hotel Paisano, where there is still an Elizabeth Taylor Suite. But the origin of the colony itself was the arrival in 1979 of Donald Judd, the legendary "nonrelational" artist, a minimalist master who has become so cultishly revered that "WWDJD?" (What Would Donald Judd Do?) bumper stickers and buttons have become a kind of Masonic handshake in the art world.

Judd perfectly fit the role of art colony pioneer. He started his career in New York, establishing a studio in SoHo long before it was branded with high-end galleries. Colony founders must be iconoclasts, and after two decades of promoting himself to the top of the art world—he

garnered a retrospective at the Whitney before he was forty—he was
ready for a turn as a visionary.

He was first introduced to Marfa as a young man, during a long trip
west from Alabama to Los Angeles en route to a military deployment. The
year was 1946. The place made enough of an impression then for him to
telegraph his mother with a glowing comment about the landscape. He
returned three decades later, fleeing what he called the "harsh and glib
situation within art in New York."

Like my boho cohort in Joshua Tree, Judd marveled at the real estate
prices, which, compared to those in lower Manhattan, were astonishingly cheap. Marfa, like the ranching that had sustained it, was well
past its prime, and its population was in steep decline. Judd snatched
up some 40,000 acres of ranchland with the help of the Dia Art
Foundation—bankrolled by the Houston oil heiress Philippa de Menil
and her husband, Heiner Friedrich, a German art dealer. And in the
town itself he bought property that had once comprised Fort D. A. Russell and earlier military facilities dating back to 1911. After a successful
suit against Dia for breach of contract, the land became his.

The counterculture at the time revered such acts of "dropping out,"
and Judd was simultaneously dipping into some of the oldest tropes of
the American colonial imagination: the trip west, the close encounter
with a hard land and its ghosts, the lonesome figure on the far plain.
That he was walking into a place that still bore the marks of severe segregation along the lines of race and class does not figure into any of the
accounts—almost all hagiographic—of Judd's journey.

As for Judd himself, he would probably have been irritated by any
critic attempting a historical and social contextualization. (And he might
have defended himself by arguing that his politics were on the right side
of history—decrying U.S. interventionism abroad and the conditions of
impoverished inner cities at home in the 1960s and '70s.)

In Marfa, Judd created permanent works that he meticulously sited
on the land, most notably, an array of aluminum boxes in an old military installation. In his will he stipulated that they never be moved.
There is no evidence that he considered the possibility that his work,
and the fulsome attention it generated, would result in a wave of gentrification that re-created in Marfa the very atmosphere that drove him
from New York in the first place.

By the time I came to Marfa, the Chinati Foundation, which Judd founded after his feud with Dia, was a bona fide site of international art pilgrimage. An independent bookseller, the Marfa Book Company, had established itself in a smartly rehabbed building next to the town's only stoplight. A high-end restaurant called Maiya's had snagged a Rhode Island School of Design graduate for a chef. Galleries with brilliant white walls and track lighting displayed lots of canvases with anything but a recognizable figure on them. And hot young kids were hanging out, some of them with real money and some of them flirting with it.

And this was just the beginning. Before the economy pitched into the abyss in 2008, more haute eateries arrived. The most notable was Cochineal, housed in a converted adobe, featuring a chef imported straight from Manhattan who picked the ultraorganic lettuce himself from his own vegetable garden. Even the more down-home places kicked it up a notch; the town's pizza joint served salads with designer greens, strawberries, walnuts, and feta in a fine vinaigrette. From a vintage 1974 Butter Krust bread truck parked a block from the bookstore, a scruffy art couple sold Mediterranean-themed lunch fare with a sound track of Americana wafting from a tinny horn speaker. (Everyone highly recommends the Marfalafel plate, falafel and tahini transformed with Tex-Mex peppers and wrapped in local color—a white-flour tortilla, *mais sans* lard.) The overall effect of the galleries, eateries, and postmodern art cowboys and cowgirls was *The Last Picture Show* meets Silver Lake or Williamsburg, with Texas-sized investment portfolios and trust funds.

Marfa had all the ingredients for a latter-day colony. The landscape was perfect: the town sat on an immense grassy plain. There was oil several dozen miles north, around Balmorhea, but Marfa had been cattle country, and the waning of the industry tantalized the imaginations of liberal Texan millionaires (there are a few) with the possibility of buying up hundreds of thousands of acres to create huge swaths of land that could be reclaimed to a "pristine" state. The Davis Mountains, painterly with their combination of lyrical and violent features—notches and domes, faces of stone and bands of forest—were far enough away to shade blue with distance.

Marfa's second boom began slowly after Judd rolled into town; his arrival brought a few other artists, who also bought up land on the cheap. The newcomers were romanced by the signs of the past. There were railroad tracks, upon which trains clacked through a couple of times a day, meaning you could hear bona fide train whistles. The tracks, of course, also meant that there was another side of them, where the "Mexicans" lived; that's what they called themselves, and what everyone else called them, too, in spite of the fact that many of them were second- or third- or fourth-generation on this side of the border, speaking Spanglish, English with a Mexican accent, and Spanish with a gringo accent. On that other side of the tracks sat the adobe ruin of the town's old segregated school.

So: lots of land, lots of old adobes, lots of light and space, Old Mexican and gringo "characters"—the salt of the earth working farms and nurseries, crusty ranchers and ranch hands, guy-guys. And the Rio Grande was just below the plain, John Wayne and John Ford's Great River, on the other side of which was Mexico.

There was a fair amount of iconic Western history in the area, too, bandits and revolutionaries and refugees streaming across the river during the Mexican Revolution. You could see the aesthetics of the first boom in the fabulously ornate Second Empire architecture of the Presidio County Courthouse, which anchored the town center. There was plenty of iconic Western-style action in the present as well, with the smuggling of drugs and people. The Border Patrol Sector Headquarters was just a few blocks away from the art scene downtown, and a large aerostat, a tethered blimp equipped with radar, floated over the plains on the main highway leading to town from the north. Smuggling was a border enterprise, involving legions of people on both sides of the line, brown and white, powerful and powerless. The Mexican narco legend Pablo Acosta had operated out of Ojinaga, the major Mexican town across the river from Presidio. In the 1980s, Acosta's operation shipped massive amounts of coke, heroin, and marijuana, inspiring many a narco ballad. But the Americans were not to be outdone. Presidio County sheriff Rick Thompson was a self-proclaimed "drug buster" and a man with impressive political connections, all the better to provide cover for his own narco operation, which involved storing 2,241 pounds of cocaine—worth hundreds of millions of dollars (up to $1 billion by one estimate)—in a horse trailer on the Presidio County Fairgrounds. Thompson is currently serving a life sentence.

There was even some Western-weird kitsch, an important ingredient in the recasting of the town as an art center and tourist destination. The Marfa lights drew a stream of people altogether distinct from the Judd crowd and probably in greater numbers. The lights were a genuine Western mystery. From a viewpoint on the highway outside town, one could see balls of pale luminescence appear and disappear on the horizon in what was thought to be a completely uninhabited area. A recent scientific study posited convincingly that the phenomenon could be attributed to a mundane source: car headlights on a distant highway, distorted by an optical illusion. But that study didn't deter the visitors, who wondered whether the lights weren't really troubled Indian spirits or the ghosts of Spanish explorers still searching for gold out there on the searing plain.

(The ghosts were in the material world. The study did not specify who was actually driving that lonely road in the middle of the night, but it was really no mystery at all—most of the traffic on it was related to trade, legal and not. Trucks hauling goods assembled cheaply in Mexico, trucks hauling drugs, trucks hauling the bodies of Mexican laborers.)

The landscape is as John Fordesque as Monument Valley, and Hollywood arrived for several productions, before and after *Giant*. On a lonely scenic route that parallels the Rio Grande into the Big Bend sits an abandoned movie set that dates back to the 1931 shoot for *Contrabando*, a pioneering Mexican talkie. The set includes the façades of a church and other rustic village buildings, on a bluff just a few dozen yards off the river. Practically any shot taken in the village is crowned with a dramatic butte. The TV miniseries adaptations of Larry McMurtry's *Dead Man's Walk* and *Streets of Laredo* were shot here in the 1990s.

Most of all, there was space, Western immensity. The area has one of the vastest stretches of land in the Lower 48 with the fewest people and roads and human-built structures. Almost all the land (aside from Big Bend National Park) is privately held and fenced. It had been heavily grazed for generations, Texas-style, with ranchers buying entire mountains, such as the pinto-colored domes and folds of Chinati Peak, which surges dramatically from the plain and dominates the landscape even from a hundred miles away. Although the ranching life was greatly diminished, there were still several working operations in the area.

The region had been branded Far West Texas in the late 1880s by geologists in Austin, and the moniker symbolically served the area well. It was way out there. Distance equals difference, and in the West, difference is one of the few sustainable commodities.

All Marfa needed to really take off was a major piece of journalism in a national medium. The *New York Times* obliged, publishing an article in 2005 by a writer named Julia Lawlor, who authored several travel-and-real-estate pieces for the paper during the boom. Most of her stories sold destinations and properties to the gentry of what the *Times* itself heralded as the New Gilded Age.

The story begins with Mary Farley, a Manhattan psychotherapist, buying three "decrepit one-story adobe buildings" whose only inhabitants were a "family of bats." Farley plans to renovate all three, keeping one as her residence and converting the others to art studios. There follows a quick cautionary tale about fellow Manhattanites Tom Rapp and Toshi Sakihara, who buy an adobe without looking inside it only to discover structural disaster. But the couple, who eventually open Marfa's toniest restaurant, turn the property around to another second-home seeker, for a $30,000 profit.

The story includes a brief mention that the newcomers are arriving in a town with severe social schisms: "Marfa real estate is beyond the means of lower-income residents, many of them Latinos who make up about 60 percent of the population." But that did not slow the invasion the article helped foment.

The final paragraph contains a classic of the genre: the older gentry's lament about the new. Two early investors talk about arriving when Marfa was still an "unspoiled beauty." One of them is Eugene Binder, a New York art dealer. "I liked it the way it was," he says. "I got here before they put in street signs." Binder spends four months of the year in Marfa. The other grump is Aedwyn Darroll, another New York artist, who moved in not long after Judd's death. "There's all the phoniness of the art world," he laments, "the art-speak stuff. It's exactly what I was trying to get away from in the city."

It was, of course, the likes of Judd, Binder, and Darroll who brought the art world they're now lamenting when others of their ilk followed them. But they could not see in themselves the despoliation they attributed to others, even though that is likely what the Mexicans and old Anglo families thought of them.

In all, the story was free publicity for Marfa real estate agents, in particular native-born Valda Livingston, who had been handling properties in town for three decades and was perfectly positioned when the storm hit. The *Times* ran the piece in the news section online but barely made an effort to conceal its raison d'être, adding an appendix of property listings, including the names and phone numbers of the realtors.

After the *Times*' front-page treatment came other stories, most of them indulging a syrupy Old Western mythos even as they promoted the postmodern art town, but a few mined a much more critical vein. One case in point was a weighty article in the online magazine *Salon*, detailing the growing rift between the affluent newcomers and the native families over future development. (The Chinati Foundation, for example, vigorously opposed a subdivision on which a developer would have built relatively affordable cookie-cutter ranchettes, while many of the natives welcomed the plan.) But stories like those ultimately served as more publicity for the very phenomenon they were nominally critiquing, and they, too, erased the other Marfa—the town of old ranchers, Mexicans, and the poor—since almost every word represented the new one.

## 2.

Valda Livingston is from the other Marfa, the one before Judd and even *Giant,* and she wants to set the record straight. She is a big woman with brittle blond hair and a face that seems drawn by stress. This is her hometown, and she has sold a good part of it to the new gentry. She is Marfa's top real estate agent.

Marfa, she wants the world to know, is not some cornball place, which is the impression that comes across in a lot of "those articles," she says, glancing at my notebook. Marfa has been ranching people, she tells me, honorable, hardworking people. Marfa has been families that sent their kids to good schools.

"There was, you know, a certain sophistication."

When Judd was alive, a trickle of people came through, but only a handful thought of buying in. The Old Western town was still dying. Judd became more famous in death, however, and his departure (1994, of lymphoma) occurred just as the economy began to recover from the recession of the early part of the decade, building the ramp for the tech bubble a few years later. Then they arrived, from Houston and Dallas and New York and California.

When I interview her at the Marfa Book Company, it is only a few months since the *New York Times* article, and she is still playing "catch-up."

"Sometimes I felt like I was hanging people on hooks," she says. "Someone seated in front of me, someone outside the door, someone on the phone, a fax coming in and e-mail jammed."

Properties that sold for $25,000 the year before are currently on the market for $100,000—and the bubble is still inflating. Now Valda has an assistant working for her.

"Someone from town?" I ask.

"No, she's from New York. She's bought three places herself."

In the window appears a man with a bottlebrush mustache and a big yellow-white Stetson-style hat. He is not an artist. He is a rancher, a cowboy. But he looks like a painting.

The town's population has remained stable, at about twenty-five hundred, which means that, generally speaking, for every person moving in there is another moving out—outlanders replacing the natives, largely the creative class replacing ranching families.

Valda is facilitating much of this movement, but even she's ambivalent about the new money pouring in from the "fat cats." Not the ones she's selling Marfa to, but the *really* rich ones, like Austin gazillionaire Steve Smith, who pumped $100 million into the Lajitas Resort, on the banks of the Rio Grande just north of Big Bend State Park. Previous to Smith, the land included a nine-hole golf course and an RV park. Smith bought in 2000, and what he wrought here was an outsized variation of what the new haute classes were doing all over the country: the nine holes became eighteen; he built the exclusive Ultimate Hideout, a ninety-two-room luxury hotel specifically with burnt-out CEOs like himself in mind, those men hard at work making and remaking the world; and he envisioned selling lots and homes on the 27,000-acre holding.

But Lajitas is on the border. Wherever you go on the resort, you have a view of Mexico and Mexicans, which means that Smith's hideout couldn't avoid being in the known world, after all. Lajitas never turned a profit and ultimately declared bankruptcy. There was another über-resort in the area. Cibolo Creek Ranch was reserved for A-list Holly-wood and rock 'n' roll royalty.

Valda just wishes they'd go back to where they came from.


Borunda's Bar is one of the few places in Marfa these days that is not haute.

When I walk in, there is no one around but the proprietor, Pancho Borunda, and a life-size cardboard cutout of a trio of Budweiser girls in black minidresses. Pancho cuts a Falstaffian-biker figure, with a long, gray-and-white beard. The first thing he wants me to know is that he does not serve specialty drinks.

"I have people coming in all the time asking me for mineral water with lime," he says, rolling his eyes. "They even ask me what I cooked my beans in."

The "artsy-fartsy types," he says, are disappointed to learn that he uses "manteca"—lard. "You want Mexican beans? You have to use manteca," he says.

Pancho's aunt ran a restaurant in town for years. She cooked on a woodstove. There was one hard rule if you ate at her place: no spirits. She allowed her patrons to bring in two beers and no more. If anyone was caught nipping, Tía would come running from the kitchen with a frying pan.

Pancho says he left town for the navy, was stationed in Spokane, and led a whole life up there, twenty-three years. He returned to Marfa ten years ago, "before all this happened."

When he left Marfa, the town was barely emerging from segregation.

"The Mexicans couldn't go across the railroad tracks after ten at night," Pancho tells me.

And the only place the Mexicans could swim was a little sliver of Alamito Creek that wasn't fenced in—a miracle in these parts, where there is so little public land and every inch of the private is fenced off. Alamito Creek runs across the entire Marfa Plain and tumbles down the escarpment that ends at the Rio Grande. At the wettest points, cot-tonwoods and grasses grow, stunning oases amid the brutality of the surrounding desert. Pancho remembers monsoon storms when he was a kid, big thunderheads letting loose over the Davis Mountains, ribbons of water flowing down the canyons and filling the creek.

"That was like our entertainment," he says.

If Valda Livingston were in the bar right now, there would be a great reality-TV moment, because a fight would break out. When I asked her about Marfa's segregated past, her cheeks reddened. "I don't think there was any discrimination until someone put that in their heads," she said. "They had the same opportunities as everyone else."

Notwithstanding Livingston's claims of equal opportunity, the town was and is neatly divided by the railroad tracks. Long past *Brown v. Board of Education*, Mexican students could only attend the Blackwell School from kindergarten through eighth grade; Marfa's movie theaters and churches were also segregated.

Now there is a lot of brown movement, in and out. Some of the older Mexican-American families have sold to newcomers and left town altogether. But Marfa needs Mexican labor, much of which is transported in from across the border in Ojinaga. Big yellow school buses bring the paisanos to work in two large greenhouse nurseries. There is also work in construction, landscaping, and the food industry. Sometimes the newcomers opt for the pre-boom regional cuisine. Paul Thomas Anderson has just left town after shooting parts of *There Will Be Blood*, and the catering job went to a Mexican family that runs a tiny restaurant called Marfa Burrito. Jesús and Ramona Tejada are mexicanos from Ojinaga with decades' worth of work on this side of the line. They have children in Abilene, mexicanos leaning toward americanos. But when I visit the Tejadas, they tell me they're on the verge of selling themselves.

"Before the houses were $17,000, even $10,000," says Jesús. Now there are places selling for $300,000, even $400,000. People have paid $150,000 for houses in ruins, roofless eroded adobes, nothing more than a mound of old dried mud.

"If they offer $400,000, vámonos," he says. These are the days when people knock on your door and make offers in cash.

And the artists, how do they treat the paisanos?

"Son bonitos," says Ramona. "Some of them speak Spanish so well you'd think they were mexicanos."

According to the Tejadas, the boom has remade Marfan society.

"We're all equal now," says Jesús. "You can't even tell who the really rich people are, since so many of them dress in rags."

"Now, in Chihuahua," he says, elongating the name, making the distance all the greater, "in Chihuahua, you know who's rich and who's not."

One of the part-time residents from New York City missed his second home so much that he called in from his Manhattan office and asked for fifty burritos to be flown out.

Pancho Borunda, on the other hand, gives me an earful about the "theys."

"*They* come in and set up their nonprofits and don't pay taxes, and we don't get any tax break. *They* don't have any children. *They* fly in only for the weekends."

Marfa is a small town, and the rumor mill turns swiftly. The latest piece of gossip is a big one, Pancho says, and all the "theys" are in on it.

It's about La Entrada al Pacífico, a free-trade superhighway that will connect the port of Topolobampo, in the Gulf of California, with Midland-Odessa, an accessible transportation hub on Interstate 20 about two hundred miles northeast of Marfa.

According to the rumor, the new money in town had inside knowledge of the superhighway and bought up land throughout Far West Texas for nothing—stealing it from senile ranchers who had no clue about what was coming. In turn, *they* would sell the land to the government, turning a huge profit.

The rumor doesn't make sense to me. (How much profit can they make with eminent domain prices?) But Pancho is serious. If *they* can come in here and turn the town upside down in a couple of years, there's nothing *they* aren't capable of.


The Galleri Urbane is another of the monuments of the new Marfa, tweaking an existing building from utilitarian rustic toward clean lines. Walk through the door and you could be inside one of Judd's famous aluminum boxes. Mostly, there is white space, which tends to swallow the art on the walls.

The gallery is run by a young couple, Jason Willaford and Ree Estrada; he is white, from rural Florida, and she is Mexican-American, from San

Diego. They are as clean and as cool, in their bodies and in their dress, as the gallery itself, which seems under strict environmental control. No stray mote troubles the air or the floor. And indeed, for a town as dusty as Marfa—the wind is always blowing dust off the plains—the gallery looks practically surgical.

I introduce myself as a writer, and Jason receives me without an appointment.

The couple had made scenes elsewhere. For a few years, they'd worked in Silver City, New Mexico. (Of all places: where my mother-in-law's people are from, old mining families, mexicanos clawing the earth for copper.) Around 9/11, Jason was working on one of his own projects, which he called *Bathroom Walls*.

"You know," he says, "bathroom walls, like the last frontier of free expression."

I nod.

So a client bought a bathroom wall and told Jason, "You should show at Chinati"—Judd's Chinati Foundation in Marfa. Jason and Ree visited Far West Texas.

"The landscape," says Jason, "you expect it to be like El Paso, emaciated and overgrazed. And then you get here and the light, the space, the nature . . ."

Jason and Ree knew about Judd, had heard that there was a scene here, but had assumed that it would have been "done," as in "over" or "overdone," Santa Fe or Taos plopped down on the Marfa Plain.

"But there was nothing here," he says, echoing Andrea Zittel in Joshua Tree. "Oh, there were a couple of restaurants, like a time capsule, you know? Back then you could buy a house for thirty, a building for a hundred."

They thought about buying in; but the *New York Times* beat them to it. Every month there seemed to be another article in a different section of the newspaper—in National, Style, Real Estate, Art, or Movies. Marfa's virtual life was very busy. The *Times* made a deal with Frommer's, the travel guide corporation, so that every time you typed "Marfa" or a closely related phrase (say, "Donald Judd") into the paper's search engine, not only did the articles appear but also Frommer's briefs on tourist attractions in town and in the region—the Presidio County Courthouse, the Hotel Paisano, the Marfa lights.

Jason, Ree, and their investor partners were set to buy a place for $300,000, but the owners pulled out five days before closing. Prices were changing day to day, Jason says. The owners probably thought they should wait for another bump in the boom. Then Jason and Ree found this place, he tells me, and offered the asking price. Two days later, the owner asked for $10,000 more. Sold.

Today they do five times more business here than they ever did in Silver City. But it was not exactly a smooth transition. In New Mexico, the Hispano elders of Silver City were not the welcoming kind, and Jason and Ree got the usual treatment afforded outsiders from the "since forever" crowd.

The reception in Marfa was more mixed. "The locals," says Jason, "would say that the newcomers were coming in arrogant and pissing over everything. But there were other locals that were tickled to death. You know, more jobs, more money in town."

There are two kinds of old-timers, Jason says. The kind who will sell you the family homestead and retire with the profit. And the kind who will blame anyone they can for their hardship.

"Just look at this country and how it was founded," Jason goes on. "The East Coast got crowded and people started moving west."

In Marfa, he's been called a neocolonialist. "Well," he says with a shrug, "that's the story of America."


I go to visit the boxes.

In the visitor center there is merchandise for sale. Judd books, Judd T-shirts, Judd coffee mugs. There is a bona fide piece of art for sale as well—a two-sided flag that hangs from the ceiling, the red, white, and blue of America on one side and the red, green, and white of Mexico on the other. The words "imperialism," "nationalism," and "regionalism" are crudely stitched with thread on both sides, in English on the American side and in Spanish on the Mexican. It is the only aesthetically refined reference to the borderlands that I ever see in Marfa. Judd did not create the work—it's far too figurative for him—but part of the concept flowed from him. The three words form the title of a well-known essay from October 1975, four years before he moved from Manhattan to Marfa. In it Judd, who wrote voluminously, discusses everything from "local cultures" and Frantz Fanon to his displeasure at the dictates of political art.

Our tour guide introduces himself by his first name only. "Chris" is every inch an art student, aloof and laconic.

We head straight for the main attraction, the Quonset huts that house the boxes. Chris gives us a thumbnail history. In 1911, he says, Camp Marfa, the precursor to Fort D. A. Russell, was established here in response to the ferment of the Mexican Revolution spilling over the border; the fort was commissioned in 1930. During World War II, prominent German POWs were held here, some of them assisting the United States in conducting research on chemical weapons. The base was decommissioned in 1946.

Chris leaves out a crucial part of the history: in 1924, with anti-Mexican sentiment boiling after years of refugees streaming across the border—and with Prohibition-era smuggling in full swing—the United States established the modern Border Patrol. Facilities for personnel in the area moved several times over the decades, but various parts of the complex have been used continuously by the BP since it was founded. The building that houses the Marfa Sector Headquarters, which coordinates twelve stations and substations in its 135,000-square-mile area of operations, remains on land that was once Fort D. A. Russell.

Chris opens the door to the first Quonset building. Corrugated tin arches above simple brick-and-mortar walls. Evenly spaced vertical concrete pylons support a series of horizontal concrete pylons to hold the ceiling in place. The floor is a grid of plain concrete slabs. An even number of windows on the long sides of the building bring in magnificent natural light.

Here are the boxes. I am shocked at my first glimpse of them, even though I've seen photographs. What astonishes is the repetition, an array radically focused on four-sided forms. They are not literally all "boxes" but dozens of permutations of rectangles fitted together with industrial rivets. There are boxes within boxes, boxes divided by slanted panels, boxes that look like IKEA entertainment-center hutches.

The effect of so many rectangles is overwhelming, and not just because of the boxes themselves. The windows, the doors, the support columns, the ceiling panels, even the rectangles of light pouring through the rectangles of windows onto the rectangular slabs of concrete that make up the floor create a rectilinear universe of frames and of frames within frames. I notice that the bricks in the walls are rectangles. Now I see rectangles in the space between boxes. Is Judd messing with the viewer? Daring you to relate his nonrelational art to some kind of, any kind of, human narrative? No, Judd would insist, it is just form. Purely, simply, grandiosely, and maddeningly form.

But then why did Chris tell us that German POWs were held here? Surely I'm not the only one who immediately thought of repetition being an element of fascist architecture. Above the entryway there is an inscription in German that is also inextricably part of the tableau, a message to the POW chemical weapons techs: "It is better to use your head than to lose it."

Here is all this narrative creeping across the horizon of form. How can we *not* relate the art to the war that defined Judd's generation and set up the Cold War, which sent Judd to Korea via a cross-country trip with a stop in Marfa that left such a strong impression on the young art- ist that he wound up moving there more than thirty years later?

Judd had strong ideas about the importance of setting for his art: "Frequently as much thought has gone into the placement of a piece as into the piece itself." And so I look. The windows! Hundreds of frames bring in the fantastic light of the Marfa Plain, which is anything but a plain form: a landscape sculpted by cultural memory and the modes of production that have exploited it—ranching, drugs, oil, Mexicans, Hol- lywood.

Now I imagine text everywhere, bleeding across the perfectly buffed metal. I see and hear and feel Judd, his place, his time, his war, the kid Judd listening to radio Westerns and watching Westerns on the screen, taking in the West, which calls out to the more adventurous New Yorkers.

A young woman in the group—horn-rimmed glasses and braids, miniskirt, alabaster legs, Converse sneakers—takes a call on her cell phone. She opens the door on the far side of the building. It is a heavy door. The slam causes a thunderous echo that lasts for what seems like a minute. Sun and shadow dance across the rectangles.

I notice an imperfection. A gap of about a sixteenth of an inch between two aluminum slabs that reveals enough of a screw for me to see its threads.

A faulty box. Maybe the boxes are fragile, after all.

Judd also built some boxes outdoors, laid out in a precise arrangement like the ones in the Quonsets. These are of concrete, reminiscent of World War II pillboxes, unavoidably military. And ultimately that's how I read the work, given its context: in their inflexibility, in its absoluteness, I find the narrative of authoritarianism, the implied precision of weaponry, the echo of an officer's order—and the question of whether the subject follows it.

Chris pushes on. We are done with the boxes.

Outside, mesquite and hard earth.

The sprawling complex, set amid the immensity of the Marfa Plain, summons the idea of owning the vastness: Judd, the mad emperor of the rectangles filled with the soul-stirring vistas of the Chihuahuan Desert, the beauty that lured him and would become the object of desire of the kind of money Judd became worth only in death. (Christie's auctioned thirty-six of his sculptures for $20 million in 2006.)

We end in the Arena, another massive tin-roofed building, formerly an indoor rodeo at Fort D. A. Russell, entertainment for the troops. It is midmorning and the sun bears down on the roof, causing it to pop and ping, the sounds expanding in the natural echo chamber. Judd spent some of his creative energy on furniture-making, and here are his tables and chairs. Minimal designs; terribly uncomfortable.

In the Arena's kitchen there is a large table with a metate and pestle on it, and a few glazed earthenware bowls—the only touch of Mexico on the grounds of Chinati. Did Judd put those there? Maybe it's not a representation of a kitchen but an actual kitchen? I want to ask Chris, but he's been buttonholed by other visitors. Maybe I'm crazy for wondering—the representational border patrolman, always on the watch to catch sins of commission and omission, as obsessed with the color of history as Judd was with form.

As the tour winds down, a white Chevy pickup truck pulls up outside the Arena. An actual Mexican jumps out of the cab and pulls an industrial-sized weed whacker from the pickup's bed.

"Thank you for visiting the Chinati Foundation," Chris shouts above the sudden noise as the Mexican tames the weeds. The great whir and whine of the machine reverberates wildly inside the cavernous Arena, which now buzzes like a billion bees.

## 3.

No matter which way you turn, there is a spectacular and iconic view, and it all looks so . . . pristine. There is not a particle of visible pollution in the air. There are only a handful of streets in Marfa, and the few ranch roads in the area are mostly hidden by the yellow immensity of the plains surrounding town. If you have the means, you can own this view, the vastness itself, and frame it: your own private gallery of the West. The problem is that the border—the contraband, the bodies, the technology, the poverty—always lurks at the edges of the frame.

But the Marfa boom began when the border was still relatively innocent—before the walls shunted migrants into the deadliest corridors, before the drug war took its bloodiest turn. The local boom began with the arrival of people like John F. "Jeff" Fort III, the former CEO of Tyco Industries. Yes, *that* Tyco Industries, whose onetime CEO Dennis Kozlowski was at the heart of the first wave of executive pay scandals, in the early 2000s. Kozlowski is serving a prison sentence of up to twenty-five years on convictions of grand larceny, conspiracy, violation of business law, and falsifying records. But Fort had nothing to do with any of that; he'd retired long before the scandal broke. If anything, he stood for the old-school patrician style of wealth antithetical to the Gordon Gekkos of the New Gilded Age.

Fort was married to Marion Barthelme, widow of the famed fiction writer Donald Barthelme and a major patron of the arts in Houston, where I teach during the early years of the Iraq War, which is just when we are ramping up the boom. In Houston my story glancingly intersects with Judd's. The Menil Foundation—established by Philippa de Menil, who also headed the Dia Art Foundation, which initially bought the old army base in Marfa for Judd—is an early supporter of the University of Houston's creative-writing program. I rent a house once owned by de Menil, directly across the street from the Menil Museum, home to one of the world's most important collections of surrealist art.

I meet Jeff at a Houston fund-raiser, and we get to talking about northern New Mexico—Jeff and Marion have another house in Santa Fe—and then he mentions Marfa. I have just read the story in the *Times* about the art and real estate boom there. I tell him I am interested in visiting, and he extends an invitation for me to see his spread, which, with its several properties, comprises a quarter of a million or so acres of land. The next time we're both in New Mexico, he says, we will fly to Marfa by plane, his private plane.

When I meet him at Million Air, a private airstrip outside Santa Fe, Jeff is wearing a white shirt with light blue stripes and pearl buttons. In his lap he holds his cowboy hat, of tightly wound pale yellow straw, ringed by a leather band encrusted with half a dozen five-pointed stars. He has thin brown hair and brown eyes and a long face, both plain and plaintive. Well into his sixties, he stands about five foot nine, has a fair amount of hair on his chest, and, as I will soon discover, is in excellent physical shape.

The plane is a Beechcraft Beechjet 400. Beige suede walls, gray leather seats, brass cup holders on the armrests. There are four seats in the main cabin, plus a jump seat in the bathroom and the seats for the pilot and copilot, who are hired hands.

The jet takes off only a few seconds after the captain gives it full thrust, and it is a smooth ride. Below are the Sangre de Cristos and the Jemez and the San Juans and the valleys between them, the land I've grown accustomed to on ground level. Now the land reveals itself in another way, with different shapes and colors. What is immense down below becomes minute. From thousands of feet up, the Black Mesa is a little smudge in a vast sea of pale earth dotted with innumerable pin-pricks: juniper and piñon trees. I fancy I can see the buttes and ravines that I hike in the BLM land surrounding Velarde. At cruising altitude, the villages of the north are all but invisible, swallowed by the land itself.

About fifteen minutes into the flight, an alarm goes off in the cock-pit. The pilot and copilot glance at each other and converse via their headsets. I cannot hear what they are saying. Jeff explains that the alarm is a warning that the plane's radar has detected another plane in the vicinity, one with which there is a potential for a collision.

"Resolve conflict," says the alarm's robot voice.

We make an evasive maneuver, up and to the south.

The alarm goes off again.

Could it be possible that the other plane also took an evasive maneu-ver that kept us on the collision course?

Once more: "Resolve conflict."

Another maneuver.

For the next few minutes both pilots lean forward in their seats, hands on the dash, faces glued to the windshield, scanning the skies for the phantom plane that we may or may not have been on a collision course with. I, of course, imagine the terrible instant: being conscious for a few seconds as I catapult into the frigid, oxygen-deprived air at thirty thousand feet and begin my death plunge to the land, that land that we paint, that we film, and imagine into being—I will finally come to it with the full force of my desire! My blood, bone, and sinew will suffuse it!

The alarm shuts off in mid-whine. We never see the other plane.

Jeff did not start out as a cowboy. He appears to have had the perfect launching pad of a family. His father was a Manhattan lawyer who moved the family to what was then a rural suburb outside of Washington, D.C. It was a segregated area, Jeff says, and he has childhood memories of walking by a black Baptist church. He never went in, of course. "But my God," he says, "the sound coming from in there!"

He graduated from Princeton and was granted a deferment from the military when he enrolled in grad school at MIT. In the early 1960s he began working for a communications cable firm called Simplex that held military contracts in Southeast Asia—a lucrative market back in those days of the buildup to full-scale American intervention. So instead of going to Vietnam in a grunt platoon, because of his smarts and connections, he got a job laying cable far from the war zone. Returning to the States, he took the helm at Simplex, a wunderkind. A few years later, the industrial giant Tyco acquired Simplex, and then Jeff topped Tyco. During his tenure, the company became a vast multinational through a dizzying run of acquisitions.

He retired at the age of fifty-one in 1992, breaking away from a life he says was killing him. He quit smoking. He got in shape. He started climbing mountains, tall ones, all over the world.

In 2002, the Kozlowski scandal broke at Tyco, and it nearly sank the company. Stock and morale plummeted. A corporation, a brand, a tradition—and the livelihood of thousands of families—all of that was on the brink. The board asked Jeff to return. He righted the ship even as

Tyco and Kozlowski continued, for the next several years, to remain in business news headlines and became enshrined as a symbol of corporate cupidity. (Kozlowski spent $6,000 on shower curtains and $1 million on a birthday party in Sardinia for his wife; in all, he stole $400 million from the company and the shareholders.)

"The CEOs these days!" says Jeff. "The ones who take those crazy bonuses—I don't understand them." In 2007, Tyco claimed nearly $19 billion in revenue. Jeff remains an adviser.

He arrived in Marfa in the early 1990s, and the landscape seduced him immediately. "I walked around for a couple of days," he says, "and my jaw dropped."

On one trip Jeff noticed a place for sale, which turned out to be a piece of Judd's property. He and his wife, Marion, were friendly with Tim and Lynn Crowley, fellow Houston sophisticates; the Crowleys also happened to be looking for rural property in Texas, and Jeff told them to come to Marfa. At least that is Jeff's version of the genealogy; most published accounts credit the Crowleys with the founding of the new colony. Jeff is largely absent from the recent journalism on Marfa, which is curious given that he became, in a matter of a few years, one of the biggest landholders in West Texas.

After Judd's place, Jeff bought another parcel up by Fort Davis, and then a house in town. The Crowleys also went on a shopping spree, purchasing a good portion of downtown Marfa as well as rural property. Then Jeff bought the legendary Chinati Hot Springs, which Judd had previously owned and had closed off to the public for the first time in recorded history, causing tremendous ill will among locals and countless regular visitors.

Jeff needed a West Texas native to teach him about the land he now owned and found the perfect mentor in Jason Sullivan, who picks us up at Marfa's tiny airport, where, in addition to the jets of the new gentry, Border Patrol helicopters land and gas up. In his thirties, Jason is a cowboy's cowboy, tall and lanky. He wears a dark brown suede hat with the rim curled tight and high, a long-sleeved blue denim shirt, and Wranglers, with a pistol in a leather holster on his right hip. His face is angular, his eyes pale blue. His reddish-blond hair is trimmed short. His work boots are of brown leather, well worn in and scuffed on the toes. When addressed with a question, he almost always begins his answer with a "yessir" or a "nosir," especially with his boss. He spits out the window of his red Tacoma often. He confesses he's "closet dipping" (sneaking snuff, which, along with cigarettes, he has tried to give up—Jeff, the former smoker, is now a zealous anti-tobacco activist).

What does a man who owns a good part of Far West Texas do with it?

He *looks* at it.

We make the drive to Chinati Hot Springs from Marfa down Pinto Canyon Road, Jason at the wheel, crossing the yellow plain toward what feels like the edge of the world. Suddenly, the grass is gone, as is the pavement, and the dirt track starts a steep, rocky descent toward the Rio Grande. The lyric plains of knee-high grass give way to a frijol-colored land, as the name of the road suggests; this craggy place is populated most prominently with brilliant stalks of sotol shooting up from their beds of splayed yucca-like leaves.

I ask what direction the Rio Grande is. Jason points straight ahead, which, judging by the afternoon sun, is west.

I am looking west into Mexico.

This is exactly where the river makes its Big Bend, screwing with the imagined compass of history, the long-standing North-South embrace of the United States and Mexico. Here, Mexicans come east to get into el norte, wading across the river, which can be a drought trickle or, during the monsoon, a terrible torrent.

Just the other day Jason encountered a couple of mojados—he actually uses the word, Spanish for "wetback," and pronounces it clearly. Somehow in his mouth it sounds not like an epithet at all but a borderlands colloquialism, said casually, almost the way a Mexican would say it, the word summing up the confluence of human bodies, the economy, the river, the history of the border.

"Saw a couple of mojados right around here the other day," he says. "One of them was ready to give up; the other was telling his buddy that it's only forty miles to Marfa. As far as I'm concerned, anyone who can walk all the way from the river to Marathon deserves a job." From the river to Marathon is one hundred miles.

We arrive at the springs and ponder the hubris of the artist who fenced them off. Jeff opened them back up to the public, spruced the place up a bit. The handful of guest rooms and barely rustic pools make

up the most modest resort in the area. Camping is $15 a night, includ-
ing use of the springs; the cheapest room is $75. A communal kitchen
is available; everyone packs in and prepares their own food. The man-
agers are Dave and Krissy Sines, an art couple who moved here from
Dallas when a friend bought an abandoned church in town and converted it into a studio. Dave has dirty blond dreads and Krissy long, silky
yellow-blond strands; together, they look like a couple at Woodstock.
They live full-time at the springs and get to make their art in their spare
time (he does large-scale metal sculpture; she paints). They are pleasant
and plump and ruddy-faced from the Chihuahuan sun—we are within
a couple of miles of the river now, having dropped a few thousand feet
in elevation from the temperate plains.

Now that the boss has arrived, there is a whirl of activity. A big Western meal is prepared for the tired travelers: chicken and beef fajitas,
flour tortillas, fire-roasted chipotle salsa (bottled, from Dallas), and a
thick pineapple upside-down cake for dessert. All cooked up by Dave
and Krissy. There are no stores or restaurants for dozens of miles.

It is monsoon. A series of thunderheads bear down on the Mexican
side of the river, their billowing tops brilliant in the late sun, their bellies heavy and gray. The wind rises, bringing the breath of the rain from
across the border. I watch lightning fork down into the river, but the
storm stays on the other side.

"Hasn't rained nearly enough around here," Jason says.

When darkness comes, it hits fast. Under a huge tamarisk, I sneak a
cigarette, then retire to one of the rooms (on Jeff's tab). After a careful
inspection, I kill a small scorpion. (And think of *The Appaloosa*, the
1966 border Western in which Marlon Brando engages in a macabre
arm-wrestling match that results in his losing and getting bitten by a
scorpion—a scene in which the celebrated Mexican director and actor
Emilio "El Indio" Fernández plays a sadistic voyeur, an utterly dirty, evil
Other, the way he was usually cast in gringo productions.)

I nervously turn out the light.

The rain finally crosses the river in the wee hours. The wind shrieks
through the tamarisk, and lightning bounds up toward the springs
from the riverside, closer and closer, followed finally by the first fat drops
of a hard, fast rain.

At dawn, it is still drizzling, and water drips from the eaves of the old adobe. Sparkling beads hang from the tips of the tamarisk needles.

Jason starts up the "quad," a Polaris Ranger high-end ATV with massive shock absorbers. There are two seats in front and a crash bar that a third person can hang onto standing up in the back, which is what I eagerly volunteer to do, to no complaint from Jason or Jeff.

The road leading out of the canyon where the spring is hidden heads west for a few miles, leaning down toward the bottomland, where the river has been cutting the canyon for millennia, before hitting another road, which will take us north and deep into Jeff's parcel. Jason steps on the gas and soon we're flying down the pebbly path at thirty, maybe thirty-five miles an hour. Rain slaps my face, a cool, sweet sting.

I look toward Mexico. Dim flashes of lightning. Several layers of gun-gray clouds swirl along the stratified mesa-mountains. One lone low cloud, foglike, hangs over the Rio Grande. The rain comes harder, just as the sun breaks through a bank of clouds in the east. Sunset comes in a sudden silver flash that illuminates the mesas. A rainbow erupts, a wide band of yellow rising from the pot of gold in Mexico. The arc hurls itself across the zenith and into the American sky. Now another rainbow comes, concentric, slightly less brilliant, an echo to the first.

Just like Jeff's, my jaw drops.


We are out all day on the land, along the dirt roads and off them, covering dozens of miles. There are dome hills and spires and rocky rims. For most of the day, everything we can see, unto the horizon, belongs to Jeff.

We are out "messing around," as Jeff puts it, which amounts to looking.

Here we are on a road heading east, slightly uphill, and to the south the land curls down into a big draw, a cleavage between hills that helps drain the higher terrain.

"Jason?"

"Yessir?"

"Have we seen that draw before?"

"Nosir."

"Let's have a look."

To get a peek over the edge all the way down into the channel would mean a walk of maybe a quarter of a mile, through a thick patch of ocotillo and a nasty thorn plant (low to the ground, tubular branches, black spines) that Jeff calls "Indian toothbrush," apologizing for the politically incorrect name. But the nastiest is the tasajillo cactus, a big chollalike dome of one-inch thorns that tends to grow close to other plants and thus is impossible to hop over or even walk around.

So Jason steers the Polaris off the stony open dirt of the road and, at barely a couple of miles an hour, heads toward the edge of the draw. Now I think of the Polaris as a tank. Nothing slows it down; the terrific thorns do no damage whatever to the thick, rubber tires. The ride is as smooth over the vegetation as it is on level dirt. But the sound—the snapping and crunching and popping—is thunderous.

We arrive at the edge. The draw looks essentially like the downslopes of two hills coming together, thick thighs joining, a narrow sandy wash carved between them by generations of rain showers. I hop off the back of the Polaris and promptly snag my jeans on an Indian toothbrush.

Jason and Jeff walk over to get the view, Jason out front by a few paces. They move slowly, deliberately, almost gingerly. Jason stops. He places his hands on his hips and spits. Jeff stops, mirroring Jason's posture, but he does not spit. They peer down, wordlessly. The wind aahs through the ocotillos.

Jason turns away from the draw and starts looking down at the ground, here and there toeing a stone with his boot, and Jeff does the same.

They are looking for the things Indians left behind, long ago, and I begin looking too, for arrowheads, for "debitage," the shards that resulted when stones were fashioned into tools. Through "lithic analysis," I learn, archaeologists can tell a lot about the people who made the tools hundreds or thousands of years ago—their technology, trade routes, social organization.

It doesn't take me long to find my first piece of debitage, a sliver of greenish stone obviously chipped off a larger piece by what could only have been a human hand. As I look at the stone, in my mind a scene takes shape: it is 7000 B.C., and my arm belongs to an Indian. At the same time I'm standing behind the Indian, looking at the back of his and my head, our hair black and coarse. When I turn him around in my imagination, "he" is no longer, because suddenly—I have just seen about half an hour of *Dances with Wolves* on cable—the face of the actor Graham Greene appears.

Jason comes up with what might be an actual arrowhead. We find evidence of other passages, too. Empty water bottles, soda containers clearly from the other side (a Coke bottle with the ingredients listed in Spanish), a can of coctel de tomate. Jason says the travelers were probably headed toward Highway 90, which is about forty miles away.

We are on Judd land. Jeff now holds the title, but Judd framed it.

We arrive at one of the casitas the artist once used. Rustic minimalism, modest touches of cowboy, Mexican. Jeff delights in telling Judd stories, the kind of lore writers and artists of a certain school spin around themselves consciously or not and that ultimately sells more books or paintings. This type of character we can call "artist as lout," though some would insist on "artist as free spirit." One story has Judd, bottle in hand, stripping his models like the photographer in Antonioni's *Blow-Up*. Others cast Judd in a demonic light, appropriate to the devil mythology in nearby Ojinaga, where the Evil One is said to be holed up in a mountain cave. Legend has it that when they tried to dig Judd's grave on this very ranch, at a site with an arresting view of the land's decline into the riverbed, the ground was impossibly rocky and the workers needed heavy tools to break it. The Mexicans said (in a romantic variant of the lore) that this was because the earth itself did not want the likes of Judd. Still another tale is about the dirt of his burial mound sinking because, apparently, his casket had imploded. (Maybe the devil himself pulled Judd down to the only place hotter than the Chihuahuan Desert.)

Few people get access to this particular Judd site (he owned three large holdings in the region). It's not that Jeff doesn't want to show it to the world; it's the sheer inaccessibility of the place. Pinto Canyon itself is no road for old men, but the path up from the springs is barbaric, fit only for a Polaris and guys like Jeff with guides like Jason.

Here, too, Judd made art. With dark volcanic rocks the size of shoe boxes, fitted perfectly to one another and forming—what else?—rectangles. Stone walls of rectangles. Because of the scale and the technical difficulty of his projects, Judd almost always worked with assistants. A man named Jesús Vizcaíno helped him build the walls.

Oh, the land! We have scaled a rocky promontory with a fantastic view of the rolls and folds and domes and crags and strata, the vicious flora somehow attached to it all, the perfectly spaced cumuli glaring white in a hard blue sky. Look up toward the rim, look down to the river. Where land and sky meet is the most painful edge. There is no relation whatever between them, their border utterly fixed, their difference absolute.

The biggest of Judd's structures here forms a corral—that is, a simulacrum of one, with ornamental touches like arches and even a faux trough. I am more moved by this piece than any box I've seen at the Chinati Foundation. Here, the rectangles look human. Out here, where no one can see him, Judd is no mid-twentieth-century American modernist messiah. He's just the guy who raised up these pretty walls of stone and was ultimately swallowed by the unyielding earth they sprang from.

We spend the afternoon scouting for archaeological sites, especially Indian "shelters," natural cover from the elements created by rock formations. We get out of the vehicle a few times, hiking as much as half a mile off the road in the heat and the light. Jeff is agile and fast; it's impossible for me to keep up with him. Jason is a little slower and more deliberate, so I'm usually at his side.

At one promising place, a steep hill maybe two hundred yards off the road with a cairn of boulders that looks to provide good shade, Jeff sends Jason on recon with a walkie-talkie. It takes Jason a good fifteen minutes to clamber up, and there is time for Jeff to take off his cowboy hat and talk to me. About the child that he was, fascinated with archaeology from the moment he heard the story of the boys who stumbled upon the caves of Lascaux the year after he was born. About how he really came to life after retiring as CEO of Tyco, how "unhealthy" he'd been all those years. He climbed Mount Washington, in New Hampshire, and the friend who accompanied him lit a cigarette at the summit. Then and there Jeff challenged him to climb Mount McKinley within one year. For training, they climbed lower-elevation peaks with "three years of *National Geographics*" in their backpacks for weight. After

McKinley, Jeff bagged peaks across the continent (including Aconcagua, in the Andes) and even in Nepal. Though not Everest. Not yet.

The walkie-talkie crackles: Jason reporting back on the cairn.

"Looks to be between three and a half and five and a half feet high," he says.

"Five and a half feet?" says Jeff.

"Yessir. It looks all right."

"Take GPS and take photos."

"Yessir."

Jeff turns back to me. Now he talks about arriving here, his origin myth.

"This little world out here," he says, "this little backwater, it's undiscovered. It blows me away to think you can own this."

He fingers his hat delicately, traces the points of the metal stars on the leather hatband. "The landscape," he says, "was totally new for me. Learning to get around took a good while. I'd never spent any time in the desert."

There it is—the encounter with a new world, radical difference.

He bought this ranch, his first, in 1995. He started making friends in town and hired people to help him run things. Like the guy named Apache Adams, who was Jeff's first ranch manager.

"Now, Jason," Jeff says, "Jason loves this land, *just loves it.*"

The walkie-talkie again.

"It's three feet," Jason says. "There's a metate."

"Good," says Jeff. Another GPS point on the land, another shelter. Here, the Indians ate. Here, they slept. Here, they ground seeds into meal.

He wasn't quite so retired in 1992, after all.

"I was worried I'd get bored," he says. "I bought a bunch of companies. You know, leveraged buyouts with Donaldson, Lufkin & Jenrette."

I have no idea what he is talking about. I look it up later. There were lawsuits from companies DLJ took control of. There was talk of insider trading. But no indictments.

It is hard to reconcile the man before me—the mild-mannered cowboy from the prep school East, the good steward of the vast land, the child still enchanted by the ghosts of Indians—with the man who played hardball in business and, by all accounts, played it well.

Jason: "There's a feature. Potential burial."

Jeff scribbles in his notebook.

"This world out here," he repeats, "is a little backwater, it's undiscov-ered. But it's bound to be discovered."

Yes, I think to myself—over and over again.

Jeff takes me to one of the most striking geological features of the entire spread. Two rows of fifty-foot-tall columns of yellow sandstone form a spectacular arroyo channel. The place already had a name when Jeff arrived: Arroyo Chupadero, "Sucking Arroyo," because to a Mexi-can's eyes it looked, perhaps, like an accordion contracting. To Jeff, he of the *National Geographic* eye, the columns looked monumental and Egyptian, very Cecil B. DeMille, like upright sarcophagi. He renamed it Valley of the Kings.

We dismount the Polaris.

"A production scout was just here," says Jeff. "It'll be in someone's movie someday."

Jeff will be glad to open the locked gate of the ranch to Hollywood. The land made his jaw drop, and he wants others to experience the same. He discovered it, and now he will share it with the world. The problem with discovery is that you have to keep on discovering. No sooner has the novelty of the latest find worn off than the desire for the next starts burning in you. And so the acreage grows.

Next we visit what he considers his greatest find, a prehistoric mural on a sheer rock wall deep inside a crevasse so hidden from view of any road or trail it is highly unlikely anyone could have come upon it, even with the intent of looking for such a thing.

"It was chance," Jeff admits. "You can't see it from anywhere."

And it is not easy to get to. He guides me in, tells me where to step, where I need to plant my toe and find support with my hands. In the reddish-brown rock, yellow-orange pigment renders a grandiose figure with outsized hands, carrying a bundle on his back (firewood? freshly hunted game?), a large penis between his legs.

The Indians were, are, everywhere. In addition to the shelters and debitage sites, Jeff shows me several ash piles, places where rocks were heated with fire and served as stoves to roast sotol roots and the like. In one, trapped in the sediment that makes up the bank of an arroyo, the band of ash is several inches wide, possibly indicating that this site was used over a long period of time.

I am listening to Jeff and writing notes and walking along the arroyo when suddenly part of a human skeleton appears, protruding from the sediment; Jeff talks about it in the even tones of a tourist guide. A saucer of pelvis, a couple of knots of vertebrae, a quarter moon of skull. I notice a piece of vertebra at my feet, probably carved out of the wall by a recent monsoon flow. I try to pick it up. It is so old that it crumbles, and now there is Indian dust on my fingers.

Jeff calls on his old friend Lynn Crowley at her house on the outskirts of town.

It is the only house I've ever visited that has a two-mile driveway between front gate and front door, a straight-arrow road where Tim Crowley occasionally lands his plane. On the ride over I notice that Jeff has my favorite Dwight Yoakam CD in the car, *This Time*, which contains the hit "A Thousand Miles from Nowhere," a song that made the sound tracks of several 1990s films (*Big Eden, Lawn Dogs, Me and Will*) and served as the background for a relationship of mine that died in the desert. He also has CDs of Tanya Tucker and Bill Monroe. Cowboy music for a cowboy landscape.

The Crowley house was designed by Carlos Jiménez, a renowned Houston-based architect and Rice University professor. The simple, sleek look recalls Richard Neutra's famous Kaufmann House in Palm Springs, where the modernist master achieved a sublime balance between structure and desert space. The house establishes itself with long, low-slung rectangles that seem as if they're partially submerged in or emerging from the Marfa Plain. The exterior is a chalky Mediterranean white trimmed with tile speckled like quail eggs. Judd himself could have placed the magnificent windows with their dramatic angles and views.

The discoverers who don't want this place to be discovered did not lose their business sense, and neither do they plan on their sympathy for the Nature Conservancy to deny them profit margins. Tim and Jeff went in together on 11,000 acres on the plains, breaking it up into square-mile lots. As of yet no one has built on them, but that's what they're for.

Local environmentalists urged the Houston speculators to write conservation easements into the land titles, placing restrictions on structures (no three-story McMansions) and outdoor lighting (to keep the skies dark for the nearby McDonald Observatory). Prospective buyers will also have to maintain fences that wild antelope can easily get through, will be prohibited from overgrazing the land with cattle, will have to protect archaeological features, and cannot further subdivide. If this was a colonial venture, it was done with liberal earnestness. Fort and the Crowleys took pains to be good citizens.

Lynn is young in the way of the new middle age, blond and tan and fit. She ran a successful art gallery in Houston before moving to Marfa with Tim. Diagnosed with multiple sclerosis, she came to the desert, as so many of us did, thinking of it as a place of healing.

But the couple did not come out here to hide. They began remaking the town center in her image. Lynn's Marfa Book Company stocked coffee-table editions of art and architecture, a smattering of serious fiction and poetry, and a strong section on scholarship about the Big Bend region; WWDJD bumper stickers were for sale next to the cash register. Another major rehab project in downtown Marfa transformed an old feed store into the Goode Crowley Theater, a space for avant-garde performances.

What else did Marfa need?

A public radio station. Far West Texas was the last NPR "black hole" in the Lower 48. As if taking part in an Amish house-raising, the new denizens pooled their resources to buy the FCC license and yet another building downtown, and stocked it with radio personalities: themselves.

Haute cuisine, for the foodies. Forthwith Maiya's, with its fennel tartlets and *petits plats de fromage*.

And millionaires. The Crowleys had friends, and they invited them over and said you should buy and they did.

All this happened in roughly a decade, during which time an old adobe in town that might have sold for $30,000 in 1994, the year of Judd's death, commanded $300,000 in 2005, the year the *New York Times* became the town's biggest booster.

Lynn and Jeff greet each other warmly, like the old friends they are.

The first stop is the kitchen, with its immense island, upon which are strewn the many wine openers Lynn has tried (including one that looks like an intergalactic weapon), without success, to open a red with. Jeff lends a hand.

Since my hepatitis C diagnosis, I have spent a lot of mental energy trying to negotiate my way out of quitting alcohol, accepting anecdotal, nonprofessional advice that says cutting down is good enough. I can no longer drink without thinking about drinking, but I still drink.

The red Jeff opens is good.

Glasses in hand, we head to the living room, passing back through the entry, where a skylight focuses the last of the day's light on a mini-exhibit curated by Lynn, including a word sculpture by Jack Pierson (four letters, of different fonts and sizes, spelling "fate").

Van Morrison is on the stereo with "Did Ye Get Healed," a number with a bright, bouncy horn riff doubled by female backup singers that is instantly recognizable and an excellent accompaniment to the art, the wine, the sophisticated company.

I am alone on a long sofa that could seat ten, and still I have to move several throw pillows to get comfortable. The living room is a huge vault of a space drawn toward the picture window, which is divided by muntins into horizontal thirds, the top and bottom panels further divided into vertical thirds. The middle frame is thus the largest and produces a colossal Western view. The Marfa Plain begins literally on the other side of the window—bunchgrass grows just a few feet beyond it—and extends dozens of miles, an expanse of yellow-brown-gray-green, sotol and tasajillo and ocotillo and a wide variety of other Chihuahuan Desert succulents, a few of the plants alive but most dead. The Davis range forms the horizon line about halfway up the frame, and the rest of the picture is sky streaked with cirri and dotted with cumuli, a few veils of rain sweeping across the steep flanks of the mountains. At the very center of the window—that is, at the center of what we can see of the mountains—there is a peculiar notch, the kind of feature an artist invents to bring balance to a composition or, in this case, anchor it. I focus my eyes on that notch and the rest of the vista swirls around it. It is space and light, but it is also time because the composition keeps shifting as the sun sets (unseen to the west; the view is to the north). At the base of the window are two matching tables with four chairs each, the tables, like most of the furniture in the house, topped with wood and anchored with steel. This is what money does in Marfa: it sets you up to view the land in high-def, in 3-D, in vistas that would have made John Ford's jaw drop. A fantastic amount of money met a fantastic amount of space, and framed it. One's house is more vantage point than living quarters.

We are joined by an art dealer from Brussels, playing the part with a spiky, short haircut and big-framed glasses. She has been here all along but was outside admiring the garden. She comes in through a glass door, emerging from the cloud produced by the misters. In the garden, we hear, there are tomatoes, beans, lettuces, and rows of young fruit trees. Lynn says she has a local tend to it.

The dealer knew Judd, and I inquire.

"He was a genius," she says, "with or without Marfa." She notes that economy, to a great extent, determined his move to West Texas. For Judd, who wanted to work on a massive scale, and in whose art space was as important as structure, cheap land was fundamental. Of course he fell in love with it, too. "And so did we," she says, "though not with the landscape—this is a landscape to fear, to be angered by perhaps, but love? Only the Americans could love a place such as this."

Judd, she goes on, was an "imperial man." She means he was an American, an American in the West. And those of us who come in his wake are the same.

"Owning this!" she says in a theatrical huff, her hand sweeping across the landscape framed by the window.

I ask where she's living.

She shrugs her shoulders. She just bought herself an old Fort D. A. Russell officer's quarters. She is renovating now. She is of the art world, after all, and this place—this town, this landscape—*this* is the art world today. She says, "You've got to make a living, don't you think?"

Indeed. The art world has come west—or, more accurately, continues coming west, generation after generation, seeking, like Judd, to reauthenticate itself. In the early twentieth century, this often meant an encounter with the ethnic other—portraits of Native Americans (or, less often, of Hispanos), as in Santa Fe and Taos. In the early twenty-first century, it most often means an encounter with the land itself.

I am drunk.

I was going to allow myself one glass.

That was three glasses ago. Or was it four?

Lynn asks me where I live, and I give her a complicated answer: teaching in Houston part of the year, commuting from northern New Mexico, I'm from Los Angeles, worked a lot on the border in southern Arizona, over the last decade spent a lot of time in Joshua Tree . . .

"Joshua Tree!" Lynn exclaims. "The next Marfa! And Marfa," she says, "is the next South Beach."

I ramble on: I spent a lot of my twenties in Central America, writing about the wars. I was inspired by liberation theology, you know, the priests who married Catholicism and Marxism . . .

A dim self-awareness arrives: I've just used the M-word. But maybe that is precisely what my hosts want of me: to show them the margins, bring them a whiff of the authentic life out there on the far plain where the water jugs run empty, touch some troubled place in their consciences.

And just what is it that I want from them? To stick, as the late Texas governor Ann Richards said all those years ago of Bush senior, their silver feet in their mouths? Reveal their inner racists? Confess their business crimes? Become my literary patrons? Maybe I just want them to want me, in the way I've felt desired by white liberals most of my life.

Lynn breaks in.

"Let's talk about movies!" she says, and she mentions that she hosted the Coen brothers while they were shooting *No Country*. "The older one was creepy. The younger one is okay." And she also caught sight of Daniel Day-Lewis in sweats, jogging around the town, muttering to himself in character; preparing for scenes in *There Will Be Blood*.

I ask if anyone saw *The Three Burials of Melquiades Estrada*, which was also shot in the area.

"It was a bit of a mess," Lynn says. "But I liked it because of the landscapes."

Yes, it does begin with the landscape of Far West Texas. But the film is about a body upon the land. Tommy Lee Jones's American ranch hand Pete is best friends with his homologue from Mexico, Melquiades Estrada. Most of their relationship is played against Old Western type— tenderly, including tears, very New Western, edging up to homoeroticism. Fate places Julio Cedillo's warm Mexican cowboy, Melquiades, and Barry Pepper's icy, alienated Border Patrol agent together at the wrong place and time, resulting in Melquiades's death. Tommy seeks justice for his friend from the town sheriff (played as an oaf by Dwight

Yoakam), but there is none to be had. So Pete kidnaps the patrolman and forces him to dig up Melquiades from a potter's field grave and haul him back to his old pueblo across the border. Most of the film has the two riding burros across the borderlands and ultimately deep into Mexico, Melquiades's body steadily decomposing along the way, recalling Peckinpah's exquisitely morbid *Bring Me the Head of Alfredo Garcia*. Melquiades's fetid corpse symbolically carries the thousands of migrants who've died in the deserts. The film is a true border production. Tommy Lee—who speaks good frontier Spanish—stars and directs, and the screenplay was written by the Mexican New Wave figure Guillermo Arriaga. It is a work of fiction with a strong historical core: the killing of Esequiel Hernández, an eighteen-year-old native of Redford, a small town south of Marfa on the Rio Grande, who was out herding his family's goats and got caught in the crosshairs of a Marine patrol unit on reconnaissance for drug smugglers. The film received top honors at Cannes and was then almost completely ignored in the United States. The following year, the Coen brothers and Cormac McCarthy would sweep the Oscars with the deeply reactionary *No Country for Old Men*— both the book and the film eschew history and minimize political context in favor of rendering implacable, Old Testament–style evil and its hapless victims. McCarthy and the Coens also obscured P. T. Anderson's *There Will Be Blood*, which restored history and, above all, political economy to the West.

I am not quite drunk enough to make a scene, but in my head I'm pointing at the center of the dinner table and shouting, "Don't you see the body?! It's Melquiades, you decadent bourgeois! Don't you smell him? And the stench of thousands of bodies more, the border dead, deaths in which you are all complicit!"

Soon enough I'm enjoying dessert, a classy whipped ricotta dribbled with honey. For the first time I become aware of the darkness in the living room windows. There is not a single light out on the plain. Now the frame is like one of Mark Rothko's black canvases hanging in the famous chapel in Houston. A picture of nothing. Or of everything you are haunted by or long for.

As we leave, it is storming outside. The monsoon. In El Paso they are evacuating flood-prone areas along the river. The Rio Grande is about to crest the levees.

## 4.

During my Lannan residency I eat a lot of Marfalafels at the Food Shark. At the Get Go, the gourmet shop in town, I buy organic chickens, which I bake according to Angela's recipe, stuffed with rosemary and lemon, and I also get my favorite Garden of Eatin' Blue Chips there. But for other sundries—decent flour tortillas (made with lard), jalapeños, and corn on the cob—I go to Pueblo Market, way out on San Antonio Street. Far from the Judd core of Marfa, San Antonio Street is on the other side of the tracks, in the Mexican barrio. While the center of town has been remade in Judd's image, the outskirts remain largely in their pregentrified state; if anything, the town's historic segregation between white ranching families and the Mexican help has been redoubled by the arrival of the art scene. Demographically speaking, most Marfans live on the other side of the tracks. The 2010 census shows the "Hispanic or Latino" population in and around Marfa dipping from about 70 percent in 2000 to 67 percent, and the white population edging up by about 4 points to 31 percent—a small but significant swap that partially accounts for the arrival of the new gentry and the displacement of the native population. The new Marfa obscures the persistence of the old one.

Marfa is the land of *Giant*, after all, where Dennis Hopper's doe-eyed Jordan Benedict III falls for the brown beauty of Juana, a Mexican-American played by the Tijuana-born actress Elsa Cárdenas; the ensuing miscegenation registers the leitmotif that climaxes with the brawl between Rock Hudson's Jordan Benedict and Mickey Simpson's "Sarge," a cigar-chomping vet who refuses to serve a Mexican family at his restaurant, while a strident rendition of "The Yellow Rose of Texas" punctuates the punches.

The Supreme Court's striking down of "separate but equal" in 1954 did not bring any rapid changes to Marfa. De facto segregation in education continued until the Blackwell School, the "Mexican" school on the other side of the tracks, closed in 1965 and the "white" school was integrated. Housed in an old adobe, Blackwell had been mostly shuttered since. It was a real estate inquiry by the new Marfa that opened its doors again. Word was that the building would be torn down and an art gallery would rise in its place.

Blackwell alumnus Joe Cabezuela (class of 1960) thought the town had more than enough galleries already and not enough public space for Mexican Marfa. Cabezuela, every inch a retiree in his glasses, khaki shorts, and tennis shoes, gives me a tour of the old school, whose lime façade is literally crumbling, exposing the old mud brick beneath. We are joined by fellow Blackwell alumnus Richard Williams, whose great-grandfather, a black man and one of the Buffalo Soldiers stationed at Fort Davis, married a local Mexican woman.

"No dejaban que se junataran los alumnos mexicanos con los de Marfa Elementary," he says. "Allá habían puros güeros, los chavalitos de los rancheros." The Mexican students weren't allowed at Marfa Elementary; the students were all white, the kids of the ranchers.

White kids, ranchers, Mexicans: Cabezuela has set the historical stage with the leading roles of race and class.

The foundation for the building was laid in 1889, for a Methodist church. The school was kindergarten through eighth grade. "Back then," Joe says, many Mexicans thought that school, for them, "only went to the eighth grade."

Ironically, for decades the Blackwell School stood next to Fort D. A. Russell, which had been founded as Camp Marfa to act against Mexican revolutionaries straying across the border and later served as a post for the Mounted Watchmen, an early incarnation of the Border Patrol. Then Donald Judd arrived and made it Art.

The plan to tear down the building crystallized ideas about Marfa and history for the Blackwell alumni. The problem was simple: although they are a large majority, Mexicans are largely invisible in Marfa— invisible, that is, mostly north of San Antonio Street, where the government buildings and most local businesses are located, and where the galleries and restaurants of the boom alighted. This erasure was so absolute and reflexive as to be unnoticeable to those who performed it. Take the Presidio County Museum in Marfa, housed in a Victorian building on San Antonio Street itself. The chronological exhibit runs from the ancient fauna of the area to the Indians, then jump-cuts to the arrival of the railroad, the ranching era, and the filming of *Giant*. The narrative bypasses the Mexican period, with no mention of Mexican-American war veterans in the military history section, no nod to Mexico the country or to the shared border, and no reference to the Blackwell School.

The remedy was simple, the Blackwell alumni strategized: turn the school into a museum and bring back history.

Cabezuela and the alumni approached the county government, which still owned the building, and secured a symbolic $1 annual lease for ninety-nine years. A call went out for memorabilia. Williams, a computer whiz, started restoring old class photos using Ulead software. Someone found two of the original student desks. One of them has the name "Henry Leyva" carved into the wood, with the final "a" barely outlined. ("Maybe he got caught," says Joe.) A large portrait of old man Blackwell himself, the founder, turned up. He cuts a Rockwellesque figure, silver-haired, beady-eyed, unsmiling.

The museum's inaugural event was billed as a big reunion, everyone invited. To get the word out locally, Richard made up flyers with blown-up black-and-white images of the old class photos. The posters were hung in storefronts across town—in the old Marfa (Pueblo Market, Corder Lumber), but also in the new, at the galleries and chic restaurants, where kids with toothy grins and horn-rimmed glasses now stared out of postmodern frames, a new kind of art installation.

The alumni undertook a big cleanup of the building, weeks of depositing worthless stuff in dumpsters around town. During an inspection of the foundation, Joe found a Ping-Pong paddle; he thinks a kid might have dropped it through a crack in the floor, hoping to spare himself and others corporal punishment. Richard found a pencil in a forgotten corner, just a nub of it left—people were poor. Seats from an old school bus turned up in the attic. Alumni pitched in by handing over prom memory books, a report card from 1948, a commencement program from 1952.

Nearly five hundred people turned out for the first reunion in the summer of 2007.

"If we don't do this ourselves," Joe says, "we're going to lose our history."

The Mexicans had been doing it for themselves all along. Starved of support and resources for the school, generations of Blackwell families had organized "coronations," selling tacos, menudo, and tamales to raise money. At its peak in the 1950s, the Parent Teacher Association had 180 intensely active members.

Reconsecrating the school prompted memories, and reckonings.

Richard Williams tells of using the surname Espudo at school so that he would fit in and not have to constantly explain away "Williams." Now he's proud of his lineage, of being a black Mexican of the border.

Joe Cabezuela's memory unearthed the erasure of an erasure. The year was 1955; the teacher's name was Evelyn Davis. Joe was in first grade. Davis thought that to improve the academic prospects of her underachieving students, she needed to get them to stop speaking Spanish. She devised an elaborate symbolic event for the students, the burial of "Mr. Spanish." A small coffin was fashioned out of cardboard painted black. The effigy was textual: students were asked to write down a Spanish word (many of them couldn't, since they'd never been taught Spanish spelling or read a book in their native language); then they were told to place the word in the coffin. The students were assembled at the foot of the flagpole, Old Glory whipping in the fall wind off the Marfa Plain. The elaborate ceremony included "pallbearers" and a "minister."

Evelyn Davis herself chronicled the event with a recollection entitled "The Last Rites of Mr. Spanish." She had taught high school and college in Seguin, Texas, where she'd "found it difficult to correct the heavy German accent of my students and so was determined to do a better job in speech instruction at Blackwell.

"Conning my seventh graders and other pupils, I convinced every one we would bury Spanish and perfect our English every hour at school."

She describes the preparations for the burial and arrives at the time to close the casket and lower it into the grave: "Everything had been perfect up to this moment until two pallbearers, who had not rehearsed, were to lower the casket with dignity. They started pulling against each other in disagreement, which was followed by anger, and then a volley of Spanish cuss words #%!*$*? The solemnity turned into titters, then giggles followed by hilarious laughter as the bearers threw dirt at each other.

"What a GREAT FIASCO."


One day in 1965, without ceremony or even advance warning, Blackwell students were told to pick up their desks and move to their new integrated school across the tracks. The move is remembered as chaotic and traumatic. Six-year-olds dragged desks larger than themselves; parents rushed into the street to help.

The year of desegregation, Joe Cabezuela decided to run for Marfa High's student government on a Mexican slate. Initially, the cohort was told that Mexicans couldn't vote because they had not paid their freshman dues. So they paid their dues. They thought victory was assured, since Mexicans outnumbered whites almost two to one, but the whites won president, vice president, and secretary. Joe canvassed the Mexican student body and discovered that only three or four had declined to vote for their own, evidence that the election had been rigged. A budding activist, Joe didn't relent until he reached a compromise with the administration: that year and that year only, Marfa High School seated two presidents, two vice presidents, and two secretaries, each office held by one white and one Mexican student.

When the new Marfa started hearing stories about the old, there were some pledges of support. Lynn Crowley contributed cash to fund a documentary about the Blackwell School. And then there was the Big Read, an NEA-sponsored program in which the new elites read Rudolfo Anaya's *Bless Me, Ultima*. One local literatus approached the organizers with the idea of presenting a lecture comparing "conceptions of space" in the famed Chicano novel and the work of Marfa's own Donald Judd.

In the culminating moment of the reunion, the alumni assembled around the flagpole as many of them had fifty-three years earlier, and watched as Mr. Spanish was symbolically disinterred. (It wasn't the coffin from all those years ago, of course; the original had long since disintegrated.) The reborn Mr. Spanish took his place inside the old school, in the new museum. The small coffin lay against the wall, open, revealing a pocket Spanish dictionary, a small vaquero-style hat, and a typical Mexican serape.

Now Joe Cabezuela is looking for major funders, and Richard Williams has taken the title of archivist for the Blackwell School Alliance. Trying to put together the definitive list of Blackwell alumni is a challenge. There was no yearbook until the early 1960s. Attendance lists were shredded as their government time limits expired. Many of the school's trophies from hundreds of regional and state tournaments have simply been thrown away. So Richard combs through forgotten boxes, looking for photographs of students, alone or in groups, searching for faces he can place a name to. The ones he cannot name he posts on the alumni website, hoping someone will reclaim them.

One afternoon he sits at the computer and scrolls through the photo collection. These are the visages that stared out from the storefronts to announce the reunion. A boy with a Pendleton plaid jacket (it was winter) and a long wave of black hair crossing his forehead, shining with pomade, smiling through thin lips, his eyes brilliant under woolly eyebrows. Another boy wears a fedora with the brim folded back, like a *Little Rascals* character, looking like the class clown. A girl about ten years old with her perfect "trenzas," braids, hanging halfway down her chest. Another young girl wearing a dress of chiffonlike material, her face turned up and away, giving us a three-quarter profile, an innocent's gaze toward heaven.

None of them have been identified yet. Richard has faint recollections of some of them. Sometimes he feels like he's on the verge of pronouncing a name.

For now, the alumni work on a shoestring, investing the hours of their retirement, but another kind of gallery has been born in Marfa.

"It's going to be a new one," Joe Cabezuela says, but what's inside it "is all going to be old."

## 5.

Fernando Carrizales, a ranch helper at Chinati Hot Springs, joins Jeff, Dave, and Krissy for dinner one night. He commutes to work from San Antonio del Bravo, which lies just across the Rio Grande from Candelaria, a village several miles north of the springs. He is a tall, graying paisano, as formal in manner as the Old World señor he is. He is dressed like the American cowboys, who, after all, arrived at their style via the Mexican "vaquero." He does not speak much English, and I become the interlocutor. (Jason's good border Spanish could get the job done, but he cedes me the role.)

Jeff is curious about making a visit to San Antonio del Bravo, which is connected to Candelaria by a modest footbridge. It is one of the last informal crossings left along the U.S.-Mexico border. Within days of

9/11, most of these crossings were officially closed, which generally meant a Border Patrol officer putting up a sign warning people that entering into the United States without passing inspection at an official port of entry could result in six months in prison and a $10,000 fine. At the Candelaria bridge, the BP took the extra step of tearing out the planks—half of them, that is, beginning on the American side and extending to the plank that the officers estimated was halfway across the river. The Border Patrol stopped because the rest of the bridge was over the Rio Bravo, not the Rio Grande, the raging river of Mexico, not the big river of America.

But the residents of Candelaria and San Antonio del Bravo simply replaced the planks. Most families have relatives in both villages and go back and forth regularly. Children who live on the Mexican side attend school on the American side.

As for Americans crossing the bridge into Mexico, they can walk over to San Antonio del Bravo, where there is no Mexican federal police presence, and hang out with the natives as long as they want to—but the BP might catch them on their way back. If people really want to use this particular bridge and not risk apprehension, their only option is to make the fifty-mile trip to Ojinaga (over a road that often washes out during the monsoon) and answer the U.S. Customs officer's questions about their nationality and what they might be bringing back from Mexico (fifty tons of cocaine, sir).

Fernando is a reminder of Old Mexico in the context of a new order. Before 9/11, Mexico had always been a convenient escape for us Americans, providing cheap sex, drugs, vacation. All of which was mirrored in Western films, which often took a turn across the river.

El otro lado was certainly there for the Martínez family. Our border home away from home when I was growing up was the Rosarito Beach Hotel in Baja. The place was well past its heyday (when Hollywood regularly called—Welles, Hayworth, Monroe), its grandiosity grown dusty and quaint. We'd take two rooms, one where us kids would sleep with my grandmother, the other for my parents. I remember falling asleep listening to the thud of disco music from the ballroom, where my parents danced and drank; somehow they were always capable of acting like parents through their hangovers the next morning. During the boom years, Baja became a popular second-home opportunity for Americans, and today three immense luxury condo-hotel towers loom over the original hotel. When the cartel wars exploded in the borderlands, decapitated bodies started showing up not far from the resort, which meant the end of that particular tentacle of the boom. Vacations are cheaper than ever in Rosarito Beach these days.

Fernando Carrizales has houses in Candelaria and in San Antonio del Bravo, both places just a couple hundred yards off the river. When there is no BP around, he crosses the bridge; when there is, he either waits for the migra to move on or wades across the river in a quiet spot. The only complication is during monsoon season, when a migra presence near the bridge might coincide with the river becoming impassable. Sometimes he must wait for days.

Fernando says that earlier today, crossing was not an epic, not even difficult. He simply walked over on the bridge, past the bilingual sign warning of consequences—what's left of it around the bullet holes that locals have plugged into it since 9/11. He knew there was no migra because residents on the American side use walkie-talkies to keep their relatives informed. But the fact is that there are fewer and fewer people who live full-time in San Antonio. Years of drought have devastated dryland farming and ranching. As a side job, Fernando uses his van to run foodstuffs from Ojinaga up to San Antonio on the bone-rattling road.

All of this sounds very romantic to the Americans listening to him—especially when he talks of village life on the other side. We like the idea of the isolation, the rough roads, the river rolling low with drought and suddenly high with the monsoon. We like the idea of the other side, a parallel universe of difference. Oh, how we want to go to Old Mexico! Even more so now that we're in a locked-down New West, because we're liberals and we want to thumb our noses at Homeland Security.

Fernando says that there is a fiesta coming up in San Antonio—will we give him the honor of coming as his guests?

We will.


As it happens, Jeff cannot join us for the trip. On the phone, he sounds torn about not being able to come, but Lynn Crowley is throwing herself a big birthday party in Marfa and he feels obligated to attend. He would rather come with us, he says; the trip over the footbridge is something he's wanted to do for a long time. During the trip, I'd meant to ask him if he's read any of Cormac McCarthy's border trilogy. I wonder if, like me, he's imagined himself as a young John Grady Cole, crossing the river on horseback, riding toward love and trouble in the South.

We hop into Dave and Krissy's Dodge pickup, running a little late at four in the afternoon—we were supposed to meet Fernando about this time in Candelaria. The undulating road is both dusty and muddy, from the monsoon rains and the blasting West Texas sun; Dave is intent on keeping the speed above fifty, and I close my eyes every time we approach a torrent of muddy water—how many times have I read the warning about never driving during monsoon season when water, even just a little, is running across a road? Dave doesn't even slow down as he rams straight through, great fans of water jetting up from the tires.

In Candelaria we meet Fernando Carrizales Jr., who will guide us to his father's village on the other side. A handsome man in his thirties, Fernando junior has a Zapata mustache and a thin, tightly braided tail of coarse black hair trailing to a point between his shoulder blades. He wears a woven straw hat that is stained with work and sweat but still shines in the sun, exactly like Jeff Fort's. What makes his outfit are his boots, tannish yellow, of lizard skin; they blend well with the monsoon mud. We are presently slogging through it as we walk down to the riverside along a dirt road that looks to be impassable to vehicles when it rains. Every few feet we have to chart a new course to avoid the pools of water and ridges of mud, which threaten to suck the shoes off our feet.

It is early summer, just a few days after the solstice, and the hottest hour of the day comes late in the afternoon. The sky is clear but for a few scattered cumuli. There is little breeze. Dave and especially Krissy are ruddy and sweaty after only a few minutes in the heat. I immediately regret not having packed more water. I'd debated, as I always do, between traveling light and coming prepared for a survival scenario. What if the BP descends on us on our return from the other side? I am struck by the theoretical possibility of a borderless existence: if I sit on the bridge at the midway point, with my body half in one country and half in the other, then neither one can detain me.

The narrow road, lined by tall tamarisks sucking hard on the river, gives way to a large clearing, and I'm shocked to see that several trucks with horse trailers have actually made it through the mud and parked. And there it is: a humble suspension-style bridge over the Grande/Bravo, a span of about thirty feet. The river is running at a good pace, the very color of Fernando's boots. A large family crosses before us, all smiles. The occasion for the fiesta is the inauguration of a new rodeo ring built by a town patrón.

Now it's our turn. The bridge bounces slightly, and I flash through a detailed fantasy of tumbling into the turgid waters and being swept downriver along the invisible line, where each country is swallowed into the nothingness of the border. A few of the weathered planks are loose, but overall the bridge is perfectly sound. When I near the halfway mark I slow my step just a tad, not enough for anyone to notice; there are people ahead of me and behind, all Mexicans who are crossing without giving it a second thought. I wonder if the BP knows about today's fiesta and whether the absence of patrolmen is a neighborly gesture. I imagine the line that bisects the river, and I give a tiny skip over it.

The rodeo fiesta is at the house of the town's richest family. The metal of the corral gates is shiny new. In the shade of the handsome brick house the family members sit in collapsible chairs, the kind with pockets for drinks. The poor of the village—that is to say, practically everyone else—are offered no shade, no chairs, no drinks, and no food, even though there is plenty of everything. The heat is merciless, the light blinding, but the people whoop it up for the rodeo.

Then it's on to Fernando's house, offers of menudo and Bud Light, to spend the night, to return to the rodeo, to come back whenever we want, that their house is ours.

In late afternoon, the clouds gather for the storm. It's starting on the American side. Krissy nudges Dave. Time to go.

Fernando makes a joke about Krissy being "la jefa."

Krissy laughs but not really. She is smarting from the sun, upset about the way the animals are treated in the ring, nervous about the migra or a narco shootout.

And right on cue, a semiautomatic goes off, about a dozen rounds, no more than a hundred yards away. No one ducks. But even Fernando seems perturbed. After a few moments of silence, Fernando shrugs it off. It's a fiesta, after all.

And now heaven and earth reveal each other. The sun breaks through the weaker part of the storm in the west, casting a brilliant spotlight on a butte on the American side of the river. A rainbow arcs across the eastern sky, and soon a second one, fainter, mirrors it, the two forming a great gateway to the American mountains with the anglicized Spanish name derived from the hispanicized Indian word that Judd gave his empire: Chinati.

We, the illegal Americans, get a ride to the bridge from acquaintances of Fernando's in the back of a pickup, swerving through the mud. When we arrive at the riverside, a middle-aged woman wearing a long white dress is standing halfway across, just staring at the water, mesmerized by the flow. She turns and smiles at us.

It is just another summer Sunday afternoon in West Texas, in north-central Mexico, on the Rio Bravo where it musters up the courage to course into its Big Bend. There is no narco shoot-'em-up, no Western darkness. There is no coyote—neither the smuggler nor the mythic trickster. There is no demarcation between one world and another. The river does not divide. Right here, right now, the river unites the land.

A year later, Candelaria is on edge. Homeland Security has served notice to the landowner on the American side of the bridge to remove it—or have it dismantled by the federal authorities.

On the porch of a house a few hundred yards from the bridge, I sit with Olivia Lozano and her daughter Rosa María. It is around midday, terribly hot, and the power is out for miles around. There is nothing for mother and daughter to do but rest and fan themselves.

The Lozano family has straddled the river since forever. Olivia had children born on both sides. Her husband was born here; she was born there. As far back as they can remember, there has been some Border Patrol presence in the area, but the officers knew the residents, and you could walk across the bridge for a doctor's appointment or for shopping. Then came 9/11.

"Who knows," Rosa María says, giggling, "maybe one of us is a terrorist."

She went fishing the other day. There is plenty of carp and catfish. The good spot to throw the line from was on the other side. When she walked back across the bridge, an agent caught her and hassled her, but ultimately he let her go.

"Is the fish illegal, too?" Rosa María says.

Someday, says Olivia, someone's going to die because of the border that's suddenly become real. For life-threatening illnesses, the people of San Antonio del Bravo have always used the bridge to get to the clinic in Presidio, the closest American border town with medical services, about an hour away by car. Without the bridge, the ride to Ojinaga, the closest town with a clinic on the Mexican side, takes up to three hours.

Rosa María's father is confined to a wheelchair on this side; one of her brothers lives on the other, tending crops. When the migra was around and he didn't have time to drive the round-trip to visit the old man, they would meet halfway across the bridge. The father was wheeled out and the son would bring a chair, and there the two would sit, face to face, talking as the sky dimmed and cicadas hummed, the muddy flow gurgling beneath them.

A week after my visit with Olivia and Rosa María, Homeland Security removed the bridge, invoking the authority of the war on terror to dismiss any pieties about whether half of the bridge was in Mexico.

At the crossing today there is only the old, shot-up sign warning that transgressions of the law will be met with consequences.

## 6.

My writer friend, Denise Chávez, says I absolutely must meet with her cousin Enrique, who lives about an hour's drive from Marfa. He is a living encyclopedia of border history, "muy especial."

Over the phone she says that he likes sweets. "Bring him something dulce."

I pick up a dozen sweet rolls, the kind with heavy icing and a list of unpronounceable ingredients. From Marfa I take Highway 67 through the ghost-mining town of Shafter, to Presidio, on the Rio Grande. The road begins on the high, grassy plain and plummets a few thousand feet to the valley floor. There are only a handful of villages in the area. Presidio County, which includes Marfa, comprises 3,855 square miles and has a population of barely seven thousand people. It is also one of the poorest counties in the United States, making it a close relative of New Mexico's Rio Arriba. And like in Rio Arriba, that poverty is largely invisible, lost in the immensity of both the land and the Western mind that imagines it. The county seat of Presidio is a small American border town, and like all such towns it is filled with Mexicans—about 95 percent of the population.

The lowlands hugging the river are an inferno compared to Marfa's temperateness—"tierra caliente," as they say in Spanish—and the river helps create the perfect storm of heat, humidity, and mosquitoes. The grasses of the plains give way to the spiny reeds of the ocotillo and tall stalks of sotol. The draws that drain the higher country give the impression that the land is being sucked down into the river valley, as if a hand is pulling a sheet off a bed, down toward the floor.

This is Enrique's country: Redford, Texas, population 136.

Enrique is home when I arrive. He almost always is. When he's not, he's at the post office—he is the town's postmaster—just a few dozen yards away. He lives on the main road, in a house whose rooms would feel spacious if the space weren't taken up with Enrique's collection. Almost every wall is lined with bookshelves, sometimes two deep, floor to ceiling, every inch filled with books and magazines and photocopied articles.

He receives the tray of sweet rolls with a smile. He invites me to sit, and I wait for him to carve out a space on the sofa, which is also piled high with books and papers. The dogs sniff my shoes. A cat leaps onto the sofa through a hole in a window screen.

Enrique wears a red guayabera detailed in white, probably the least common color scheme in the guayabera genre. Reading glasses hang from a chain around his neck. He has a full head of hair beginning to gray; a band of thick strands slices across his forehead and bushy eyebrows.

There is not much time for small talk—or for my questions, for that matter. The presentation, the performance begins.

He drops a book in my lap: *The Militarization of the U.S.-Mexico Border, 1978–1992: Low-Intensity Conflict Doctrine Comes Home*, by Timothy J. Dunn. The book is open to a particular page, and Enrique points out a paragraph. He reads part of it out loud, from memory and verbatim, as I read along.

The image of the U.S.-Mexico border region that emerges from . . .
alarmist portrayals is that of a vulnerable zone in urgent need of
numerous, serious security measures, to repel an "invasion" of "illegal
aliens," to win the War on Drugs, and even to counter the threat of ter-
rorism. Complex international issues such as undocumented immigration and illegal drug trafficking were reduced to one-sided, domestic
border control problems and framed as actual or potential threats to
national security, which in turn required strong law enforcement, or
even military responses.

Before I can go further, on top of the open book he places a clipping
from the *Denver Post*, October 13, 1991. It is an article about the war on
drugs, the theater of which is imagined to be on the border (out in the
desert, where Cormac McCarthy conjures his darkness, where Mexicans slither across the sand at night) rather than in the typical American living room where the drugs are consumed. As I read, Enrique
quotes, again verbatim, one Michael Lappe, a U.S. Customs officer, who
says that Redford, Texas, is "the drug capital of the Southwest."

On top of the *Post*, Enrique places a copy of the *Big Bend Sentinel*, the
paper of record in Far West Texas. The lead article details the killing of
Esequiel Hernández by U.S. Marines on patrol with a unit called Joint
Task Force 6, charged with drug interdiction efforts on the border, near
Hernández's house in Redford; this is the event that *The Three Burials of
Melquiades Estrada* is based upon. The tragedy occurred in the wake of a
key point of escalation of the war on drugs ordered by President George
H. W. Bush.

Now an issue of *National Geographic* is added to the pile in my lap.
The writer, a man named Richard Conniff (who on another assignment
swims with piranhas in the Amazon), gets himself and us close to the
danger at hand. In a helicopter flyover of the region he describes how
the people of this fallen corner of the world live. Enrique recites: "The
homes looked like a scattering of rotten teeth in a damaged old mouth."

He repeats the phrase three times.

"So," Enrique asks, his voice rising, his mouth dry, "what kind of
people live on the border? Cavity people? Pus people? What do you do
with rotten teeth? You pull them out and destroy them."

There are indeed rotten teeth on the border, Enrique says, but they are not the subject of Conniff's article. Who could be more rotten than former Presidio County sheriff Rick Thompson, the one with tons of cocaine in his horse trailer? The Marines who trained for the assignment that resulted in Hernández's killing were given the same imagery and ideas as the magazine's readers, to justify their operation on the border. Not only were they told that Redford was the "drug capital of the Southwest"; they were also informed that 75 percent of Redford residents were involved in drug trafficking.

"Seventy-five percent," Enrique repeats. "One hundred people live in Redford. That means that seventy-five of them are drug smugglers."

Off a shelf comes a General Accounting Office report on the border, a profile of the place and its people. Enrique recites as I read, an eerie echo: "1/4 of the population on the U.S. side lives in poverty. Along the line in Texas, 35 percent live in poverty."

Nearly half of children and seniors live in poverty. In Redford, the per capita annual income is $3,577, with over 80 percent of the population living under the poverty line.

"If seventy-five percent of us are drug smugglers," Enrique says, "we better get in another line of business."

Enrique presents me with a photograph of his mother, Lucía Rede Madrid, taken in the cross-border lending library—pre-9/11, of course— she founded in the building that once housed the Madrid family's general store. The project brought her many commendations, including a medal from the first President Bush for being one of the nation's "thousand points of light." She started the library in 1979 with twenty-five of her own books. By the time she arrived at the White House in April 1990, she had fifteen thousand titles. Among the hundreds of children she mentored was one Esequiel Hernández.

Now he shows me the discharge papers of his uncle Sergeant Alberto Rede, who served with the Army Air Corps in World War II, receiving the Distinguished Flying Cross for combat missions in the South Pacific. Another uncle, Ruben Rede, served in the army and was awarded three Bronze Stars for service in Tunisia, Naples, Rome, and Arno.

"The Marines that killed Esequiel Hernández were not in Europe or in Vietnam or in Iraq, or in Mexico with General John Pershing's Mexican expedition," Enrique says.

Esequiel Hernández was American. His death was the first instance since Kent State in which American military personnel killed an American on American soil.

Esequiel Hernández was herding the family's goats on a bluff above the river. He carried his .22 with him—of World War I vintage, a single-shot rifle. Unbeknown to him—indeed, to all of the residents of Redford—a four-man Marine unit was on reconnaissance duty in the area. They were dressed in Special Operations Reconnaissance ghillie suits.

"This is what they looked like," Enrique says, handing me the G.I. Joe version, still in the box with the clear plastic window. The doll went on sale four months before the Marines arrived in Redford. The Hasbro Corporation had composed the following pitch for its new line: "The U.S. Marine Corps Sniper must be a superb marksman and a master at field craft and aggressive tactics. Outfitted in a ghillie suit, this G.I. Joe soldier carries a Remington 7.62 MM M40A1 sniping rifle, and a Colt arms assault rifle. He also comes with binoculars to spot his target."

Esequiel was standing by an old dry well, the goats nearby. On the bluff he was within sight of his family's home. Nobody knows exactly what Esequiel Hernández saw in the minutes before he was hit with a single round from Corporal Clemente Banuelos's rifle. Maybe movement in the matorrales. A bushy thing amid bushes. One green against another.

Or worse: a hulking, stringy Medusa. It was 1997, and the chupacabra was center stage in the folklore of the moment. The legendary creature was said to kill farm animals, especially goats, by sucking their blood, like a rural vampire. The incidents coincided with devastating droughts in northern Mexico and the borderlands, the disruption of the Mexican rural economy because of free trade, the increasingly violent war on drugs.

The Marines were two hundred yards away, a distance that remained constant until just before the fatal shot was fired, when the Marines closed the gap to 140 yards.

The Marines did not see a human form, either. They saw a drug smuggler, because they'd been told that 75 percent of Redford residents were drug smugglers and that Redford was the drug capital of the Southwest.

Esequiel fired his rifle once, maybe twice. What direction he fired in later became a point of contention. Whether he readied to fire a second

or third time, as Corporal Banuelos claimed, was also a point of contention. Another man in Banuelos's unit first testified that he did not see
Hernández aim in the direction of the Marines, but he later changed his
story and corroborated Banuelos's version of events.

Corporal Banuelos radioed headquarters about the situation. The
rules of engagement stated that the Marines could fire only when they
were in imminent danger and had exhausted other defensive options,
such as retreating from the threat. These rules had been written for
Joint Task Force 6 anti-drug operations in general, and Banuelos was
told to follow them. There was no guidance for Marines on patrol within
yards of American civilians who had no idea that the military was in
the area.

The Marines only knew that Redford was "hostile" and its residents
almost certainly involved in the drug trade. There were no "friendlies"
in Redford. Banuelos fired at what he imagined was a fearsome smuggler who was firing at him. Esequiel Hernández spun with the impact
and plunged into the well.

The autopsy established that he had his back to the Marines when the
fatal shot was fired. Investigators also determined that at no time did
Esequiel advance on their position. From the moment visual contact
was made, he was moving away—almost certainly because he feared
whatever it was that was lurking in the matorrales.

The corps' own internal investigation found "systemic failures at
every level of command." The Marines never offered Hernández medical aid. Forty minutes elapsed between the shooting and the arrival of a
rescue helicopter. The forensic examination established that Hernández
would have died of his wounds regardless. But, according to the Marines'
report, that should not have mattered to Banuelos and his men. It was
a "basic humanitarian responsibility" to offer aid in such a situation. The
report found that the Marines had not been adequately trained to do so.

Corporal Clemente Banuelos was a Mexican-American only four
years older than Esequiel Hernández; he was a young man who had much
in common with the man he killed, but on the day they came together
on the hard red earth on the bluff above the Rio Grande, neither recognized the other. Esequiel probably saw a monster, and that is certainly
what Banuelos saw, manufactured masks obscuring the truth that when
he pulled the trigger, Banuelos was shooting at himself.

• • •

On another visit, I notice that some of the books and articles Enrique piles on my lap have passages highlighted in yellow marker—a concession to his weakening eyesight.

Today we begin with geography.

"The border," Enrique says, "is two thousand miles long." And it is much wider than the line that represents it—because of free trade, because of migration, because of the intricate commercial and human relationships between the towns on either side of it. The border, Enrique says, is a vast realm.

The population of this place—communities on both sides within sixty miles of the line—was 10.5 million in 1997. By 2017, it will have doubled. No border, Enrique says, can remain one given that fundamental demographic fact. "And what do they bring us here in Redford?" Enrique says. "The National Guard. Army Reserve."

They have returned. This is an unthinkable reversal for Enrique. Largely because of the brilliant activism he and his cohort waged following Esequiel Hernández's death, all military personnel were pulled off the line. But ten years have passed since then, and it seems that the memory has faded enough for the troops to return with the same justification as before, embellished with post-9/11 paranoia. Six thousand National Guard troops were dispatched to the border as part of Operation Jump Start to offer tactical support—to staff observation posts, install new fencing and vehicle barriers, build new roads and Border Patrol stations. But at several points along the line, especially in New Mexico and Texas, they are allowed to carry arms. According to the authorities, the weapons are for self-defense.

"That's what they said the last time," Enrique remarks.

Now he is weaving together big historical moments, the Nuremberg Trials, Kent State. Then he looks to passages in the Old Testament that spell out the ethics of hospitality. He thunders and shudders like a fire-and-brimstone preacher. He leans in toward you, gets uncomfortably close; spittle flies from his lips.

"It's racist blindness!" he shouts.

It is as if he seeks, with the stories, the numbers, the arguments, the lives at stake, to raise the body of Esequiel Hernández, a son of the border, named for the Old Testament prophet who in a vision saw the Valley of Dry Bones—the place where the dead took on flesh when Ezekiel spoke the Word.

After such an outburst Enrique sits down heavily, with a grunt. He might walk out of the room for a long while, pace the kitchen in the terrible heat, or sit with his head bowed over his hands, his elbows splayed on the table.

He carries the pain of the border in his head.


In one session Enrique hands me two pictures. Emiliano Zapata, the sad-eyed Mexican revolutionary, sits astride his horse. Subcommandante Marcos, nearly a century later, stands among the indigenous leadership of the Zapatista movement in Chiapas.

With the pictures still in my lap, he piles on a new GAO study on poverty in the region. It has worsened since my last visit. Now 48.1 percent of people in Presidio County live below the poverty line, in the same county as the Marfa Book Company and Maiya's restaurant.

"We've been Americans since 1848," says Enrique. "It doesn't pay to be an American."

And yet, billions of dollars may soon pour into the region for the transpacific superhighway. By one estimate, 1.5 million trucks a year will roar through the Big Bend.

"And the border will fall," says Enrique.

This is counterintuitive. As Enrique is envisioning the Americas' version of the euro (the "amero") and a borderless state from Canada to Tierra del Fuego, the walls are going up. The Secure Fence Act of 2006 brought eight hundred miles of fencing and National Guard troops to the line.

Another article in my lap. From an essay by Richard Rodriguez: "To placate the nativist flank of his Republican Party, President Bush has promised to brick up the sky. But that will not prevent the coming marriage of Mexico and the United States. South and north of the line, we are becoming a hemispheric people—truly American—in no small part because of illegal immigrants."

"This is the future," Enrique says. He believes that 9/11 was just a brief parenthesis in the process of integration. This coming together is more than trade and politics. He hands me a study of border DNA. Literally. Samples were taken from residents of Ojinaga, and the typical resident was determined to be 5 percent African, 3 percent European, and 91 percent Native American.

"This is our genetic history," Enrique says. "We're still Indians."

He is now lobbying for his people—the Jumano Apache—to become a federally recognized Native nation. The name of his tribe is spelled out in branches of mesquite lashed together on the roof of his house.

"You must read this book," Enrique says, handing me *The Conquest of Texas: Ethnic Cleansing in the Promised Land.*

I read: "The justification for attacks upon such non-Anglo groups evolved out of an imagined fear that such groups would somehow pollute what Anglos perceived as their superior culture."

He shuffles over to me with a framed document. It says, "In the Name of the State of Texas, to all whom these presents shall come, know ye . . ."

It is a land grant to Secundino Luján. Enrique's great-grandfather.

Enrique veers back and forth from his grand vision of continental integration—so Whitmanesque, so Bolívaresque—to the moment Banuelos pulled the trigger, the negation of integration. Now he's talking of Pershing's "punitive expedition" into Mexico, the refugees of the revolution coming across at Presidio, marching through the desert for three days without bread or water, the women bearing it better than the men.

And nearly a hundred years later, war came again, except it was citizen upon citizen. "Just like when George the Third sent British soldiers to make war on British subjects in Boston," Enrique says. "Like sending the National Guard to Kent State. There is a word for that. Tyranny."

He puts a Bible in my hands, open to Leviticus.

He recites chapter 19, verses 33 and 34, from memory: "When a stranger sojourns with you in your land, you shall not do him wrong. You shall treat the stranger who sojourns with you as the native among you, and you shall love him as yourself, for you were strangers in the land of Egypt."

"You have to be hospitable in a desert culture," Enrique says.

Now Montesquieu is on top of the pile, *The Spirit of Laws,* with its ideal of political liberty, which Enrique sums up as "If I'm afraid of you, and you're afraid of me, there is no political liberty."

Here is *Native Science*, by Gregory Cajete, which urges us to consider objects as they are seen in Native cosmology, not in isolation but "in relationship." And Steven LeBlanc's *Constant Battles*, the Harvard archaeologist's effort to deconstruct "noble savage" myths. Ancient Native peoples were anything but Edenic creatures, he writes. They were as complex, as bloody as "us." And naturalist Frederick Gehlbach writes in *Mountain Islands and Desert Seas* that there was another kind of desert before the arrival of Europeans and their livestock, one lush with grasses and cottonwoods along the riparian belts of the rivers in the region— the Bravo, the Conchos, the San Pedro.

Finally, Emmanuel Levinas and his "ethics as a first philosophy."

*Do not kill me . . . make room for me.*

It all adds up to fragmented madness. To a search that ends where it started, to a senseless death in the desert, to a man who has become his library. Yes. And it is also more than that; there is a truth amid the clashing signs. The desert Enrique Madrid lives in is not the Big Empty, not the "spiritual" place of gilded clouds, not cowboys and cacti in silhouette, the desert of the Western or the Travel section. Enrique's desert is crammed with history. An emptiness filled to bursting with stories in search of voices, ghosts in search of bodies.


I spend the night at Enrique's, in a spare bedroom at the back of the house. There is a huge hole in the window screen, and the cats jump over my head, going in and out all night long, which means the mosquitoes get free passage. Their whining attacks remind me of my first trip to Big Bend, which was with Angela. Like most desert parks in the United States, Big Bend is most popular during its cooler seasons, fall through spring. We'd arrived in the middle of August, the devil's breath scorching the land. The campground was a massive asphalt disk that would've driven Ed Abbey to apoplexy. There were no other campers, but a lot of vultures hanging out on the picnic tables, waiting for clueless tourists like us. We were bombarded with mosquitoes in spite of having slathered ourselves with repellent, so we pitched camp quickly to take refuge inside the tent. Of course it was stifling, but we killed the few mosquitoes that had followed us in and settled down for what we thought would be a relatively comfortable night's rest, leaving Bear outside to stand guard.

Just as we were dozing off, he let loose his operatic bark. Then we heard what he'd heard: the unmistakable rhythmic grunting of javelinas. Knowing that they roamed in packs and could be aggressive, I opened the tent fly and dragged Bear inside with us. The grunting increased, and seemed to be coming from several different directions at once. *They're surrounding us*, I thought. Bear started barking again, his nose pressed to the fly screen of the tent. I shone the flashlight into the dark and could see the compact, tusked creatures trotting toward us. Bear became increasingly agitated. In Joshua Tree, Bear played with coyotes, but the javelinas were something else. They stank, and they wanted our food. Now I heard a hoof click on rock only a few yards away. Bear couldn't stand it anymore. He took a couple of steps back from the fly and then charged forward with such force that he tore it open.

Chaos. Bear chasing the javelinas in one direction, then the javelinas chasing him back in the other, me with the flashlight, shouting, cursing the runty thugs, thinking of fetching my old .22 from the bed of the pickup and then remembering the strict laws against firearms in national parks. I finally caught Bear. He was our hero; he'd chased away the javelinas.

But the tent fly: worthless. And we could think of no way to patch it. And even if we could have mended it somehow, the tent was already swarming with mosquitoes. Angela headed for the metallic cocoon of the truck. I wrapped myself in a sheet, leaving only a hole for my nostrils, determined to sleep on the land.

Bear didn't sleep a wink, his ears perked up all night long, listening for the javelinas.

Enrique and his wife, Ruby, often sleep on a bed out on the land behind their house, the only way to get a whiff of cool air at night. No one has air-conditioning in Redford, no one can afford it, and swamp coolers are largely useless because of the humidity from the river. Mosquitoes don't bother Enrique and Ruby; the only animals that do are rattlesnakes. Especially the pygmy variety, Enrique says; they are so small, you can barely hear the rattle even when you're about to step on one.

One night Enrique and Ruby were awakened by the roar of an engine. The camouflaged beast crested a ridge on their property and bore down on their desert bed. A Humvee. The Border Patrol claims that it has the right to cross private property proximate to the border in pursuit of smugglers.

Enrique, of course, contests that. "In the United States," he says, "you need a search warrant even to watch a person through binoculars."

Now, in the unsparing heat at Enrique and Ruby's, I think about going outside and looking for the bed in the desert. But it is a moonless night.

You have to be hospitable in the desert. In the desert there is danger and death, so it is critical to bring to it what redeems us: our ethics.

Out in the desert tonight, there is a migrant trying to get his bearings and a Border Patrol agent hunting the migrant, and there are others: the man who owns a mountain, and an environmentalist, and a film crew shooting humans swallowed by the land, and there is the land, and the dead and the living upon it, and time wheeling them all toward sunrise.

In the wee hours, the bedroom door, which I opened to allow the cats free passage, slams shut with such great force that I feel the bed shudder. I shoot upright. Immediately I think, *The wind. Yes, the wind must have picked up and blown the door closed.*

But there isn't the slightest breeze. It is pitch black and hot. The devil must have sneezed in his cave.

The last time I saw Enrique Madrid was the only time I met him outside his house in Redford.

While I was at the Lannan house in Marfa, I heard about a conference on the construction of the border wall where Enrique was scheduled to give the keynote speech. The conference had been organized by a band of young progressive artists and activists who lived in the Big Bend area and seemed to have little in common with the Marfa gallery crowd—none of whom I would see at the conference. They called themselves the ReViva Collective.

I drove over to the nearby town of Alpine and walked into the meeting hall. I noticed the red guayabera first. Enrique was seated at a table, his back to me. As usual, it took him a short while to remember who I was. When he did, he quoted verbatim a passage from a book I'd written.

I was surprised by his face, the skin pale and tight across his cheek-bones. It hadn't been long since the last time I'd seen him. Then I realized he was sitting in a wheelchair, which he now maneuvered away from the table to face me. I saw that his right leg had been amputated at the knee, the pant leg folded and held in place with paper clips. Diabetes.

I remembered Denise Chávez telling me that I should take her cousin Enrique something sweet.

"You know what they say about amputated limbs?" Enrique asked me. "Well, I can feel my foot. Right now. I can curl my toes.

"They're not down there," he said, pointing at his phantom foot. "It's all in here." He pointed at his head.

When it came time for his presentation, helpers materialized, moving a long table into place, and then Enrique wheeled himself behind it. The contents of several boxes were emptied, and soon there were seven piles across the table: books, magazines, clipped articles, bound reports, framed photographs, and a cardboard box containing G.I. Joe in a ghillie suit. Enrique had brought us his living room.

For the next two and a half hours he wheeled himself around the table, picking up texts, reading, weaving. His voice rose to preacherly cadences and fell into fragmented whispers. In the end, he came back to the underlying theme of the conference, which was the central theme of his life's work: the question of the neighbor.

"What do you do with your neighbors?" Enrique asked. "What do you do with your neighbors?" he asked again. And once more, shouting: "What do you *do* with your neighbors?"

"You talk to them," he said, now in a gentle voice. "You love them. You marry them. You become them."

# CONCLUSION: NEIGHBORS

I lived in Velarde for almost three years, seeking out elders to interview, checking the post office box in the neighboring village of Alcalde, growing vegetables in late spring and summer, and splitting wood in the fall and winter. Several times a month, I filled the bed of my pickup with oozing bags of garbage for disposal at the transfer station. I drove the 68 at least once a day, usually to Española—to Walmart, to the Indian tobacco store, to Walgreens, to the Mexican tortilla place—and now and then to Embudo to see Estevan Arellano or Taos to visit Miguel Santistevan. Sometimes I'd keep going all the way across the Colorado state line into the San Luis Valley and gaze up at Culebra Peak, the Everest of the southern part of the state, which norteños say is really just far northern New Mexico (many since-forever families straddle that border) and where activists recently won an epic fifty-year battle to regain rights to the commons of the old Beaubien-Miranda grant.

In those three years the economic boom peaked and the cost of homes in the desert soared. But the boom never reached the Española Valley, where the only dramatic increase was in the rates of heroin addiction and overdoses.

Death was all around us. People died in head-on collisions on the 68 and on the holy road to the Santuario de Chimayó, most of the accidents alcohol- or drug-related. People died from cancers related to toxic jobs at Los Alamos National Laboratory or from diabetes and cardiac disease because their rural diets had deteriorated with the arrival of fast food, or from alcohol and tobacco. They died of depression, which came from loss.

Every morning when I went upstairs to my office in the attic I'd pause at the window and scan the view. At Lena's place, the carport was empty after she and Joe split up and she disappeared after her overdose. The old Rendón adobe remained abandoned, a hundred shoots of sumac growing wild in the yard. Finally, my eyes would settle on Rose and Jose's place, his black sedan and her red Chevy parked alongside the house. They were almost always home.

We had listened to Rose scream in the dusty heat of summer, in the frigid stillness of winter mornings, and above the rush of the river during the thaw. But when she became pregnant with her second child, things got quieter. I still heard Rose cough on the patio, and Jose was often in the yard, busying himself with the usual chores. He put in a lawn, which he tended carefully. After Rose gave birth we saw the stroller out in front of the house a few times, but never saw the baby, who they named Dion, never even heard him cry.

In three years, the longest conversation I'd had with Jose was about the pipe from our kitchen that drained close to their property line. I didn't realize the kitchen plumbing didn't empty into the septic tank until several months after we moved in. The pipe simply dumped the dirty water at the bottom of the hill behind the house, available to all the neighborhood animals, including our dogs. Someone at Lowe's had suggested spraying the water, which gathered in greasy, detergent-laced puddles, with bleach to repel pets and wildlife. I tried it once, and the next day I saw one of Joe Rendón's dogs lapping it up as usual. Then I came up with the idea to create a kind of canal with river rocks, the heavy, eggplant-sized ones that were strewn all over the area and that told the story of the Great River that flooded and meandered across the valley. But the dogs simply pushed the rocks away with their paws or noses.

One morning I was trying to get heavier rocks into place when Jose came out of his house. We nodded at each other, as we always did, and I called him over. I asked him if there were many drains like this in the area, and whether they were legal. He said that there were, and that surely any new construction wouldn't permit such a setup, but that the old ones—who knew how far back they went?—were probably grandfathered in. I thought of the hundreds of old adobes throughout the valley, and how their waste leaked into the aquifer, which residents tapped with their private wells. Jose said that I should dig a deep ditch where the pipe ended, say four feet down, and then fill it in with rocks; the dogs wouldn't be able to get at the water. It sounded like a good idea. For the first time, I thought of Jose not as a small-time gansgsta, but as a norteño, a man of the land, someone who belonged here.

The encounter also made me think, again, of attempting more of a relationship with our neighbors. But we didn't, for reasons both practical and ethical. This was where we lived. Getting closer to their lives could mean compromising our own. Did we want Rose knocking on our door, hysterical after a fight? Would we be making our house, our possessions, our safety vulnerable because of their business? And then there was the matter of my motivations. Was my desire less about compassion than about literary ambition—gleaning more material for my book? But not opening our doors to them was also a moral issue. Weren't our ideals of solidarity and hospitality, which imbued the articles and books we wrote, about situations precisely like this one? There was no way to look out the window at Rose and Jose without recognizing their profound sadness and pain.

Rose and Jose were our neighbors; we lived within a few hundred feet of them as they fought, made love, ate, as her belly grew with her second child, as their customers pulled in and out of their driveway, as she dragged hard on her joints and coughed and popped her pills, as he snorted and shot up.

There were some beautiful moments. A Fourth of July where Jose bought a big box of fireworks and lit up the night for his eldest son Domonic; I saw the look of delight on the child's face in silver flashes. The family had a bonfire one freezing New Year's Eve. And I remember a few times, which stood out as unusual, when they all lounged outside together on warm spring or summer evenings. On these occasions there was no shouting, no customers, no coughing. In spite of everything—or perhaps precisely because of the precariousness of their lives—they were a family. There was a big plywood sign hanging outside their front gate, facing the dirt road we all shared. In large yellow and orange letters, circus-style script, it read:

SLOW DOWN: CHILDREN AT PLAY.

Four years after we moved into the Velarde house and a year after we left, I woke up at my grandparents' old house in Los Angeles—the one with the Western diorama in the entryway—where Angela and I were living until we could find a place of our own. The desert that I'd begun writing about during the boom now personified the bust. Many of the Western cities that had seen the greatest population growth as well as the biggest increases in real estate values and concentrations of sub-prime mortgage loans were making headlines with soaring rates of unemployment and foreclosures. At the same time, the migrant flow across the border had fallen dramatically, although the number of deaths in the desert had not. (Fewer people now made the journey, but it was just as dangerous, if not more so, because of the fencing that shunted migrants farther and farther out into the remotest wilderness.) The nativists held sway in Arizona politics and had even gained ground in New Mexico, where Susana Martinez parlayed anti-Mexican sentiment among Hispanos and Anglos into winning the governor's office. From Joshua Tree to Marfa, the season of wild speculation was over, but the effects of the boom—that is, the chasm that it opened between haves and have-nots—stood in sharp relief. And although the great recession was forcing many people to move (just as gentrification had a few years earlier), the demographic of the desert West had been fundamentally altered. There were new neighbors across the landscape, and neighbors they would remain.

We continued to follow the news in Velarde, often checking the *Rio Grande Sun*'s website for the latest from the Española Valley. I happened to be scrolling through the news briefs, when I read this:

Deputies Investigate Death of 2-Year-Old
Sun Staff Report

The death of a 2-year-old Velarde child is the subject of an ongoing investigation being conducted by the Rio Arriba County Sheriff's Department. An ambulance met up with the parents of the little boy, Dion Martínez, on State Road 68 as they rushed him to the Hospital May 8, Deputy Freddie Trujillo said. The couple, Jose Martinez and Rose Garcia, told investigators the child had been sick since May 7, suffered from sleeplessness, and finally fell asleep around 5 a.m. May 8. When Garcia went to wake the baby up around 12 p.m. May 8, he was already cold, Trujillo said.

Stunned, I called Angela over to the computer. Our twin daughters had just been born, and we grieved for Dion, the baby we never heard or saw, with the raw emotional intensity of new parents.

We imagined the scene over and over again in the coming days and weeks.

Jose and Rose probably got into his sedan, since he often parked it behind her SUV. He would have driven, talking to the dispatchers on his cell phone while she would have cradled the baby and screamed. We would have heard her, if we had still lived there.

It happened on a spring day. Around noon, it would have been warm, in the upper seventies and windy, with the winds of spring that people in the valley celebrate, the warm breath of the breeze announcing the end of the long winter. The sky was probably clear, and there would have been the smell of young grasses and leaves in the air. The acequias would have been running fast and full, and perhaps there was a tractor out on the camino de en medio.

I could imagine the sedan's engine revving and the cloud of dust plowed up along the dirt road. The sirens would have grown louder as they come north on the 68. Jose must have pulled over to the side of the highway as the ambulance made a U-turn, and Rose would have run to the paramedics, Dion's arms hanging limp. And then the interminable ride to the hospital—all in the shadow of the Black Mesa.

Over the following weeks and months, there was more news from Velarde. The toxicology reports showed traces in Dion's system of chlorpheniramine (an antihistamine common in allergy medication), ibuprofen, ethanol, and cocaine. The cause of death was ruled "multiple drug and drug toxicity" and "global hypoxic-ischemic brain injury." The drugs likely caused cardiopulmonary failure and cut off oxygen to the baby's brain. Dion's death was caused by a drug overdose and ruled a homicide.

He had fallen ill the day before he died with what Rose and Jose described to investigators as severe diarrhea and vomiting. There was fever; they had bathed him in cold water several times through the night to get his temperature down. Rose and Jose said they administered teething tablets, amoxicillin, Dimetapp, and Children's Motrin. They denied knowingly giving him cocaine. When confronted with the evidence, Rose, according to the police report, "became hysterical and shouted that it was not possible," while Jose, informed in a separate interview, "started to cry and could not believe what the [investigator] was saying."

Jose conjectured that there might have been cocaine residue in the bottle containing the teething tablets, which he said had been given to him by someone else.

Early on in the investigation, detectives noted some contradictions in Rose's and Jose's statements. Jose initially said that he went to work early on the morning of his son's death, while Rose said that she took Domonic to school at around the same time, raising the question of who stayed at home with Dion. Eventually Jose admitted to lying. He had not gone to work. (During our entire time in Velarde, he never appeared to be employed.) He'd driven the short distance to the Lyden Bridge over the Rio Grande, where he'd smoked pot and taken a dose of methadone. He said he'd lied because he didn't want investigators or Rose to know what he had been doing. He insisted that Rose was at home with the children when he left the house, and that Dion was still alive.

It sounded as though Rose and Jose had desperately tried to treat Dion in the hours before his death. It sounded as though a terrible mistake had been made—a small ball of cocaine mistaken for a teething tablet, perhaps. It seemed that there were drugs all over the house, legal and contraband, and that, after a sleepless night with Dion, Jose snuck out of the house to get high down at the river's edge.

For two years the case wound its way through the legal system, resulting in a plea bargain. Rose and Jose were ultimately sentenced to three years of probation, which outraged people all over northern New Mexico.

Dion's death and its aftermath made Rose and Jose look both monstrous and pathetic. But something was omitted from the frame, which is the responsibility of the rest of us. I lived next door to this family, and though I was troubled by what I saw, I never thought it was my place to intervene, to use the lingo of rehab. Intervention could have taken many forms, from the intimate to the juridical to the political, from urging Rose and Jose into the recovery program just down the street, to demanding action from the state on behalf of their children, to organizing the community to advocate for comprehensive treatment and prevention services.

I could not abide the thought that I was a useless witness to a crime in which we had all played a part. I had been close. This was a death in my neighbor's house.

We visit Velarde for the first time since leaving for Los Angeles. We return often in the months and years ahead, since we come to see our family in Albuquerque frequently. Each time we do, it feels like we're coming home.

I accompany Angela on a visit to Hoy Recovery at Piñon Hills, her former place of employment. There is a sign announcing the facility at the intersection of the 68 and Lyden Road, out in front of the adobe festooned with red chile ristras that belongs to Rose Garcia's mother. The sign—which includes Hoy's logo, a sun rising into a rainbow dawn—is a landmark for clients, friends and family of clients, cops, paramedics. An arrow points down the road toward the Rio Grande.

Ben Tafoya is Hoy's executive director, a boot-wearing, Spanglish-speaking Hispano. He has held the post for a decade, coinciding with the onset of northern New Mexico's heroin epidemic. From the beginning, Tafoya envisioned "culturally appropriate" strategies to end the revolving door of treatment and make a lasting impact. He wanted to start a long-term residential facility to complement the detox program, a sustainable community where addicts would figuratively bury their disease in the land. They would sow and reap crops, tend animals. They would sell at the farmers' market in Española.

But over the last ten years, most of Tafoya's energy has been spent trying to staunch the bleeding of his funding and fighting off managed-care administrators. Ultimately, Governor Bill Richardson turned the state-subsidized facility over to an out-of-state bottom-line corporation, ValueOptions. The company took one look at Hoy—unlicensed personnel doling out meds and some even accused of getting high with the clients—and promptly stripped the funding for its detox program.

Tafoya persisted. In the end, he didn't need much money or permission from ValueOptions to start up a gardening program for long-term rehab clients. The land was already there: Hoy sat on a dozen acres of rich Rio Grande bottomland.

Ben brought in Robert Espinoza, a local middle-aged farmer, to head the project. The first task was to get the land working again. It had lain fallow for a long time and was nowhere near level, which made drawing water from the acequia impossible. So Robert brought in a pump and hooked up drip lines. The initial crop was chiles, corn, calabacitas, tomatoes, peas, melons, and cucumbers. The same chapulines that had devoured my garden in Velarde arrived after a big wet winter and feasted on every shoot that broke the ground. A very unorganic spraying saved the crop.

Ben had told Robert that he wouldn't have to do much work, that Hoy's clients would be his labor force. But things didn't work out so smoothly. The male addicts, Robert said, were no good to him. They smoked cigarettes in the shade of the cottonwood trees; they flirted with the women. The women, on the other hand, turned out to be serious farmers. So he segregated the work crews—a smart move, since the women worked so hard that they shamed the men into making more of an effort. Still, Robert wound up doing most of the work himself. It's not easy when your work crews are constantly being disrupted as clients finish their thirty-, sixty-, or ninety-day stints and leave, or run away in the middle of the night, get high, and get kicked out of the program. Still, Ben, the optimist, thought he had made a good start.

When Angela and I arrive, the corn stalks are a few feet high and the first batch of calabacitas is being harvested. The tomato plants have been pruned. The chapulines have returned after the pesticide spraying, but the garden is big enough to survive the assault with a decent yield.

We meet a crew of clients handpicked by the staff to show off the success of the gardening program. We sit at a table across from three men and three women. They fidget with sunglasses and cough their cigarette coughs and laugh and smile.

They are all counting the days. A white girl from Santa Fe with an Hispano boyfriend in Dixon is at day twenty-five out of sixty. A famous Hispano carpenter—he's made furniture for prominent politicians in Santa Fe—is at seventeen out of thirty. They list their addictions: alcohol and coke, alcohol and heroin, and plain alcohol.

They say it's good to be out in the garden among the plants, it's good to be quiet and not have to tell their life stories or listen to anyone else's, the litanies of abuse, the victimization, the violence and the depression.

Each of the Hispano clients has some memories, received or real, of being on the land. Ana, a young woman from Chimayó, had rolled her eyes when she first heard about the gardening program. She's been on the land her whole life. It bores her. You can't snort dirt or shoot water, although, she says, once in a while, the land looks good when you're high.

To an extent Angela and I share Ana's skepticism. When Angela first told me about the idea when we'd lived in Velarde, she jokingly referred to it as the "chicos" program because Ben was obsessed with the dry-roasted corn kernels norteños add to just about any dish. Ben was going to save the addicts of the north with chicos—yeah, right. But now, a few years later, the land brings forth what the sun and rain have summoned; the corn stalks rustle in the humid breeze of the monsoon. And our cynicism falls away, as has Ana's: pruning the tomato plants, she senses her place on the land. She remembers the stories of her childhood, of elders a generation and more ago plowing, sowing, irrigating, harvesting under the great deep-blue dome of norteño sky.

The recovery process hasn't been miraculoulsy transformed by chicos, but at Hoy there are moments when the heaviness lifts from the land, when working it brings a deep satisfaction that eases the craving for heroin and cocaine and alcohol and rejoins a circuit that was long ago broken.


I came to the desert to clean up and heal, like the consumptives once did, following the deep symbolic lineage of the desert as destination of restorative pilgrimage, a place to soothe the soul and cleanse the body.

I was an addict, and addiction is a disease—that's what we'd come to call it by the end of the twentieth century. It is an illness of body and mind, and, as Angela argues in *The Pastoral Clinic*, her book on our time in New Mexico, one that is socially and historically situated. Tranquilizers and antidepressants can help to alleviate the worst of corporal detox, but the mental weaning is something else again. For the long-term treatment of addiction, there are only ideas, like surrendering to a higher power or affirmations or taking responsibility. All of these are clichés, and the rates of relapse are much greater than those for staying clean. The massive body of literature around addiction hasn't made any dent in the reach of the disease, in northern New Mexico or anywhere else. It is fairly obvious why, though you never hear it discussed at a caffeine-and-nicotine "meeting."

What is missing from most of the literature is the subjective experience of alienation from places and relationships and representations shaped by power—that is, by the way power violently and unevenly distributes wealth, determining who lives in the trailer and who lives in the adobe chalet and assigning not just the corresponding real estate value but the value of human lives across the social geography. Call it the ethics of boom and bust, the dialectic of the American dream in which there truly is no failure like success—in which boom is predicated on bust. The desert knows this process intimately, having been conquered and colonized over and again. The gap in income inequality has grown steadily over several generations—during times of growth and recession—and did so that much more dramatically during the boom of the aughts.

What is left but to rebel against all of it by dropping out of a process that has already dropped you, even if the rebellion takes its toll on the powerless rebel and not on the powerful. You are low, so you get high.

Of course, there are many others in parallel and radically different realms of alienation. They have turned away from American materialism; their spirits yearn for something more. They, too, search for the high—on the land itself; on Jeff Fort's "jaw-dropping" vista of the Candelaria Rim; on the awe Sam Hitt feels in the Tusas Mountains; on Miguel Santistevan's intimacy with the earth and water and seeds; on Ike de Vargas's ferocious love of the trees he once felled and the animals he still hunts; on the "spirit" Elizabeth Robechek communes with in the woods above Santa Fe; on the biblical landscape animated in Mike Wilson's eyes; on Fred Drake's House of the Moon.

What unites these encounters is the desire borne of alienation: the urge to imagine for ourselves a new life, another country where we will no longer be strangers to ourselves or to each other.

Early one morning during our visit I go to the BLM commons that I used to hike with Bear and Chino. I drive through the gate and over the cattle guard, and for a moment it feels just like my morning ritual in New

Mexico. But there are no dogs in the backseat, and I will not be going home to our house in Velarde. I park at the mouth of a gully that drops down from the hills of juniper and piñon.

I take an old favorite route. There are no human footprints, no hoof-prints, and only very old, dry cow pies. The land looks less stressed than it did when we lived in Velarde. The good rain and snow of the past winter have helped the many piñon shoots, whose needles are green and sturdy. Maybe a generation from now, the piñon will recover from its drought-related die-off—that is, if the drought is truly over and we aren't in the midst of a megadrought.

Throughout the area there are signs of human habitation and land use going back at least hundreds of years. A cave in the side of a butte might have been used as an ancient Pueblo sweat lodge; its entrance is in the shape of a crude cross, perhaps a natural formation that was later enhanced by Catholic penitentes. Cattle and sheep have grazed here since Oñate's arrival; for centuries this land was the commons of the Sebastián Martín grant. A couple of miles northeast of here there is an ojito, a natural spring, and a ranch that was the site of a hippie commune in the 1960s. I am just the most recent arrival.

I gain some of the higher ridges of the route and am greeted by gusts from the prevailing west-southwest winds blowing in from the Jemez. Here is the place where I found what I called the "flying piñon," snags broken off at the root that I'd find several yards and sometimes much farther away from where the tree stood when it was alive. I'd asked some old foresters about this, but no one was familiar with the phenomenon. It seemed to have been caused by a great gust of wind snapping the snag, bearing it aloft for a few seconds, and then tossing it back down. That was the best theory I could come up with—there were no drag marks. The snags were not light, though, so a perfect alignment of conditions would have had to occur: wind direction, a certain level of dry rot in the tree trunk, a particular formation of branches that made for airworthiness.

More than likely no one has ever been present in the actual moment to see a piñon take flight. Maybe a researcher somewhere has studied the phenomenon, but I never looked it up. I want to imagine the moment as one of violent, unexpected beauty. Occurring under circumstances that I cannot fully explain, the flying piñon sets me on an emotional journey that carries me to what I imagine as the border of matter and spirit. I muse that the phenomenon might have struck Lawrence the same way had he come upon the scene a hundred years ago; a fitting emblem for a place that is seen and felt in so many different ways, between the flying piñon and Ike's can of Bud.


At the end of our trip we visit our old street. We take the longer, prettier route from Ohkay Owingeh, heading north along the Lyden Road, and stop at the bridge where Jose got high as Dion was dying. As we turn on to Endalecio Rendón Road, we see the sedan that belongs to Josie, Joe Rendón's wife, parked in front of their trailer. Next door at our old house is the unsettling sight of the exterior wall with a fresh coat of deep-purple paint. The house itself has been painted, too, a shade of earth brown slightly darker than most norteño adobes. The carport at Lena's old place remains empty. The gate is closed at Rose and Jose's, the big CHILDREN AT PLAY sign still there.

We park alongside the Rendón wall and knock on the door of the trailer. Josie answers and recognizes us immediately, invites us in. She is wearing a big T-shirt and shorts. Her grade-school-age son Little Joe is skinny-brown, shy and cute wandering around in his underwear. It is still summer vacation.

Yes, she was here when Dion died. She heard cars charging up and down the dirt road past her trailer, but she didn't think anything unusual was happening.

"It sounded just like when there was heavy business over at Rose's," Josie says. "Or when they'd had a fight, you know what I mean? And that was it until Joe came home later in the afternoon. He walked in and he was crying. And I thought, Oh my God, what happened—who was it this time?"

There was a wake at Club Lumina, and Josie and Joe paid their respects. Most of the village showed up for the funeral at the Velarde cemetery.

And Lena? I asked.

She was dead, too. After her breakup with Cuchi, Lena had overdosed again. "They say it was that drug you take for depression, what's it, Zoloft, and alcohol," Josie says. "Just too much of everything, you know? Now they're both buried up in the cemetery, Dion and Lena, right by

each other, and I told Joe that now we got a lot more people to visit up
there. It just seems like it gets more and more crowded."

Our former landlady Lisa is back in our old house, making improvements, and now planning to move in herself, permanently.

"Joe's all mad at her because she put up this big wall," says Josie. "You
remember that it was just a fence? Well, now it's a wall of tree trunks."

When we say good-bye I tell her to say hi to Joe for us, and she says,
Stop by anytime.


It doesn't take long to find the graves in the village cemetery, which is
tiny and, like Josie said, crowded. Burials here are still conducted as they
were four hundred years ago, with a mound of earth over the grave. We
see Lena's first. There is a simple white cross with her name and the words
"Daughter and mother."

Then we see Dion's grave. None of the mound of the earth is visible
because it is covered with teddy bears and Matchbox cars and cowboy
and Indian figurines and little blond angels and kiddie Hallmark cards
with handwritten notes inside. There are dozens of crosses and Jesuses
and Virgins and pinwheels that turn in the breeze.

It is monsoon, and the thunderheads are building up over the Sangres, the San Juans, and the Jemez. In the shadow of the Black Mesa, the
land is green and the cicadas are buzzing. We can hear the river. It is a
modest rush, thick and slow.

# ACKNOWLEDGMENTS

I consider myself part native and part stranger to the desert, and sought knowledge from people who have lived it far more deeply than I have. Many of them appear in the narrative of this book: I am very grateful for the generosity and hospitality with which they received me during my sojourn.

My parents lived in Sedona during many years and their home there was a loving red-rock refuge for my sister Rossana, my brother John, Angela, and me: gracias Mom and Pop. In Albuquerque, for the Christmas "tamaladas" and cigarettes on the porch, for shooting hoops and for Freddie Fender on the stereo: gratitude and love to Wilma, Kristina, Noah, Zak, and Keith.

My agent Susan Bergholz became a "neighbor" during this project and our many, many conversations about the West were integral to the process.

My editor Riva Hocherman and I got lost a few times in the desert, but every page reflects her keenly close reading, for which she has my sincere gratitude.

David Reid and Jayne Walker, as always, provided an abundant fount of friendship and many ideas of where and how to look.

The Lannan Foundation presented me not just with a generous fellowship but also with a month of writing time at its residency program in Marfa, where Douglas Humble and Ray Freese hosted me with great West Texas warmth. Many thanks also to Patrick Lannan, Jaune Evans, Christine Mazuera-Davis, and Martha Jessup for their openhandedness over the years. I am thankful also for the insights of Tim Johnson at the Marfa Book Company and the neighborliness of Rachel Manera, Alice Jennings, and my residency cohort: Cyrus Cassells, José Manuel Prieto, and Pamela Bridgewater. Miguel Díaz-Barriga at Swarthmore College has written incisively about the erasure of detention history at Chinati in Marfa and his ideas helped hone mine on the subject.

Elia Arce first invited me to the "House of the Moon," and just in the nick of time—gracias, niña Elia, por ese regalo. John Pirozzi was a great housemate in

Joshua Tree, and I thank Vasili and Katherine Varelas for letting us rent their wonderful house for many years. Joshua Tree might be something of a boutique desert today, but Ted Quinn and Tony Mason keep it real, as they say—and they have the memory of Fred Drake in safekeeping. My friend Johnette Napolitano arrived in the Mojave with a Chihuahua and struck a desert-artist figure as inspiring as it was cool.

Norteño forester and activist Luis Torres does not appear in the narrative, but his guidance was indispensable (and his friendship so very appreciated). Estevan Rael-Gálvez, who was the State Historian of New Mexico during my time in Velarde, was very kind to show this newcomer around the block. Among northern New Mexico's progressive cohort I consulted Chellis Glendinning, Moisés González, and especially Kay Matthews and her late husband Mark Schiller, who received Angela and me very sweetly and offered their deep knowledge of the land and people. Peter Nabokov, who encountered the norteños and the Pueblos long before I did, offered crucial advice—and wonderful texts—from early on in my journey.

The Loeb Fellowship at Harvard University's Graduate School of Design (saludos, Jim Stockard and Sally Young!) provided me with contacts throughout the borderlands, including Arnie Valdez of San Luis, Colorado, who shared his profound understanding of Hispano history and politics.

I taught at the University of Houston while I lived in Velarde, and my colleagues and students there provided me, as I began this project, with a wonderful literary community and camaraderie. Thank you, Hosam Aboul-Ela, Raj Mankad, Miah Arnold, Mark Doty, Kristine Ervin, Jesse Salmeron, Chitra Divakaruni, Claudia Rankine, Nick Flynn, J. Kastely, Kathy Smathers, and Tatcho Mindiola. Off campus, Rick Lowe and Sehba Sarwar had the perfect mix of politics and art. The late Marion Barthelme extended uniquely gracious support, and Rich Levy and the crew at Inprint always made me feel at home.

In Tucson, Tom Miller and his partner Regla Albarrán have always received me with kindness, as has Jack McGarvey in Rio Rico, just on this side of the borderline. On the far Western edge of the Tohono O'odham reservation, Ofelia Rivas welcomed me into her home and showed me the price we have all paid for the "wall." I also had the privilege to break bread with O'odham poet Ofelia Zepeda, whose verses capture both the tragedy of the border and the path to overcome it. Reverend John Fife has retired from Southside Presbyterian Church, but he remains a beacon of activist charisma in the borderlands, a voice in the desert I have been listening to since the Sanctuary Movement. Likewise, Ernesto Portillo Jr.'s columns at the *Arizona Daily Star* are a cry in the wilderness against the neo-Know-Nothings. Thank you, Aurelie Sheehan and Alison

Hawthorne Deming at the University of Arizona for hosting my gratifying and edifying visits there.

Since my return to Los Angeles I have had the honor of working with my colleagues at Loyola Marymount University, among whom I would like to especially thank Juan Mah y Busch and Douglas Burton-Christie, both of whom in their own ways have shown me paths across deserts I hardly knew. The Jesuits at LMU provided me with not just an academic home, but a mission that I hope this book lives up to.

I would also like to thank for their aid from near or afar, for a moment, or across the many years this book took shape with friendship, a chat, a meal, a hike, a place to stay, a word of encouragement:

Joe Rodriguez, Betto Arcos, Joe Garcia, Joanna Fodczuk, Yael Flusberg, José Luis Paredes Pacho, Elisa Bernard, Roberto Lovato, Ofelia Cuevas, Marcus Kuiland-Nazario, Debbie Winski, mi primo Mario Castaneda, Ardell Broadbent, Mike Davis, Sandra Cisneros, Sandy Close, Ana Castillo, Demetria Martinez, Fr. David Ungerleider, Ry Cooder, Luis Alberto Urrea, Charles Bowden, Lynell George, Sesshu Foster, Greta Anderson, Peter Young, Josh Kun, Jim Fogelquist, Sasha Anawalt, Carolyn Forché, Nicholas Herrera, Tom Lutz, Linda Arias, Olivia Harrison, Luis Rodriguez, Ephraim Cruz, Dove Haber, the late Howard Zinn, Anthony Arnove, Paul Harris, Tom Hayden, Juan Galván, Cecilia Ballí, Billy Bizeau, Dana Bowen, Victoria Williams, Gary Bowden, Sue Bradley, Fred Burke, Carl Byker, J. Michael Walker, David Kipen, Olga Briseño, Steve Orlen, Sue Horton, Robin Rauzi, Marisela Norte, Randy Williams, Stephen Wu, Lisa Cacho, Jose Matus, Isabel García, Katherine Wells, Neil Cambpell, Chuck Moshontz, Daniel Hernández, Willy Herrón, Jesus Velo, Juan Felipe Herrera, Guillermo Gómez-Peña, John Martinez, Eloy Casados, Xan Cassavetes, Joey Burns, Julia Goldberg, Dave Catching, Dean Chamberlain, Martin Cox, Judith Lewis, Ernesto Chávez, Christina Cisk, Dave Royer, Roman Coppola, Victor Nunez, Rick Ross, Don DiNicola, Lupita Domínguez, Martín Espada, William Estrada, Michael Marizco, Mark Fairfield, Reed Johnson, Agustín Gurza, Adolfo Guzmán-López, Penny Holland, Adrienne Jenik, Beth Ann Sánchez, Louise Steinman, Maureen Moore, Margaret Thompson, Judy Wishart, and Elliot Young.

# ABOUT THE AUTHOR

RUBÉN MARTÍNEZ, a writer and performer, is the author of *Crossing Over* and *The New Americans,* among other works. He lives in Los Angelos, where he holds the Fletcher Jones Chair in Literature and Writing at Loyola Marymount University.